Unmaking Mimesis
Essays on feminism and theater

Elin Diamond

ROUTLEDGE

Leabharlanna Poibli Chathair Baile Átha Cliath
Dublin City Public Libraries

London and New York

First published 1997
by Routledge
2 Park Square, Milton Park, Abingdon, Oxon, OX14 4RN

Simultaneously published in the USA and Canada
by Routledge
270 Madison Ave, New York NY 10016

Transferred to Digital Printing 2008

Typeset in Baskerville by Poole Typesetting (Wessex) Ltd

British Library Cataloguing in Publication Data

A catalogue record for this book is available from the British Library

Library of Congress Cataloguing in Publication Data
Diamond, Elin.
    Unmaking mimesis : essays on feminism and theater/Elin Diamond.
    Includes bibliographical references and index.
    1. Feminism and theater.   2. Mimesis in literature.   3. Feminist theater.
    4. Drama – Women authors – History and criticism.
    I. Title
    PN1590.W64D53   1997
    792'.082 – dc20
    96–8881

ISBN 0–415–01228–7 (hbk)
       0–415–01229–5 (pbk)

Publisher's Note
The publisher has gone to great lengths to ensure the quality of this reprint
but points out that some imperfections in the original may be apparent

For Hannah Zoe

Contents

Acknowledgments

During the years of manuscript preparation, I benefited greatly from an Andrew W. Mellon Faculty Fellowship at Harvard, a residency sponsored by the Kentucky Foundation for Women, and the Faculty Academic Study Program at Rutgers. Barry Qualls, that most artful of department chairpersons, magically uncovered pockets of unofficial time during which I was able to move the manuscript toward completion. A year-long seminar at the Rutgers Center for the Critical Analysis of Contemporary Culture, in stimulating conversation with Carolyn Williams, Diana Fuss, Marcia Ian, and Jay Geller, spurred key discoveries in my research. Cora Kaplan, at the Institute for Research on Women at Rutgers, offered support and an invitation to speak about my work. David Glover and Jonathan Diamond gave timely advice on the closing chapters. With deadlines pressing, Carolyn Williams produced a meticulous, inspiring reading of a draft of the final chapter, and Marianne DeKoven spent precious summer days on a read-through of the entire book. My thanks to these colleagues and to Wesley Brown for, over many years, sharing his library and his wisdom on drama, theater, and politics.

Since 1984, casual conversations with Sue-Ellen Case have propelled me into long bouts of thinking and writing. My private dialogues with her and with Herbert Blau are everywhere in this book. I salute my feminist comrades in the Women and Thasrer Program of ATHE, Vicki Patraka, Jill Dolan, Amy Robinson, Kate Davy, Glenda Dickerson, Gayle Austin, Ellen Donkin, and Sue-Ellen Case, for many years of critique, passion, fights, and dancing. This book germinated during our conferences. My sincere gratitude to Tim Murray, Cheryl Wall, Christina Zwarg, Hersh Zeifman, Elisa Diamond, Valerie Diamond, Celia Diamond, Mary Lowe, and Risa Denenberg for upbeat and steady encouragement. And I thank my Routledge editor and team, Talia Rodgers, Patricia Stankiewicz, and Hannah Hyam for endless patience with a finicky author.

The worst turns in life make for amazing responses. In the definitive loneliness of illness, when work on my anthology and on revisions of this book nearly came to a halt, Robert Lowe, Wendy Salkind, Joshua Diamond, Randa Diamond, Deborah Bloom, Harriet Davidson, Marianne DeKoven, Wesley Brown and Deb Margolin kept the doors open and the phone lines warm, and created mimetic networks in which I might locate a fading subjectivity. I thank them here, heartfully.

Finally I give my deepest thanks to Robert Lowe for his wit and loving friendship and for the inspiration of his talent, in view on this volume's paperback cover. To my adored dedicatee I acknowledge that no one should have to wait her entire life to date (five-and-one-half years) for a parent to finish a book. I wish I could promise it would be the last time.

Elin Diamond
Plainfield, NJ

Portions of this book appeared first in academic journals. I thank the journal editors for permission to use this material in revised form: 'Rethinking Identification: Kennedy, Freud, Brecht,' *Kenyon Review* 15:2 (Spring 1993), pp. 86–99; 'Realism and Hysteria: Toward a Feminist Mimesis,' *Discourse* 13:1 (Fall-Winter 1990–1992), pp. 59–92; '*Gestus* and Signature in Aphra Behn's *The Rover*,' *ELH* 56:3 (September 1989), pp. 519–541; 'Mimesis, Mimicry and the "True-Real',", *Modern Drama* 32:1 (March 1989), pp. 58–72; '(In)Visible Bodies in Churchill's Theatre,' *Theatre Journal* 40:2 (June 1988), pp. 189–205; 'Brechtian Theory/Feminist Theory: Toward a Gestic Feminist Criticism,' *The Drama Review* 32:1 (Spring 1988), pp. 89–94.

Introduction

What in us really wants the truth?

Friedrich Wilhelm Nietzsche

In Plato's diatribe against image-makers in Book X of *The Republic*, he creates, typically, an image. A craftsman walks through the ideal city waving a mirror. Socrates has just set up his tripartite distinction between ideal Forms, the phenomenal object world and the contemptible activity of *poietes* who subvert the Republic's ideals by corrupting its fragile guardians. Into this infamous group he suddenly thrusts his interlocutor Glaucon:

> Don't you realize that in a certain way you yourself could be the maker of all things? (And what way is that?) The way is not difficult. It can be quickly managed anywhere on earth – most quickly if you are prepared to carry a mirror with you wherever you go. Quickly you will produce the sun and the things of heaven; quickly the earth; quickly yourself; quickly all the animals, plants, contrivances, and every other object we just mentioned.[1]

In response to Socrates' 'quickly' Glaucon answers not just quickly but correctly: 'But they would be appearances only.' 'Excellent,' says Socrates, then quickly moves on, perhaps hoping to haul out of view what suddenly has come into view: a small but significant scene. Usually the passive interlocutor, Glaucon has slipped through the master's discursive net and landed in a performance. What's worse he's playing around with a mirror. Socrates invented him, now he must get rid of him.

We do appreciate Socrates' larger purpose. Here is mimetic activity in all its perniciousness. Mocking the transcendent authority of the supreme maker with his own phoney largess, this fantasy 'craftsman,' this pseudo-Glaucon mocks as well the creator's product, changing an admittedly second-order but rational nature into flickering incoherent images. The dazzling, turning mirror, grabbing and scattering particulars in its wake, upsets the vital order of objects and deprives the sun of its magisterial role as 'offspring' of the cosmic logos. More seriously it lures the senses of the mirror-holder (and of any passing impressionable guardian), particularly the superior optical sense, by transmitting untrue judgments about reality.

Aristotle will calm this scene. He will describe mimesis as a means of selecting from the particulars of human behavior those purposeful actions which, if imitated appropriately, guide listeners and spectators to the recognition of ethical universals. In the *Poetics*, the onus of mimesis as falsifying reality, Plato's truth-illusion matrix, is dropped – only to be replaced by a normative teleology that governs parts to wholes in the artwork.

This sums up, rather conventionally, a few points about Plato and Aristotle and mimesis.

But suppose we read Plato's 'scene' differently. Outside the precincts of the theater Glaucon knowingly mimes the environment by 'reflecting on' and particularly displacing the singularity of forms. He moves among the population entertaining young men and bothering their elders. With our postmodern eyes, we might say that fracturing objects and spectators in the mirror (as Virginia Woolf's Miss Latrobe did) is interesting, but equally compelling is the manipulating of the mirror, the making and breaking of relations, montages, contiguities. There's Glaucon and a passing goat. The goat and some stones of a temple ruin. Glaucon, the foot of a passerby, and my fantasy of the 'scene,' everyone/thing both in and out of the frame.

These two uses of mimesis underpin the discussions in this book. One, mimesis as representation, with its many doublings and unravelings of model, subject, identity (Irigaray, Derrida). Two, mimesis as a mode of reading that transforms an object into a ·*gestus* or a dialectical image (Brecht, Benjamin). In both senses an unseen bears on the scene. But the first depends on the truth of the model and its creative revisions, the second on truths produced in engaged interpretation. As practices, both lavish attention on performer as well as production – in our scene a composite entity named Glaucon who, let us note quickly, brings gender into view. Because he acts mimetically Glaucon, for Plato, descends into 'Glaucon,' a non-entity, and as such womanish, a woman. Is s/he then a woman? Or like a woman? In mimesis, remarks an anthropologist, 'one conforms with something one is not and also should not be.'[2]

I

This book is an inquiry into the possibilities of a feminist mimesis. I explore the connections between theories of mimesis and feminist theories of sexuality and representation, and I do this through readings of a number of Western theater texts. In the most basic sense, I put into dialogue what I believe to be the most pressing questions in feminist theory with the oldest questions of theatrical representation: Who is speaking and who is listening? Whose body is in view and whose is not? What is being represented, how, and with what effects? Who or what is in control?

In the last twenty-five years, feminism has struggled with psychoanalytic-semiotic constructions of the female subject in sometimes explosive juxtaposition with empirical approaches to women's lives, histories and politics. One result of this agon has been a risky but exciting inclusiveness – the split and desiring female subject demands recognition of her gendered body, her race, her ethnicity, her nation. Yet these designations imply, problematically, the exclusivity of mimetic modeling. Similarly, in proposing universal frameworks of sexual, political, and economic liberation, white US feminists working with African American, Asian American, and Latina feminists must continue to ask, who is speaking? who is listening? who is in view, and who is not? When 'third world' and Western women convene in global conferences or across a lunch table, such questions are the implicit conditions of meaningful dialogue.

Work on art practices limited to Western theater texts can hardly account for the multitude of inquiries that constitute feminist politics today. Nor is 'feminism' the stable referent for my readings of texts written for performance. I do, however, presume that representation and social-historical reality are fully imbricated; that discourse and its products (gender, identity, politics) are caught up in fantasies, identifications, and frictional models passing as truths; and that the utopian strain in feminism depends on the performative 'as if' – all of which bring theater and its own paradoxes into the debate. Desire, politics, and gender struggle are persistent irritants in Western theater and its literature. Historically women have been denied power in the theater apparatus yet signs of female sexuality have been crucial to that apparatus's functioning – a contradiction that can be read into the signifying processes of almost any play. Theater itself may be understood as the drama's unruly body, its material other, a site where the performer's and the spectator's desire may resignify elements of a constrictive social script. Theater may also be understood as a symptomatic cultural site that ruthlessly maps out normative spectatorial positions by occluding its own means of production. And yet – any set of seemingly rigid positions is available for revision. Conservative and patriarchal, the theater is also, in a complex sense, the place of play, and unlike other media, in the theater the same play can be played not only again, but differently.

But what of mimesis? Given its long association with neoclassical *imitatio* in both its didactic and idealist directions; given too, in our late twentieth-century view, its link with conservative tendencies in dramatic realism, why would a self-consciously evolving feminism concern itself with mimesis? Let's look at a recent damning definition: 'Mimesis . . . posits a *truthful* relation between world and word, model and copy, nature and image . . . referent and sign in which potential difference is subsumed by sameness.'[3] While A.O. Rorty situates Aristotelian mimesis between 'representation' and 'imitation' ('neither separately captures it'), most scholars want to shear off mimesis from the cruder connotations of imitation – fakeness, reproduction, resemblance.[4] Stephen Halliwell's new translation of the *Poetics* consistently prefers 'representation' over 'imitation.'[5] But suppose we follow a far longer tradition that interprets mimesis as not only the act of imitating but an imitation *of*. 'Imitation indicates a constant relation between something which is and something made like it . . .'[6] Tangled in iconicity, then, in the visual resemblance between an originary model and its representation, mimesis patterns difference into sameness.[7]

From this notion, a feminist critique has followed. Same as what? For feminist historians, philosophers, and literary critics in the last three decades and, in fact, much earlier, truth and the sameness that supports it cannot be understood as a neutral, omnipotent, changeless essence, embedded in eternal Nature, revealed by mimesis. Rather Truth is inseparable from gender-based and biased epistemologies. The model of imitation may be the Platonic Ideal or Aristotle's universal type, Truth may be conceived as model-copy adequation, or, conversely, as an unveiling (that which shows itself or appears), but in all cases the epistemological, morphological, universal standard for determining the true is the masculine, a metaphoric stand-in for God the Father.[8] 'Phallogocentrism' (Derrida's coinage, following Lacan) further embeds this hierarchy; in the logos, the language of universal reason, the phallic signifier organizes the production of meaning. Luce Irigaray, as we will see, links phallic power to Platonic mimesis. Lacking the organ of privilege, unable to represent their desires in a male symbolic, women are positioned as the mirror to reflect back the masculine 'Self-Same.' Irigaray calls this specular operation 'mimesis imposed,' a term with provocative resonance for resistant practice.[9] Derrida posits play as primordial mimesis; Irigaray trumps that, shadowing mimesis with *mimétisme*.

Before turning to Irigaray's potent reconfigurations of mimesis as mimicry, we need to pause. The truth-model axis of mimesis is only one piece of classical mimesis. As Lyons and Nichols remind us, there is always a tension between understanding mimesis as guaranteeing 'the objective nature of the work of art, its truth value' (and, by extension, the truth of the represented), and understanding mimesis as representing, as generative, as performance – a powerful instantiation of 'the role of subjectivity [and cultural specificity] of artist and viewer, speaker and reader . . .'[10] 'Neoclassical,' of course, refers to the veneration of antiquity and the belief in its superior sense of beauty and art, but resistance to mimesis as normative modeling arose as soon as Aristotle's *Poetics* was translated (and distorted) by Italian critics in the sixteenth century.[11] While the 'mirror of nature' trope is consistently used in Renaissance and neoclassical theories (fifteenth to eighteenth centuries), it is tied complexly to shifting definitions of nature, and the emphasis typically falls on the artists' distinctive embellishments – we might say, their signifying on tradition – not their subservience to models. Indeed imitation (*imitare*) was distinguished from copying (*ritrarre* or portraiture), the former deviating to 'improve' on the model, the latter reproducing it.[12] 'Leave to art the freedom of a deviation,' opines Diderot (echoing Plato's *Cratylus*), '. . . the painter's sun is not that of the universe and could not be. . . .'[13] Yet elsewhere in his work and in that of Diderot's contemporaries, Tzvetan Todorov finds an unresolved 'hesitation between imitation as representation or staging, and imitation as production of an object that resembles its model.'[14]

This 'hesitation' finds its roots in the mimesis wordgroup in Greek, and in its earliest uses. According to Göran Sörbom, *mimema* or *mimemata* are the concrete products of the verb '*mimesthai*' (the activity of representing,) at the 'origin' of which, as Aristotle seems to note in Chapter 4 of the *Poetics*, is the *mimos* or *mimetes*, the person(s) performing (and improvising) the activity.[15] Sörbom situates the performer at rich men's banquets doing imitations of social inferiors (23). Presumably Plato knew about this banquet circuit and would have known the conceptual play on words these terms produce. *Mimos* is both the performer and what is performed (a mime), just as *mimesis* denotes both the activity of representing and the result of it – both a doing and a thing done; both the generative embodied activity of representing (including improvising in music and dance) and a (true) representation (of a model).

Mimesis, then, is impossibly double, simultaneously the stake and the shifting sands: order and potential disorder, reason and madness. As a concept mimesis is indeterminate ('representation, imitation . . . neither separately captures it') and, by its own operations, loses its conceptual footing. On the one hand, it speaks to our desire for universality, coherence, unity, tradition, and, on the other, it unravels that unity through improvisations, embodied rhythm, powerful instantiations of subjectivity, and what Plato most dreaded, impersonation, the latter involving outright mimicry. In imitating (upholding the truth value of) the model, the *mimos* becomes an other, *is being* an other, thus a shapeshifting Proteus, a panderer of reflections, a destroyer of forms.

II

As an evolving movement that self-consciously theorizes its practice, feminism must I think embrace this doubleness. Let's elaborate a bit more on Plato's fantasies and proscriptions. The ideal city is based on upholding boundaries; indeed mimesis first enters the *Republic* in a discussion of property, what will be included and excluded in the ideal city.[16] What is proper to the self (that which insures the self-same) follows immediately: every individual must be 'at one with himself [one and not many]' (423d). The guardian proves his self-mastery, the ascendency of reason, by rejecting mimesis, not only because it involves him with resemblance and appearances – the transitory elements of the physical world – but because it involves him in trangressions against the 'proper' of identity itself. For Plato and Aristotle, mimesis is inherent in any learning process, but for Plato, the distractions in obtaining true knowledge, the knowledge of the unseeable Forms, are palpably risky.

Plato attempts a parsing: there is (good) mimesis and (bad) mimesis. To Adeimantus comes the famous injunction that philosophers should fix their minds

> on eternal realities . . . and on those things that belong to the unchanging and eternal order. Seeing that they neither inflict nor suffer wrong but abide instead in that harmony which reason enjoins, he will try to imitate them. As far as is in him to do so, he will make them his models and assimilate himself to them (500c).

But the young guardians following the poets, who impersonate others rather than simply narrate stories, will violate their own proper boundaries. Further, they may be contaminated by impersonating inferior others, namely women and slaves:

> Then those we are educating ought not – since they are men – to play the parts of women, young or old . . . nor may they play the roles of either female or male slaves nor perform any slavish act . . . neither should they impersonate a coward nor any other kind of bad man whose behavior is repugnant to [our] standards (395d,e).

Finally, looming too near to the guardian is his potential double, that is, himself doubled, an operation that, in Derrida's words 'splits what it doubles,'[17] displacing the authority and authenticity of the original. Mimesis begins by proposing a stable model-copy relation to reinforce the good of the Republic, then turns to reveal no model, no copy, but rather a destructuring, intransitive repetition.[18]

Feminist theorists and classicists have long since given both mimetic double and 'the person' a gender. Sue-Ellen Case has linked the gender bias across social organizations in ancient Greek culture to Plato's and Aristotle's proscriptions, concluding that as Aristotle denies women the capacity to exemplify tragic virtues (*Poetics*, ch. 15), the erasure of women from social representation means that 'mimesis is not possible for [them].'[19] To turn Case's phrase slightly, if mimesis was not possible for women, it was not possible without them. As Froma Zeitlin writes, for the Greeks 'Woman is the mimetic creature par excellence, ever since Hesiod's Zeus created her as an imitation with the aid of the other artisan gods and adorned her with a deceptive allure.'[20] Anticipating the misogynist anti-theatricalism that took root in Patristic writings, Plato considered women susceptible to illusionism and most likely to deceive. But more influential, Zeitlin argues, is the rhetoric of his condemnation: 'by a whole series of innuendoes and juxtapositions' poets are compared to 'male trickster figures' and branded with feminine attributes of pandering and corrupting. Mimetic behavior, especially in the Republic, is explicitly feminine:

> when heroes are shown to weep and lament their misfortunes, they are not only endorsing a false theology about the justice of the gods but are weakening themselves and others by their indulgence in womanish grief.[21]

To seem womanish in behavior is to become womanish. To seem is to be. Plato has revealed the serious play of drag, and of all mimicry.

The problematic of mimesis in the *Republic*, says Lacoue-Labarthe, is not a 'problematic of the lie' of the simulacrum, but instead involves the subject – and 'the feminization' of that subject.[22] Ultimately mimesis has little to do with a mirror held up to nature or reality – the aesthetic of realism – but rather suggests – if we follow Platonic anxiety to its limits – a trick mirror that doubles (makes feminine) in the act of reflection.

Is this a true (mimetic) history of mimesis or a fantastical undecidable (mimetic) genealogy? And where would a feminist want to be or to seem in relation to it? These questions lead to some well-traveled territory, but perhaps we might travel it again. Postmodern conceptions of the subject derived from deconstruction and Lacanian psychoanalysis are polemically antimimetic. Since language, in Saussurean terms, is a system wherein meaning is arbitrarily produced in relations of difference, the subject represents her desire in the signifier which, in the logic of signification, can refer only to another signifier, and so on. To understand language not as a mirroring tool of communication but as a dense web of signification means, in the simplest sense, that a speaker can no longer lay claim to a stable system of reference, can no longer rely on language to mirror (express, represent) her entire thought. But feminism, whose empirical, historical project continues to be the recovery and analysis of women's texts and experiences, has a stake in truth – in contributing to the accumulation and organization of knowledge by which a culture values or forgets its past and attends to the contradictions in the present. Such contributions entail universalist thinking, which means generalizing from particulars, whether in conventional discursive form or in multivocal performatives (storytelling, self-interruption).

Whether a feminist views the problematic of the signifier and of representation through a postmodernist prism or a historical-materialist lens, the critique of patriarchy carries with it an ethical commitment to the value of one's own position, however complex and nuanced that position might be. As many have pointed out, feminism has gained much from postmodernism.[23] The decentered subject implies the dismantling of the self-reflecting cogito/self, whose inferior other has been traditionally gendered female. And yet feminists, in our different constituencies – we speak emphatically of 'feminisms' now – with our different objects of analysis, want to intervene in symbolic systems, linguistic, theatrical, political, psychological – and intervention requires assuming a subject position, however provisional, and making truth claims, however flexible, concerning one's own representations. Indeed feminism, like theater, finds it difficult to rid itself of the classical mimetic structure. Tragic drama was of course Aristotle's specific object for articulating the precepts of mimetic art. But there is a deeper connection. The discourse of theater, like the discourse of feminism, cannot rid itself of the temptation to refer, to emplot, to remember, to show. The actor's body cannot forget its gender (in the most exciting contemporary practice, performers remember with a vengeance), cannot shake off the referential frame imposed by text, mode of production, and spectators' narrativity – those trajectories of scopic desire and identification that performer and performance text can only partially control. For example, certain texts of early realism provoked excitement when middle-class women found, for the first time, mimetic models that sparked (and contained) their political desires. Of Elizabeth Robins's performance, as the first Hedda Gabler on the London stage (1891), an acquaintance commented: 'Hedda is all of us.'[24]

As we will see in Chapter 1, such intense identifications are solicited by realism. But stage realism is mimesis's positivist moment. If historicized, it can be codified and critiqued even as we acknowledge that its appeal is as strong in the 1990s as it was in the 1890s. Mimesis, however, cannot so easily be seen, framed, gotten around, partially because it is continually embroiled in cultural desires and politics. Dryden may seem to echo Jonson and seems in turn to be echoed by Pope and Diderot in describing nature as the sign of order and perfection that the artist 'imitates.' But the mimesis of this 'nature,' in its production and reception, will be fully marked by the political, literary, and gender ideologies of the critic, the artist, the audience, and the social contexts that interconnect them. The Restoration dramatist's prologue is exemplary of such interconnections: the playwright's mouthpiece utters witty/serious praise of high poetic ideals whose imitation is sadly prevented by the lowbrow, loutish, wig-combing spectators before whom she or he stands. Because it produces a (fictively) true (therefore false) relation to the real, mimesis is as much a historical-ideological flashpoint as an aesthetic concept. When A.S. Schlegel sounds the romantic rejection of imitation by making the familiar Platonic move of reducing mimesis to trivial copying; when Karl Philip Moritz announces that 'the *born artist* is not content to observe nature . . . he has to . . . create as nature does,' both were announcing a change in more than aesthetic philosophy.[25] They were suggesting that assumptions about nature or universal order, the legitimacy of which neoclassical mimesis seemed to reproduce, were now in doubt. Romantics, they imply, will offer truer truths, although to use the soul rather than the landscape as model only shifts direction, produces yet another mimesis. In this sense mimesis leaps beyond aesthetic precincts, beyond parsing its energies between upholding a model (representation) or improvising a variation (representing). It has always made this leap. Since Plato sought to cleanse his Republic of histrionic display mimesis has been a political practice, inseparable from interpretation and contestation.

III

This is why Bertolt Brecht and Walter Benjamin are Irigaray's dialectical partners in this study. Irigaray's deconstructions of Plato will echo throughout these pages. But with Brecht comes the urgency to understand mimesis (not to mention feminism and any other critical concept) as historically mediated. As we will see (Chapter 2) Brecht theorizes a performance model geared to the pleasures of interpretation, the production of political agency. Epic theater theory provides ways to expose illusionism, to pry actor/signifier from character/signified, to defuse realism's narrativity, but importantly Brecht never denied referentiality; he aimed rather to expunge the ahistorical referent. In Brecht's plays the subject's dialectical struggle ceases only in a socialist future, but that his much wished-for proletarian spectators could imagine themselves as new referents is immanent in the Lehrstück mode of address. In effect Brecht insisted on *more mimesis* not less: 'The first thing therefore is to comprehend the new subject-matter; the second to shape the new relations.

The reason: *art follows reality*. . . . Can we speak of money in the form of iambics? . . . Petroleum resists the five-act play' (my italics).[26]

Benjamin's notion of complex temporality in image production and reception will help us think and feel through the auratic presence of 1990s performance artists (Chapter 7). For Benjamin and Theodor Adorno mimesis is a bio-anthropological behavior rooted in adaptive mimicry and magic and completely divorced from a truth-model matrix. In Frankfurt School mythopoesis, mimesis reaches 'back' beyond the 'mimetic taboo' put in place by Plato and Aristotle when they subordinated artistic play to philosophical truth, sensuousness to rationality.[27] In their different ways Brecht and Benjamin situate their materialist truths within, not anterior to, mimetic practice. Given the reification of human and commodity relations under capitalism, mimetic truth must be pried open through interpretive labor. Mimesis is this labor: a sensuous critical receptivity to, and transformation of, the object.

It has become commonplace in Brecht criticism to suggest that his anti-Aristotelianism disguises key connections with Aristotle, especially the latter's emphasis on cognitive pleasure. But it is Benjamin's text that connects crucially with Aristotle's, where Aristotle is not parsing the objects, manner, and means of mimesis but describing behavior. In 'On the Mimetic Faculty,' Benjamin imbricates a Platonic negative with an Aristotelian positive: '[The human] gift of seeing *resemblances* is nothing other than a rudiment of the powerful compulsion in former times to become and behave like something else.'[28] 'Resemblance' signals the epistemological side of mimesis: the congruence of representation to represented, the truth-model matrix, but then it shifts: 'Children's play is everywhere permeated by mimetic modes of behavior . . .' (333). Here are Aristotle's opening lines in Chapter 4 of the *Poetics*:

> Poetry in general can be seen to owe its existence to two causes, and these are rooted in nature. First there is man's natural propensity, from childhood onwards, to engage in mimetic activity (and this distinguishes man from other creatures, that he is thoroughly mimetic and through mimesis takes his first steps in understanding). Second there is the pleasure men take in mimetic objects . . .[29]

A pleasure that turns out to be noting resemblances. Stephen Halliwell's glossing of these lines sounds distinctly Benjaminian.

> When Aristotle mentions the observations of likeness in these ways, he clearly does not have in mind a superficial or passive matter of merely registering the existence of similarities. . . . The discernment of likenesses means at its best, then, an active and interpretative process of cognition – a perspicacious discovery of significances in the world, or in representations of the world.[30]

This emphasis on mimesis as 'discernment of likenesses' and interpretive effort, on discovering the world through/as interpretation, recalls Benjaminian topoi. For Benjamin the discernment of 'similars' constellates past and present in a singular sensuous moment of discovery.

Chapter 4 of the *Poetics* is as tantalizing as any section of that fragment. Aristotle will soon get rid of this interest in resemblances and improvisation, or rather his teleology does. Mimetic activity becomes coherent art that will, like philosophy, refer us to the universals of type and action. Aristotle plants the effeminate body of the *mimos* firmly in a unified *muthos* that elicits and regulates the emotions toward appropriate rational standards. Yet this 'planting' is crucial, for feminists if not for Benjamin. It demonstrates why, in Alice Rayner's words, mimesis is 'an ethical accounting, not simply a reflection or imitation.' In the mimetic, 'the perception of acts adheres to prior assumptions about the relation of agents and acts. . . .'[31] Realism will conceal and reveal those 'prior assumptions'; Brecht will attempt to historicize them. A feminist theatrical practice, mimetically embodying/ interpreting the other, will do, at the very least, all three.

However dynamic he becomes (again) in recent criticism, 'Aristotle' is also the history of Aristotelian interpretation. Benjamin's philosophical roots in Kantian aesthetics and romanticism make Aristotle's rationalism and his mimetic tradition deeply suspect.

Irigarary's suspicions are deeper. The gender blindness of Brecht and Benjamin and their apologists may be as profound as that of the grand philosophical masters of antiquity and the Enlightenment. The impulse of this study mimes Irigaray's own scholarly procedure: to read mimesis theory with/against/through feminist skepticism and desire. Chapter 6 pairs Irigaray with Benjamin; below she pairs herself with Plato.

IV

Women imitate the earth
Plato

According to many commentators, Irigaray is shedding her essentialist skin.[32] After rereading 'Plato's Hystera' in *Speculum* it is difficult to understand the all-too-convenient subsumption of her theorizing to the ecstatic alterity that Hélène Cixous imagined in the early 'The Laugh of the Medusa.' In *Speculum*'s first long section, 'The Blind Spot of an Old Dream of Symmetry,' Irigaray rereads Freud's 'Femininity' through Lacan's mirror stage (although Lacan is never mentioned) and condemns the specular logic by which the female is seen as lack because she lacks what is 'like a man.' Condemned to the Law of the Same, to reflect back the male's image, she must 'abandon her relation to her own primal fantasy so that she can inscribe into those of men' – which will in turn become the 'origin' of her desire. In Freud's account of the phallic phase, the little girl is 'a little man,' or in Irigaray's words, a normal female is configured as 'a man minus the possibility of representing [her]self as a man' (27).[33] In a brilliant move, Irigaray accounts for penis envy as an epiphenomenon of Freud's specular logic. It is not enough for women to lack the penis, they must be envious, driven by the desire to have it, thereby confirming to men that they still possess it. It is her female envy that in effect fills out the mirror reflection, making her look like the male looking at himself.[34] In 'Plato's Hystera,' coming after 'Speculum,' ten short dense meditations on desire, ontology, and the speculum as favored tool for probing the secrets of female sexuality, Irigaray transforms the mirror into a political weapon: 'mimesis imposed' becomes mimicry unleashed.

Irigaray's intertext is of course Plato's allegory of the cave in the *Republic*, Book VII, in which the cave wall with its projected images serves Plato as a metaphor for the illusory nature of wordly objects that keep man from contemplating true Forms, the unseeable Ideal. Only when forced to leave the dark cave (the expulsion is painful) are the symbolically chained men allowed to see the Truth. Making explicit the birth metaphors implicit in Plato, Irigaray exchanges metaphor for metonymy; cave as embedded enclosure becomes the womb or hystera embedded in the maternal body/earth. And this *hystera*, by Plato's own account, is nothing less than a fully operational theater whose illusionistic apparatus is, as in conventional mimetic theater, designed to obscure the mode of production: the chained men cannot see the fire or the parade of whispering, object-carrying men behind them, whose voices, melding perceptually with the object-projections, are taken for true presences. As in the conventional proscenium set-up, 'chains, lines, perspectives oriented straight ahead – all maintain the illusion of constant motion in one direction. Forward' (245).

But in this womb/theater, what is ahead (the cave wall) is in fact behind (the opening to the cave). Thus Irigaray concludes: 'You will always already have lost your bearings as soon as you set foot in the cave; it will turn your head, set you walking on your hands . . .' (244). In this ocular funnyhouse of thrown images and ventriloquized voices, Irigaray gives us a 'mimetic system' that completely belies the concept of origin or model, for to the prisoners no origin of the image projections is imaginable; or, to put it another way, what they experience as origin is already mimicry, a representation of repetition. Hence mimesis without a true referent: mimesis without truth (see Chapter 1). With this reconfigured womb-theater, Irigaray wittily retrieves and confirms Plato's worst fears about theater, female duplicity, and, by implication, maternity. Platonic philosophy wants to place man's origins, not in the dark uncertain cave, but in his recognition of the (Father's) light. The philosopher wants to forget – wants to prove illusory – his female origins. Irigaray turns that wish into a playfully anarchic scenario; philosophic man discovers that, horrifically, mother is a theater.

This audacious womb-theater has resonant meaning for feminist theory and performance. To imagine a theater, whose 'mimetic system is not referable to one model, one paradigm . . . dominated by Truth' (292) is to undermine the ideality of logos as truth, the basis of Western thought and mimesis theory since Plato. At the origin of human existence, the mother, Irigaray situates Nietzsche's irreducible conundrum: the nontruth of truth. In Plato's allegory, reality, the 'real' of the prisoners' experience, is a shadow-and-mirror play (recall 'Glaucon,' our imaginary *mimos*). But Irigaray exacerbates Plato's vision. Her cave/hystera 'is already a speculum. An inner space of reflection. Polished and polishing, fake offspring. Opening, enlarging, contriving the scene of representation, the world as representation' (255). Plato's *Timeaus* presents the visible world as, in each particular, representing its appropriate form. Irigaray's version, however, makes representation itself originary; the womb opens and delivers . . . fake offspring.

This notion of a womb-theater in the business of representation poses interesting possibilities for feminist mimesis. In the 1970s and 1980s, in the feminist theater theory many of us were writing, the 'scene of representation' was generally understood as a narrativization of male desire. Representation, we tended to say, *inevitably* transforms female subjects into fetishized objects whose referent is ideologically bound to dominant – heterosexual – models of femininity and masculinity.[35] After spending most of *Speculum* denouncing the specular reflection status imposed on women by the male eye/I, is Irigaray proposing that representation should be claimed by women? The answer to this question, indeed to any question posed to Irigaray's text, is unambivalently double. 'Plato's Hystera' posits two mimetic systems, one repressed by the other. The patriarchal (classical) mimetic system, articulated by Plato and Aristotle, assumes a model, an invisible Form or a universal, beyond or at least distinguishable from empirical particulars, and far from 'shadows – images in the mirror – mere copies (289).[36] Unraveling patriarchal mimesis is Irigarayan mimicry, in which objects, shadows and voices are excessive to the philosophers' rational models and spill into mimicry – 'fake offspring.' Is this a Mom and Pop mimetic system? Yes, but typically 'mimesis' has no *being* unto itself; Irigaray's revisionary hystera-theater has lain in the 'womb' of Western thought since Plato, generating promiscuous fake offspring: an incessant Medusan mimicry of the patriarchal, truth-knowing/seeing 'eye.'[37]

Rewriting Plato's allegory as womb-theater, Irigaray also challenges critics of her essentialism. The womb-theater is no passive vessel of male creative seed (Aristotle's assertion in 'De Generatione Animalium') but a site of material production. While Irigaray insists on the mother as forgotten origin, erased from psychic history, she also metonymically links matter, earth, body to the illusionistic theater apparatus – its mirrors, fetishes, lights, voices, the whole 'stage set-up' (243). 'Plato's Hystera' forestalls recuperation by feminists who valorize maternity and nurturance as the defining elements of female subjectivity. A theatricalized hystera necessarily de-essentializes both female anatomy and maternal experience, for if the maternal womb is a theater, then ideas of essence, truth, origin are continually displaced onto questions of material relations and operations.[38] Nevertheless, this displacement, like all displacements, is slippery. As Meaghan Morris has so aptly put it, Irigaray 'is very far from confusing the anatomical and the social, but she works with a deadly deliberation *on* the point (the site and the purpose) of the confusion of the anatomical and cultural.' *Speculum* thus resists definition as feminine; for her the feminine is conditional or future tense, an interrogative mood . . . [she] remains the recalcitrant outsider at the festival of feminine specificity – she lounges ironically at the door.[39]

As we will see in the course of this study, women playwrights and feminist performers have taken up Irigaray's ironic disturbance of the unitary Self-Same. If Irigarayan *mimétisme* has no specific ontology, it is nevertheless productive: like the mirror-play of Plato's effeminate poet, the theater writing discussed in this book dislodges the referent from its idealized moorings and, to some extent, women from their prisonhouse of otherness. Yet because it is *theater* writing, women's plays and performance cannot occupy an Irigarayan 'elsewhere,'[40] or if they do, this elsewhere is never *not* interrupted by an unruly theatrical clamor. As I read 'Plato's Hystera,' this clamor is the sound of historical pain, contestation, and resistance.

V

It turns out that the participial 'unmaking' is not just an attribute of a deconstructive turn of thought – an unraveling from within. Rather 'unmaking' resides solidly in the *American Heritage Dictionary* with three, fortuitously relevant, meanings: (1) to deprive of position, rank, or authority; (2) to ruin, destroy; (3) to alter the characteristics of.

When I began *Unmaking Mimesis*, I had only the first in mind, because like many I viewed mimesis as a version of dramatic realism and linked them both to a rather simple referentiality – a view reductive to both realism and mimesis. In the ubiquitous feminist critiques of representation in the 1980s, it became clear to me that feminism was also a kind of realism, seduced by the desire to represent the truth about social reality, but was constantly in the process of questioning that position. I begin this book with a long section on realism, not merely to 'deprive' dramatic realism of its 'authority' (definition 1) – modernism has surely done that – but to explore realism's connection to feminist theory and practice. Attacks on dramatic realism are familiar: setting out to offer truthful versions of experience, realism universalizes but one point of view, ignoring the force-field of human-social contradiction. In the process of exploring social (especially gender) relations, realism ends by confirming their inevitability. But any critique of a representational practice needs to situate itself in the historical materials and desires of that practice. Part I of this book is organized as a discursive formation, bringing together the 'new' Ibsen and Ibsenite realism of the late nineteenth century and an equally powerful adjacent discourse, the 'new' science of psychoanalysis launched in Freud and Breuer's *Studies on Hysteria* (1895) and related texts. I argue that realism and early psychoanalysis are both theaters of knowledge – sites charged with the pleasure of positivist inquiry. Both share a similar object (the hysteric/fallen woman), a common claim to truth (the discovery of her secret), and a common genealogy (nineteenth-century melodramatic and clinical spectacles). I then suggest that in exploiting the signifiers and medical models of the hysteric, realism catches her disease, that is, produces the malady it is supposed to contain and cure. Reading Ibsen with a feminist contemporary, Elizabeth Robins, stretches the boundaries of our understanding of realism while, necessarily, depriving it of its prodigious authority. The section concludes by briefly suggesting what Robins's methods 'auger' for twentieth-century theater, namely body-centered performance, feminist 'semiotic' realism, and Brecht.

Part II, 'Gestic feminist criticism,' moves from a discussion of a powerful form of theater representation (realism) to consider the agents and apparatuses of representation. Each of Chapters 2, 3 and 4 rethinks the feminist controversy over the body or body-as-text by introducing historical density into the acts of reading and seeing. Here I propose a materialist approach, 'gestic criticism' which derives from Bertolt Brecht's theory of the *gestus*, the moment in performance when a play's implied social attitudes become visible to the spectator. To read a gesture, a line of dialogue, or a tableau gestically is to draw into analysis the author's history, the play's production conditions, and the historical gender and class contradictions through which stage action might be read. Brecht's *gestus* is not a reading of classical mimesis, however. Brecht intended to 'ruin' and 'destroy' (definition 2) conventional mimetic practice, understanding that that meant overhauling the apparatus of production and reception.

Chapter 2, 'Brechtian theory/feminist theory: toward a gestic feminist criticism,' investigates topoi of feminist theory in relation to Brecht's epic theater theory. I argue that Brecht's alienation-effect, the 'not . . . but,' historicization, and *gestus*, reconsidered through feminism, can reinvigorate Brecht's tropes and, in turn, alert feminist and culture critics to critical tools fashioned in the specificity of theater. The flash point in this discussion is the actor's body. When the Brechtian-feminist performer 'alienates' her/his own gendered, racial, or ethnic history, when that body is 'historicized,' spectators are invited to move through and beyond imaginary identifications, to rethink their own differences and contradictions. Chapter 3, '*Gestus*, signature, body in the theater of Aphra Behn,' looks back to the lavish perspectival displays in Restoration theater which coincided with the playwrighting career of Aphra Behn. I consider the ways in which the professionalization of the dramatist, the new Scenes and machines, and the admission of women as theater workers and alluring ornaments signify in Behn's theater. Behn's explicit theme, the cruelty of forced marriage, should be viewed, I argue, in the light of her manipulations of the theater apparatus; specifically her highly contradictory practice of exposing the bodies of female performers in the upstage Scenes of the theater, thereby intensifying their commodity status.

Chapter 4, 'The *gestus* of invisibility,' investigates the relationship of body to space in a way that is both post-realist and post-Brechtian. Caryl Churchill, I suggest, subverts modernity's 'theater of knowledge,' even as she stays within its precincts. The chapter opens with a deliberately schematic trope, 'orificial/artificial,' to refer to the apparently accessible body in postmodern performance, and the actor's disciplined artificial body in representation.

Churchill's plays pose the problem of feminist agency by tracing a fine line between these positions. In her later plays, the body's discipline and release became a metaphor for the constraints on laboring women, and like Behn she uses theater space to concretize this metaphor. Churchill's 'death-spaces' toy with the vanishing point, that 'point' in a perspectival drawing at which, to the viewer, parallel lines converge or seem to converge. This is the imaginary site where appearance is closest to disappearance, where 'life' touches 'death.' Churchill makes the vanishing point a feminist *gestus*.

Part III, 'Toward a feminist postmodern,' 'alters the characteristics of' mimesis (definition 3). The spatial investigations of the middle sections give way to the rich and varied temporal explorations in Adrienne Kennedy's plays and recent performance art by Peggy Shaw, Robbie McCauley, and Deb Margolin. In Chapter 5, 'Identification and mimesis: the theater of Adrienne Kennedy,' I read this playwright's oeuvre with Borch-Jacobsen's concept of mimetic identification and Paul Gilroy's historico-philosophical concept of the 'black Atlantic.' From her earliest plays Kennedy demonstrates the historical valence of identification and the powerful temporal dissonances such identifications produce. Cultural simulacra and historical figures pleasurably and torturously inhabit Kennedy's characters, resulting in a shocking overlay of political history and psychic crisis. Her latest works, I argue, intensify these effects, creating a mimetic network of spatio-temporal inscription that draws together Fanon's texts and Bram Stoker's *Dracula*, family loss and colonial struggle. Kennedy's brilliant autobiography, a postmodern artifact of enormous suggestiveness, weaves through all these analyses, recalling us continually to the imbrication of identity and identification. Chapter 6, 'Performance and temporality: feminism, experience, and mimetic transformation,' takes up a recent trend in feminist performance art: the return to the auratic body and a kind of storytelling that emphasizes not only the contingency of the present but also historical figurations composed of lost or forgotten artifacts, the detritus of commodity culture. In these pieces, auratic bodies transform into 'dialectical images' – embodied montage-like constructions, not unlike Brecht's *gestus* – that bring conflicting temporalities into view and into (the concept of) experience. The performance art of McCauley, Shaw, and Margolin allows me to tease out a feminist mimesis based not on truth-models or psychic projections but on contiguities: subjects-in-relation, subjects-in-time.

VI

I want to continue in the tradition of performance art which encourages people to learn from the past and to challenge the stories. I want to follow a tradition that heightens the connection of art to life.

Robbie McCauley

Because feminist performers voice such sentiments, we who write about them need to keep mimesis circulating. The connection of art (with its false simulacra, its irrationality) to life is precisely what Plato feared, and what Aristotle sought to regulate (while expunging the immoral dithyramb from poetic tradition, and women and slaves from 'life'). Still, for Halliwell, Aristotle's belief that art 'can nourish understanding and move the emotions with ethical force' means that 'mimesis makes art outward facing'[41] – an enticing formulation for feminism. The question, of course, is how. A feminist mimesis, if there is such a thing, would take the relation to the real as productive, not referential, geared to change, not to reproducing the same. It would explore the tendency to tyrannical modeling (subjective/ideological projections masquerading as universal truths), even in its own operations. Finally, it would clarify the humanist sedi-mentation in the concept as a means of releasing the historical particularity and transgressive corporeality of the *mimos*, who, in mimesis, is always more and different than she seems.

Part I
Unmaking mimesis

1 Realism's hysteria

Disruption in the theater of knowledge

DOLEFUL REFERENTS

Morbid pessimism, subdued or paroxysmal, is the dominant role of the
. . . new psychological drama . . . . The ideal writer of the neurotic school
is a sort of literary mosquito, probing greater depths of agonised human
nature than anybody else . . . . And this same process of needless self-torture is at work in some women's minds now. It is difficult to explain on any
other hypothesis their craving for the literature of hysteria . . . the doleful
squalor of Ibsen.

H.E.M. Stutfield

Noticeable immediately in this statement is the ease with which the writer
identifies not only a genre, 'the literature of hysteria,' and its characteristic
strategies and tone, but also its characteristic audience/reader: women whose
minds are engaged in 'needless self-torture,' who perversely indulge their 'craving' for unhappiness – who exhibit, in other words, the very symptoms of
hysteria they were seeing enacted on stage.[1] To this late Victorian critic, the
hysteric was alarmingly on stage *and* in the audience, responding mimetically
with 'sobs and tears' to the titillating and tearful revelations of Rita Allmers
during the first London performances of Ibsen's *Little Eyolf*. As he sat surrounded by women at a matinée in the Avenue Theatre, November 1896,
H.E.M. Stutfield was no doubt reacting to more than an unseemly adoration
for Ibsen and other 'semi-insane' writers. The 'new woman's' demands for suffrage, better education, employment, and more sexual freedom, accompanied
by major changes in late Victorian law and culture, were, Stutfield believed,
connected to the very disease he was witnessing at the Avenue Theatre: hysterical ego-mania.[2] In his *Blackwood's* article, authoritatively entitled 'The
Psychology of Feminism,' Stutfield borrows the inflammatory medico-ethical
terminology of Max Nordau's *Degeneration* (1895) to denounce those 'self-cen-
tered, neurotic, and egotistical' women both on and off the stage who have
fallen prey to 'the Ibsenite theory of female individualism' (108). In fact the
enormously popular *Degeneration* substantiated Stutfield's claim for theatrical influence: Nordau's long chapter on hysteria contains the sub-heading 'Ibsenism.'

The year 1895 marks the appearance of another analysis of neuropathology in women, Freud and Breuer's *Studies on Hysteria* (translated into English in 1909 but discussed in British medical journals as early as 1896), and from 1889 to the end of the century a rash of English translations and productions of Ibsen's 'literature of hysteria' appeared (six Ibsen performances in 1893 alone), infecting indigenous imitators who broke out with their own versions of the 'new drama.'[3] What I am pointing to is a discursive formation whose fields of enunciation are the new science of psychoanalysis and the new 'sex-problem play,' both at the end of the nineteenth century, both targeting the 'women with a past.' My first thesis is that Ibsenite realism guarantees its legitimacy by endowing the fallen woman of popular melodrama with the symptoms and etiology of the hysteric. In deciphering the hysteric's enigma realism celebrates positivist inquiry, thus buttressing its claims for 'truth to life.' In effect, hysteria provides stage realism with one of its richest and, ideologically, one of its most satisfying plots.

My second thesis, that realism is itself a form of hysteria, needs a wider preface especially in relation to feminist theory. Realism's putative object, the truthful representation of social experience within a recognizable, usually contemporary, moment remains a problematic issue for feminism, not least because theatrical realism, rooted in part in domestic melodrama, retains the oedipal family focus even as it tries to undermine the scenarios that Victorian culture had mythified – the angel in the house, the lost child, the poor but faithful husband, among others. In line with Diderot's tragedy for the common man, late nineteenth-century social realism establishes its authenticity against, on the one hand, the 'artificiality' of neoclassical rules, and, on the other, episodic, histrionical, visually excessive melodrama. With the box-set and picture-frame stage that came to dominate theater design in the latter half of the century, realism could carve out a 'natural' present; the walls of the family drawing room and later the family living room, particularly the fourth wall, create the only space for breathing what Zola calls 'the free air of reality.'[4] The notion that realism offers, as Shaw puts it, 'ourselves in our situations,'[5] follows the curve of Plato's condemnation of mimesis but inverts the valuation. The lifelike stage sign is not only validated by, it reinforces the epistemology of an 'objective world,' for the referent does not simply exist (the historical drawing room on which Hedda Gabler's is modeled), it is reaffirmed in the activity of reception. Realism is more than an interpretation of reality passing as reality; it *produces* 'reality' by positioning its spectator to recognize and verify its truths: this escritoire, this spirit lamp affirms the typicality, the universality of this and all late Victorian bourgeois drawing rooms. Human signification is no less teleological. The actor/signifier, laminated to her character/signified, strenuously seeks admission to the right class of referents.

With Brechtian hindsight we know that realism, more than any other form of theater representation, mystifies the process of theatrical signification. Because it naturalizes the relation between character and actor, setting and world, realism operates in concert with ideology. And because it depends on, insists on a stability of reference, an objective world that is the source and guarantor of knowledge, realism surreptitiously reinforces (even if it argues with) the arrangements of that world. Indeed 'arrangement' is a crucial concept in realism. The picture-frame or proscenium stage (which still dominates theater design) reinforces the pleasures of perspectival space, in which each object has a measured and appropriate position within the whole – a 'whole' produced by a 'single and immobile eye [I],' positioned to see/know the relations between, and meanings of, the objects in view.[6] For nineteenth-century middle-class audiences duly impressed by the authority and methods of positivism, theatrical realism fed a hunger for objects that supplied evidence, characters who supplied testimony, plots that cried out for interpretive acuity and, pleasurably, judgment. Realism as literature and as mode of production urged and satisfied the pursuit of knowledge, the production of truth.

Hysteria, on the other hand, has become the trope par excellence for the ruination of truth-making. Whether we situate the hysteric empirically, as a historico-medical object, whose unreadable symptoms derive in part from the material and gender constraints of bourgeois life (particularly, as Breuer noted, the Victorian tendency to channel young women into jobs as governesses or nurses to the dying),[7] or discursively, as a 'speaking body' that defies the grammar of the patriarchal symbolic, hysteria in feminist discourse has become meaningful precisely as a disruption of traditional epistemological methods of seeing/knowing.[8] Cixous and Clément's *The Newly Born Woman* remains one of the best feminist readings of hysteria because it interweaves empirical and figural explorations, Clément drawing on anthropology and psychoanalytic history, Cixous mythmaking and deconstructing through a spiraling series of fantasmatic (hysterical) identifications.[9] In both authors' sections, Freud's theory of bisexuality, a prominent feature of his formulations on hysteria, is rewritten as a refusal of correct gender positions, although for Clément such refusal is efficacious only in the short term ('Every hysteric ends up inuring others to her symptoms, and the family closes round her again,'[5]), while for Cixous, hysterical discourse explodes the binary logic of logocentrism ('It is you, Dora, you who cannot be tamed . . . your words will . . . write themselves against the other and against men's grammar,' 95). If the female subject is the 'repressed that ensures the system's functioning' (67), hysteria throws a wrench into the system, upsetting its socio-linguistic and gender arrangements.

Sarah Kofman's *The Enigma of Woman* explores Freud's need to criminalize the hysteric in order to break through her narcissistic self-sufficiency and reveal her secret (her sexuality). As early as *Studies on Hysteria* Freud understands, through his interpretation of hysterical symptoms, the sexual origin of all neurosis. But according to Kofman, psychoanalysis cannot penetrate woman's 'enigma'; by Freud's own account, female sexuality is double, undecidable.[10] When Freud attempts to fix a position for the instability of female sexuality, he is led to theorize (illogically, defensively) the binary of gender (active/male versus passive/female) and, more outrageously, to posit penis envy, as the only result of the girl's passage through the oedipus. In effect Kofman, like Irigaray, rejects the castration complex, female sexuality as lack, as the inevitable scenario of female identity. Elizabeth Berg, in her reading of *The Enigma of Woman*, draws out three positions in Kofman's argument. The first is the sick hysteric who, ignorant of her own truth, 'enter[s] into complicity with the doctor in order that he may reveal it.'[11] Second is the narcissistic woman who knows the truth and will not tell. Her most salient feature is her muteness; embodying the truth, she cannot speak it: 'the narcissistic woman silently grounds the discourse of the philosopher or psychoanalyst who verbally interprets the truth that she bears' (19). The second hardly improves on the first; to be inscribed in the economy of truth is always to reinscribe the very phallic oppositions that feminism attempts to undermine. The third woman is 'both masculine and feminine, [thus] no longer the incarnation of truth' (19). Berg elaborates: 'the third woman is not a synthesis of masculinity and femininity . . . it is not that there is no sexual difference; rather sexual difference is seen as undecidable, producing an irresolvable oscillation between masculine and feminine' (19). Nietzsche emerges here. The third woman is 'affirmative,' dionysian, like the god of mythology whose contradictions (god/(wo)man; masculine/feminine) dissolve the have/have not binary of penis envy and gender opposition, those truths of phallic structuration. The third woman has no referent, except in feminist theory. Of course Berg's one-two-three schema sets out its own truth, but it will be useful in our account of a dramatic form that legitimizes itself through its ability to know, to respect, to reflect the truth – 'an undistorting and unexaggerating mirror of real life.'[12]

I have said that the new realism, like the new science of psychoanalysis, establishes its truth by reading of the enigma of hysterical symptoms. Freud found an exemplary psychoanalytic dynamic in Ibsen's *Rosmersholm*, in which the interrogation of Rebecca West (a 'new woman') glorifies the pursuit of knowledge as Rector Kroll peels off layers of repressed material about her past. Figures of male authority, however ironized, read the enigmas of two other Ibsen hysterics, Ellida Wangel and Hedda Gabler; and a similar if cruder dynamic occurs in plays by English Ibsenites, A.W. Pinero's *The Second Mrs. Tanqueray* and Henry Arthur Jones's *Mrs. Dane's Defence*. But if hysteria is signified and narrativized, has it been cured? Or is it possible that even as realism contains and puts closure to the hysteric's symptoms, it catches her disease?

The first English audience of Ibsen's *Hedda Gabler* disgusted the Stutfields but enthralled middle-class women. In her memoir of her Ibsen years, Elizabeth Robins, an American who first acted Hedda and other major Ibsen roles in London in the 1890s, confirms Stutfield's impressions of the imaginary identifications and the gender divisions that Ibsenism produces:

> How should men understand Hedda on the stage when they didn't understand her in the person of their wives, their daughters, their woman friends. One lady of our acquaintance, married and not noticeably unhappy, said laughing, Hedda is all of us.[13]

What should be our response to such confident projection – such absolute identification of self with group, group with a fictional imago?[14] On the one hand this one-to-one mirroring, so typical of the Lacanian imaginary, offers yet another example of both the pleasure and the ideological distortions of realism. *Hedda Gabler* produces a subject who sees, and reproduces, a real relation between signifier–signified–referent. Hedda is all of us, says the spectator, and the pleasure of participating in that group reference is the self-gratifying sense that one's knowledge of the world and the text has been confirmed. Robins's spectator is merely the flip-side of Stutfield, using Ibsen as empirical evidence to validate her own 'truth'. If the early texts of realism seem to gender its spectators, dividing men who snigger (according to Stutfield) and fail to understand Ibsen, from women who weep and do understand, realism is just doing its job, mirroring and reproducing society's most conservative ideological positions. On the other hand, there is something volatile in this woman's statement: a narcissism that deconstructs the mimetic referent upon which it is insisting. If Ibsenism empowers women to recognize themselves as the referent for Hedda, the truth of referentiality passes through the signifier of hysteria. The question, then, is this: can feminist theory make use of the observation that realism, at its inception, can be construed as a form of hysteria?

By historicizing the relation between hysteria and realism, by recovering an early connection between the thematics and semiotics of medical and popular theaters, between Freud's well-padded couch and the ottoman upon which so many heroines of early realism collapse, we might discover some informing contradictions. The drama of 'ourselves in our situations' exists only by repressing other selves, other situations. In Archer's simple narrative, 'new drama' replaces 'old'; 'logical' realism separates off from the false, illogical melodrama. But traces of melodrama's irrationality and its hallucinatory effects still cling to the teacups and upholstered divans. Melodrama provides in fact a crucial link between popular and psychoanalytic theaters. By historicizing Stutfield's particular example we uncover one of realism's most common features, the erasure of the apparatus of representation. For Stutfield, the Avenue Theater production of *Little Eyolf* represented only the delusions of a group of well-meaning Ibsenites, unaware of their own disease.[15] Stutfield was, in fact, an excellent audience for the new realism, for he thought he was seeing *all*. He did not see, or did not choose to mention, the attack on the hegemony of actor-managers of which this independent production, through the impetus of Elizabeth Robins and William Archer, was a notable contribution.[16] Robins, too, needs to be historicized. Her importance in popularizing Ibsen, the fact that to Shaw, Archer, Henry James, Oscar Wilde, and many suffragette colleagues, her life and work seemed exemplary of Ibsenite individualism, has been only recently noted.[17] My immediate interest lies in her contribution to the hystericizing of realism. In May 1893, the highly praised *The Second Mrs. Tanqueray* by A.W. Pinero and the controversial *Alan's Wife* by Elizabeth Robins and Florence Bell were performed within weeks of each other in very different venues, to very different responses, and with very different relations to the referent. In order to appreciate this odd juxtaposition of theater events, it will be helpful to look at realism's past, to 'excavate,' as Freud would say, the theatrical secrets it represses.

FALLEN WOMEN: THE MEDICAL MELODRAMA

Semiotically, discursively, the hysteric has always been a fallen woman. Since ancient Greek physicians named the 'disease' for the female womb (*hysteron*), the hysterical woman has been guilty, not only of sexual aberrations that undermine her proper role in family and culture, but also of symptoms whose etiology could not be explained. No medical narrative could contain the sheer diversity of symptoms – depression, withdrawal, bouts of uncontrollable laughter and crying, muscular tics, shortness of breath, nervous cough, attacks of blindness, mutism, vomiting, cutaneous anesthesia, abasia, tremors, deafness, an assortment of neuralgias, contracture of limbs, hair-tearing fits, and seizures – some or all of which arose and vanished erratically, or lasted for years. Unable to assign verifiable causes to these symptoms, doctors since Galen have blamed female biology. The notion that woman, by her 'nature,' is susceptible to disease underlies much medical discourse on hysteria, becoming especially vociferous among eighteenth- and nineteenth-century physicians who thought that menses and pregnancy produced a deficiency of blood which impeded mental functioning and thus moral development. Such thinking slides into tautology: women are hysterics because they are women. Even those seventeenth- and eighteenth-century physicians like Sydenham and Whytt who attempted to reroute the etiology of hysteria through a genderless nervous system could not escape some form of the uterine theory. As Michel Foucault succinctly puts it: 'The woman's body [as constructed in medical discourse] encloses a perpetual possibility of hysteria.'[18]

The search for the etiology of a disease is the search for an originary cause from which predictions can be made, treatment determined. The truth of a disease, its status *as* a disease, waits upon such a narrative, yet truth eluded even those, like Thomas Sydenham, who wrote most sympathetically about hysteria:

> The frequency of hysteria is no less remarkable than the multiformity of shapes it puts on. Few of the maladies of miserable mortality are not imitated by it. Whatever part of the body it attacks, it will create the proper symptom of that part.[19]

Like an itinerant mime, hysteria takes on behavior (symptoms) suitable to the region (part of the body) in which it resides. The Greeks attributed such movements to a wandering womb seeking nourishment. In the findings of the Harveian Society, published in the *British Medical Journal* in 1887, malnutrition of the uterus was again posited.[20] After two thousand years, the only point of agreement among physicians was the identity between hysteria and female duplicity – a duplicity grounded in the body and in cultural discourse. As

Carroll Smith-Rosenberg notes, bourgeois Victorian society demanded that its women be 'chaste, delicate, and loving,' protectors and purveyors of bourgeois values, but

> behind this modest exterior lay a complex network of reproductive organs that controlled her physiology, determined her emotions, and dictated her social role. She was seen, that is, as being both higher and lower, both innocent and animal, pure yet quintessentially sexual.[21]

Hysteria marks the eruption of the lower, the animal, signifying a sexuality that is anti-social, even criminal, and – worst of all – inexplicable. Hence the combination of rage, disgust and frustration that often occurs in medical discourse. Francis Skey writing in the *Lancet* calls hysteria a 'factitious condition of the body that mocks the reality of truth,'[22] and over fifty years later Hughlings Jackson wrote in the *BMJ*, 'Many so-called cases of hysteria were cases of nothing.'[23] Without an etiology, a theory of causation, hysteria was indeed a case of nothing, that is nothing that medicine could treat. And yet in the last quarter of the century middle-class women were taking to their beds in increasing numbers with depression, analgesias, uterine pains – the assorted symptoms of 'hysteria.'

Accusations of fakery ('cases of nothing') were as common as the claim that women, prisoners of their uteruses, were by nature hysterical. If hysteria was a factitious condition of the body, then women claiming the existence of such pains had to be faking. Smith-Rosenberg quotes George Preston in his 1897 monograph: 'There is only the bald statement of the patient . . . . No confirming symptoms present themselves . . . and the appearance of the affected parts stands as contradictory evidence against the patient's word.'[24] A.J. Nairne, whose circumspect analysis of hysteria in the *BMJ* separates him from most of his colleagues, acknowledges that in the 'popular view' cases of 'so-called' hysteria had 'come to be associated with the idea of female disorders of a rather discreditable type and which no woman of a self-respecting character would be subjected to.'[25] This opinion combines two inseparable but distinct constructions of hysteria: the sexual, animal nature of the disease and the moral weakness of women who gave into it. If this was 'the popular view,' and presuming the average citizen did not read medical journals, how was it reinforced? French physician Jules Falret writing in 1890 gives us a clue:

> These patients are veritable actresses; they do not know a greater pleasure than to deceive . . . the life of the hysteric is nothing but one perpetual falsehood; they affect the airs of piety and devotion and let themselves be taken for saints while at the same time secretly abandoning themselves to the most shameful actions.[26]

If the hysteric is an actress, she is acting in a melodrama whose episodes are numbered by the exotically unpredictable pains crisscrossing her body, always one step ahead of the physician, who, like the unflinching hero, pursues anxiously, true to his word to cure even his ungrateful patients. Typical of melodrama – and hysteria – actions are writ large: the hysteric chokes, she writhes on the ground, she pulls out handfuls of hair, her back is arched, her limbs contracted, her face twitching. In full melodramatic expressiveness the body speaks. But what does it say? To physicians, like Skey, Jennings, Falret, and Preston, 'the appearance of the affected parts stands as contradictory evidence against the patient's word.' Where are the lesions? Where are the ruptures? The doctor pursues until he stands defiantly like the sinned-against George Talboys in *Lady Audley's Secret* and proclaims: 'You are a traitress . . . I will expose you, woman.'[27]

My interpolation into medical discourse of one of the most popular Victorian melodramas is not fanciful. In the extravagant, sensationalistic melodrama that dominated the first half of the century in England and on the Continent, we find not only the intensely judgmental ethos that pervades medical opinion on the hysteric, but also figural projections of the battle between doctor and hysteric.[28] The features of melodrama are well known: episodic fast-action plots strung together with chases and absurd coincidences in which vice and virtue clash through the agency of instantly recognizable type characters against a background of thrilling spectacle and musical effects. Bernard Shaw long ago observed what many critics have elaborated, that melodrama gives full play to the spectators' most savage fantasies about power, vicitimization, and heroics, before installing a heavenly (and politically conservative) peace at the end.[29]

The pleasure the spectator experiences before these unleashed heroes and villains is suggestive of the Lacanian imaginary, the pre-lingual moment of dyadic identification between mother and infant, infant and its mirror image, which forever attaches the ego to an illusory imago even after its entry into language and culture. Melodrama's vice–virtue dichotomies, embodied in clearly coded type characters, the intensely visual nature of the *mise-en-scène*, with its waterfalls, sea battles, explosions, its full-throated, broad-gestured acting, all were engineered to provoke passionate binary identifications. The semiotics of class – villains as lecherous aristocrats or wealthy landlords; heroines as poor but faithful wives – naturally gratified the imaginary of a disenfranchised, newly urbanized working class. Melodrama's imaginary offers, in Peter Brooks's words, 'a complete set of attitudes, phrases, gestures coherently conceived [to dramatize] essential spiritual conflict'; such conflict reaffirms the values and meanings that material and class inequities had distorted.[30]

It is possible that such iconography supported 'the popular view' of hysterical women as both victims and degenerates. Indeed the nineteenth-century melodramatic actor and the hysteric shared a similar repertory of signs; the facial grimace, eye-rolling, teeth-gnashing, heavy sighs, fainting, shrieking, shivering, choking. *'Hysterical laughter'* is a frequent stage direction, usually an indication of despair and abandonment, also a symptom of guilt. In the medical melodrama described above, the doctor symbolizes truth, health, the moral and spiritual foundations of society while the hysteric is the fallen woman/villainess, infecting the social body, vamparizing its lifeblood.

Interestingly in the 1860s, domestic melodrama, which vied for popularity with nautical and romantic varieties, offered a variation on the long-suffering heroine: the heroine who dies of sin. In *Lost in London* and *East Lynne*, famous vehicles for the heroine's fall, suffering, and demise, innocent wives are seduced and carried off, only to return repentant and miserable, to die for-given in their husband's arms. In *East Lynne* (adapted from Mrs. Henry Wood's novel), Isabel Archer returns home as governess, disguised only by her sin-worn face and dark glasses; her poverty, her symbolic blindness, most of all her demotion from propertied lady to governess are, to use Brooks's phase, the 'morally legible' signs of punishment and suffering (44).

Is Isabel Archer a hysteric? Max Nordau would have found her impres-sionableness a sign of incipient ego-mania, especially as this symptom emerges in a scene of mistaken judgment. Through the stage-managing of her seducer, Isabel watches her husband and a family friend strolling the garden in deep conversation and, misreading the signs ('how ardently he looks at her'[31]), pre-sumes they are in love. Isabel's orphaned status has already been emphasized. As these silent figures pass before her, and as her seducer suddenly produces written (forged) confirmation of their betrayal, the melodramatic signifier cre-ates in bold strokes a primal scene of separation and abandonment – a scene from a cultural as well as a subjective imaginary. As Martha Vicinus has point-ed out, scenes of domestic betrayal and remorse coincide with the domestic upheavals and material insecurity that accompanied the change from country to city life for the new urban working force. In domestic melodrama, incessant appeals to 'home', to strife and reconciliation between generations, and the reiteration of stern moral messages all offered positions of pleasurable identifi-cation, especially to female spectators who responded, as did the Englishwomen viewing *Little Eyolf*, with tears of recognition.[32] (Aging actresses would perform Isabel Archer as a farewell role, assured that Isabel's journey from happiness to misery to suffering repentance would earn them passionate applause.)

If *East Lynne* shows a hysteric as victim of her emotional, impressionable nature, *Lady Audley's Secret* (adapted from Mary Elizabeth Braddon's novel) is dominated by a darker hysteric, a defiant, violent, seductress and interloper. Abandoned to poverty by her husband, Helen Talboys fakes a death announcement, enters the employ of old Lord Robert Audley as a governess, and soon cajoles him into marrying her. When her first husband George Talboys returns, she pushes him down a well and attempts to incinerate and stab all who interfere. Finally she dies raving and unrepentant – albeit in a 'tableau of sympathy' (266). A true Auerbachian demon, Lady Audley violates all the gender rules of the etiquette books and marriage manuals.[33] Lady Audley 'married for love,' but the 'sweets of wealth and power' drove her to bigamy. She performs the hysteric's hypocrisy as described by Falret: all 'piety and devotion' to her aging husband, soon abandoning herself to 'secret actions' – murder, arson – the likely effects of sexual corruption. *Lady Audley's Secret* has been called a society melodrama, a prototype of the bourgeois problem play that was to dominate London theater in the 1890s. Indeed the play features an interrogation scene in which the fallen woman incriminates herself by revealing her secret. It also produces an ambiguity which was untypical of melodramatic endings. Lady Audley's lapse into hysteria, signified by a hallucination of her dead husband and benefactor, refers back not to bigamy but to the allure of wealth and comfort which started her on a life of crime.

> LADY AUDLEY (*vacantly*) . . . I have a rich husband. They told me he was dead – but no, they lied – see –, he stands there!
>
> (266)

George Talboys's role in this scene, as opposed to the discovery scene mentioned above, is one not of abused husband, but of sympathetic mourner, a change that suggests the public's fascination with madness and sexual rapacity and their relation to criminality.

Two extremely popular Victorian melodramas, Paul Potter's adaptation of Du Maurier's *Trilby* (1894, adapted 1895) and Leopold Lewis's *The Bells* (1871), emphasize, in the case of the former, the criminal hypnotist or mesmerist, Dr. Svengali, who kidnaps, marries, and transforms the innocent Trilby, and in the latter, the criminal in hiding who is drawn out and incriminated by hypnotism.[34] Mathias, a rich magistrate, is haunted by the sound of bells that no one else hears, and in a scene in which he *imagines* himself under hypnosis, he reveals that his riches derive from his murder and robbery of a wealthy Polish Jew, whose horses' sleighbells have become forever associated with the crime. As played by the histrionic actor Henry Irving, the pathology of Mathias's hallucinations and final breakdown far outweighed interest in his crime. Similarly, in her limelit 'tableau of sympathy,' the red-haired (a sign of devilishness) Lady Audley attains a kind of eerie transformation; she becomes both murderess and victim, morally guilty but also pathetically sick. The conclusion of *Lady Audley's Secret* satisfies the binary ethos of melodrama, but suggests an etiology based not on inherent degeneracy but on material want. Her hallucinatory hysteria can be read as both conventional and problematic.

> LADY AUDLEY   Aye – aye! (*Laughs wildly.*) Mad, mad, that is the word. I feel it here! (*Places her hands on her temples.*) Do not touch me – do not come near me – let me claim your silence – your pity – and let the grave, the cold grave, close over Lady Audley and her Secret.
>
> *Falls – dies – Music – tableau of sympathy – GEORGE TALBOYS kneels over her Curtain*
>
> (266)

Lady Audley's secret, her bigamy, has already been told: George Talboys's presence is living proof that she has married two men. Presumably she fails to see Talboys because she is mad. But why does she merit the tableau of sympathy? Unlike Isabel Archer she is not repentant. The tableau sanctimoniously covers over, as the grave will cover her, the guilt of bigamy without exacting penitence or confession from the guilty woman. Perhaps Lady Audley's secret is not that she committed bigamy but that she violated gender regulations by making her own fortune independently from her husband. *This* secret has to be buried because melodrama cannot tell it, cannot explore the social, political, and gender problems it raises. In Ibsen and the Ibsenite drama of the 1890s, such secrets will be told and debated, although the taint of female degeneracy will never be expunged. The crime of bigamy will simply be displaced and 'internalized' as a pathology like bisexuality or the hypnoid state.

Fifteen years after the first production of *Lady Audley's Secret*, a real mesmerist captivated his spectators:

> The subject exhibits hysterical spasms; Charcot suspends an attack by placing first his hand, then the end of a baton, on the woman's ovaries. He withdraws the baton, and there is a fresh attack, which he accelerates by administering inhalations of amyl nitrate. The afflicted woman than cries out for the sex-baton in words that are devoid of any metaphor.[35]

Jean-Martin Charcot's famous *leçons du mardi*, which Freud attended, offered lurid spectacular demonstrations intending, among other aims, to prove the nonorganic etiology of hysteria. Charcot would induce a hysterical affect, such as an analgesia or anesthesia, on one side of the hysteric's body, then move it to the other side with the help of a magnet,[36] a mechanized imitation of the wandering womb. Freud credited Charcot for stressing an originary psychic trauma in his etiology of hysteria, thus lending prestige to the attempt by many physicians to debunk the uterine theory. And yet Charcot also associated hysteria with sensitivity in ovaries and mammary glands (labeling them hysterogenic zones) and he reinstated the idea of woman as inveterate deceiver, casting himself as the victimized doctor. He notes 'the ruse, the sagacity, and the unyielding tenacity that especially the women, who are under the influence of a severe neurosis, display in order to deceive . . . particularly when the victim of the deceit happens to be a physician.'[37]

The episode cited above contains effects worthy of the best sensational melodramas: the woman's jolting spasms quelled then renewed by the magic wand of a Svengali-like physician, who with the help of potions brings the demonstration to a screaming climax. In this highly charged theater the bipolar forces of pain and pleasure, sick and healthy, patient and doctor, and (because the Salpetrière was primarily a hospital for women) female and male, interact in a medical orgy fired by laughing gas and erotic language 'devoid of any metaphor.' The audience of male doctors and students, 'their bodies tensed to see the tensed body of the possessed woman,' occupy the position of learner and voyeur, the scopophilic position that permits them to identify both with 'the great Charcot' and with a hero who can maintain the arousal of a screaming, heaving woman, aided by a few carefully chosen props. The citation (from Foucault's *The History of Sexuality*) ends with the dry stage direction: 'G. is taken away and her delirium continues' (56).

This performance–demonstration, or one similar, is captured in the famous lithograph which hung in Freud's office. In it, an expressionless Charcot lectures on hysteria at the Salpêtrière, next to a swooning, partially disrobed female figure supported by his assistant Babinski, surrounded by male physicians arranged in stylized randomness, their eyes fixed on the woman. Her back, suggestively arched, combines the signs of *grand mal* seizure and sexual orgasm.[38] If melodrama tableaux imitated precisely such pictorial arrangements, Charcot's patient conforms just as iconographically to melodrama's figurations of the hysteric: collapsed (passive victim), but with bosom exposed (active seducer), she balances both the victimized Isabel and the thrilling Lady Audley: she is both fixed in an etiological narrative and the star of her own spectacular theater of suffering. Charcot and Babinsky present the dispassionate faces of science, but the physicians, some with backs partially turned toward the viewer, occupy our position. A mid-century spectator's account of a melodramatic heroine's suffering may help us read the painting's iconography:

> [her] hair, like a mantle of flame, streamed over her fair shoulders, while from the simple tunic of white muslin, which fell from head to heel, gleamed forth a pair of statuesque arms and a superbly moulded bust which rose and sank tumultuously as though about to burst with the agonies of a tortured, despairing heart.[39]

Foucault sees other meanings in such demonstrations: 'The essential point is that sex was not only a matter of sensation and pleasure, of law and taboo, but also of truth and falsehood. . . . What needs to be situated is the . . . interplay of truth and sex' (56–57) – and this interplay, Foucault suggests, occurs most clearly in the confession, a ritual of discourse in which, with great emotional distress, past sins are articulated to an authority figure, who then grants absolution and forgiveness. Foucault's account of the discursive power of sexual confession helps us account for the significant change in the theatrical and therapeutic construction of the hysteric. It is on the basis of the confession that the fallen woman blossoms out of melodramatic unifacity into a figure who, by allowing figures of cultural authority to strip her of falsehood, creates a theater of knowledge, makes possible the production of truth. It is on the basis of the hysteric's confession that Freud discovers the traumatic event that triggers the somatic conversions of hysteria.

TRANSLATION AND THE HYPNOID STATE

> I cannot think that these are all the reasons for your feelings . . . . I believe that you are really in love with your employer.
>
> Sigmund Freud, *Studies on Hysteria*

> Woman, you're lying! . . . I say you're lying! You are Felicia Hindemarsh!
>
> Henry Arthur Jones, *Mrs. Dane's Defence*

In the private practice of a physician working in a large town, the quantity of such patients [with organic nervous diseases] was nothing compared to the crowds of neurotics, whose number seemed further multiplied by the manner in which they hurried, with their troubles unsolved, from one physician to another.

Sigmund Freud, *Collected Papers*

Oh! oh! oh! I believe, to be a woman is to be mad.

A.W. Pinero, *The Notorious Mrs. Ebbsmith*

The discourses of psychoanalysis and the late nineteenth-century problem play share a similar emphasis on newness and on the theatrical production of truth. Sigmund Freud and Josef Breuer label their innovative treatment of hysterics 'the cathartic method,' in which hysterical patients verbalize the scene of originary trauma, thus eliminating or purging the debilitating symptom. William Archer, Ibsen's major English translator, promotes the 'new drama' because it 'casts out the foreign elements of rhetoric and lyricism' – the overblown language of melodrama – in favor of 'natural' dialogue and a 'purification or *katharsis*' of dramatic form. For Freud, Breuer, and Archer catharsis is the effect that vindicates an epistemology and a practice. All are eager to associate their projects with a venerable and powerful cultural monument, Attic tragedy, and to impress their readers with a concomitant feeling of pity and wonder. But there is a more specific similarity; the new therapy and the new theater depend on exploring and exposing the woman with a past. Realism and psychoanalysis celebrate precisely what melodrama and farce, and uterine-theory physicians had ignored; motivation arising from the complications of an 'individual,' shaped by inherited traits, social contexts, and forgotten traumas. Gone is the medical magnet drawing analgesias from one side of the body to another. Gone are hair-tearing fits and chases before moving painted panoramas. But perhaps 'gone' is too strong a word. If in their object-laden rooms Ibsen and his imitators give prominence to etiology (causal and probable action) the explosive melodrama of hysteria remains only barely repressed. And Freud, in the privacy of his consulting room, follows his mentor Charcot in charming away some unwanted pains. In both sites, the woman with a past is the object of discovery.

The 'Preliminary Communication' to the *Studies on Hysteria* is an ambitious, optimistic document. Freud and Breuer announce with certainty that 'hysterics suffer mainly from reminiscences' and report that hysterical symptoms will disappear 'immediately and permanently' when the event that produced the originary trauma is remembered and articulated and the accompanying affect released or 'abreacted' (7–10). In these first therapies Freud and Breuer use hypnosis (at which Freud was untalented), massage, and firm urgings to coax out the traumatic memory, discovering in the process resistance or repression, the first step toward mapping the unconscious. The process of verbally remembering and re-reacting was christened the 'talking cure' or 'chimney sweeping'

(30) by Breuer's famous patient 'Anna O.' (Bertha Pappenheim), the result of which was catharsis, abreaction, and the disappearance 'immediately and permanently' of the hysterical symptom. This seems as far a cry from the juiced-up demonstrations of Charcot's *leçons du mardi* as the exciting but human-scale dialogues of realism were from the constant teeth-gnashing, swooning, gesturing and shrieking of melodrama.

Which is not to say that Freud saw his work as any less theatrically effective or powerful. In his case studies of Frau Emmy Von N., Miss Lucy R., Fraulein Elisabeth Von R., and Katharina, which he admits read like good stories, Freud's tone is confident, even exultant, as he begins to understand the unconscious as a realm of potential discovery and to develop the tools for – to use his own metaphor – excavating through layer upon layer of memory to arrive at the originary trauma. The conclusive proof of the patient's putting 'the affect into words' is that the stimuli connected with the affect, be they spasms, neuralgias, or hallucinations, *reappear once again with the fullest intensity and then vanish forever* (7). During this performance, while the patient speaks, recreating the memory, experiencing the hysterical symptom with doubled intensity, Dr. Freud observes, monitors, and legislates: it must be a truthful performance, otherwise there can be no catharsis:

> As a rule the patient was free from pain when we started work. If, then, by a question or by pressure upon her head I called up a memory, a sensation of pain would make its first appearance, and this was usually so sharp that the patient would give a start and put her hand to the painful spot. The pain that was thus aroused would persist so long as she was under the influence of the memory; it would reach its climax when she was in the act of telling me the essential and decisive part of what she had to communicate, and with the last word of this it would disappear. I came in time to use such pains as a compass to guide me; if she stopped talking but admitted that she still had a pain, I knew that she had not told me everything, and insisted on her continuing her story till the pain had been talked away.
>
> (148)

In his treatment of Elisabeth Von R., Freud plays both director and audience, judge and witness, which casts the patient in the role of performer, if not criminal. At several points in the *Studies*, Freud refers to his patients' 'confessions' (8, 79, 139, 144, 151), and near the end of the volume to himself as a father confessor (282). In *The Enigma of Woman*, Sarah Kofman stresses the magisterial authority Freud exercises in obtaining confessions, arguing, as we noted earlier, that when she consents to reveal her secrets, the hysteric 'collaborates with the doctor and . . . recognize[s] *his* word as the voice of truth.'[40] In the *mise-en-scène* of Freud's Vienna office – actually the anteroom where his patients awaited a preliminary interview – this lopsided 'collaboration' was stunningly orchestrated. According to Diana Fuss and Joel Sanders, directly opposite and at eye level to the chair on which the waiting patient sat, was a mirror, that time-honored instrument of (self-)reflection, mimetic doubling, identificatory rage, and vanity. When Freud took his seat directly opposite the waiting patient, the latter's image was suddenly erased by Freud's face – and gaze.[41]

In the above passage concerning Elizabeth Von R. the production of this truth depends upon the hypothesized 'somatic conversion,' a process Freud will call 'translation.'[42] Through his verbal question or hand pressure, Freud introduces a memory that is immediately translated into another medium: bodily pain, signalled by a 'start' and a hand gesture. The verbal revelation is obviously more vital, but the word must be *verified* by the body's visible mimesis. Without this physical signal Freud cannot be sure that he has heard the secret – 'the essential and decisive part' of the story. Elisabeth's body language is Freud's 'compass to guide me' as he travels into the unconscious (148). It tells Freud the truth even when Elisabeth herself resists, when she stops talking but still admits to pain. The result of this performance is cathartic climax and completion: no more words, no more pains. The hysteric's body language, her tics, her contractures, can be represented, their messages translated, the representation concluded.

A lot is at stake here. Freud desires scientific validation of his method; he and Breuer are formulating if not an etiology (for he hadn't yet postulated infantile sexuality or the theory of dreamwork), at least a reliable method by which the analyst can peel away the resistant material and arrive at the origin of the symptom. Miss Lucy, the English governess suffering from unpleasant olfactory sensations, remembers that she smelled burnt custard while reading a sad letter from home; Anna O.'s thigh neuralgia began when she had to bandage her father's leg as it rested across her thigh; Katharina's shortness of breath relates to a sexual scene that shocked and depressed her. Freud is after, in his words, no less than 'a completely adequate set of determinants,' a 'causal chain' (139) to justify the conversion of traumatic affect into hysterical symptom. Only such causality could produce the desired *anagnorisis* which, once again, is translated into theater:

> The sulky unhappy face had grown lively, [Katharina's] eyes were bright, she was lightened and exalted.
>
> (131)

> In the spring of 1894, I heard that [Elizabeth] was going to a private ball for which I was able to get an invitation, and I did not allow the opportunity to escape me of seeing my former patient whirl past in a lively dance.
>
> (160)

The absurd avuncular tone of these passages occasions an apology from Freud who notes that his case histories 'read like short stories . . . and lack the serious stamp of science' (160). But the happy ending is a logical extension of Freud's spectacular maneuvers in *Studies on Hysteria*. There are two narrative personas Freud makes use of: one, the restless, relentless detective:

> But I was not satisfied with the explanation thus arrived at. It all sounded highly plausible, but was there something that I missed, some adequate rea-

son why these agitations and this conflict of affects should have led to hysteria [in Miss Lucy] rather than anything else?

(116)

and two, that of powerful, Svengali-like healer: '[Frau Emmy's] period began again to-day after an interval of scarcely a fortnight. I promised to regulate this by hypnotic suggestion and, under hypnosis, set the interval at 28 days' (57). In the same vein, in a lightning-quick analysis on the side of a mountain, Freud questions a country girl suffering from suffocation 'in the confident expectation that she would think of precisely what I needed to explain the case' (129). This satisfying mimesis between the analyst's theory and hysteric's response is the scientist's version of the happy ending, which retroactively confirms the truth of the methods and theories by which it was achieved: the theory of the unconscious and repression, the 'talking cure' and its 'catharsis,' all discoveries in *Studies on Hysteria*. With 'Fragment of an Analysis of a Case of Hysteria' (Dora's Case, 1905), such certainties are exploded, not least of which the magisterial role of the analyst, who, too late, discovers the transference (the analysand's projection onto the analyst of infantile wishes, imagoes, past scenes) and cannot conceive of the counter-transference (analyst's projection onto the patient). When Freud tells of his inability, in Fraulein Elizabeth's analysis, 'to get hold of any scene [from the past that would explain her symptoms]' (147), we can't help wondering, with Freudian hindsight, if the scene in question wasn't being enacted right in front of – and with – him. However, unlike Dora's 'fragment,' *Studies on Hysteria* is about successful translation: as trauma is translated (somatically converted) into symptoms, former patients are translated into happy young women, their cases translated into readable and instructive 'stories' that tell the truth about hysteria.

It is not surprising that when Freud needs to illustrate a problematic etiology he raids other fictions, including what he calls the 'new psychological drama,' which molded itself on a dynamic of excavation, repression, and revelation. For Ibsen and his English imitators, A.W. Pinero and Henry Arthur Jones, the conventionalized fallen woman became more than automatic sinner. Her social position, her desires, her confusion, most of all her secret sexual past, were a problem, *the* problem or enigma, that has to be solved. Like Freud's case histories, the new realism progresses by going backward, revealing the psychobiography of nervous women. Through confessions and self-exploration, woven into dialogue and action, an etiology emerges. One might say the search for an etiology is basic to realism's departure from the episodic melodrama. The events of the past, filtered through memory and desire, form part of the 'motive-complex' of Mrs. Alving, Rebecca West, Nora Helmer, Ellida Wangel; in their (self-)discovery lies the play's claim to truth.

Of course Freud would have found another fascination to the theater: the fact that the symptomatology of hysteria is always 'translated,' theatricalized, putting the spectator into the position of analyst/discoverer. Of the three Ibsen plays, written in succession, that deal with female hysteria, *Rosmersholm* (1896),

The Lady from the Sea (1888), and *Hedda Gabler* (1890), Freud focuses on the first, with its 'new woman,' Rebecca West, as an ideal exemplum not only of the oedipal taboo, but of the analytic dialogue – Dr. Kroll's interrogation of Rebecca West – and the way in which repression functions to 'dissimulate' motives that the patient (character) finds unacceptable. Rebecca can confess to what Strindberg called the 'psychic murder' of Rosmer's wife Beata, but not to what she must repress: that she has been her father's mistress. This is the secret that the play withholds. Because he can rely on Ibsen 'to have arranged his conscious dramatic [material] in logical accordance with unconscious possibilities,'[43] Freud finds 'complete agreement' between literary and 'clinical experience' (331). In effect, Freud translates *Rosmersholm* into a case history filled with synoptic dazzling insights and the unmistakable tone of the stern detective/analyst:

> Let us listen to [Rebecca], and consider whether we can accord her our full credence.
>
> (325)

> Laws of poetical economy necessitate this way of presenting the situation, for this deeper motive [the knowledge that Rebecca has committed incest] could not be explicitly set forth . . . We have, however, *a right to demand* that the ostensible motive shall not be without an inherent relation to the dissimulated one . . .
>
> (329) (my italics)

Rector Kroll, Freud acknowledges, shows 'analytical perspicacity' (329) when interrogating Rebecca, but 'Kroll is mistaken' (327). Dr. Freud will pick up where he leaves off. This 'right to demand,' which Freud grants himself and all reader/spectators of Ibsen, echoes the impatient enraged physicians who take the position of George Talboys in *Lady Audley's Secret*. 'I will expose you, woman' (246). This is positivism's demand, rooted in the medical melodrama and driving the 'new drama,' infecting characters, spectators, and analysts alike with the desire to see/know the absolute truth.

Interestingly, both Helen Talboys and Rebecca West insinuate themselves through deceit and bold action into the households of wealthy men; both have secrets that the plays reveal and mystify; and both die as a consequence of that secret. In melodrama, however, there is complete adequation between the symptomatology of hysteria and the actor's language, body, and motive, allowing the spectator *instantly* to decipher the signs and messages (melodrama's 'coherent aesthetic'); there is no ambiguity. Realism retains some of melodrama's thrilling signs – Ellida Wangel like Lady Audley beats her temples with fists; Nora rips into a wild tarantella (a dance which Catherine Clément, and conceivably Ibsen, linked to hysterical abandon) – but the gestural range has diminished to the suggestive signs of a complex, changing interior state. Instead of adequation, there are gaps, feints, evasions, and ambiguous physical translations, such as Hedda's thin hair, Mrs. Dane's hand-wringing, Paula

Tanqueray's pallor. The next section will take up this point more fully. For now let me note that what Freud manifests in his reading of Rebecca West is one of the pleasures of realism; the analyst's magisterial role in translating the hysteric's signs is transferred to the audience. The spectator takes on the role of seeker/knower, is assured of completing the narrative, of discovering the secret, of judging its truth.

The Rebecca West analysis occurs in 1916 when Freud was interested in affirming the centrality of the Oedipus complex. Had he been casting about for examples of the hysteric's secret, its repression, its medical discovery, and the patient's reinsertion into conventional society, he might have looked to *The Lady from the Sea* – although, as Raymond Williams points out, the problem of this play is seemingly solved *by* the play; Freud is not needed. Also, unlike the scientific Kroll in *Rosmersholm*, the doctor/analyst of *The Lady from the Sea* is a husband with a drinking problem, and in his counter-transference he produces wrong guesses, thus ironizing the authority and insight, not to say the conventional morality, which he is supposed to represent.

Nevertheless, Ellida Wangel, 'the lady from the sea,' is Ibsen's optimistic 'case history' of the hysteric. Married to a provincial physician whose two daughters have little affection for her, Ellida is depressed, withdrawn, so fixated on the sea of her childhood that her only pleasure is to swim in the fjord. She is fixated too on a mysterious attachment to a sailor whose origins are deliberately obscured in the play but who had promised to return and reclaim her. Minor characters either comment on Ellida's 'morbid state of mind,' her self-absorption, or embody it, as in the figure of the consumptive sculptor, who hopes to represent the unplayable scene of this mystical marriage. Ibsen even supplies an insane mother and an originary trauma – the death of Ellida's son – whose eyes she connects with the stranger's eyes, so that sexual contact with her husband has become an uncanny replay of the earlier unconsummated union. Ellida is haunted by repetition. The sea, with its connotations of sensuality and death, overwhelms her thought, objectifies her crisis and, simultaneously, undermines sexual relations with Wangel (a typical symptom of hysteria, as Ibsen would certainly have known).

The first scene of confrontation between Ellida, her physician husband, and the Stranger reads like a session of moral therapy. Ellida must choose between the helpful but conventional husband and the 'freedom' of the sea – that is, the freedom to continue her hysteria. In their last meeting with the Stranger, Wangel gives his wife the freedom to go; he also gives her responsibility, and with this sudden sense of being empowered to make her own decisions, Ellida banishes the intruder and assumes her appropriate role in marriage and motherhood – translating, as Freud put it, 'hysterical misery into common unhappiness.' With Ibsen's typical density, the signs of Ellida's hysteria, accumulating through dialogue and confession, are counterpointed by hints about Dr. Wangel's drinking, his hypocritical attention to his daughters, the possibility that he may be drugging his wife. But in the play's closing lines, Ellida's return from the brink of the sea, from deeper involvement with the 'terror' and

'horror' of the Stranger, to home and family, the theme of healthy responsibility is sounded again, if somewhat ironically now, by her husband/doctor.
Ellida concludes: 'How very true!' That is the truth of bourgeois duty and conformity which the hysteric puts in jeopardy and which, therefore, requires
Ellida's affirmation to rebuild. Was there any doubt that she would 'return'?
Ellida's instructive adjustment from 'morbid' frigidity to the 'truth' of responsibility is not so much a change as a demonstration, the routing of an 'incompatible idea' in a normally healthy mind. In other words, Ellida's illness is evidence of a double self or, in Freud and Breuer's terms, a 'hypnoid state.'

Before *Studies on Hysteria* was published in full, the 'Preliminary
Communication' appeared in a German periodical in January 1893; and in
April of 1893 an account of it was delivered to a meeting of the Society for
Psychical Research in London, then printed in the *Proceedings* the following
June. Another account, by a physician called Michell Clarke, was published in
Brain in 1894. What impressed Clarke was the concept of 'double conscience'
(Pierre Janet's term) or what Freud and Breuer called the 'hypnoid state.'
Freud and Breuer first thought that pathenogenic or incompatible ideas were
in a sense stored in the unconscious and could only be addressed and abreacted if the patient were hypnotized. Hysterics, they theorized, had a kind of
secret, sick self, although Freud soon abandoned this idea for a more complex
theory of the defense mechanism. Clarke makes only brief mention of abreaction (which he calls 'reaction'), but he stresses the 'double consciousness' that
produces separate and different psychical states in the same person.[44] Much
later, in *The Psychopathology of Hysteria* by a Boston physician (1913), long after
Freud had published his findings on infantile sexuality, the chief symptom of
hysteria was identified as the 'splitting of consciousness.'[45] Why did this receive
such currency?

Perhaps the idea of 'double personality' allowed doctors to ignore the sexual etiology that Freud so disturbingly proposed in infants. Equally likely, the
idea of dramatic duality reinforced the popular epistemology of the double
woman: frail saint and animalistic whore. With the theory of the hypnoid state,
the two conditions could exist side by side until 'the products of hypnoid states
intrude into waking life in the form of hysterical symptoms' (13). The hypnoid
state in effect frees the hysteric from the opprobrium of fakery. It accounts for
the observable fact that, as Freud and Breuer note in their Preliminary
Communication:

> hysterics may be . . . people of the clearest intellect, strongest will, greatest
> character and highest critical power. This characterization holds good of
> their waking thoughts; but in their hypnoid states they are insane, *as we all
> are in dreams.*
>
> (13) (my italics)

The ecumenical view that hysteria crosses gender lines and, more significantly perhaps, the frontiers of health was contradicted by Freud himself.[46]
Nevertheless, the notion that a good woman contained within her a bad

woman represented to the profession enlightened opinion. It permitted physicians to see the woman as simultaneously innocent and guilty, pitiable but meriting severe correction. The playwright Henry Arthur Jones, anxious to establish his credentials in the movement for the 'new drama,' published a lecture he delivered before J.S. Mill's ethology society, expressing fascination for the rich material of the hysterical personality. The puzzle of human character – which Jones thinks the new drama should reflect – is exemplified by

> the strange and bewildering fact of multiple personality. We find that certain men and women (more women than men) manifest wholly different personalities and characters during certain divided portions of their lives. Instances of double personality are, I daresay, familiar to you all; where a certain person leads two wholly separate lives, manifesting in each of them wholly different dispositions; being wholly oblivious in the one state of everything that happens in the alternate state.[47]

Though he does not mention hypnosis, this sounds, in layman's language, very like a summary of the hypnoid state.[48] With a Victorian faith in empirical science that Foucault has so conscientiously documented, Jones asserts that 'only by the careful study and exploration of disease [do] we learn the laws of health.'

After the landmark English production of Ibsen's *A Dolls's House* in 1889, virtually every play that took itself seriously as innovative new drama with regard to sexuality in social life thematized and theatricalized the hypnoid state.[49] Pinero's *The Second Mrs. Tanqueray*, *The Notorious Mrs. Ebbsmith*, and *Mid-Channel*, Jones's *Michael and his Lost Angel* and *Mrs. Dane's Defence* feature female characters with double natures, one sick or sexually tainted, the other well, responsive to society's 'laws of health.' Usually the woman in view is inferior to, a sick simulacrum of a purer self constructed in language; and the past is invoked as the moment of originary splitting. Marguerite Gautier, the consumptive courtesan in *La Dame Aux Camélias*, a prototype of the realism so admired in post-Ibsen England, offers this early version of the trope:

> par moments, j'oublie ce que j'ai été, et le moi d'autrefois se sépare tellement du moi d'aujourd'hui, qu'il en resulte deux femmes distinctes, et que la seconde se souvient à peine de la première.[50]

Marguerite can no more resolve her intractable twoness than the hysteric can read her hypnoid state. So one forgets the other: the radical forgetting of an incompatible idea that it takes its revenge by returning, as a symptom – Freud's first conception of repression.

Jones and Pinero, Archer's favorite English Ibsenites, wring serious pleasure from the hypnoid state.[51] In Jones's *Mrs. Dane's Defence*, a fallen woman tries to win a place in respectable society by marrying a correct, well-connected young man who adores her. Mrs. Dane is a woman with an unimpeachable past. No one knows Felicia Hindemarsh, yet another governess compromised by her employer, a scandal that prompted the wife to commit suicide, the husband to go mad. The play begins and is driven by questions about Mrs. Dane's past. Jones makes ridiculous Mrs. Dane's flamboyant persecutor, but he takes great pains with Sir Daniel Carteret, who wants to keep his adopted son from marrying Mrs. Dane. An unabashed mouthpiece for dominant ideology, he is also the doctor/sleuth who discovers the disease from apparent symptoms and stamps it out. In the famous third-act interrogation scene, Sir Daniel proceeds as Freud does in the case histories, hunting down details and inferring a pattern from chance remarks. Sir Daniel digs deeper into the past, excavating layer upon layer of material until he arrives, with a great show of authoritative temper, at the secret:

> SIR DANIEL Woman, you're lying! . . . You are Felicia Hindemarsh! (*He looks at her steadily. Her eyes drop. She sinks on her knees before him, seizes his hand in supplication, looks at him appealingly; he angrily withdraws his hand.*)[52]

Making explicit the necessity of his harshness, Sir Daniel reiterates the Victorian patriarchal ideal: 'A man demands the treasure of a woman's purest love. It's what he buys and pays for with the strength of his arm and the sweat of his brow' (268). And in response to Mrs. Dane's last plea for forgiveness and acceptance Sir Daniel invokes 'the law, the hard law that we didn't make, that we would break if we could – for we are all sinners at heart' (272). Mrs. Dane walks off alone. She has been cured of her hysteria (her secret 'incompatible self') and society has been cured of her. The hysteric's disruptions of the social economy, says Catherine Clément, amount to nothing. The family becomes inured to her symptoms.

'At last, at last, at last! A really strong English play has been written. . . . *The Second Mrs. Tanqueray* is the finest modern play of our time . . . a play of men and women, of high passions, a rare study of character.' The *Pall-Mall Gazette*'s enthusiasm derives partly from pride in the hometown talent and partly from the fact that Pinero's Paula Tanqueray so fully satisfies the aesthetic requirements for the true: she is two Paulas, seducer and violator, her hysteria both her own and society's disease. Of course Shaw's criticism stands, that Pinero succumbs to an archaic ideology when he makes his heroine commit suicide, but a more relevant observation would be that Pinero's 'tragedy' has the limitations, if not the interest, of *Studies on Hysteria*, in which certain symbolic positions are filled (doctor–patient, knowledge–ignorance, truth–deception, sexual –virginal) and hierarchies maintained. The plot, as with the *Studies*, is the text's most dubious feature. A fallen woman, Paula attempts to rehabilitate herself with the help of her long-suffering husband, Aubrey, but faces up to her sickness (her sinful past) when one of her former lovers shows up to woo Ellean, Aubrey's innocent daughter by his first marriage. Realizing the futility of hiding from her past, Paula throws herself out of her bedroom window.

On the way to this point, however, Pinero demonstrates the new drama's respect for the complexity of moral issues. The rehabilitation of Paula *produces* a hypnoid state; that is, Pinero provides a parallel possibility that Paula's pain and eventual suicide are the result of society's split consciousness – its double standard – as well as her own secret past. Figures of doubleness abound before Paula enters, beginning with Aubrey's splitting of his life's narrative into the present and the 'next chapter,' and of his future wife into the unnameable 'lady' and 'Mrs. Aubrey Tanqueray.'[53] The allegory of scandalous Mabel Hervey who has become 'the new Lady Orreyed' is another double representation: 'Paint [Mabel's] portrait, it would symbolize a creature perfectly patrician; lance a vein of her superbly-modelled arm, you would get the poorest *vin ordinaire!*' (87).

As Paula attempts entry into this environment of doubles, she develops hysterical symptoms – insomnia, anxiety, hand-wringing – and most of all a hypnoid personality, not just sharp swings in mood, but evidence of another repressed being.[54] Like the Victorian doctors, Aubrey enjoins her to forget the past, to exert will power, but in the claustrophobic drawing room an unseen Paula emerges. She tells bawdy jokes fit 'for the smoking room,' not Ellean's virginal ears. She blurts out facts about former lovers; she has, says Aubrey, strange 'out-of-the-way thoughts' (109) – that is, antisocial, disruptive, incompatible ideas bearing the taint of sexual knowledge. Aubrey calls her 'incurable' (101). When Paula claims she has 'two sides' to her nature, and that 'I've let the one almost smother the other' (107), she implies that Ellean's acceptance of her as a 'second mother' would mend the rift. But Aubrey forces a definite split, reminding Paula that she is second, not to the first wife and mother, but to herself: the virginal 'she' who is irretrievably lost but whom Aubrey worships in Ellean. Instead of encouraging a relationship between the two women, which Paula wants, Aubrey continually separates them, enjoying conjugal rights with Paula while lavishing intimate attentions on Ellean.

The play is redolent with sexual displacement; in fact Paula's desire for Ellean's desire ('why don't you look on me as your second mother?' 107), far outweighs any gesture of passion toward Aubrey: 'Ellean, you seem to fear me. Don't! Kiss me!' (107) – and earlier 'Love me' (106). Pinero diverts attention from this passion by positioning Ellean in the phallic role of analyst/judge. When Paula enters she is 'innocent-looking' but like Clément's construction of the hysteric her body 'is a theater of forgotten or repressed scenes,' and the stepdaughter as spectator reads and translates her symptoms accurately: 'I have always known what you were . . . . It's in your face' (147). Judged as a criminal by the one whose desire she most craves, Paula kills herself.

Just before, though, she delivers what for realism is the equivalent of a *grand mal* seizure: the confession. Not of a single event which produces the fall as with Mrs. Dane, but to something late Victorians found much more fascinating: the spectacle of the hypnoid state. In its final-act manifestation, the incompatible idea entering consciousness is ugliness, with the effect that Paula is once again 'seen' as divided: the still-attractive woman in view, the hideous wreck in the future. Pinero takes pains with this speech, dwelling on, indeed fetishizing, the methods of deception: 'paint and dye and those messes' (149).[55] The 'irresistible truth' that propels Paula out of the window is 'physical repulsion,' the anticipated vulgarity of a 'body too thin or too stout . . . cheeks raddled and ruddled – a ghost, a wreck, a caricature, a candle that gutters, call such an end what you like!' (150). *The Picture of Dorian Gray* had appeared in *Lippincott's Magazine* by 1890, and may have partially inspired this verbal picture of internal degeneration, projected away from a visibly healthy body. Another possibility is that Pinero needed to solve the problem of the hysterical body in the only way that realism would permit. If hysteria broadens, makes 'serious' and 'real' the fallen-woman stereotype, it also dangerously disrupts the subtle discussion on which realism thrives. The signs of guilt are the signs of the body, and it is precisely this revolutionary body that must be silenced, de-materialized, *translated* into a morally acceptable etiology. The last act of that etiology is the physical corruption of the sick self, the hypnoid other. Yet language has already effected this displacement. Paula, Pinero directs, '*deliver[s] this speech staring forward, as if she were looking at what she describes*' (150). Her body in full view Paula speaks of a body not present: a referent which, in the play's 'double conscience,' is more real than the one we see. Nowadays the most hackneyed of method-actor ploys, Paula's 'staring forward' underlines the fact that at realism's inception, at the cathartic moment of one of its most popular texts, the body's 'reality' with its potential for 'physical repulsion' is confirmed as illusion.

REALISM'S HYSTERIA

It may be [that certain] psychopathic characters are as unserviceable on the stage as they are in real life.

Sigmund Freud, 'Psychopathic Characters on the Stage'

The female underground revolution in thought. The slave's fear of the outside world.

Henrik Ibsen, Notes on *Hedda Gabler*

In Ibsen's preparatory notes for *Hedda Gabler* (1890), more copious than for any other play, three ideas recur: one, Lovborg's 'double nature'; two, the 'burlesque note' of Lovborg's anarchic ideas being pieced together by bourgeois 'philistines' who have no idea of their meaning; three, Hedda's hysteria.[56] The three ideas are related, although in the play Ibsen publishes their connection is repressed. Lovborg, not Hedda, dramatizes the hysteric's hypnoid state: he has a double nature (the masterful thinker, says Ibsen, who cannot master himself); 'two ideals' (woman as object of desire; woman as companion), two books (conventional and revolutionary), and two suicides (romantic: bullet to the temple, and sordid: misfired bullet to the groin). About Lovborg's inspirational manuscript, Ibsen's notes give Tesman a line which he deleted from the play: 'The new idea in E.L.'s book is that of progress *resulting from the comradeship between man and woman*' (167; my italics). This is quite different from the abstract uninformative description the play gives: '[My book] is divided into two sections. The first is about the forces shaping the civilization of the future. And the second part . . . suggests what lines of development it's likely to take.'[57] At one time Ibsen imagines the value of Lovborg's text to lie with its revisionary speculations on sexuality and gender, but in the published play that writing is domesticated into an object in an envelope and then symbolized as a 'child,' which Hedda burns. The text is then revived in a ludicrously aborted state, as bits of notes that Mrs. Elvsted has kept in her body – her pockets – and that, through the agency of Tesman, will now be (re)delivered. The dark 'burlesque' of the manuscript/child, the fact that Tesman's cobbled-together mediocrity will not translate Lovborg's inspirational thought, is a metonym for Ibsen's own text, which cannot hope to translate Hedda. Hedda, too, is an unread-able text. In his preparatory notes Ibsen announces, 'The play shall deal with the "impossible" ' (159), and further on, 'Brack understands well enough that it is Hedda's repression, her hysteria that motivates everything she does' (166); followed by 'On her part, Hedda suspects that Brack sees through her with-out believing that she understands'; and a few lines later: 'She really wants to live a *man's* life wholly. But then she has misgivings' (166).

If hysteria motivates all Hedda's actions, then her attachment to her mili-tary father's pistols, her betrayal of the sensual ('abundant hair'), loyal Thea, her destruction of Lovborg's manuscript/child, her disgust with the bourgeois smugness of her husband and his aunts, and, most of all, her horror at her own pregnancy are features of hysterical discourse. They are also the radii of *Hedda Gabler*, for only Aunt Rina's death is untouched by Hedda's agency. As Bert States observes, Hedda's first lines in the play (and, he might have said, the first lines of most drama conceived for realism's eternal room) posit a 'Ptolemaic universe – that is, a world whose center is *here*, will remain here, and the elsewhere will revolve obediently around it.'[58] Never leaving the room until the last moments of the play, Hedda is the centripetal center, and her hysteria – like the peripatetic Galenic womb – wanders into every corner of the play's perimeter, imitating the discourse of her interlocutors – the language of womanly confidentiality with Thea; of wifely devotion with Tesman; of romantic dualism with Lovborg – infecting and destroying: 'Why is it, this – this curse – that everything I touch turns ridiculous and vile?' (773) In Hedda Lady Audley's demon lives again. Ibsen wrote to the head of the Christiana Theater naming the only actress who could 'express the demoniacal basis of the character.'[59] Even the invalid Aunt Rina's death can be seen as a mimesis of Hedda's death-grip on the action; Hedda's mourning black in the last act joins the aunt's death to Lovborg's and to Hedda's own demise. Ibsen delib-erately diminishes the socio-legalistic checks on this rampant disease. Judge Brack is the Ibsen surrogate who 'understands' that hysteria 'motivates every-thing Hedda does,' but his insight produces no etiology. In line with other patriarchal fictions (Sir Daniel Carteret, Dr. Wangel, Rector Kroll) Brack is empowered to 'read' the hysteric but his 'inquest' has the undesirable effect of the hysteric escaping his control. Ibsen debunks Brack, who does not know that Hedda knows that he knows. The little moral tale that the play and its commentators provide, that cowardice and lack of an 'object' or mission in life accounts for Hedda's boredom and destructiveness, is a Brackian idea ('Brack represents the personal bourgeois point of view') and represses the horror of the '*here*' in realism: the room/womb, which in *Hedda Gabler* is both the body's hysteria and the play's action.

Those pistols. Perhaps they are Hedda's 'object' in life – not just the tired 'phallic symbol,' but what Lacan would call the little *object a*, the substitute for the Other to which/whom the subject's desire is really addressed. The convenient explanation is that Hedda's Other is the Father; and certainly in the realm of culture, the Lacanian symbolic, all subjects are subjected by, positioned in relation to, the Name-of-the-Father. But the question of hysteria, the question *in* hysteria is, as Sarah Kofman notes, the question of femininity. Refusing the oedipal formation of which the referent is always the Father, the hysteric asks, unforgivably, 'Am I a man or a woman?'; indeed after Dora, Freud finds an instability of gender identification in all his hysteria cases: 'an hysterical symptom is the expression of both a masculine and a feminine unconscious sexual phantasy.'[60] Kofman argues that such 'bisexuality' has no 'expression' except as a metaphor for the undecidability of female sexuality, which occurs precisely when, in Freud's narrative, the female must give up active (phallic) tendencies in order to take up her correct passive gender position. In Kofman's reading of Freud, normal female sexuality retains the masculine–feminine imprint, hysterical symptoms resulting when phallic repression has been too strong. In a sense Kofman rewrites the theory of the hypnoid state, for the masculine/aggressive element that exists within femininity must not, she argues, be routed out: it is the excess of repression of masculinity that produces hysterical symptoms.[61] Linked throughout the play with paternal signifiers – the pistols, the father's portrait, the father's name, Hedda, says Ibsen, 'really wants to live a *man's* life wholly. But then she has misgivings.'[62] The misgivings produce marriage, and the choke-chain of convention: family routine, visiting aunts, and finally an unwanted pregnancy. In the play's social fiction, Hedda Gabler is erased by Hedda Tesman just as the cultural fiction of 'femininity' suppresses all tendencies deemed unfeminine. With her overdetermined connection to the father, Hedda Gabler troubles the representation of the wife.

But Hebba Gabler cannot be viewed as 'freer' than Hedda Tesman; in effect it is the patriarchal 'Gabler' of her identity that causes her to become the 'Tesman.' Ibsen's notes offer glimmers of a troubled daughter–father story, a scandal involving the General which leaves Hedda exposed and vulnerable in the sophisticated world of 'her set.' Firing pistols at Lovborg and Brack has little to do with her desire to be her father; it is rather a way of seizing phallic power to destroy phallic power, specifically the power of gender specificity which the father, Lovborg, and Tesman demand in the name of normative heterosexuality. Hedda is caught between her swelling (mother's) womb and her father's pistols and identifies with neither.

Realism, the mimesis of a true self, has no ability to represent or translate this undecidable state, which is perhaps why *Hedda Gabler* has a double ending, a hysterical ending that calls into crisis the seeable field of realism's stage – a stage, as Bert States says, where 'everything is in view, lying in wait' (68). After Judge Brack taunts her with his new power to blackmail, Hedda circles the stage, stopping by the new 'parents,' Tesman and Thea, as they assemble their fragmented 'child.' She grazes Thea's feminine hair and '*imitates Tesman's intonation*' (776), a quick reprise-pantomime of hysterical mimicry, and then retreats to the inner room, pulling the curtain. She has left the visible space for the first time since arriving on stage. She has not exited, however, but has drawn the spectators' eyes to the vanishing point, the stage within a stage, a space present but out of sight like Freud's topography of the preconscious/conscious mind's separation from the unconscious. From this latter unseen 'space,' Hedda projects not words but sound, 'a wild dance melody' (777) on her childhood piano, which earns a rebuke from the 'parents.' Then, using the oldest proscenium-stage object, the curtain, as a prop, she pops her head out like a grand guignol puppet to make one last insolent remark. With Head-da in fragments, Ibsen comes close to translating the 'impossible.' The old puppet trick shivers the wholeness and completeness of the mimetic body, in which actor is subsumed in character, and for one moment the hysterical body is explicitly equated with the unseen: that which realism represses. After the gunshot, Brack closes the play with the famous line, 'But good God! People don't *do* such things!' People don't, but actors do. Hedda's gesture of obvious miming – recalling Diderot's image of Garrick's face thrust between two doors – ruins the seamless world of 'real' people – a world that has already been dis-figured, made 'ridiculous and vile,' by the infections of hysteria.

Or is 'the female . . . revolution in thought. The slave's fear of the outside world' a better way of expressing hysteria's infection? These lines from Ibsen's notes to *Hedda Gabler* (166) are Zarathustrian in their veiled power and sexual ambiguity: subjects without predicates, ideas without referents, heads without bodies. Who or what is the Other, the addressee, of these phrases? It seems that the world-famous master of prose realism was unable to write the 'female . . . revolution' and the 'slave's fear' into the grammar of a sentence. But 'in [his?] thought,' we detect traces of disturbance, the signifier's tarantella.

When first produced in London, *Hedda Gabler* joined other Ibsen plays in inciting wonderfully florid accusations of immorality, criminality, and disease. *A Doll's House* had a 'hideous . . . atmosphere . . . an abuse [of] wholesome minds';[63] *Ghosts* was 'an open drain, a loathsome sore unbandaged, a dirty act done publicly, a lazar house with all its doors and windows open' (38); *Hedda Gabler* promoted 'heartlessness and overweening vanity [typical of] the daily police reports' (39). The London production of *Hedda Gabler* in April 1891, following hard upon *Rosmersholm* in February and *Ghosts* in March of that year, was a triumph of Elizabeth Robins's and Marion Lea's entrepreneurial skills, and by late Victorian standards a commercial triumph as well: a five-day run was extended to five weeks. To the H.E.M. Stutfields, however, success merely confirmed that Ibsenism was no mere fad but an ideology attracting neuropaths who thrived on images of sexual aberration and rebellion. Typically,

William Archer countered these charges with realism's deadly credo: Ibsen's 'individuals' represent 'no systematic body of doctrine'; Ibsen's sole task was to 'make the stage a sincere, undistorting, unexaggerating mirror of real life.'[64] That Ibsen's most famous apologist should defend his bard by depoliticizing him seems appropriate to realism's mystifications as we understand them today. The hackneyed 'mirror of life' conceit erases agency and ideology – the point of view in the angle of the mirror, in the holder of it, and in the life it reflects. Archer's nervous efforts at appeasement also cover over Ibsen's mysteriously coded but politically suggestive 'female revolution in thought.'

However, some responses to *Hedda Gabler* raise fascinating questions about specularity, spectatorship, and mimetic representation. A.B. Walkley provides one part of the picture:

> The 'hard-shell' Ibsenites, who insist upon regarding Ibsen as a moralist rather than as a dramatist, will be sore put to it to find the moral of 'Hedda Gabler'. More wary persons, who recognize that the purpose of art is not to point morals, but to create impressions, will be content to accept the play as a picture of a peculiar type of revoltee, a dramatic study of a mental pathology, a nineteenth-century tragedy . . . . 'Hedda Gabler is a masterpiece of piquant subtlety, delicate observation, and tragic intensity. . . . Its heroine may be, as our judicial critic[s] [assert] "a monstrous specimen of unfettered womanhood"' but I can only ask, 'What then – so long as she is interesting?' She is a very complex, very modern, very morbid type; and if you ask me whether she is to be praised or blamed, I put aside your question as a pure irrelevance – she is to be watched with interest.[65]

Adroitly reshuffling his adversary's buzz-words, 'modern,' 'complex,' and 'morbid,' with pseudo-Kantian sophistication, Walkley announces that moral questions should not interfere with aesthetic (and scientific) appreciation; the 'masterpiece,' the 'tragedy,' 'the type,' communicate to the spectator through 'impressions,' 'intensity.' Like the medical observers in Charcot's theater, Walkley can indulge in the harmless perversion of voyeurism, taking his pleasure in the separation from and mastery over the object: Hedda 'is to be watched with interest.' (The phrase is striking considering his response to another Robins performance, in *Alan's Wife*, two years later.) Robins's Hedda was undoubtedly responsible for some of Walkley's pleasure. Known for her detailed, precise, and, according to Shaw, 'intensely self-conscious' acting,[66] Robins translated Hedda, enabling the critic/spectator to take on the role of spectator/analyst, gathering clues (the pistols, the portrait, the thinning hair), and to trace the outline of a 'mental pathology.' Testimony of the density of her performance comes from Robins's own memoir, *Ibsen and the Actress*, in which she retroactively fleshes out Walkley's 'dramatic study' with her own etiology, exactly as though she were writing a psychoanalytical case study – filling in the gaps which the play leaves ambiguous: Lovborg's sensuality 'made her [Hedda's] gorge rise . . . the man who had wallowed in filth must not touch Hedda Gabler.'[67]

What Robins creates here is an ontological alternate 'that no critic . . . ever noticed' (30) – which was precisely Konstantin Stanislavsky's goal in the 'psychotechnique' that he formalized after years of acting in the plays of Ibsen and Chekhov. An actor 'after a long and penetrating process of observation and investigation' creates 'an inner life,' a 'subconscious' for his/her character. To do this, the actor must pay particular attention to the character's '*traumas of the past*' and synchronize these, through 'emotion memory', with her 'own motivating desires' (my italics).[68] Interpreting and relaying her character's desires, the actor solicits the spectator's desires to read and interpret her, to 'watch with interest.' One need only read Elizabeth Robins's promptbooks to understand how systematically she laid the groundwork for her discovery. When Brack recounts the shabby scene of Lovborg's actual death, Robins, according to Archer, gazed out to the audience 'evidently not taking in what Brack was saying.' In her promptbook, next to the line 'Illusion?,' Robins wrote 'grave and absent' and next to the line 'Not voluntarily?' she indicated 'sad, far-looking eyes and a smile that says softly how much better I know Eilert than you.'[69] Marking moments when her body translates the secrets of 'emotion memory,' Robins consciously represents hysteria's signifier, not for her interlocutor Brack, but for the Other, the spectator who will complete the circuit of signification and read her truth. As Stuart Schneiderman puts it:

> In the hysterical symptom a part of the body is sacrificed to fill in a gap in the Other, to make him understand or respond. The symptom is signifying. It speaks a reply that the hysteric cannot pronounce – this is because she must await it from another body.[70]

Is this not the relation of the realist actor to his/her audience – the actor produces symptoms addressed to spectators, who gradually understand their meanings? In this sense, realism creates the theater equivalent of the transference; the actor joined to character through 'emotion memory,' re-experiencing past relations, past emotions in the presence of, as Lacanians say, a 'subject presumed to know.'[71]

However, the pleasure of realism as with psychoanalysis, as with any process of interpretation, is not only the achievement of knowledge but its deferral. What if the subject presumed to know is, like Henry James when *he* watches Robins's Hedda, not sure?

> And then one isn't so sure she is wicked, and by no means sure . . . that she is disagreeable. She is various and sinuous and graceful, complicated and natural; she suffers, she struggles, she is human, and by that fact exposed to a dozen interpretations, to the importunity of suspense.[72]

If realism sets up the transference, the re-experiencing of past relations, past emotions in the presence of an analyst/spectator, it also induces a counter-transference, an identification of spectator with actor/character whose infinite variety exceeds the judgment of any single spectatorial moment, and who permits, as Freud notes in 'Psychopathic Characters on the Stage,' that delicious masochism of feeling at one with a hero whom Fate or Society destroys.[73] One of the sexual perversions, masochism in Freud's typology falls under the rubric of the feminine. To experience pleasure only through pain and humiliation is to be, according to Freud, in the feminine, or passive position.

Freud's short essay on theater was published not long after he published 'Fragment of an Analysis of a Case of Hysteria,' which was terminated in December 1899. The history of Freud's revisions and detours has been well documented;[74] what concerns me is the crucial revision, planted in the periphery, in a footnote. Freud had initially assumed that Dora, but for her hysteria, would have been attracted to her father's surrogate, Herr K. In his footnotes, however, Freud reveals that Dora's attraction had become identification. In her sexual desire, Dora acts the 'man' adoring the woman. The hysteric's bisexual symptoms, then, are linked to the desire to move (like the 'wandering womb') into another position, to identify fully with another's subjectivity.

'Hedda is all of us.' The married woman's response to Elizabeth Robins's portrayal of Hedda differs from Walkley's interested scrutiny in the power of its imaginary identification, opening access not only to masochistic satisfaction in Hedda's suffering and defeat, but also to the more dangerous disturbance of counter-transference: Hedda is the imago of plenitude, extending beyond me and other individuals; we meet in Hedda, discover ourselves in Hedda. This inflated group identification ('I' becomes 'we' becomes 'Hedda') bears little relation to the mastery of voyeurism and interpretation, or even the desiring engine ignited by ambiguity. In the context of Robins's narrative, the object 'us' in the spectator's formulation refers to 'women.' What happens when females occupy the masochistic position? Is the quest for the true interpretation deflected? If the hysteric's truth is her undecidability, are the women who take pleasure in this gender disturbance reifying it, reducing it, or extending it?[75] In *The Newly Born Woman* Cixous writes, 'The hysterics are my sisters' (99). Again, in contradistinction to the voyeuristic position, the position of mastery over the object, Cixous plays in the narcissistic mirror: 'As Dora I have been all the characters she played' (99), but near the end of the book she asks, 'What is identification? When I say "identification," I do not say "loss of self." I become, I inhabit, I enter' (148). To what extent can the spectator enter, pleasurably, knowingly, into the hysteric's undecidability – or are 'knowingly' and 'undecidability' an oxymoronic pair? What happened to Lady Burne-Jones?

> We had been told that exceedingly critical person, Lady Burne-Jones, had been saying remarkable things about [*The Master Builder*]. No one, least of all she herself, had expected it to take such hold of her. When some time later I met her this is what she said: After the final curtain I remember being disturbed by the applause. When I got up to go, I was bewildered to find the theatre empty; and I never knew how long I'd been sitting there alone.[76]

'I remember . . . I was bewildered . . . I never knew how long I'd been sitting. . . .' This testimony echoes the 'absences' of the hysteric's hypnoid state, a form of losing oneself. Cixous's protean dance of entering, inhabiting, and becoming represents a fantasmatic hysteria, a theorist's hysteria, which deliberately navigates around the mirror and beyond the self-scripted secrets of the realist actor. Cixous's theater celebrates the undecidable and admits no spectators. Robins's theater, on the other hand, representing Ibsen, welcomes her female spectators to the pleasures of the mirror. Her married friend happily sees her imago, not Hedda, just as Robins gratifyingly sees her imago, 'grave and absent,' as she fills out the portrait of 'Hedda Gabler.' The enormous pleasure of such illusory flights is that we 'know' they are true: Hedda *is all* of us.

However, a sweet irony of history plays havoc with these truths. Robins's Hedda was really no one's imago but William Archer's. Translating (in both senses) *Hedda Gabler* for the London stage in 1891, Archer deleted all references to Hedda's being 'filled out.' Thirty years later, in her detailed memoir *Ibsen and the Actress*, Robins again suppresses any mention of pregnancy. Without the dialectic between her body's terrifying 'room' and the dead room she shares with Tesman, could there be any possibility of representing Hedda's sexuality? Perhaps Archer understood that doubleness, of a certain kind, at a certain historical moment, ruins the intensity of identification and transference, and the pleasure of masochism. That a Victorian gentleman felt justified in censuring a cluster of signs alluding to hysterical disturbance is hardly surprising. What is noteworthy is that the first great success of Ibsenism on the English stage was achieved by partially repressing the hysteria that Ibsen had imagined. Yet perhaps the married friend was responding to this repression as, precisely, *Hedda Gabler*'s actual referent when she said, 'Hedda is *all* of us.' For all of us, at what Lacan calls the 'primordial level,' the mother had a phallus, had it 'all.'[77] Ibsen, Robins writes, gives 'his actors the clue – the master key' (26) to his plays. This favorite Victorian metaphor serves Freud to make an emphatic point about Dora's hysteria: 'Sexuality is the key to the problem of the psychoneuroses and of the neuroses in general. No one who disdains the key will ever be able to unlock the door' (136). If Archer and Robins had the keys, they found it too dangerous to unlock Ibsen's *Hedda*.

HYSTERIA'S REALISM

> Which body? We have several.
>
> Roland Barthes, *Barthes by Barthes*

Of course the juxtaposition of dates is intriguing. Like the hysteric's hypnoid state *The Second Mrs. Tanqueray* and *Alan's Wife* occupy a near-identical temporality, both appearing in London theaters in May 1893, but one is well, the other sick. Pinero's *The Second Mrs. Tanqueray* is produced in the mainstream St. James Theater, receives critical raves: 'the finest modern play of our time; a landmark play in English new drama,' a 'true character study,' says William Archer, with smooth, natural plotting.[78] Elizabeth Robins's *Alan's Wife*, also 'a study,' is produced in J.T. Grein's financially shaky Independent Theater, and is denounced by Shaw's friend A.B. Walkley as false, sensationalistic, not art. Elizabeth Robins, considered, after her success in *Hedda Gabler*, the most important 'new drama' actress in London, was offered the part of Paula Tanqueray and turned it down, rehearsing and performing instead in *Alan's Wife*. Both plays deal in a representation of hysterical behavior, but the first successfully narrativizes the hysteric's deviance as a truth while the second writes from *within* hysteria's truth. Given this distinction it is perhaps not surprising that *The Second Mrs. Tanqueray* has a long, successful run from which Pinero makes £30,000, and *Alan's Wife* plays for two afternoons and earns Robins nothing – except notoriety due to the highly unusual format of the play's publication. In fact the play's contribution to contemporary theory has to do with the peculiar polyvocality of the text in an era when textual relations to performance took on singular importance.

Yet another of the epistemological dividing lines between realism and melodrama is the site and status of the drama text. In stage practice before Ibsen, the written text was little more than a plan with speeches. Like Nahum Tate and countless lesser hacks, actor-managers rewrote, recast, reconceived plays to conform with public taste and the exigencies of the theater company. The public hunger for the latest well-made Parisian success, especially rampant in London between 1850 and 1880, meant that the text was always a patchwork; actors usually worked from 'sides,' texts containing only their lines. The passage of the American Copyright Bill in 1891 protected both authors and the integrity of the text. As Gay Gibson Cima observes, the detailed study of the whole text became a feature of Ibsenism, actors worrying the knots of references, evasions, allusions to reconstruct the full case history of their characters. Said one performer, 'in the study of Ibsen, I had to devise what was, for me a new method. To learn what *Hedda was*, I had to imagine all that she had *ever* been ... [for example] the scenes of Hedda's girlhood with her father,' the early relationship with Lovborg, 'and all other meetings that packed his mind and hers with imperishable memories all the rest of their days.'[79] Minnie Fiske's transference onto the text is an actor's prologue to the status of the text in literary modernism – the unique and irreducible source of unlimited meaning, the site of knowledge to be studied, analyzed, unlocked, understood. The text initiates the desire to interpret; as Elizabeth Robins puts it:

> By the power of his truth and the magic of his poetry [Ibsen] does something to the imagination that not only gives the actors an impetus, but the impetus in the right direction . . . Ibsen knew better [than his critics about the suffering of women]; he saw further than the special instance.
>
> (31)

Not surprisingly these impressions are materially rooted in the new material relations of theatrical production: the passage of new copyright laws, coupled with Ibsen's popularity/notoriety, created a resurgence of play-reading in the 1890s, which encouraged Shaw, Pinero, Jones, and others to publish the true texts – in Archer's case the 'true translations' of Ibsen's plays – as distinct from the unreliable promptbooks through which their plays reached the stage. In the published plays, stage directions, merely functional in promptbooks, became novelistically precise, a means of visualizing the details of rooms, importing metonymically a social and psychological atmosphere into objects and geography.

> A large, attractively furnished drawing room, decorated in dark colors. In the rear wall, a wide doorway with curtains drawn back. The doorway opens into a smaller room . . . .

In the first two sentences of his stage directions, Ibsen defines the sites of Hedda's life and death, the latter taking place in the main room's inner theater, the body's smaller room. Jones, Pinero, and other realists were less subtle but no less absorbed by the naturalistic reproduction of material life. Pinero was typical in supplying Aubrey Tanqueray's address even before describing his room.[80]

The manipulation of stage directions will be an issue in our reading of *Alan's Wife*, a play written collaboratively by Elizabeth Robins and Florence Bell, opening 2 May 1893, with Robins playing the lead role. Robins had already published fiction under the pseudonym C. Raimond; in attempting to win a hearing for *Alan's Wife* she went further, removing all signs of authorship. As William Archer tells the story in his long introduction to the published text, he supplied Robins with the story, *Befriad*, by the Norwegian writer Elin Ameen, along with his advice about adaptation. No doubt in collusion with the authors, he also recommends 'one or two young dramatists,' but the title page lists no author and Archer coyly offers no explanation.[81] On her side, Robins did not miscalculate the benefits of anonymity.

Exploiting the rage for medico-criminal naturalism, Robins and Bell subtitle *Alan's Wife* 'a dramatic study in three scenes.' In scene 1, Jean Creyke is pregnant and sexually radiant, setting out dinner for her young husband while extolling his virtues and beauties to her mother, who nevertheless wishes she had married the weaker but wealthier village curate. The scene ends with Alan Creyke brought home on a stretcher, hacked to pieces by a new mill saw. In scene 2, Jean sits to the side while her mother and neighbor attend to her crippled baby boy: she has reproduced the trauma of her husband's mutilated corpse. The women leave. After agonizing doubt, Jean smothers the child so that he won't suffer into adulthood as a cripple. In scene 3, Jean is in jail. She refuses to speak to the magistrate until the end of the play when she affirms the logic of the murder and walks off unrepentant to her death. Remarkably, in this scene, Jean doesn't speak but the script in effect 'translates' her gestures. Ignoring this crucial point, Archer is at pains to point out other authorial changes to the story: one was to situate the action in the north of England, the other, far more significant, was to keep the protagonist on stage alone in the second scene, to intensify the horror of her hysterical hallucinations and the gothic infanticide – Jean gives the infant a mock christening by candlelight, then snuffs the candles, and advances stealthily toward the crib clutching the quilt with which she will smother him, as the lights dim. Archer, of course, would have preferred an Ibsen-style discussion between Jean and the curate, who still loves her, in which the audience could learn about their relationship while they debate the future of the infant.

Considering that in February–March of 1893, Robins had played Hilda Wangel to enormous acclaim in the first London production of *The Master Builder*, and that at the end of May, the very month of the opening and closing of *Alan's Wife*, she was to star in repertory performances of *Hedda Gabler*, *The Master Builder*, *Rosmersholm*, and *Brand*, her co-written *Alan's Wife* is surprisingly, even vehemently un-Ibsenite. It rejects entirely the formal arrangement of retrospective action, the process whereby the past remembered produces or explains a hysteria, its necessary confession, and its cure. Unlike Hedda, Ellida, Mrs. Alving, Nora, and even Hilda, Jean Creyke has no nervous symptoms or fearful secrets but rather an irrepressible eroticism based in a dialectic of strong, blond health (Alan and Jean) versus sickly, Christian, conservatism (the curate and Jean's mother). *Alan's Wife* reads in fact like a Nietzschean morality play, and though Robins and Bell may not have read *Twilight of the Idols* (1889), the closing sentence of 'Morality as Anti-Nature' – 'an attack on the roots of passion means an attack on the roots of life: the practice of the church is *hostile to life*' – glosses the play's attitudes throughout.[82] Alan is Jean's proud, swaggering 'master,' a natural leader who 'loves the hills and the heather, and loves to feel the strong wind blowing in his face' while Warren, the curate, peddles his joy-killing vale-of-tears conformism. In this dialectic Jean is not merely Alan's support but his twin, equally strong, reckless, handsome, a female, as Kofman would say, who does not accept her castration, who in fact fetishizes the *likeness* between herself and the male ('What would *I* have done with a good boy who never got into mischief?' 8). Significantly her pregnancy is mentioned only near the end of the scene, as that which will, if such a thing were possible, make her even happier. Suitably, the godlike Alan does not appear (except as a corpse on a stretcher), but when he dies, the play's discourse is dominated by doctrinal injunctions from her mother and Warren: 'you must put off that hard, rebellious spirit, and put on a meek and submissive one, else you will be punished' (27). When their voices are joined by those of the secular authority that hang Jean, and when Jean's (semiotically dense) silence is broken by her Brontean fantasy of a transfigured heaven where Alan and a straight-limbed son wait to welcome her, it is clear that Robins and Bell are attempting to reimagine socio-ethical conventions. What is the referent for *Alan's Wife*? Not Ibsen's ironical but coherent drawing rooms in bourgeois society, but rather one woman's hallucination of transcendent power – hysteria itself. Put another way, in *Alan's Wife* hysteria is no longer a means of affirming the methods and ethics of a benign but authoritarian patriarchy; rather it energizes the heroine's moral iconoclasm, evacuating the Father's power by denying his structures, semiotically and textually. *Alan's Wife*, more than any play we have reviewed in this chapter, dramatizes and allegorizes hysteria's progress.

Ignoring the typical drawing room of late nineteenth-century realism, with its naturalistic opulence, its sign-heavy objects, Robins and Bell design a lower-class exterior more typical of classic naturalism, but with an unusual signifying geometry. A 'village street' bisects the stage 'transversely' from the front right corner to the back left. At right angles to the street, starting from the left corner, is the outside of the Creyke cottage; and 'in the angle' between the street and the cottage, the 'central portion of the stage,' is the cottage garden where Jean's mother sits, where Jean prepares the table for an outdoor meal. The central part of the stage bodies forth a female space – a triangle – the site of food and nature, where the male will enter and be served ('Is anything too good for him? Is anything good enough?' 6). Into this domestic imaginary – Jean glorying in the reflected power of the phallus – comes the trauma, the mutilated male, and from this moment, Jean's world is defined by the Father's Law, what Nietzsche calls 'castratism': 'The church fights passion with excision in every sense: its practice, its 'cure,' is *castratism* . . . . It has at all times laid the stress of discipline on extirpation (of sensuality, of pride, of the lust to rule . . .)' (484).

Scene 2 shows the effects of the extirpation of sensuality and pride in Jean's life. Taking on the hysteric's demoniacal pallor, the *'suppressed wildness,'* the *'wide vacant eyes'* (36) of Lady Audley and Robins's Hedda Gabler, she smothers the baby while uttering *'a long wailing cry'* (37), the song of monstrous violation. In his introduction, William Archer defends the play as Greek tragedy, pointing to Orestes' fated matricide, but of course the relevant tragic character is Medea, the sorceress child-killer, whose wild cries open Euripides' play. For Catherine Clément, the hysteric's symptoms hide the figure of beast, the repressed in all women, and indeed Jean destroys not only the crippled infant, but the Victorian angel-mother, whose desire is perennially deposited in the lackbank of phallic structuration. The anticultural, anti-oedipal 'mercy' which Jean shows her child by killing it, is an act of truthfulness wholly consistent with the values of *Alan's Wife* but wholly inconsistent with the laws of gender and society.

The final phase of the hysteric's progress displaces the method (mimesis) and the textual autonomy of realism. In scene 3, Jean stands silent like Clément's hysteric, a woman with her words cut off, or like Kofman's narcissist, a woman who won't tell what she knows. She rejects the succor of the lawgivers, minister and magistrate, and of her religious (castrated) mother. It is tempting to compare Jean's silent rejection to the orchestrated moves of Freud's Dora as she terminates her analysis before the doctor can complete his history. But far more Dora-like is the confusion of figuration and representation and the unstable identifications that result. In the stage performance of *Alan's Wife*, Jean is silent under questioning, but in the text, these silences are *translated* into prose sentences, the accuracy of which would be impossible to represent. Here is a typical exchange:

> MRS. HOLYROD [Jean's mother]   Oh, my dear, if you could tell him something that would make them let you off – now think Jean, think, honey! it may be you could tell them something that would save you.
>
> JEAN *(Silent – stares vacantly into space)*   I can tell him nothing.

(42)

Collapsing the semiotic distinction between authorial stage direction and Jean's speech (here neither is spoken), Robins and Bell not only subvert the conventions of realist texts, they insist on the untranslatability of a woman's (body) language before the law – the law represented by the dramatic fiction and the representational law of realism. Any competent performer can mime a 'vacant' stare, but how does one represent somatically a declarative sentence ('I can tell him nothing')? In effect, Robins and Bell have produced a hysterical body in the theater: *they have given the actor's body a language that cannot be 'read'*. Moreover the visible body and the invisible text are mutually destabilizing. Just as the signifying body forces itself into the written text, the text invades the space of representation. There can be no translation of Jean's symptoms; figuration writes over mimesis producing a realism without truth: hysteria's realism.

What happens to the spectator of hysteria's realism? A.B. Walkley, the critic/analyst who watched Hedda Gabler 'with interest' (who was encouraged by *Hedda Gabler* to assume that comfortable position), in letters appended to the text, claims that he had *seen* a bloody body on stage, that he had seen the baby's corpse after it was strangled. Archer writes back, using testimony by Robins and the stage manager, that there was no bloodying of (streaks of red paint applied to) the actor impersonating Alan's hacked-up corpse, and that the doll-baby never emerged from the solid oak crib. In other words, Walkley hallucinated these appearances. In the public theater, he has, like Anna O., created a private theater, transferring his own fantasies and wishes into the space of representation. How different is this from the women who weep over/identify with Ibsen's female protagonists? Walkley's imagoes are castrated males, the mutilated husband and the dead baby, and so his identification produces something much more powerful than the enthrallment of mirroring; he has entered into the real according to the hysteric, that which cannot be symbolized or represented. The entire apparatus of seeing and knowing, especially his privileged seeing as a critic, has been dismantled; he is not simply assuming the behavior of the hysteric (Stutfield's women), he has become hysterical, hallucinating a world that is not there. Freud warned that modern drama which allows the repressed to come too close to the surface will only be pleasurable for neurotics.

In *Alan's Wife*, Robins and Bell have produced a limit-text of Ibsenite realism: mimesis gone wild. A body imitating hysteria generates other hysterias, and the solid geometry of representation, the theater of knowledge, is radically disturbed. Jean's speaking but unhearable body is 'impossible' as a fetish object of Walkley's journalistic analysis, she/it becomes a space that collapses the subject–object relation. It is the unmaking of realism in the name of realism that Robins and Bell offer contemporary feminism. By wedging a space between the body and the text of the body they displace the imaginary wholeness of the actor in realism, making her truth provisional, contingent. *Alan's Wife* does not abandon the referent, but it refuses to allow the 'hysteric' to become recuperated as the necessary stake in realism. It does not abandon narrative, but it refuses the closure of positivist inquiry. It does not dismantle the text as a unique source of meaning, but it destabilizes the relation between text and performance, each contaminating the other. What are the implications of a contaminated text, a realism-without-truth? We might imagine, for example, a *different* mimesis – one in which the actor's body becomes a material signifier that speaks not for, but before, the referent.

BEFORE THE REFERENT . . . TOWARD THE *GESTUS*

Other examples would no doubt do, but in one short and biased version of twentieth-century drama and performance, *Alan's Wife* is augury. There are three reasons. First, the intrusive presence of Elizabeth Robins's body in *Alan's Wife* recalls the anarchic potentialities of the ancient *mimos*, who makes and simultaneously unmakes representation. Twentieth-century performance dreams of the body that will gesture and present, not imitate and represent, a body of 'subjugated knowledges' (Foucault) that resists social discipline. Meyerhold's biomechanical exercises (1920s), Brecht's epic theater training (1920s–1950s), Artaud's 'affective athleticism' (1930s) with all their differences, seek to destroy the body/mind split that authorizes the bourgeois cogito and its regime of power/knowledge. In his metapsychological papers (1914–17), Freud, too, inflicts more damage upon the cogito with his theory of a drive-riven instinctual body in rebellion against the ego's repressive tactics. In the environment of political experimentation in the 1960s and 1970s, the Living Theater, the Open Theater, the Performance Group, the Omaha Magic Theater, and many others, developed their own versions of 'psycho-physical exercises' to release the body's unauthorized truths.

The performances of early second-wave feminists helped shape this scene: in the 1970s, performance art by Valie Export, Linda Montano, Judy Chicago, Martha Rosler, Theodora Skipitares, and the performance cabaret of Split Britches in the early 1980s, though each quite different, produced critiques of the aesthetic dematerialization of the woman's body precisely to disturb the rationalizing, fetishizing gaze of late twentieth-century A.B. Walkleys. In these years, too, women performers such as Glenda Dickerson and Spiderwoman sought, through body rituals, access to the alterities of goddess myths, folklore, spirit-magic, dreams, all of which, Dickerson notes, 'are at the other end of the spectrum from realism.'[83]

The second legacy of *Alan's Wife* is the intrusion of text into performance, a mode of feminist theater production that took shape in the 1970s and 1980s. In Simone Benmussa's *mise-en-scène* of Helene Cixous's *Portrait de Dora* (1976), in Joan Schenkar's *Signs of Life* (1979), the hysteric (Dora and Alice James respectively) returns to representational space, but in text and *mises-en-scènes*, neither her character nor any other is a unitary object under scrutiny but rather a tangle of textual-cultural references, what Benmussa calls 'texts from elsewhere.'[84] We might label these theater pieces 'semiotic realism,' for the referent is not expunged but rather rerouted through voices, film, photographs, patterns of light, musical phrases.[85] The 'presence' of historical figures – Freud

(Benmussa), P.T. Barnum and Henry James (Schenkar) – creates a sense of history as an assemblage of patriarchal narratives that are ripe for revision. If there is a referent in these texts it is historical experience, never fully describable, but invoked as nodal points of memory and desire. (See Chapter 6 for a discussion of the 1990s version.) Culture critics who imagine that such postmodernist styles as pastiche, attention to surface not depth and polyvocality mean that postmodern art practices offer no understanding of history and no political edge, have simply ignored feminist experimental theater of the last two decades.

Finally Robins's body in *Alan's Wife*, because it appears on stage, asks to be read, and in the impossibility of a 'true' reading of psychological motive, we are diverted into a reading of historical motive. We might observe that twentieth century drama was an exceedingly mixed bag; modernist hunger for 'primitive' experience was already unraveling well-made plots into dream plays and folk drama. We might suggest that Robins was less interested in formal innovation than in rejecting the Kantian art-life breach which realism, with all its mundaneness, reinforces. The opacity of Jean Creyke's silence foregrounds the question of interpretation, and if we don't happen to share the views of A.W. Walkley we might read her silence as multiply signifying. Into Jean Creyke's silence, we might suggest, Robins concentrates the much-criticized (and much feared) spirituality of the British suffragettes whose struggles she joined and whose mass marches, sit-downs, and hunger strikes helped define the embodied resistance from civil rights to AIDS activism we practice today. We might mention that in 1907, Robins 'translated' the hysteric's private pathological innervations into the political pulsations of one of twentieth-century drama's first crowd scenes: Act II of *Votes for Women!* (1907) – a scene that reminded every reviewer of meetings they saw in the street. Here is mimesis that doesn't depend on the guilty secret, the bourgeois ego, or the private drawing room (although Acts I and III contain all three!). It is this mimesis that Brecht refunctions into the *gestus*, in which an actor's body is trained to encode historical resistance. The next section proposes a critical practice based on this body, through Brecht's theory and the plays of Aphra Behn and Caryl Churchill.

Part II

Gestic feminist criticism

Part II
Gestic feminist criticism

2 Brechtian theory/feminist theory
Toward a gestic feminist criticism[1]

If resistance to realism provokes a silent unreadable body (Chapter 1), it is fitting that a chapter on Brecht should begin with a short text on pointing.

> In the 1930s, Gertrude Stein and Alice Toklas on their American lecture tour, were driving in the country in Western Massachusetts. Toklas pointed out a batch of clouds. Stein replied, 'Fresh eggs.' Toklas insisted that Stein look at the clouds. Stein replied again, 'Fresh eggs.' Then Toklas asked, 'Are you making symbolical language?' 'No,' Stein answered, 'I'm reading the signs. I love to read the signs.'[2]

One might devote a chapter merely to unpacking this statement for its historical, discursive, and sexual resonances. Let me just say that Toklas's irritation seems justified. She is pointing to clouds; they have an ontological, referential status *as* clouds but Stein playfully crosses ontology with textuality, object with symbol, referent with sign. Acting the self-conscious spectator, Stein produces a reading and says that *that* is more pleasurable than any Massachusetts clouds. In this chapter, I am concerned with how we point to and read signs in the theater, and by 'we' I mean feminist critics and theorists and also students of Brecht's theater theory – an unlikely group, but then this is part of my argument. I would suggest that feminist theory and Brechtian theory need to be read intertextually, for among the effects of such a reading are a recovery of the radical potential of the Brechtian critique and a discovery, for feminist theory, of the specificity of theater.

At the outset I should say that, like Gertrude Stein's clouds, feminist theory and Brechtian theory are moving, changing discourses, open to multiple readings. The umbrella term 'feminist theory' covers feminist theater theory, literary theory, film theory; black feminist theory, lesbian feminist theory, psychoanalytic feminist theory, postcolonial feminist theory, many of which combine under different rubrics with different topoi, different political inflections. Yet perhaps all theories that call themselves 'feminist' share a goal; an engaged analysis of sex and gender in material social relations and in discursive and representational structures, especially theater and film, which involve scopic pleasure and the body. Brecht's theater theory written over a thirty-year period constantly reformulates its concepts but it too has certain concerns: attention to the dialectical and contradictory forces within social relations, principally the agon of class conflict in its changing historical forms; commitment to 'alienation' techniques and deliberate discontinuity in theatrical signification; 'literarization' of the theater space to produce a spectator/reader who is not interpellated into ideology but is passionately and pleasurably engaged in observation and analysis. Brechtian theory posits a theater of knowledge, but without realism's focus on the private secret, the exploration and recontainment of difference, or the satisfaction of narrative closure.

Feminists in film studies were quick to appropriate elements of Brecht's critique of the theater apparatus. In Summer 1974, the British film journal *Screen* published a Brecht issue whose stated purpose was a consideration of Brecht's theoretical texts and the possibility of a revolutionary cinema. In Autumn 1975 Laura Mulvey published her influential essay 'Visual Pleasure and Narrative Cinema' in which, employing psychoanalysis 'as a political weapon,' she argues that Hollywood film conventions construct a specifically male viewing position by aligning or suturing the male's gaze to that of the fictional hero, and by inviting him thereby both to identify narcissistically with that hero and to fetishize the female (turning her into an object of sexual stimulation).[3] In rejecting this dominant cinematic tradition, Mulvey powerfully invokes Brechtian concepts:

> The first blow against the monolithic accumulation of traditional film conventions . . . is to free the look of the camera into its materiality in time and space and the look of the audience into dialectics, passionate detachment.
>
> (18)

Demystifying representation, showing how and when the object of pleasure is made, releasing the spectator from imaginary and illusory identifications – these are crucial elements in Brecht's theoretical project. Yet through the 1980s we feminists in drama and theater studies have attended more to the critique of the gaze than to the Brechtian intervention that signals a way of dismantling the gaze. Feminist film theorists, fellow-traveling with psychoanalysis and semiotics, have given us a lot to think about but we, through Brechtian theory, have something to give them: a female body in representation that resists fetishization and a viable position for the female spectator.

This chapter, then, has two purposes. One, an intertextual reading of key topoi of feminist theory – gender critique and sexual difference; questions of authority in women's writing and women's history; spectatorship and the body – with key topoi in Brechtian theory – *Verfremdungseffekt*, the 'not . . . but,' historicization, and *Gestus*. Two, emerging from this intertexting, a proposal for a theater-specific feminist criticism. I call it 'gestic' feminist criticism and follow this chapter with two chapters that demonstrate its possibilities.

Some qualifications and clarifications. I realize that feminists in theater and performance studies might greet this coupling with some bemusement. Brecht exhibits a typical Marxian blindness toward gender relations, and except for some interesting excursions into male erotic violence, created conventionally gendered plays and too many saintly mothers (one is too many). Moreover the postmodern critique of Brecht by the late Heiner Müller should not be ignored, particularly the rejection of the Brechtian 'fable' which Müller describes as a 'closed form' that the audience accepts as a 'package, a commodity.'[4] This chapter brackets both Brecht's plays and their retrograde (and un-Brechtian) stagings in the former GDR and the West over the last three decades. My interest lies in the potentiality of Brecht's theory for feminism, and, as I mentioned above, a possible re-radicalization of his theory through feminism. In current literary theory, especially from the British Left, Brecht's concepts have become weapons in campaigns against mimetic linearity,[5] bourgeois naturalism,[6] and, in a fine reading by Terry Eagleton, on the side of deconstructive rhetoric.[7] Toril Moi, in her notorious *Sexual/Textual Politics*, parses the feminisms by enlisting Brecht's debate with Lukács on the question of socialist realism to challenge Anglo-American critics of Virginia Woolf.[8] Strange bedfellows perhaps, but the point I wish to make is that these critics have understood that Brechtian theory in all its gaps and inconsistencies is not literary criticism, but rather a theorizing of the workings of an apparatus of representation with enormous formal and political resonance. I think we in theater studies should be long past the point of accepting Martin Esslin's view that Brecht's theories 'were merely rationalizations of intuition, taste, and imagination',[9] or Eric Bentley's view that the theory is a didactic distraction from Brecht's true art.[10] Herbert Blau has the best if not the last word on theory versus practice debates: 'Theater is theory, or a shadow of it . . . . In the act of seeing, there is already theory.'[11]

GENDER, *VERFREMDUNGSEFFEKT*

The cornerstone of Brecht's theory is the *Verfremdungseffekt* ('alienation-effect'), the technique of defamiliarizing a word, an idea, a gesture so as to enable the spectator to see or hear it afresh: 'A representation that alienates is one which allows us to recognize its subject, but at the same time makes it seem unfamiliar';[12] '[the] A-effect consists in turning [an] object . . . from something ordinary, familiar, immediately accessible into something peculiar, striking, and unexpected' (143). In performance the actor 'alienates' rather than impersonates her character, she 'quotes' or demonstrates the character's behavior instead of identifying with it. Brecht theorizes that if the performer remains outside the character's feelings, the audience may also and thus freely analyze and form opinions about the play's 'fable.' *Verfremdungseffekt* also challenges the mimetic property of acting that semioticians call iconicity, or the conventional resemblance between the performer's body and the object, or character, to which it refers. This is why gender critique in the theater can be so powerful.

At the risk of simplifying a heavily worked terrain, let me offer a few formulations: gender critique refers to the words, gestures, appearances, ideas, and behavior that dominant culture understands as indices of feminine or masculine identity. When spectators 'see' gender they are seeing (and reproducing) the cultural signs of gender, and by implication, the gender ideology of a culture. Gender in fact provides a perfect illustration of ideology at work, since 'feminine' or 'masculine' behavior usually appears to be a 'natural' – and thus fixed and unalterable – extension of biological sex. And yet, as Judith Butler argues, 'the "body" is itself a construction; [that is,] bodies . . . *come into being* in and through the mark(s) of gender.'[13] This rigorously antifoundationalist argument insists on the fictionality – yet the persistence – of gender taxonomies and the critical role of performance. Gender, as Butler so compellingly puts it, is

> *a stylized repetition of acts* . . . which are internally discontinuous . . . [so that] the *appearance of substance* is precisely that, a constructed identity, a performative accomplishment which the mundane social audience, including the actors themselves, come to believe and to perform in the mode of belief.[14]

A feminist practice that seeks to expose or mock the strictures of gender, to *reveal* gender-as-appearance, as the effect, not the precondition, of regulatory practices, usually uses some version of the Brechtian A-effect. That is, by alienating (not simply rejecting) iconicity, by foregrounding the expectation of resemblance, the ideology of gender is exposed and thrown back to the spectator. In Caryl Churchill's *Cloud 9*, crossdressing that is not quite perfect, in which the male body can be detected in feminine clothes, provides broad A-effects for a gender critique of familial and sexual norms in Victorian and present-day society. More to Butler's point, when (male) Betty announces, 'I am a man's creation as you see / And what men want is what I want to be,'[15] she 'alienates' (foregrounds) the '*appearance* of substance' and the 'mode of belief' (ideology) that keeps it in place. In the gender structure Churchill is framing, the female body cannot even appear, only its masculine citation. In lesbian performance at New York's WOW cafe – I'm thinking of Holly Hughes's *Lady Dick* and Split Britches's *Upwardly Mobile Home* – and in the broadly satirical monologues of Italy's Franca Rame, gender is relentlessly exposed as 'performativity,' as a system of regulatory norms which the subject 'cites' in order to appear in culture.

In her recent *Bodies that Matter*, Butler works to correct what she perceived to be a misunderstanding of earlier formulations: some readers of *Gender Trouble* seemed to think that 'performativity' assumed a humanist subject that could choose her gender and then perform it. Thus in the new work Butler is careful not to personify norms, discourse, language, or the social as if they were new subjects of the body's sentencing.[16] She rejects discussion of performativity that involves theater since performance, or rather the performer, implies one who ontologically precedes and then fabricates gender effects.[17] On the one hand, this charge is irrefutable. Even performance art that refuses scripting and archiving, that works to separate repetitive nonsignifying acts from a performer's intentionality *precisely in order to reveal subjectivity and the body as effects of discourse(s)* – even the most antihumanist performance exists in a bounded time/space, in the realm of the visual, where what is seen is taken as evidence of being. On the other hand, Butler's charge simplifies the complexity of practices that constitute cultural and social existence. Though 'performativity' is not an 'act' but a 'reiteration' or 'citation,' why should we restrict its iterative sites to theory and to the theorist's acts of seeing? Theater, too, is theory, 'or a shadow of it.' Does that shadow always mean humanist recuperation into representation? Performance, as I have written elsewhere, is the site in which performativity materializes in concentrated form, where the 'concealed or dissimulated conventions' of which acts are mere repetitions might be investigated and reimagined.[18]

Despite Brecht's loathing of the bourgeois subject, he needed (and feminists need) to retain, theoretically and politically, the notion of agency. But in Brecht agency does not signal a return to the old intentional subject – no coherent ego's intentions 'saturate' (Derrida's term) a given context.[19] The character is never the focal point on the Brechtian stage, but rather the always-dissimulated historical conditions that keep her from choosing and changing. The actor *shows* this, and shows his showing, displacing attention from virtuosic impersonation to demonstration – demonstration not *of* authority, but *as* praxis. A-effects are not easy to produce. But the payoffs, especially where gender is concerned, can be stunning. When gender is 'alienated' or foregrounded, the spectator is able to see what s/he can't see: a sign system *as* a sign system. The appearance, words, gestures, ideas, attitudes that constitute the gender lexicon become illusionistic trappings that are *nevertheless* inseparable from, embedded in the body's habitus. Understanding gender as ideology – as a system of beliefs and behavior mapped across the bodies of women and men which reinforces a social status quo – is to appreciate the continued timeliness of *Verfremdungseffekt*, the purpose of which always is to denaturalize and defamiliarize what ideology – and performativity – makes seem normal, acceptable, inescapable.

SEXUAL (ETC.) DIFFERENCES, THE 'NOT . . . BUT'

Gender critique in artistic and discursive practices is often and wrongly confused with another topos in feminist theory: sexual difference. When the article on which this chapter is based first appeared, I proposed that 'sexual difference be understood not as a synonym for gender oppositions but as a reference to differences within sexuality' (85).[20] I was of course not alone. The rejection of heteronormative ideologies has come to suggest, not without contestation, the embrace of heterotopic subjectivities. In Teresa de Lauretis's words: 'the female subject is a site of differences . . . that are not only sexual or only racial, economic, or (sub)cultural, but all of these together, and often enough at odds with each other.'[21] If theorists learned to seek and continually mark difference by way of deconstruction's privileging of 'differences within' all representational systems, the social, cultural, and political meanings have been harder to think through and practice.[22] Border disputes about difference are not only metaphorical.

Still the political value of deconstruction lies in its interrogation of identity. Deconstruction posits the disturbance of the signifier within the linguistic sign; the seemingly stable word is inhabited by a signifier that bears the trace of another signifier and another, so that contained within the meaning of any given word is the trace of the word it is not. Thus deconstruction wreaks havoc on identity, with its connotations of wholeness and coherence; if an identity is always different from itself it can no longer *be* an identity. Sexual *difference* in this sense destabilizes the bipolar oppositions that constitute gender identity. The concept of 'differences within' complicates as well identity narratives (of nationhood or racial purity) and *their* bipolar structure of (true) self versus (alien) other. Psychoanalysis offers other similar cues. Despite the normative tone of his gender distinctions, Freud also makes clear that the drives and desires that constitute human sexuality fail to produce a stable identity:

> we are accustomed to say that every human being displays both male and female instinctual impulses, needs and attributes; but though anatomy, it is true, can point out the characteristic of maleness and femaleness, psychology cannot. For psychology the contrast between the sexes fades away into one between activity and passivity, in which we far too readily identify activity with maleness and passivity with femaleness, a view which is by no means universally confirmed.[23]

To paraphrase Gayle Rubin, women and men are certainly different, but gender coercively translates the nuanced differences within sexuality into a structure of opposition.[24] In my reading of Rubin's 'sex–gender system,' the trace of non-normative desire is kept alive within the sterile opposition of gender. Similarly, the trace of the social affiliation I am not enacting stays alive within the one that I do enact. Difference is where we imagine, theorize, while gender is where we live, our social address, although some of us wish (and some of us have the privilege) to leave home. Let me put it another way: no feminist can ignore the social and political battlefield of identity, but neither can she or he forget that the words and positions of the battlefield contain traces of what they are not, and these traces contain our most powerful desires.

Keeping differences in view instead of conforming to stable representations of identity, and *linking those differences to a possible politics* are key to Brecht's theory of the 'not . . . but,' a feature of alienated acting that I read intertextually with the heterotopia of difference.

> When [an actor] appears on stage, besides what he actually is doing he will at all essential points discover, specify, imply what he is not doing; that is he will act in such a way that the alternative emerges as clearly as possible, that his acting allows the other possibilities to be inferred and only represents one of the possible variants . . . . Whatever he doesn't do must be contained and conserved in what he does.[25]

This mention of 'conserve' sounds like the Hegelian *aufhebung* but Brecht was too much of a modernist-Marxist to endorse a systematic dialectical progression toward the Absolute. Dialectic in Brecht is a 'zigzag' of contradictions. Each action must contain the trace of the action it represses, thus the meaning of each action contains difference. The audience is invited to look beyond representation – beyond what is authoritatively put in view – to the possibilities of as yet unarticulated motives, actions or judgments. Brecht's early plays, particularly *In the Jungle of Cities*, thematize the 'not . . . but': 'I'm never anything more than half' says Mary Garga, who doesn't have the pleasure of joining the men in what Brecht called 'the idealist dialectic' of the play or 'the pure joy of fighting.'[26] Contemporary feminist plays by Simone Benmussa, Caryl Churchill, Marguerite Duras and Joan Schenkar also work the 'not . . . but' into their gendered fictions and their *mises-en-scènes*, but arguably any play can be read and performed with these nuances.

The Brechtian 'not . . . but' is the theatrical and theoretical analogue to 'differences within.' As such it ruins classical mimesis: the truth-modeling that produces self-identical subjects in coherent plots gives way utterly to the pleasure and significance of contradiction – and of contradictions that, at any given moment, are emerging but unseeable. One might argue that Brecht's notion of 'the alternative' in the 'not . . . but' should not be read as postmodern difference, that his theater writing is not Derrida's *écriture*. But Brechtian theory leaves room for at least one feature of *écriture* – the notion that meaning is beyond capture within the covers of the play or the hours of performance. This is not to deny Brecht's wish for an instructive, analytical theater; on the contrary, it invites the participatory play of the spectator, and the possibility – for Brecht a crucial possibility – that signification (the production of meaning) continue beyond the play's end, even as it congeals into action and choice after the spectator leaves the theater.

HISTORY, HISTORICIZATION

The understanding of women's material conditions in history, and the problematics of uncovering 'women's history' are topoi in feminist theory that Brecht's theory of historicization greatly informs. Brecht understood social relations, particularly class relations, as part of a moving dialectic. The crux of 'historicization' is change: through A-effects spectators observe the potential movement in class relations, discover the limitations and strengths of their own perceptions, and begin to change their lives. There is a powerful dialectical movement in Brechtian historicization of preserving the 'distinguishing marks' of the past and acknowledging, even foregrounding, the audience's present perspective.[27] That is, when Brecht says that spectators should become historians, he refers both to the spectator's detachment, her 'critical' position, *and* to the fact that she is writing her own history even as she absorbs messages from the stage. Historicization is, then, *a way of seeing*, and the enemy of recuperation and appropriation. One cannot historicize and colonize the Other or, as Luce Irigaray would have it, 'reduce all others to the economy of the Same.'[28] Brecht considered bourgeois illusionism insidious because it is guilty of precisely that:

When our theaters perform plays of other periods they like to annihilate distance, fill in the gap, gloss over the differences. But what comes of our delight in comparisons, in distance, in dissimilarity – which is at the same time a delight in what is close and proper to ourselves?

(276)

In historicized performance gaps are not to be filled in, seams and contradictions show in all their roughness, and therein lies one aspect of spectatorial pleasure – when our differences *from* the past and *within* the present are palpable, graspable, possibly applicable. Plays aspiring realistically to depict the present require the same historicization. Realism disgusted Brecht not only because it dissimulates its conventions but because it is hegemonic: by copying the surface details of the world it offers the illusion of lived experience, even as it marks off only one version of that experience. This is perhaps why the most innovative women playwrights refuse the seamless narrative of conflicting egos in classic realism. Consider, to name only one example, Suzan-Lori Parks's *The America Play* (1994) which stakes the real in memory, fantasy, and verbal repetition not because historical experience is fragmented (which is true enough) but because, as Parks puts it, there isn't 'enough history' for her or her African American characters.[29] Rejecting the Brechtian fable – narrative progress is meaningless in her work – Parks concretizes historical gaps by turning the stage into a 'black hole' in which a mother and son commemorate their 'Foundling Father,' a composite of President Lincoln, absent father, and minstrelsy impersonation.

Brechtian historicization challenges the presumed neutrality of any historical reflection. Rather it assumes and promotes both unofficial histories and unofficial historians. Reader/spectators of 'facts' and 'events' will, like Gertrude Stein reading the clouds, translate what is inchoate into signs (and stories), a move that produces, not 'truth,' but mastery and pleasure.

SPECTATOR, BODY, HISTORICIZATION

Historicization in fact puts on the table the issue of spectatorship and the performer's body. According to Brecht, one way that the actor alienates or distances the audience from the character is to suggest the historicity of the character in contrast to the actor's own present-time self-awareness on stage. The actor must not lose herself in the character but rather *demonstrate* the character as a function of particular socio-historical relations, a conduit of particular choices. As Timothy Wiles puts it, actor and audience, both in present time, 'look back on' the historical character as she fumbles through choices and judgments.[30] This does not endow the actor with superiority, however, for as Wiles later points out, the present-time actor is also fragmented: 'Brecht separates the historical man [*sic*] who acts from the aesthetic function of the actor' (85). The historical subject *plays* an actor presumed to have superior knowledge in relation to an ignorant character from the past, but the subject herself remains as divided and uncertain as the spectators to whom the play is addressed. This historical subject disappears neither into a representation of the character *nor* into a representation of the actor; each remains processual, historical, incomplete. And the spectator? Aware of three temporalities within a single stage figure the spectator cannot read one without the other, her/his gaze is constantly split; her/his *'vouloir-voir'*[31] – the desire, as in realism, to see and know all without any obstacle – is deflected into the dialectic of which the divided performer is only a part. Moreover, in reading a complex ever-changing text, spectators are 'pulled out of [their] fixity';[32] they become part of – indeed they produce – the dialectical comparisons and contradictions that the text enacts.

The special characteristics of Brechtian reception emerge in relation to analogous processes in film theory. In psychoanalytic film theory, the film-text and the viewing-state are set in motion by unconscious fantasy.[33] In the darkened room, in immobile seats, the spectator enters what Jean-Louis Baudry calls a 'state of artificial regression,'[34] the womb-like effects of film viewing which confuse boundaries and send the subject back to earlier stages of psychic development, particularly the Lacanian mirror phase in which the infant, lacking controlled motor development, sees its image in a mirror or in its caretaker's eyes as a coherent whole. Misrecognizing himself (the male infant is specifically at issue here) as a complete autonomous other, he spends the rest of his life unconsciously seeking an imaginary ideal – and discovers 'it,' so the theory goes, at the movies.

Now the differences between the Brechtian spectator and cinematic spectator are obvious. The last thing Brecht wants is a spectator in a 'state of artificial regression,' in thrall to her/his imaginary ideal. Brechtian theory formulates (and reformulates) a spectatorial state that breaks the suturing of imaginary identifications and keeps the spectator independent. Much influenced by Brecht, Patrice Pavis's semiotics of the *mise-en-scène* rests almost entirely on the spectator: 'the mise-en-scène is not entirely an indication of the intentionality of the director, but a structuring by the spectator of materials presented . . . whose linking is dependent on the perceiving subject.'[35] In film theory the subject position is constructed ready-made for the spectator, only his capacity to regress is assumed. In Brechtian theory the subject's capacity to regress is suppressed. Film semiotics posits a spectator who is given the illusion that he creates the film; theater semiotics posits a spectator whose active reception constantly revises the spectacle's meanings.

But Pavis is too much of a postmodernist to theorize a spectator with total authority. He deconstructs the spectatorial position by locating its difference within: 'What we need,' he says, 'is a theory of "reception desire"' – a theory that, without positing a spectator 'in a state of artificial regression,' accounts for the spectator's unconscious desire and thereby opens the door to pleasurable identification with stage figures (158).

What does Brecht contribute to 'reception desire'? Although he talks a lot about pleasure, it is the pleasure of cognition, of capturing meaning; Brecht does not apparently release the body, either on stage or in the audience. The actor's body is subsumed in the dialectical narrative of social relations; the spectator's body is given over to rational inquiry (unless there's pleasure to be had with the Brechtian cigar). And Brecht exhibits the typical blindness of all Marxist theorists regarding sexuality and desire.[36] Feminist theory, however, insists on the presence of the gendered body, on sexuality, on the gender system, and on the problematics of desire.

It is at this point – at the point of conceptualizing an unfetishized female performer as well as a female spectator – that an intertextual reading of Brechtian and feminist theories works productively. If feminist theory sees the body as culturally mapped and gendered, Brechtian historicization insists that this body is not a fixed essence but a site of struggle and change. If feminist theory is concerned with the multiple and complex signs of a woman's life – her desires and politics, her class, ethnicity, or race – what I want to call her *historicity*,[37] Brechtian theory gives us a way to put that historicity in view – in the theater. In its conventional iconicity, theater laminates body to character, but the body in historicization stands visibly and palpably separate from the 'being' of the actor as well as the role of the character; it is always insufficient and open. I want to be clear about this important point: *The body, particularly the female body, by virtue of entering the stage space, enters representation – it is not just 'there', a live, unmediated presence, but rather (1) a signifying element in a dramatic fiction; (2) a part of a theatrical sign system whose conventions of gesturing, voicing, and impersonating are referents for both performer and audience; and (3) a sign in the system governed by a particular apparatus, usually owned and operated by men for the pleasure of a viewing public whose major wage earners are male.*

Yet with all these qualifications, Brechtian theory imagines a polyvalence to the body's representation, for the performer's body is also *historicized*, loaded with its own history and that of the character, and these histories roughen the smooth edges of the image, of representation. In my hybrid construction – based in feminist and Brechtian theory – the female performer, unlike her filmic counterpart, connotes not 'to-be-looked-at-ness'[38] – the perfect fetish – but rather 'looking-at-being-looked-at-ness' or even just 'looking-ness.' As we will see in the section below, this Brechtian-feminist body is paradoxically available for *both* analysis and identification, paradoxically within representation while refusing its fixity.

SPECTATOR, AUTHOR, *GESTUS*

The explosive (and elusive) synthesis of alienation, historicization, and the 'not . . . but' is the Brechtian *gestus*, a gesture, a word, an action, a tableau, by which, separately or in a series, the social attitudes encoded in the playtext become visible to the spectator. A famous *gestus* is Helene Weigel's snapping shut her leather money bag after each selling transaction in *Mother Courage* (1939), thereby underscoring the contradictions in profiteering and survival – for Brecht, the social reality of war. In *Mother* (1994), Patricia Spears Jones's multimedia reimagining of Gorky's novel (and Brecht's use of it), in collaboration with Mabou Mines, spectators sit in fully functional kitchen areas surrounded by television sets, enabling them to watch live action or watch TV, or both. In her closing soliloquy, an educated embittered Mother (Ruth Maleczech) grabs a video camera and films herself, face pressed up and distorted against the lens, while speaking of her yearning for 'transcendence' – a revolutionary leap beyond the suffering she witnesses.[39] In this agonized moment spectators' eyes dart uneasily between video screen and performer, creating with the latter a *gestus* that powerfully displays the contradictory relation between political agency and media manipulation, between humanist traditions of protest and postmodern environments. While the *gestus* must be readable, Brecht always emphasized complexity:

> [The] expressions of [the *gestus*] are usually highly complicated and contradictory, so that they cannot be rendered by any single word and the actor must take care that in giving his image the necessary emphasis he does not lose anything, but emphasizes the entire complex.[40]

The gestic moment in a sense explains the play, but it also exceeds the play, opening it to the social and discursive ideologies that inform its production. Brecht says that the scene of the *gestus* 'should be played as a piece of history' (86) and Pavis elaborates: *Gestus* makes visible (alienates) 'the class behind the individual, the critique behind the naive object, the commentary behind the affirmation. . . . [It] gives us the key to the relationship between the play being performed and the public . . . .'[41] If we read feminist concerns back into this discussion, the *gestus* signifies a moment of theoretical insight into sex–gender complexities, not only in the play's 'fable,' but in the culture which the play, at the moment of reception, is dialogically reflecting and shaping.

But this moment of visibility or insight is the very moment that complicates the viewing process. Because the *gestus* is effected by a historical subject/actor, what the spectator sees is not a mere miming of a social relationship, but a *reading* of it, an interpretation by a historical subject who supplements (rather than disappears into) the production of meaning. As noted earlier, the historical subject playing an actor, playing a character, splits the gaze of the spectator, who, as a reader of a complex sign system, cannot consume or reduce the object of her vision to a monolithic projection of the self. Indeed with the *gestus* Brecht ruins the scopic regime of the perspectival realist stage. While leaving the proscenium intact, while encouraging his spectators to look from a distance, he also undermines the immobility of the spectatorial eye/I, for in the act of looking the spectator engages with her own temporality. She, too, becomes historicized – in motion and at risk. Free to compare the character's signs to 'what is close and proper to [herself]' (276) – her material conditions, her politics, her skin, her desires – she is simultaneously 'pulled out of [her] fixity.'[42]

Sitting not in the dark, but in the Brechtian semi-lit smoker's theater, the spectator still has the possibility of pleasurable identification. This is effected not through imaginary projection onto an ideal but through a triangular structure of subject/actor–character–spectator. Looking at the character, the spectator is constantly intercepted by the subject/actor, and the latter, heeding no fourth wall, is theoretically free to look back. The difference, then, between this triangle and the familiar odeipal one is that no one side signifies authority, knowledge, or the law. Brechtian theater depends on a structure of representation, on exposing and making visible, but what appears even in the *gestus* can only be provisional, indeterminate, nonauthoritative.[43]

This feminist rereading of the *gestus* makes room, at least theoretically, for a viewing position for the female spectator. Because the semiosis of the *gestus* involves the gendered bodies of spectator, subject/actor and character, all working together but *never harmoniously*, there can be no fetishization and no end to signification. In this Brechtian–feminist paradigm, the spectator's look is freed into 'dialectics, passionate detachment';[44] she might borrow Gertrude Stein's line, and give equal emphasis to each word: 'I love to read the signs.'

If the *gestus* invites us to think about performers and spectators in their historical and sexual specificity, it also asks us to consider the author's inscription. 'The author's attitude to the public, that of the era represented and of the time in which the play is performed, the collective style of acting of the characters, etc. are a few of the parameters of the basic *gestus*.'[45] In the case of women writers and particularly of women dramatists, the erasure from history has been so nearly complete that the feminist critic feels compelled to make some attempt at recovery – and here Brechtian theory fellow-traveling with feminist theory suggests a critical practice – gestic feminist criticism – that could contextualize *and* reclaim the author.

A gestic feminist criticism would 'alienate' or foreground those moments in a playtext when social attitudes about gender and sexuality conceal or disrupt patriarchal ideology. It would refuse to naturalize or valorize female dramatists, but would focus on historical material constraints in the production of images. It would attempt to engage dialectically with, rather than master, the playtext. And in generating meanings it would recover (specifically gestic) moments in which the historical actor, the character, the spectator, *and* the author enter and disrupt the scopic regime of realist representation.

GESTIC FEMINIST CRITICISM: APHRA BEHN AND CARYL CHURCHILL

The following two chapters pursue this mode of reading through the work of two British playwrights, Aphra Behn (1640–89) and Caryl Churchill (1931–). Middle-class, politically engaged professional writers, both affiliated, as it were, with the Royal Court, Behn and Churchill create comic plays about gender oppression and dramatize their gender critique gestically – in ways that comment politically and historically on the apparatus of representation and the laboring body of the female actor. Separated by some three hundred years, these writers respectively help establish and help erode the foundations of the theater apparatus that Brecht sought to transform: the perspectival stage.

Marking the inception of modern theater architecture in England, Behn's plays explore the scopic regime of illusionism that fed the hunger for greater stage realism. Churchill revises realism's epistemological authority by worrying the phenomenology of illusionistic space. In Behn's plays, actor and author signal to each other across the proscribed spaces of Restoration theater, while Churchill offers a postmodern reading of the vanishing point, making and unmaking spaces for her political agents to 'live.' Churchill looks for inspiration to Behn's century when capitalism takes root in the midst of revolutionary upheaval, her aim being to explore ideological contradictions, especially concerning women. Behn, active in the male-dominated literary marketplace, works these same contradictions into both plays and theater space. Interestingly both playwrights cite or acknowledge the Roman poet Lucretius' *De Rerum Natura* (*On the Nature of Things*) drawing his antireligious materialism into images that make us see anew the relation of women's bodies to nature, to mortality and to representation.

3 *Gestus*, signature, body in the theater of Aphra Behn

Where the dream is at its most exalted, the commodity is closest to hand . . .

Theodor Adorno, *In Search of Wagner*

In the theater . . . things are always seen *from somewhere*. Here we have the geometrical foundation of representation: a fetishist subject is required to cut out the tableau.

Roland Barthes, *Image – Music – Text*

WILLMORE   I long to see the shadow of the fair substance; a man may gaze on that for nothing.

Aphra Behn, *The Rover*

In the soul of the commodity . . . a hell rages.

Walter Benjamin

In the Western theater (Gr. *theatron* or 'seeing place'), pleasure is never far from the market and its mystifications. The spectator sees what is not there – an illusion, a sign of an absent original – and fails to see what *is* there – a constructed series of images so polished and coherent that the ideological and human labor of their making is hidden from view. The splendor of Wagner's theater appeared to Adorno as both commodity-intensive and a grandiose erasure of the social and historical inscriptions marking those commodities. For Barthes, theatrical representation produced not only a consumer but a fetishist, one who *wishes* to see what is not there, who shores up mastery by 'cut[ting] out' a meaningful tableau. At the historical moment when English theater was codifying the perspectival foundations and conventions of modern bourgeois illusionism, Aphra Behn's Willmore (*The Rover*, 1677) demonstrates the links between seeing, consuming, and fetishizing. In the absence of a courtesan whom he cannot afford, Willmore 'long[s] to see' her in representation, in the form of three on-stage portraits, one of which he steals, before the courtesan herself arrives.

Willmore's gesture, I will suggest, should be read as a Brechtian *gestus*, an act that undermines the imaginary relations of classical mimesis in order to make visible the contradictory links between textual politics, authorial position, and theater apparatus.[1] In the unraveling of their intrigue plots, Behn's plays not only thematize the marketing of women in marriage and prostitution but they also reveal her own manner of authorial inscription, her passionate gestic address to the theater apparatus that she inherited and the culture in which she wrote. Brecht's account of the *gestus*, we noted, alerts us to the vectors of historical change written into dramatic texts, but he makes scant provision for gender in representation or as a ground of social struggle. But gender is writ large in Behn theater texts. Educated yet constantly in need of money, with court connections but no supporting family, a former spy and recent inmate in a debtors' prison, Aphra Behn wrote plays when female authorship was a monstrous violation of the 'feminine sphere.' Since the reopening of the theaters in 1660, Frances Boothby and Margaret, Duchess of Newcastle each had had a play produced, but no woman had challenged the Restoration theater with Behn's consistency and success. Indeed, that she could earn her living writing for the theater was precisely what condemned her. The muckracking satirist Robert Gould slandered Behn and all would-be poetesses in a pithy couplet: 'For Punk and Poesie agree so Pat,/You cannot well be *this* and not be *that*.'[2]

In 'Arachnologies: The Woman, the Text and the Critic,' Nancy Miller implicitly offers a feminist refunctioning of Brecht's *gestus*. Texts by women, she argues, encode the signs or 'emblems of a female signature' by which the 'culture of gender [and] the inscriptions of its political structures' might be read.[3] In the woman-authored text, then, the gestic moment would mark both a convergence of social actions and attitudes, and the gendered history of that convergence. Robert Gould's verse, with its violent equation of poesie and punk, provides some evidence of the 'culture of gender' in Restoration London. Like her male colleagues, Behn hawked her intrigue comedies and political satires in the literary and theatrical marketplace, and like them, she suffered the attacks of 'fop-corner' and the often paltry remuneration of third-day receipts. But in Behn's case the status of professional writer damned her as immodest and her texts as sexually tainted, virulent extensions of her gendered body. Benjamin's words suggest her response: in the 'soul' of the author and her characters, commodities both in the marketplace, 'a hell rages.'

Deciphering Behn's emblematic signature obliges us to read the social and sexual discourses that complicate and obscure its inscription. I am aiming to open her texts – *The Rover*, *The Feign'd Curtezans* (1679), among others – to what Brecht calls their 'fields of force' – those contradictory relations of gender and apparatus that signified in Behn's culture and are, as these readings will indicate, symptomatic of our own. Like Brecht in his discussion of Shakespeare's *Coriolanus*[4] I am interested less in interpretive truth than in exploring gestic moments in which author, apparatus, history and reader-spectator each plays a signifying role. Thus the following section will consider Behn's theatrical materials, the Restoration theater apparatus with its proto-fetishist positioning of 'scenes' and actresses. The next three sections consider Behn's gestic critique of female sexuality and commodification. The final section joins the signifying power of Brecht's *gestus* to Benjamin's hollowed-out allegorical emblems in order to pose the relation of body to signature, of passionate discourse to theater apparatus. How does Behn stage the relationship between female authority and public calumny – between what Robert Gould in darkly humorous euphemisms refers to as 'this' and 'that'?

THE APPARATUS

By theater apparatus, I refer to several related aspects of theater production: the physical machinery and properties of the stage; and, more elusively, the social, psychic and ideological relationships among text, stage, and audience. When Aphra Behn's plays appeared in London, between 1670 and 1689, the theatrical hierarchy, like all other cultural institutions, was almost exclusively patriarchal in control and participation. Charles II invested power in the first patentees, Thomas Killigrew and William D'Avenant. Aristocratic or upperclass males generally wrote the plays, purchased the tickets, and formed the coteries of critics and 'witlings' whose disruptive presence is remarked on in countless play prologues and epilogues. In its physical machinery and properties, the Restoration stage was a fully rationalized visual system. Although the technology was well established in Italian and French courts, and in English court masques before the Interregnum, the first two Restoration theaters featured the innovations of movable painted 'Scenes' and mechanical devices or 'machines', installed behind the forestage and the proscenium arch. The perspective was best, of course, from the level of the King's box, yet all Restoration spectators, seated in semicircular areas of pit, boxes, first, middle and upper galleries, could 'cut out a tableau' composed of actors arranged before elaborately painted 'wings' (stationary pieces) set in receding rows, and 'shutters' (flat painted 'Scenes') that moved in grooves and joined in the center. When the painted Scenes parted, characters were 'discovered' against other Scenes that, parting, produced further discoveries.[5]

Given the 'new' natural philosophy in which mathematical and mechanistic descriptions of nature became paradigms for understanding both the body's wiring and state power (Hobbesian man was a 'machine' dominated by 'motions' of fear and the desire for power); given the excitement of Royal Society intellectuals and amateurs everywhere, including such feminists as the Duchess of Newcastle and Mary Astell, over empirical methods of thought and discovery; given the general awareness of the telescope and microscope, new technologies of enhanced vision, the post-Restoration theater offered timely and perverse excitements. The seductive movement of painted flats, the 'discovery' of previously unseen interiors, introduced a powerful scopic epistemology in which the probing scientific eye was treated to an opulent simulation: the truth not of nature but of illusion. While the Elizabethan spectator was compelled to imagine the features of battlefields, parks, or bedchambers, Restoration spectators like Richard Flecknoe had Scenes and machines, 'excellent helps of imagination, most grateful deceptions of the sight'; these 'graceful and becoming Ornaments of the Stage [transport] you easily without lassitude from one place to another, or rather by a kind of delightful Magick, whilst you sit still, does bring the place to you.'[6] Restoration stagecraft created a spectator-fetishist, who expected and took pleasure in perspectival arrangements that deceived the sight, whose disavowal of material reality produced a desire for the 'delightful Magick' of exotic and enticing representations. Most of Behn's plays were written for the Duke's Theater in Dorset Garden, built in 1671 and known for its 'gawdy Scenes,'[7] a stage not unlike Wagner's in Adorno's critique: commodity-intensive, seductive and dreamlike.

In this account of Restoration reception I am deliberately conflating two uses of 'fetishism': one, Freud's description of the masculine eroticization of objects or female body parts which derives from the disavowal of a material lack (of the penis on the mother's body); and two, Marx's description of the commodity which, at the moment of exchange, appears, fetish-like, to be separate from the worker who produces it: the 'specific social character of private labors' is disavowed.[8] Nowhere do these meanings of fetishism seem more relevant than in commentary generated by that new Ornament of the Stage, the Restoration actress. In his preface to *The Tempest*, Thomas Shadwell links the new phenomenon of female performers with theatrical Scenes, both innovative commodities for audience consumption:

> Had we not for yr pleasure found new wayes
> You still had rusty Arras had, and threadbare playes;
> Nor Scenes nor Woomen had they had their will,
> But some with grizl'd Beards had acted Woomen still.[9]

That female fictions were to be embodied by beardless women would, Thomas Killigrew promised, be 'useful and instructive.'[10] What the signifying body of the actress actually meant in the culture's sexual economy is perhaps more accurately suggested by metatheatrical references in play prologues and epilogues. The actress playing Flirt in Wycherley's *The Gentleman Dancing Master* satirically invites the 'good men o' th' Exchange' from the pit into the backstage tiring-room: 'You we would rather see between our Scenes'[11] and Dryden, in the Prologue to *Marriage a-la-Mode*, has the actor Hart refer to passionate tiring-room assignations.[12]

Samuel Pepys's private writings are even more suggestive of the theater's sinful pleasures. On 5 October 1667 he attended the Theater Royal in Bridges Street:

> . . . and there, going in, met with Knipp [Mrs. Knep], and she took us up into the Tireing-rooms and to the women's Shift, where Nell [Gwynn] was dressing herself and was all unready; and is very pretty, prettier than I thought; and so walked all up and down the House above, and then below into the Scene-room . . . . But Lord, to see how they were both painted would make a man mad – and did make me loath them – and what base company of men comes among them, and how lewdly they talk – and how

poor the men are in clothes, and yet what a show they made on the stage by candlelight, is very observable.

(834)

Candlelight sutures contradictions between 'lewd' actors and an alluring 'show,' and even a habitual playgoer like Pepys is disturbed when the seams show. That actresses were pretty women was not surprising, but the transformation of women into painted representations beautifully exhibited by candlelight was both disturbing and fascinating. Pepys went behind the painted Scenes but the paint was still there. He hoped to separate the pretty woman from the painted actress, but it was the actress's body he admired – and fetishized – from his spectator's seat. On 2 March 1667 Pepys wrote little about Dryden's new play (*Secret Love*) but admired Nell Gwynn as a 'young gallant' (a 'breeches part' that exposed her legs).[13]

In this early modern theater, then, the actress's presumed sexuality disavowed her labor. Rather than produce a performance she was a piece of the spectacle, a painted representation to lure the male spectator. Not surprisingly, in her professional duplicity, her desirability, in her often public status of kept mistress, she was typically equated with prostitutes or 'vizard-masks' who worked the pit and galleries of Restoration theaters during and after performances. In Wycherley's *The Plain Dealer*, Mrs. Hoyden is disparaged for being 'As familiar a duck . . . As an Actress in the tiring-room' (407).

And yet this account of illusionism, fetishism, and gender must be dialectically mediated by other aspects of spectatorship. In the self-regarding Restoration theater, illusionism was not a matter of a performer's disappearance into a role (as it would become in theatrical realism) but an aggregation of other illusions; that is, the performer's body was a discursive site that exceeded the stage fiction. Elizabeth Barry, who acted in most of Behn's successful comedies, was, in *The Rover*, cast as Hellena, the lover of Willmore; she was also mistress to John Wilmot, Earl of Rochester, on whom Behn's Willmore was modeled. Rochester personally trained Barry to be an actress and Behn pseudonomized her as 'Amoret,' making her the recipient of published 'intimacies' and cavalier complaints. Though alluringly fetishized by the apparatus's theatrical machinery, Restoration performers invited audiences to include such extratheatrical scandal in their viewing pleasure. Restoration audiences were far more varied than once thought, including lawyers, architects, vicars, members of the Royal Society, court professionals (like Pepys), lowly apprentices as well as courtiers; respectable women and their maids as well as prostitutes.[14] But the behavior of the 'Squires, Sharpers, Beaus, Bullies, and Whores' in the pit was notorious, and hailing each other from side-box, gallery and pit, they talked, seduced, combed wigs, bought oranges, met friends, departed and arrived noisily during the performance, disputed, drew swords, 'cried down' performers and generally watched themselves watching the play.[15]

Behn and her colleagues met these challenges with fictional looking glasses held up to berate the audience. 'Observe me well,' scolds Behn's Sir Timothy Tawdrey, 'I am a Man of Show, / Of Noise, and Nonsense, as are most of you . . . . We are as like, as Brother is to Brother.'[16] The Restoration prologue typically complains about the lowly status of poetry, berates the audience for its stupidity, disparages the whores, condemns the factions of noisy fops, refers to any current political turmoil, introduces the author, and, in a vague way, describes the play. But in the prologue to her first play *The Forc'd Marriage: or, The Jealous Bridegroom* (1670), Aphra Behn turned these conventions into a *gestus*, the first suggestion of her authorial signature. A male actor enters and enjoins the audience to be leery of the 'Spies,' probably whores whom the Poetess may have planted

> I'th' Upper Box, Pit, Galleries; every Face
> You find disgis'd in a Black Velvet Case [the whore's vizard]
> My life on't; is her Spy on purpose sent,
> To hold you in a wanton Compliment;
> That so you may not censure what she 'as writ,
> Which done, they face you down 'twas full of Wit.[17]

Within moments 'Enter an Actress' who, *'pointing to the Ladies'* asks, 'Can any see that glorious Sight and Say/A Woman shall not Victor prove today?' (286). In her pointing gesture, the actress sets up an explicitly triangular structure that draws together the historical performer, the role she is destined to play, and the female spectators in the audience. She also mentions 'a Woman,' a potential 'victor,' a conventional trope of poetic love battles, but whose referent here is the new author Aphra Behn. In that shared look actress, character, spectator, and author are momentarily joined, and for perhaps the first time on the English stage all four positions are filled by women. But not for long. Casting her eye at the female spectators, the actress differentiates, and in class-specific terms. Insisting, ironically, that 'There's not a Vizard in our whole Cabal,' she condemns the lowly 'Pickeroons' that scour for prey, and scorns any financial gain ('the petty spoils') the 'victor' might claim in conquest. Yet she ends by promising: 'We'll sacrifice it all to pleasure you' (286).

I suggest that whom that 'you' designates has become as undecidable as the status of the 'Ladies' in the audience. Certainly, as we've seen, in the sexual slang of the day, actress meant whore, professional authoress meant whore, and 'pleasuring' suggests the prostitute's paid work for her client. But the interlocking look of women is also pleasurable, a signifying space for a new (preordained) 'victor' in the cultural marketplace. I would call the actress's pointing and the entire prologue a *gestus*, a moment in which author, gender history, and theater politics become readable in all their contradictions. Behn claims victory in the fight to become an author but only through the signifiers of sexual degradation. Catherine Gallagher persuasively turns this contradiction into a positive: 'Behn created a complex authorial identity by drawing on seemingly irreconcilable metaphors – the author as prostitute and the author as monarch,'[18] but her argument rests on Behn's strategic *disembodiment*. By hiding 'behind her own representations . . . [Behn] implies that her true self is the sold self's seller' (22). The *gestus*, however, is always an embodied construction; indeed I think the body's passions and pains interested Behn even as she adroitly manipulated the public signs of authorship. To achieve the alienation of an empty commodity was not Behn's pleasure but a motive for struggle.

THE WIFE THING

Near the end of Act II of *The Rover*, after the wealthy virgins and hungry gallants have been introduced, and the reader–spectator is made aware that comic symmetry is pressing toward chase and final reward, mention is made of a beautiful courtesan whom the gallants, including the affianced ones, are trying to impress. Angellica Bianca would seem to be a supplement to the intrigue plot – a supplement since one need not intrigue to visit a whore. Yet before the wealthy virgins are rewarded with the husbands they desire, they will traverse this whore's marketplace. In Scenes and 'discoveries,' they will market themselves as she does, compete for the same male affection, suffer similar abuse. The courtesan herself enters the play not in the way the audience might expect, behind an exotic vizard, or 'discovered' in her bedchamber after the parting of the Scenes, but as a portrait, as *three* portraits, a large one hung from her balcony and two smaller ones posted on either side of the proscenium door designating her lodging. Placed out in her absence but signifying her presence, these portraits titillate and lure, drawing together audiences on stage and off.

   The Rover and *The Second Part of the Rover* (1681), both drawn from Killigrew's *Thomaso, or The Wanderer* (1663), are Behn's only plays to label a character a courtesan. In her wholly original *The Feign'd Curtezans*, witty virgins impersonate famous Roman courtesans, near-debauches occur, but as befits the romantic intrigue, marriages settle the confusion of plots and the financial stink of prostitution is hastily cleared away. But if courtesans figure by name in only three plays, the commodification of women in a male-controlled marriage market is Aphra Behn's first and most persistent theme. Beginning appropriately enough with *The Forc'd Marriage: or The Jealous Bridegroom*, all of Behn's seventeen complete plays deal to some extent with the fact that women, backed by dowries or portions, are forced by their fathers into marriage in exchange for jointure, an agreed-upon income to be settled on the wife should she be widowed.

   There was a lived context for this perspective. The dowry system among propertied classes was in place since the sixteenth century, but at the end of the seventeenth century there were thirteen women to every ten men and cash portions had to grow to attract worthy suitors.[19] As the value of women fell by almost 50 percent, marriage for love, marriage by choice, was almost unthinkable. Women through marriage had evident exchange value; that is, the virgin became a commodity not only for her use-value as breeder of the legal heir but for her portion which, through exchange, generated capital. As exchange value converts commodities into fetishes or 'social hieroglyphics,' signs whose histories and qualitative differences can no longer be read,[20] women in the seventeenth-century marriage market took on the 'phantasmagoric' destiny of fetishized commodities. Margaret Cavendish, Duchess of Newcastle, the prolific, often scorned writer of the generation preceding Behn's, points out the market reduction of women to the status of domestic things: sons bear the family name but 'Daughters are to be accounted but as Movable Goods or Furnitures that wear out.'[21]

Restoration comedy from the earliest Etherege and Sedley, through Wycherley, Dryden, Vanbrugh, D'Urfey, Congreve, and Farquhar, mocked the marketplace values of marriage, promoting the libertine's aesthetic of 'natural' love, verbal seduction, and superiority over jealous husbands and fops. But Aphra Behn concentrated her energies on decoding the exploitation of women in the exchange economy, and added vividly to contemporary discourse protesting women's oppression in the marriage market.[22] 'Wife and servant are the same / But differ only in the name,' wrote Lady Mary Chudleigh.[23] 'Who would marry,' asks Behn's Ariadne (*The Second Part of The Rover*), 'who wou'd be chaffer'd thus, and sold to Slavery?'[24] The issue arises repeatedly in plays and verse of the period: not only are marriages loveless, but once married, women lose both independent identity and control of their fortunes. Ariadne again:

> You have a Mistress, Sir, that has your Heart, and all your softer Hours: I know't, and if I were so wretched as to marry thee, must see my Fortune lavisht out on her; her Coaches, Dress, and Equipage exceed mine by far: Possess she all the day thy Hours of Mirth, good Humour and Expence, thy Smiles, thy Kisses, and thy Charms for Wit . . .
>
> (152)

The feminist philosopher Mary Astell might have had no sympathy for the sensuous appetites of Behn's females but Ariadne's sentiments receive astute articulation in Astell's *Some Reflections upon Marriage*. The money motive for marriage produces in the man contempt and 'Indifferency' which 'proceeds to an aversion, and perhaps even the Kindness and Complaisance of the poor abused'd Wife, shall only serve to increase it.'[25] Ultimately, the powerless wife ends up 'mak[ing] court to [her husband] for a little sorry Alimony out of her own Estate.'[26] Two centuries later Engels merely restates these comments in his observation that forced marriages

> turn into the crassest prostitution – sometimes of both partners, but far more commonly of the woman, who only differs from the ordinary courtesan in that she does not [hire] out her body on piecework as a wage worker, but sells it once and for all into slavery.[27]

In *The Lucky Chance*, a late city comedy about two old aldermen unable to resist buying young wives, Behn dramatizes material conjugal relations as a *gestus*.

Because 'her Fortune was small, and [in] hope of a Ladyship,' Leticia is pressured to break 'sacred vows' to her lover whom she now believes dead. After
the wedding, she greets her aged spouse Sir Feeble Fainwood – *'Enter Leticia,
fine in Jewels'* – bearing on her body the commodities that purchased her,
metonymic signs of the fetish object she has become. Lady Julia, another
victim of a forced marriage, offers a sarcastic Brechtian caption to the image:
'Give you joy, my dear Leticia. I find, Sir, you were resolved for Youth, Wit,
and Beauty.'[28] Julia of course omits what the silent adorned body articulates:
that for women poverty 'resolves' all questions, especially questions of whether
and whom to marry.[29] Lady Julia's impecunious husband Sir Cautious Fulbank
will later sell her body for one night (albeit to her lover) to settle a gambling
debt, but the reduction of women's bodies to exchange value occurs even in
sexual love. Florinda of *The Rover*, fleeing an arranged marriage, plans to elope
with her lover carrying a box of jewels, a conflation of sexual parts and market value, and in *The Amorous Prince* a woman is *given* a box of jewels, here signifying her body's prostitution and the absent purchaser, who later decides to
marry her. Little wonder, then, that Mary Astell recommended celibacy to her
readers or that Margaret Cavendish imagined an all-woman world, presided
over by Lady Happy, in which the gorgeous commodities derived from the
marriage state would be lavishly available to all *un*married women of the community.

In Behn's drama, the reduction to commodity status of women in the marriage market retained the traces of a familiar libertinism, the notion that desire
must exceed (and could subvert) the marriage contract. In *The Forc'd Marriage*,
Behn produces a tableau so prodigiously gestic as to serve as an emblem for
matrimony, forc'd or not, for the rest of her playwrighting career. The stage
directions from the Summers edition merit full citation:

Act II

THE REPRESENTATION OF THE WEDDING

The Curtain must be let down, and soft Musick must play:

The Curtain being drawn up, discovers a scene of a Temple:
the KING sitting on a Throne, bowing down to join the hands of Alcippus
and Erminia, who kneel on the steps of the Throne; the Officers of the
Court and Clergy standing in order by, with ORGULIUS. This within the
Scene.

Without on the Stage, PHILANDER with his sword half drawn, held by
GALATEA, who looks ever on ALCIPPUS: ERMINIA still fixing her Eyes on PHI-
LANDER; PISARO passionately gazing on GALATEA . . . the rest all remaining
without motion, whilst the musick softly plays; this continues a while till the
Curtain falls; and then the Musick plays aloud till the act begins.[30]

In this emblematic dumb-show, the patriarchal bearer of the law constrains
but cannot contain desire. The lovers' cross-gazing not only illustrates the

notion of desire as continual displacement, it generates a structural diagram for the intrigue (or Spanish cape-and-sword) comedy that Behn specialized in, with its cross-hatching of plots and subplots, its continuous motion. Her tableau 'without motion' will be shattered by hectic intrigue and sword play, but it haunts the canon with the suggestion that if characters come to rest without 'projects,' 'designs,' and ingenious disguise, they will find themselves in this dreaded tableau, representing the law because there is no image for their desire. Obviously Behn considered this representation of enormous importance, not only framing it with music but calling for the curtain to be lowered, then raising it to continue the action – almost unheard of in contemporary theatrical practice.

Adorno's critique of dream-spectacle – 'where the dream is most exalted, the commodity is closest to hand' – might serve as the appropriate caption for Behn's sighing tableau. *The Forc'd Marriage* was staged at the Duke's Theater at Lincoln's Inn Fields, which even before moving to the lavish space at Dorset Garden continued the traditions of spectacular display introduced by William Davenant, the company's first patentee. Exploiting the most seductive devices – soft music, the carefully modeled inner space – Behn dramatized the forc'd marriage of fantasy and commerce and its immediate offspring: 'that dead commodity called a wife.'[31]

DISGUISE AND DESIRE

> HELLENA Come put off this dull humour with your clothes, and assume one as gay and fantastic as the dress my cousin Valeria and I have provided, and let's ramble.
>
> Aphra Behn, *The Rover*

> SIR TIMOTHY We'll send to the Duke's House and borrow some Habits for the Masquerade.
>
> Aphra Behn, *The Town Fop*

No playwright, and certainly not a woman playwright, could ignore the persistent denunciation of theater practice as moral and spiritual contamination. The Patristic revulsion against theater, typified in tracts from the third-century Tertullian to those of Renaissance Puritans like Philip Stubbes and William Prynne, builds on the Platonic condemnation of mimesis as the making of counterfeit copies of true originals. In a sense Prynne and his supporters were pragmatic semioticians; ignoring rationalizations from Horace to Sidney to Dryden that dramatic poetry was designed to 'delight and instruct,' they perceived that meaning was made by impersonation – the deliberate contamination of natural or God-given identity (to play a slave one becomes slavish) – and by enticing spectators to respond pleasurably to such deceptions. Moreover, the Fathers and their followers condemn actors in costume and cosmetics as hyprocrites whose shape-changing derives from the devil. 'Whatever is *born*,' writes Tertullian, 'is the work of God. Whatever . . . is *plastered on*, is the devil's work.'[32] It is Tertullian who makes an early connection between the deceptions of theater and women, since women's nature, in one persistent line of Christian thought, is second only to the devil's in the capacity to deceive. Throughout Prynne's *Histriomastrix*, theater is condemned for promoting effeminacy: 'Those Playes which are usually acted and frequented in over-costly effeminate, strange, meretricious, lust-exciting apparell, are questionlesse unseemely, yea unlawful unto Christians.'[33] Restoration actresses were so clearly identified with the pleasure of theater spectatorship that the Puritan dicta, through periods of all-male theater practice, seemed prophetic. To the Puritan mind the presence of women on stage was an affront to feminine modesty, but more damning was the fact that the means of illusionism – use of costume, paint, masking – involved specifically female vices. The nature of theatrical representation, like the 'nature' of woman, was to ensnare, deceive, and seduce.

Because the mask conventionally conceals the true, because it seduces curiosity, facilitates role-playing, putting on a mask is a metatheatrical act, emblematic of the impersonations on which theater depends. When Prynne condemned the theater for promoting eroticized deceptions, he clearly found it symptomatic of larger social excesses:

> But now there is such a confuse mingle mangle of apparell . . . and suche preposterous excesse thereof, as everyone is permitted to flaunt it out in what apperell he lust himselfe, or can get by any kind of meanes. So that it is verie hard to knowe who is noble, who is worshipfull, who is a gentleman, who is not.[34]

Disguise allows women and men to pass not only as the other gender but as members of a different class. After the Restoration in 1660, the theatricality of everyday life was strongly in evidence, extending beyond lavish court masquerade into the private lives of men and women. Pepys charged that the 'age ran by dissimulation'; royalty wore disguises to mingle with commoners; there were stories of women in men's clothes serving in military campaigns – one of Behn's prologues refers to Mary Morders who lived as soldier and ended up with a man's pension in Whitehall during the time of Queen Anne. Yet far less notorious persons, married women like Mrs. Evelyn and Mrs. Pepys, wore vizards similar to the ones worn by professional prostitutes or their theatrical mimics on stage – Pepys mentions stopping at the Exchange with his wife to buy her one.

When constructing his theory of the derivation of absolutist sovereign authority, Hobbes found it appropriate to use theater metaphors to distinguish between 'Natural' and 'Feigned or Artificial' persons. But 'person' is itself an unstable referent:

> The word Person [persona] is Latin . . . [and] signifies the *disguise*, or *outward appearance* of a man, counterfeited on the stage; and sometimes more particularly that part of it, which disguiseth the face, as a mask or vizard:

and from the stage, hath been translated to any representer of speech and action, as well in tribunals, as theatres. So that a *person* is the same that an *actor* is, both on stage and in common conversation . . .[35]

Though a person is 'he whose words or actions are considered his own,'[36] it is clear there there is leeway in that passive construction of 'consider' – one's judgment about the natural or feigned rests on highly contingent assumptions, for identity, one's own and that of one's interlocutor 'in common conversation' is explicitly theatrical, capable of shifting. As Christopher Pye notes, agency does not disappear, rather origin and agency become confounded.[37] This is precisely the Earl of Rochester's game when playing the mountebank:

. . . if I appear to any one like a counterfeit, even for the sake of that, chiefly ought I to be construed a true man. Who is counterfeit's example? His original; and that, which he employs his industry and pains to imitate and copy. Is it therefore my fault if the cheat by his wits and endeavours makes himself so like me, that consequently I cannot avoid resembling him?[38]

The assumption that the artist's copy improved on and could be separated from its model is fundamental to neoclassical mimesis, but in Restoration society 'nature' tended to be the most slippery of concepts. Hence, as Derrida puts it, 'representation mingles with what it represents' (Prynne's 'mingle mangle'), producing 'a dangerous promiscuity and a nefarious complicity between the reflection and the reflected. . . . In this play of representation, the point of origin becomes ungraspable.'[39]

Disguise operates complicatedly in Behn's intrigue comedies. On the one hand, the structure of masking–unmasking resembles the conventions of Renaissance comedy, as a plot tactic for liberating lovers from such obstacles as heavy fathers and arranged matches – that is, as concealment that defers but ultimately guarantees truthful and socially positive revelations (in three Behn comedies old husbands actually annul their own marriages in favor of younger men). Such uses of disguise function to defuse the commodity status of women in the exchange economy. On the other hand, masquerade promotes fetishization by the seductive coverings and uncoverings of the woman's body. In *The Rover* and *The Feign'd Curtezans*, Behn uses disguise not to guarantee a truthful representation of women but to represent what cannot be known about them, sexually and culturally. In this sense her masking is a gender *gestus*, a sign not just of deception but of contradictory anxieties about the meaning of the feminine.

Even as *The Rover* obscures the distinction between virgin and prostitute, Behn launches a marriage plot with all the conventional motivations. Florinda, Hellena, and Valeria don gypsy costumes – assume the guise of marginal and exotic females – to join the carnival masquerade explicitly to evade the patriarchal arrangement of law and jointure laid down by their father and legislated by their brother Pedro: Florinda shall marry a rich ancient count and

Hellena shall go into a convent, thus saving their father a second dowry and simultaneously enriching Florinda. The opening dialogue of *The Rover* is also implicitly gestic, raising questions about women's material destiny in life as well as in comic representation:

> FLORINDA What an impertinent thing is a young girl bred in a nunnery! How full of questions! Prithee no more, Hellena; I have told thee more than thou understand'st already.
>
> HELLENA The more's my grief. I would fain know as much as you, which makes me so inquisitive . . .[40]

Hellena dons masquerade because she desires not a particular lover but a wider knowledge. Given the conventions of Restoration comedy, this wish to know 'more than' she already understands is troped as a wish for sexual adventure. But if we hear this dialogue gestically – in its social register – other meanings are accessible. Women's lack of access to institutions of knowledge spurred protest from writers as diverse as Margaret Cavendish, Bathusua Makin, Mary Astell, and Judith Drake. Aphra Behn mocks a university fool in *The City Heiress* and a learned lady in *Sir Patient Fancy*; she criticizes neoclassical aesthetics in 'Epistle to the Reader,' appended to *The Dutch Lover*,[41] for having nothing to do with why people write or attend plays. When she translates Bernard de Fontenelle's *A Discovery of New Worlds*, however, she reveals as passionate a hunger for esoteric knowledge as the early English feminists. Knowledge is power, said Hobbes, following Bacon. It meant more than a fool's search to collect facts, it meant new ways of thinking, principally Cartesian skepticism and analysis. Unfortunately, the controlling conceit of Fontenelle's work – a mere woman is informally taught the complexities of Copernican theory – produces an untenable and revealing contradiction for Behn. 'He [Fontenelle] makes her [the Marchionness] say a great many silly things, tho' sometimes she makes observations so learned, that the greatest Philosophers in Europe could make no better.'[42] Insightful yet silly, wise yet a *tabula rasa*, Fontenelle's Marchionness oscillates between intellectual independence and slavish imitation. She is perhaps less a contradictory character than a projection of a male intellectual's ambivalence about female education.

Aphra Behn's Hellena seeks knowledge 'more than' or beyond the gender script provided for her. She rejects not only her brother's decision to place her in a nunnery, but also the cultural narrative of portion, jointure, and legal dependency in which she is written not as subject but as object of exchange. Yet Hellena, too, oscillates, both departing from and reinforcing her social script. Her lines following those cited above seem, at first, to complicate and defer the romantic closure of the marriage plot. To have a lover, Hellena conjectures, means to 'sigh, and sing, and blush, and wish, and dream and wish, and long and wish to see the man' (7). This thrice-reiterated wishing will result in three changes of costume, three suitors and three marriages. As with the repetitions of 'interest,' 'credit,' and 'value' – commodity signifiers that circulate through the play and slip like the vizard from face to hand to face – this repetition invokes the processes underlying all wishing, to desire that will not, like a brother's spousal contract, find its 'completion.'

If we incorporate insights from feminist psychoanalytic theory, the virgins' masquerade takes on added significance, or rather this discourse helps us decode what is already implied – namely, in an economy in which women are dependent on male keepers and traders, female desire is always already a masquerade, a play of false representations that covers over and simultaneously expresses the lack the woman exhibits – lack of the male organ and, concomitantly, lack of access to phallic privileges, to material and institutional power. Unlike the theatrical mask, which conceals a truth, the masquerade of female sexuality subverts the 'Law-of-the-Father' that stands 'behind' any representation. Underneath the gypsy veils and drapes of Behn's virgins, there is nothing, in a phallic sense, to see; thus no coherent female identity that can be co-opted into a repressive romantic narrative. Willmore, titillated by Hellena's witty chatter, asks to see her face. Hellena responds that underneath the vizard is a 'desperate . . . lying look' (56). That is, she like her vizard may prevaricate; represented may 'mingle mangle' with representer – for the spectator (Willmore) there will be no validating stake.

Yet, as Behn well knew, there is means of validation, one which guarantees patriarchy's stake in portion, jointure, and the woman's body: the hymen. In Restoration comedy no witty unmarried woman was really witty unless she had property *and* a maidenhead. Behn's virgins may re-'design' their cast of characters but they cannot change their plot. Ultimately their masquerade is dissimulation in the classic representational sense, a veil that hides a material truth. Hellena's mask merely replicates the membrane behind which lies the 'true nature' of woman: the equipment to make the requisite patrilineal heir. Thus Willmore's masterful response to Hellena's 'lying look' is a mock-blazon of her facial features, ending in a fetishistic flourish: 'Those soft round melting cherry lips and small even white teeth! Not to be expressed, but silently adored!' (56). The play in Hellena's discourse between knowing and desiring, which extends through the masquerade, completes itself in the marriage game. She exercises her will only by pursuing and winning Willmore, for as it turns out he has the 'more' she 'would fain know.'

Willmore acts not only as the rover but as signifier for the play's phallic logic. His name metaphorizes the trajectory of desire as he roves from bed to bed 'willing more,' making all satisfactions temporary and unsatisfying. Desire's subject, Willmore never disguises himself (he comes on stage *holding* his mask). Until enriched by the courtesan Angellica Bianca, he remains in 'buff' or leather military coat. In another sense, though, Willmore is already in disguise, or rather the entity 'Willmore' covers a range of linguistic and social signifiers. As noted earlier, Behn's model for Willmore (like Etherege's for Dorimont) was reputedly the Earl of Rochester, whose name, John Wilmot, contains the word (*mot*) 'will.' And we mentioned that Rochester was also the lover and mentor of Elizabeth Barry, the actress who first played Behn's Hellena. In Tory mythology Charles II, on the verge of fleeing England, disguised himself in buff – a leather doublet. Indeed Willmore's first lines refer to the offstage Prince who, in exile during the Commonwealth, was also a rover. Doubled mimetically and semiotically with both Rochester and the Merry Monarch (who attended at least one performance of *The Rover* before the play was restaged at Whitehall), Willmore needs no mask to effect his ends; his libertine desire is guaranteed and upheld by patriarchal law. Hellena's playful rovings, on the other hand, and her numerous disguises, signal both ingenuity and vulnerability. Ironically, the virgins' first costume, the gypsy masquerade, represents their actual standing in the marriage market – exotic retailers of fortunes or portions. Their masquerade defers but does not alter the structure of patriarchal exchange nor does it dismantle the economy of gender representation; rather both are firmly upheld.

> JULIO A Curtezan? and a Zittella [virgin or spinster] too? a pretty contradiction.
>
> *The Feign'd Curtezans*

In *The Feign'd Curtezans*, the interplay of disguise and desire is not ironic but deliberately gestic, a concentrated and contradictory demonstration of the impossibility of female desire in a phallic economy. Two country sisters, Marcella and Cornelia, in love with two roving Englishmen, Fillamour and Gaillard, flee from a forced marriage contract (Marcella's) and follow the men to Rome, disguising themselves as famous Roman courtesans, Euphemia and Silvianetta. Laura Lucrezia, also in love with Gaillard, assumes the name Silvianetta as well. The sisters and Laura take houses next to each other; the houses are identical, such that a lover wooing at one mistakes the house (and woman) at the other. The familiar virgin/courtesan topos, beginning as a sleight of hand, becomes 'real' since, unlike *The Rover*, virgin and courtesan plots are never separate: to woo the 'curtezan' *is* to woo the virgin. In a play where the English dolts pursue the same woman as the gallants, where double identities proliferate, Behn stages what Lacan calls the 'fantasy' of heterosexuality;[43] a relation of perpetual misrecognition, wherein the male gallant loves the 'truth' of his ideal (the phallus) and the female functions only as prop to his fantasy.[44]

In several scenes, we find Fillamour staring directly at Marcella/Euphemia, attempting to distinguish between the virgin he idealizes and the courtesan he wants to seduce:

> I've often seen that Face – but 'twas in Dreams:
> And sleeping lov'd extremely!
> And waking – sighed to find it but a Dream:
> The lovely Phantom vanish'd with my Slumbers,
> But left a strong Idea on my heart
> Of what I find in perfect Beauty here,
> – But with this difference, she was virtuous too.

(365)

Comic irony mocks Fillamour's courtly-love idealism; the courtesan, we know, is a virgin whose 'difference' is literally in his mind. Indeed Fillamour's Petrarchan flourishes are themselves the quarry of Behn's satire, for this is the discourse that both elevates and extinguishes the love object; that masks the impossibility of heterosexual mutuality by 'pretending' that an obstacle exists, in this case Marcella's presumed lack of virtue. Marcella responds by refusing to be mystified as either 'lovely Phantom' or 'strong Idea'; but unable to represent her desire except in/as masquerade, she takes the only route left open – meeting Petrarchan idealism with Hobbesian (and libertine) materialism:

> MARCELLA You only dreamt that she was virtuous too:
>   Virtue it self's a Dream of so slight force,
>   The very fluttering of Love's Wings destroys it;
>   Ambition, or the meaner hope of Interest, wakes it to nothing;
>   In Men a feeble beauty shakes the dull slumber off.
>
> (365)

There is no transcendent ideal but rather the waking from dull slumber into ambition and sensuous appetite. Virtue is indeed the 'difference' in that like 'honor,' 'honesty,' and 'reputation,' it has no ontology except in patriarchal dreams; gestic, foregrounding the impossibility of representing female desire.

In doubling virgin and courtesan Behn thus ironizes on a classical mimetic relation, a relation of sameness that subverts both patriarchy (patrilineal legitimacy) and phallic desire. This subversion accounts perhaps for the dominant rhetorical device of *The Feign'd Curtezans*: the definition.

> And yet this rare piece is but a Curtezan, in coarse plain English a very Whore, – who filthily exposes all her Beauties to him can give her most, not love her best.
>
> (312)

> These Women are whores but differ from the rest in this, they generously own their trade of Sin, which others deal by stealth in; they are curtesans.
>
> (327)

> What, Curtezan! Why tis a noble Title, and has more Votaries than Religion . . . glorious Profession with a thousand Satisfactions, more than in a dull virtuous Life: Dark-Lanthorn-Men, the Serenades, Songs, Sighs, Vows, Presents, Quarrels, all for a look or smile.
>
> (328, 329)

From Gaillard, who thinks he woos a professional, Cornelia gets music, dark-lanthorns, formulaic vows, and eventually quarrels. But in the mold of Hellena, when finally cornered by the man she is pursuing, she halts the masquerade:

I am of noble Birth; and should I in one hapless loving Minute destroy the honour of my House, ruin my Youth and Beauty, and all that virtuous Education my hoping parents gave me . . .

(379)

Cornelia is forced to uphold that which makes her marriage-marketable, just as Behn is forced to uphold the gender conventions of the intrigue plot. But the more subversive message is also voiced, virgin and courtesan are nothing more than labels which can slip and be reattached differently. Cornelia pointedly asks her sister: 'and can you be frighted with the Vizor, which you your self put on?' (328).

Of course doubling ruins truth-model mimesis (true virgin versus fake courtesan) and produces what Prynne decades earlier called the 'mingle mangle' of social discipline. Behn uses this chaos to mock gender structuration, theatricalizing Derrida's formula for the 'play of representation,' in which the double splits what it doubles . . . and the law of the addition of the origin to its representation, of the thing to its image, is that one plus one makes at least three.[45] Virgin plus fake courtesan adds up to . . . ? Instead of changing from 'the loose dress' of the city courtesan back to the clothing of the wealthy country virgin, Marcella takes on a *third* identity, '*in Man's Clothes*' (356). Similarly, Laura Lucrezia, intermittently impersonating a courtesan, more memorably pursues Galliard dressed as a strapping youth: 'call me Count *Sans-Coeur* . . . . How dost thou like my Shape – my Face and Dress. My Mien and Equipage, may I not pass for Man?' (331).

'Breeches parts' were notoriously successful in Restoration theater, and Aphra Behn wrote on average more breeches parts than her colleagues.[46] Female characters, played now by women, who cross-dressed to 'pass for man' made gender gestic, defamiliarizing the sign systems (face, dress, mien, equipage) that legitimate masculinity. As all disguise temporarily detaches sign from referent, Laura Lucrezia's 'pass for man' not only creates a gender 'mingle mangle,' it seems to produce a kind of agency. Donning breeches allows desperate female characters access to lovers they could not have had, and in several plays they carry swords and fight at their sides. Shakespeare's Viola was endearingly cowardly when confronting Sir Andrew Aguecheek's challenges, but in Behn's plays women in breeches eagerly take up the challenge to fight – Hellena in *The Rover*, Marcella and Laura in *The Feign'd Curtezans*, Cloris in *The Amorous Prince*, Hippolyta in *The Dutch Lover* (her lover having carried her off wounds her again with his sword), and most memorably, the Widow of *The Widow Ranter* who fights '*like a Fury*' alongside Daring on the exotic Virginia 'Sevana,' '*he putting her back in vain; they fight out.*'[47]

The fact that the hard-drinking Widow has just married Daring in those same breeches suggests the possibility of a new female signifying space. But the cultural semiosis of breeches parts belies such conclusions: Daring expresses the prevailing male sentiment: he 'never lik'd [the Widow] half so well in Petticoats' (292), just as Pepys, when he first saw Nell Gwynn in breeches, became interested in a play he had disliked years earlier. Women's stockinged legs on the public stage were a scandalous pleasure, a fetishist's dream. In Behn's work, females mimicking males points up, not female freedom, but the homosociality of the intrigue plots – Laura 'has' Gaillard only when she's Sans-Coeur and 'he [takes] me in his Arms, Pressing my willing Bosom to his Breast, Kissing my Cheek . . .' (346).

And yet, the gestic element in any theatrical image refers not to its unity of expression but to its unresolvable contradictions. A female performer in breeches, sword in hand, points *both* to gender slippage and to gender constraint; to a space of pleasurable female activity and to a viewing apparatus that reifies and exploits her sexuality. The gestic inference of Behn's abundant use of women-in-breeches parts is not that disguise hides a truth that will ultimately emerge (the woman's 'true self'), but rather that representation is always pressured by embodiment – and not only toward the pleasures of fetishism. Put another way, truth in Behn is always embodied, a point which, as we will see, makes the exposure of *un*disguised flesh a *gestus* requiring a different description.

PASSIONATE ADDRESS/GESTIC UNDRESS

[In] matters of love, excess is a virtue, and all other degrees of love are worthy of scorn alone.

Aphra Behn

LA NUCHE   Oh, that my sin would change this Rage into some easier Passion: Sickness, Disgrace and Pity were kinder than this.

The Second Part of The Rover

DIANA   No pain is like defeated new Desire.

The Town Fop

JULIA   I burn, I burn Jacinta, and only this charming Carlos can allay my Pain . . .

The False Count

ANGELLICA   He's gone, and in this ague of my soul
The shivering fit returns.

The Rover

She who so well cou'd love's kind Passion paint
We piously believe, must be a saint.

John Dryden, Prologue to *The Widow Ranter* written after Behn's death

However ironic Dryden's line about sainthood, he agreed with Thomas Creech that no one presented passionate love more palpably than Aphra

Behn. A prolific writer of cavalier verse celebrating pastoral seductions, Behn ostensibly followed the libertine line in her celebration of, in Gaillard's words, 'the generous indulgent Law of Nature' (312). Behn praised Creech's 1682 translation of Lucretius's *De Rarum Natura*, not only because it made a classic available to non-Latin-reading women but because the poem encouraged her to produce her own version of human social origins. In 'The Golden Age' (1684) she imagines a utopian state of nature regulated not by man-made laws, by custom or religion, but by sexual passion: 'The lovers thus uncontrolled did meet, / Thus all their joys and vows of love repeat: / Joys which were ever-lasting, ever new / And every vow inviolably true: / Not kept in fear of Gods, no fond religious cause, / Nor in obedience to the duller laws.'[48] Passion produces truth because it makes the lover incap-able of mere conformity to moral or religious conventions. The 'uncontrolled' lover's body, performative in language ('vows') and sexual affect ('joys'), speaks truth, a truth falsified by dullness or insensate motionlessness, be it in a law or a lover.[49]

In effect Behn agreed with Hobbes's fundamental tenet, that sensation ('the several motions of matter . . . which presseth our organs diversely'[50]) was the basis of knowledge and that appetite was the inevitable effect. But Hobbesian materialism was passive; sensation and feeling were mechanically induced, stimulated by fear or self-preservation. In the notorious song from her third play *The Dutch Lover* (1673), 'Amyntas led me to a grove,' Behn situates sensuous knowledge in the subjective agency of the female singer: '. . . And many kisses he did give / And I returned the same / Which made me willing to receive / That which I dare not name.' The song ends with a mock-passive consummation: '[He] layed me gently on the ground; / Ah who can guess the rest?'[51] The coyness of this final question tends to depart in the plays where female passion and generous consummation lead to rage and pain ('passionate' in its earliest usage meant 'to suffer pain'). Behn's passionate females – usually courtesans, married, or older women – speak a painful language that cannot be answered – 'I burn, I burn, Jacinta . . .' – and for them Behn found a separate semiotic, the inverse of the mask: the body in 'undress.'

'*Enter Chloris, in undress*'; '*Enter Florinda in an undress*'; '*Enter Ariadne . . . undrest.*' In play after play we find this stage direction. The undraped female body (both virgin and courtesan) seems to be passion's necessary referent, the visible sensorium of the pains, the burning, the shivering fits suffered by Behn's mature lovers. However, if passionate address was inseparable from actual undress, the ground for the body's materiality was the voracious materialism of the Restoration stage. Flecknoe and Pepys, we recall, testified to the intensity of the theater's visual pleasure, and actresses were linked metonymically to the innovation of stage properties. Let's look more closely at the distribution of such properties. The Restoration stage offered two playing spaces, the forestage used especially for comedy, where actor and audience were in intimate proximity, and the upstage area or 'scenic stage' where painted wing and shutter settings, thirty-five to fifty feet from the first row of spectators, produced the exotic illusionistic 'discoveries' characteristic of heroic tragedy.

Writing mostly comedies, Aphra Behn might be expected to follow comic convention and use the forestage area, but as Peter Holland notes, she was 'positively obsessive' about discovery scenes.[32] Holland counts thirty-one discoveries in ten comedies (consider that Sedley's *The Mulberry Garden*, 1668, uses one; Etherege's *The Man of Mode*, 1676, uses two), most of which are bedroom scenes featuring a female character '*in undress*.' Holland reasons that such scenes are placed upstage so that familiar Restoration actresses would not be distractingly exposed to the audience. The psychoanalytic version of this view would be that the exposed (and castrated) female body must be obscured in order to activate scopic pleasure. Displayed at a distance, the actress in undress becomes a fetish object, pleasuring the male spectator while protecting him from the anxiety of sexual difference. But this is incongruous. Why would Behn objectify the very bodies whose passions she upheld as natural, as the utopian alternative to gender custom and crude self-preservation?

Let's return to *The Rover* and to Behn's most famous courtesan. In contrast to the virgins' 'ramble' and masquerade are the stasis and thralldom attending Angellica Bianca. While the virgins are learning artful strategies of concealment, Angellica's entrance is a complicated process of theatrical unveiling. She arrives first through words, then through painted representation, then through the body of an actress who appears on a balcony behind a silk curtain. The first references to Angellica situate her beyond the market in which we expect her to function. According to Behn's gallants, she is the 'ador'd beauty of all the youth in Naples, who put on all their charms to appear lovely in her sight; their coaches, liveries and themselves all gay as on a monarch's birthday . . .' (28). Equated with sacred and secular authority, Angellica gazes on her suitors and 'has the pleasure to behold all languish for her that see her . . .' (28). When the English gallants group themselves beneath her balcony, they wait with the impatience of theater spectators for Angellica to appear – not in person but in representation, as 'the shadow of the fair substance' (29).

At this point the link between shadow and substance preoccupies them. Blunt, the stock country fool, is confused by the fact that signs of affluent and even noble status – velvet beds, fine plate, handsome attendance, and coaches – are flaunted by courtesans. Here once again is the epistemological and aesthetic 'mingle mangle' that Behn and her colleagues treat satirically. More to the point, Blunt's comments in the presence of Angellica's portraits allow Behn to foreground the ambiguity of female signs and to comment on the pleasures and politics of theatrical signification. Consider her adaptation of *The Rover*'s source play, Thomas Killigrew's ten-act semi-autobiographical closet drama, *Thomaso, or The Wanderer*. In both plays, one portrait is prominent and raised, two smaller versions are posted below, one of which is snatched by the rake – Thomaso in the Killigrew play, Willmore in Behn's. But there is an important difference in the relationship of sign to referent. In *Thomaso*, Act II, scene 1, anonymous parties of men pass in front of the paintings, react scornfully to the courtesan's high price, and wander on. But in Act II scene 2, with the arrival of Killigrew's main characters, Angellica Bianca is sitting on the balcony in full view of her prospective buyers. Her bawd challenges the men to 'compare them [the paintings and the woman] together.' In line with neo-classical decorum, the men agree that the woman exceeds her representation: 'That smile, there's a grace and sweetness in it Titian could never have catch'd'.[53] By the time the English Thomaso and his friends arrive, the viewing of the paintings and the viewing of Angellica are almost simultaneous:

> HARRIGO   That wonder is it I told you of; tis the picture of the famous Italian, the Angellica; See, shee's now at her Window.
> THOMASO   I see her, 'tis a lovely Woman . . .
>
> (334)

In *The Rover*, Angellica Bianca never invites such explicit comparison: Angellica's simulacra, not Angellica, preoccupy her male audience. When the English cavaliers first view the paintings, Belvile, the fatuous moralist, reads them as 'the fair sign[s] to the inn where a man may lodge that's fool enough to give her price' (33). That is, the iconicity of the paintings, their likeness to Angellica, which so impresses Killigrew's cavaliers, is in Behn's text suppressed. Gazing on the portraits the gallants rewrite the courtesan's monarchical description, now figuring her as a thing, a receptacle for depositing one's body. To underscore the point, Blunt asks the ontological question to which there is a ready answer in commodity discourse: '[G]entlemen, what's this?' Belvile: 'A famous courtesan, that's to be sold' (33). But the infinitive phrase is curious. To be sold by whom? Released by her earlier keeper's death, Angellica and her bawd seem to be in business for themselves. At this point, however, Blunt reminds us again of the object status of both woman and painted signs: '[L]et's be gone; I'm sure we're no chapmen for this commodity' (33).

Willmore, however, monarchy's representative, succumbs to the lure of the signs, believing not only in their iconicity but in their value as pleasurable objects – for the original one must pay a thousand crowns, but on the portraits one can gaze for nothing. Penury of course is not the real issue. Willmore understands that the appeal of the paintings is precisely that they are not the original but an effective stand-in. After the two Italian aristocrats draw swords in competition for Angellica, Willmore reaches up and steals one of the small paintings, in effect 'cuts out,' in Barthes's words, a piece of the representation for his own titillation. His intentions, like his actions, are explicitly masturbatory:

> This posture's loose and negligent;
> The sight on't would beget a warm desire
> In souls whom impotence and age had chilled.
> This must along with me.
>
> (38)

This speech and the act of appropriation occur *before* Willmore sees Angellica. Only in Behn's text do the paintings function as fetishes, as substitute objects for the female body. When challenged why he has the right to the small portrait, Willmore claims the right 'of possession, which I will maintain' (38).

At the outset of this chapter, I described Willmore's acquisitive gesture as a *gestus* – that moment in theatrical performance in which contradictory social attitudes in both text and society are made heuristically visible to spectators. What does this *gestus* show? Willmore removes Angellica's portrait the way a theater manager might lift off a piece of the set – because without buying her, he already owns her. Her paintings are materially linked to the painted Scenes, which were of course owned, through the theatrical hierarchy, by patentee and king – who, in Behn's fiction, validates and empowers Willmore. This homosocial circuit points to an even larger gendered network. As innumerable accounts make clear, Restoration theater participated in the phallic economy that commodified women, not in the marriage market, but in the mistress market: the king and his circle came to the theater to look, covet, and buy. Nell Gwynn is the celebrated example, but Behn's biographer Angeline Goreau cites other cases.[54] Elizabeth Farley, an actress in the King's Company, joined the royal entourage for several months, then became mistress to a Gray's Inn lawyer, then drifted into prostitution and poverty. The answer to the question, 'Who is selling Angellica?' is, then, the theater itself, which, like Willmore, operates with the king's patent and authorization. When Angellica sings behind her balcony curtain for her Italian admirers, and draws the curtain to reveal a bit of beautiful flesh, then closes it while monetary arrangements are discussed, she performs the titillating masquerade required by her purchasers *and* by her spectators. This is mastery's masquerade, not to demonstrate freedom, but to flaunt the charms that reflect (back) male power.

If Angellica's paintings signify the theater apparatus and its ideological complicity with a phallic economy, what happens when Angellica appears? Is illusionism betrayed? Interestingly, Aphra Behn chooses this moment to emphasize presence, not only of character but of body; Angellica emerges in the flesh and offers it, gratis, to Willmore, finding his scornful admiration ample reason, for the first time, for falling in love. In their wooing/bargaining scene it becomes clear that Angellica wants to step out of the exchange economy signified by the paintings: 'Canst thou believe [these yielding joys] will be entirely thine, / without considering they were mercenary?' (45). The gestic word here is 'entirely'; Angellica dreams of full reciprocal exchange without commerce: 'The pay I mean is but thy love for mine. / Can you give that?' (47). And Wllmore responds 'entirely.'

A commodity, Marx writes, becomes so only insofar as it 'possess[es] a double form, a natural form and a value form.'[55] Angellica's name contains 'angel,' a reference to both the celestial figure and an old English coin stamped with the device of Michael the archangel, minted for the last time by Charles I but still in circulation during the Restoration. Through passionate vows Angellica tries to eliminate her value-form and to return her body – passion's referent – to a state of nature. While the virgins of the marriage plot are talking 'business' and learning the powers of deferral and unveiling, Angellica is trying to demystify and authenticate herself, to step out of the paintings, to be known not by her surface but by her depth. As she 'yields' to Willmore upstairs, the portraits on the balcony are removed – a sign that the courtesan is working. In this case, though, not only does the (off-stage) 'natural' body supplant its painted representation, but the courtesan, who has been in excess of, now makes up a deficiency in, the marriage plot: Angellica labors for love. However, though the paintings disappear in Act III, the signs of commodification are still in place, or are metonymically displaced through properties and Scenes to other characters in the marriage plot. We learn that Hellena's portion derives from her uncle, the old man who kept Angellica Bianca; thus the gold Willmore receives from the courtesan has the same source as that which he will earn by marrying the virgin. Like Angellica, too, the virgin Florinda uses a portrait as a calling card, and at night in the garden, '*in undress,*' carrying a little box of jewels – a double metonym for dowry and genitals – she plans to offer herself to Belvile (65). Unfortunately Willmore not Belvile enters the garden and nearly rapes her. In Act IV scene 4, again fleeing Willmore Florinda runs in and out of the Scenes until she arrives in Blunt's chamber where another near-rape occurs. Blunt has just been cozened by a prostitute and dumped naked into the city sewer; he emerges vowing to 'beat' and 'kiss' and 'bang' the next woman he sees (99, 101), who happens to be Florinda, but now all women appear to be whores. In fact Willmore, Frederick, and even Belvile arrive soon after to break down the door and 'partake' of Florinda. If the courtesan Angellica Bianca makes a spectacle of herself through balcony curtains and paintings, Florinda's 'undress' and her proximity to the Scenes signify a similar reduction to commodity status.

ALLEGORIES OF AUTHORITY: 'I . . . HANG OUT THE SIGN OF ANGELLICA'

> In the soul of the commodity, which gives the illusion of having made its peace in its price, a hell rages.
>
> Walter Benjamin

Angellica's paintings, I have argued, form a metonymic chain linking the text of *The Rover* to the apparatus of representation. Angellica's portraits represent the courtesan in the most radical sense. They both produce an image of her and reduce her to that image. Notwithstanding her passionate address, Angellica cannot exceed her simulacra. When Willmore gestically appropriates the courtesan's painted image, he makes visible the patriarchal and homosocial economy that controls the apparatus as well as the commodity status of paintings, their model, the painted actress and the painted Scenes. The passionate body *in undress* is also gestic, making visible an alternative but recuperable economy of passionate love. Still we have to contend with the body in the Scenes, and the relation of these bodies to the author's signature. For the *repetition* of such images had in fact become Behn's theatrical signature.

I want to argue here that Behn's 'obsessive' dependence on the undressed body in the Scenes suggests an allegorical vision – here I mean allegory in

Walter Benjamin's sense – as a self-critical practice rooted in emblem, hiero-glyph and gesture; that is, in signs pointing not to a sacred or abstract truth but to an expanded sense of their own materiality. In *The Origin of German Tragic Drama*, Benjamin sought to recover the specificity of seventeenth-century baroque tragedy (or *Trauerspiel*), particularly its untragical, unclassical absorption in historical pessimism, its reliance on material and inscrutable emblematics, on 'contemplative' elements that aim not to seduce the spectator into an illusory world but rather to demand her active decoding. Not surprisingly, Benjamin found precisely these elements in Brecht's epic theater practices and linked them (in *Understanding Brecht*) to the *Trauerspiel*.[56] The materiality of the sign and its caption is another connection between baroque allegory and epic theater. Brecht thought of the *gestus* as implicitly captioned, 'set out and laid bare to the understanding of the audience.'[57] According to Benjamin, the baroque emblematist 'does not present the essence implicitly, "behind the image." He drags the essence of what is depicted out before the image, in writing, as a caption.'[58] Because they need decoding, the *gestus* and the alle-gorical emblem smash the illusion of artistic unity (the fusion of symbol and meaning, sign, and referent), and, by extension, of all imaginary relations that produce the 'harmonious' world of capitalist mythmaking.[59]

But there are differences. Allegory, as a literary form and as a mode of sig-nification, is fundamentally esoteric, while the *gestus* is an act of artistic and/or critical intention, a complex but readable sign. Benjaminian allegory says that 'life is an illusion which, when dissipated, reveals nothing';[60] the sign is empty. The Brechtian *gestus* seeks to dispel illusion, allowing us to recognize the con-tradictory 'truth' of human life under capitalism; the sign is full, excessive to itself. Perhaps most significantly, Benjamin's conception of the allegory and the allegories he studies pay homage to transitoriness, decline, dissipation, death, a world lost to spiritual redemption. The *gestus* invokes political will, the pos-sibility of change.

How do we relate the *Trauerspiel* allegories to Behn's intrigue comedies? In their social-satirical commentary, Behn's fast-paced late seventeenth-century plays have none of the spiritual melancholy of the early seventeenth-century German *Trauerspiel*, nor does Restoration comic repartee compare with what Benjamin called the 'recitative' exaggeration of the German plays, their 'antithesis of sound and meaning'.[61] But close to Behn is the allegorist's ten-dency to bring into image-laden perspective the collapse of history into nature – a nature, as Benjamin puts it, no longer 'in bud and bloom, but in the over-ripeness and decay of her creations' (174). In this secular 'empty world' there is no redemption, rather the 'profane world' is both elevated and devalued (174). I want to suggest that Behn's body in undress and in the Scenes takes on precisely this allegorical function, pointing to, and materially instantiating, the collapse of an idealized nature (the nature of Behn's paradisal, sexually 'uncontrolled' Golden Age) into the historical exchange economy that defined late seventeenth-century gender relations. In the Restoration culture of gender the mock-Platonic ideality ascribed to the courtesan (and to the virgins who imitate her) is emblematic of the profane, empty material world which, through her beauty, is simultaneously 'elevated and devalued' and remains, after the busy intrigue plots have concluded, utterly unredeemed.

Allegory, as noted above, stinks of mortality. Hence the obsession in the German baroque with the ruin, the broken fragment, the decaying object. These, says Benjamin, stand in opposition 'to the idea of transfigured nature as conceived by the early Renaissance' (177). Restoration rhetoric of bodily decay – the face in ruins – haunts Behn's seductive tableaux. The body's perfection in the Scenes can be admired, fetishized from a distance, but is mediated by the actress's known history, her potential for physical and social ruin. If, for Benjamin, the transience of secular history is figured in the death's head (166), Behn's figure, the body 'in undress' discovered in the Scenes, is a double-sided emblem redolent of seventeenth-century gender ideology.

Double-sidedness is, of course, basic to allegory. Discussing the *Trauerspiel* emplotment of the fall of kings, Benjamin links tyrant drama (producing fear) to martyr drama (inciting pity). Given the legal ideologies empowering and constraining the historical monarch, the baroque tyrant's combination of corruption and futility made him inseparable from the suffering martyr; 'tyrant and martyr are the Janus-head of the monarch,'[62] two sides of the same coin. In Behn's intrigue comedies, the angel functions as double-sided coin, imprinted with the faces of virgin and courtesan, the Janus-head emblem for the destiny of Restoration women whose distinctions in gender ideology (virgin/wife/prostitute) are belied by their common role in the exchange economy: coins clinking in the pockets of husbands and fathers. Like the baroque allegorists, too, Behn works within the dialectic of convention and expressiveness. The courtesans' passionate discourse ('I burn, I burn, Jacinta'), so crucial to Behn's extra-contractual love thematics, is mediated not only by the commodity frame through which the words are heard – but by the sheer conventionality of that expressiveness: the rhetoric of sighs, wounds, vows, gazes, love darts, and conquests so common in cavalier poetry. Allegory is *both* convention and expression, or more precisely 'the expression of convention.'[63]

Yet the question remains. Is that body-in-undress-in-the-Scenes utterly reduced to its commodifying apparatus; does it become solely a conventional sign, hollow, lifeless, exchangeable, or is there, as Eagleton puts it, a 'somatic dimension' to that sign, 'some purely sensuous residue which escapes the strict regime of sense to which all language is now shackled'?[64] In an allegorical key, the sensuous residue must be understood as the material trace of time passing; the passionate body-in-the-Scenes offers us not abstract symbolizations of Beauty or Love but the collapse of symbolic nature into history. Put another way, Behn's utopian state of nature is simultaneously an earth-bound 'subjection to nature,'[65] and this, says Benjamin, gives rise to the enigmatic question of the biographical historicity of the author. Behn's body in the Scenes, then, is profoundly dialectical, an emblem of ideal nature containing an individual's historical dust.

As a writer, Behn was continually sexualized, embodied. As poet/punk her writings were compared to veneral disease;[66] the *angel*-ic bodies she created

became, as she must have suspected, her most enduring image.[67] Behn nur-
tured her literary afterlife as best she could, on the one hand complaining that
'the Woman damns the Poet,'[68] that all accusations of bawdiness and plagia-
rism are levied at her because of her gender; on the other hand avowing she
must write 'not . . . as th' antient Poets writ, / For your Applause of Nature,
Sense and Wit, / But, like good Tradesmen, what's in fashion vent, / And
cozen you, to give ye all content.'[69] Likewise Dryden complained in prologues
throughout the 1670s that he was writing to please an immoral audience, producing work that ran counter to his temperament. But Dryden was also part
of Behn's problems. He admired her adaptations of translated works but would
never tolerate 'mongrel plots' which no doubt included her particular mixture
of intrigue, farce, and feminist satire. Further complicating her claim to
authority was the sexual attribution: 'my Masculine Part the Poet in Me.'[70] Is
it possible that the painful androgyny of authorship, the conflict between her
'defenceless' woman's body and her 'masculine part,' is allegorically staged in
play after play, in the person/image of the passionate woman cast into the
Scenes, in the visual equation of female body, fetish, and commodity? Is this
what Behn wants us to 'discover'?

In her 'Postscript' to the published text of *The Rover*, Behn complains that
she has been accused of plagiarizing Killigrew simply because the play was
successful and she a woman. Yet while claiming to be 'vainly proud of [her]
judment' in adapting *Thomaso*, she 'hang[s] out the sign of Angellica (the only
stolen object) to give notice where a great part of the wit dwelt' (130). This
compliment to Killigrew may also indicate what compelled Behn to embark
on her adaptation. Angellica Bianca, sharing Aphra Behn's initials, is the only
name from *Thomaso* that the writer leaves unchanged. As we have seen, the
'sign (paintings) of Angellica' both constitute and represent the theater apparatus, serving as metacritical commentary on its patriarchal economy, its habits
of fetishistic consumption. They also constitute Behn's authorial *signature*, what
Miller calls the 'material emblems . . . brutal traces of the culture of gender.'[71]
These emblems allegorically inscribe the mortality of the body 'in undress' *and*
the immortal life of the commodity: the death's head glares out within the
seductive image. In this sense, Behn's signature is less the painting than the
caption, another dusty hieroglyphic of the culture of gender.

Allegory, says Benjamin, 'goes away empty-handed.'[72] The critic need never
do so. The signs of Angellica not only help us specify the place of this important woman dramatist in Restoration cultural practice, they invite us to historicize the critique of sexualized representation that has informed so much
feminist theater criticism in the last decade. Certainly the conditions of women
writers have changed since the Restoration, and yet the fetishistic features of
the commercial theater have remained remarkably similar. Now as then the
apparatus is geared to profit and pleasure, and overwhelmingly controlled by
men. Now as then the arrangement of audience to stage produces what Brecht
called a 'culinary' or ideologically conservative spectator,[73] intellectually passive

but scopically hungry, eager for the next turn of the plot, the next scenic effect. Now as then the actor suffers the reduction of Angellica Bianca, having no existence except in the sensuous semblances produced by the exchange economy.

If Restoration theater marks the historical beginning of commodity-intensive, dreamlike effects in English staging, Aphra Behn's contribution to contemporary theory lies in her demonstration that, from the outset, dreamlike effects depend(ed) on the fetish-commodification of the female body. When Willmore, standing in for King and court, steals Angellica's painting, Behn genders the spectatorial economy as, specifically, male consumption of the female image. But this is not the only story. By reading Willmore's gesture of appropriation as a *gestus*, the feminist critic implicates her own act of reading/interpreting. Aphra Behn's signature becomes what Marx called a 'social hieroglyphic,'[74] a sign of a buried life whose decoding generates fresh possibilities for critique and contestation.

4 Caryl Churchill's plays

The *gestus* of invisibility

Writing is for you, you are for you; your body is yours, take it.
Hélène Cixous, 'The Laugh of the Medusa'

ALICE I hate my body.
Caryl Churchill, *Vinegar Tom*

Hélène Cixous's 'The Laugh of the Medusa,' the controversial manifesto of *l'écriture féminine*, opens forcefully: 'I shall speak about women's writing: about *what it will do.*'[1] Revolutionary myth as much as practice, 'feminine writing' celebrates the libidinal multivalence of a woman's body and imagines a uniquely female writing that disrupts, mimics, exceeds, and dismantles what is known in feminist discourse as the patriarchal symbolic.[2] Since the 1975/76 publication of 'The laugh of the Medusa,' Cixous has been accused of ahistorical essentialism, of conceptualizing a female body-scene that keeps off-stage political and material differences within and between genders.[3] For Caryl Churchill, who began writing professionally in the activist climate of the post-Brecht British fringe and the socialist debate in the women's movement, Cixous's scorn for empirical gender categories would probably be repugnant.[4] Churchill's own work of the mid-1970s (*Light Shining in Buckinghamshire, Vinegar Tom, Cloud Nine*) places historical contradiction, class ideology, and sexual politics at the center of action and rhetoric. Alice of *Vinegar Tom* (see above epigraph) hates her body because in the play's fictional seventeenth-century village, where poverty and terror are displaced into misogynist scapegoating, her body is materially and sexually abused, her desire inexpressible.

Yet to think about theater writing is to envision immediately a writing that 'will *do,*' that empowers speakers with vital words, incites bodies to move in space. The 'unheard songs' (246) Cixous imagines in the female body have a place in Churchill's theater writing, a curious place. From her early theater texts, but especially in *Fen, A Mouthful of Birds*, and *The Skriker*, the body becomes a kind of limit-text of representational information, a special site of inquiry and struggle. What I am isolating for discussion is a double strain in Churchill's work: on the one hand, a commitment to the apparatus of representation (actor as sign of character; character as sign of a recognizable human fiction) in order to say something *about* human oppression and pain – the capitalist greed that underwrites bourgeois feminism in *Top Girls*, for example, or the cyclical exploitation of workers in *Fen*; on the other hand, a consistent though less obvious attention to the powers of theatrical illusion, to modalities within representation that subvert the 'aboutness' we normally call the work's 'content.' I am referring to various representations of corporeal violence – Worsely's hacking, burning, poisoning, shooting his body, and constant reminders of stinking meat in *Owners*; the witch-hunting in *Vinegar Tom* that involves on-stage pricking and hanging; Angela forcing Becky to drink boiling water in *Fen*, among other examples. I am referring also to self-reflexive play on illusionism, from card tricks to telepathic summonings, telekinesis, shape-shifting, and, after *Top Girls*, to a dialogue style of overlapping speeches that fractures the language of the individual subject into near-cacophonic vocalizations, culminating in the literal doubletalk of *The Skriker*. This incomplete list of effects may not add up to a demonstration of Artaudian cruelty, magic, or sonority, but it indicates a certain obsession with the signifying limits of the performing body.

Mention of performance recalls the theoretical debates in the 1970s and 1980s about performance and theater, and the place of feminism in those debates. With the enormous influence of Brecht and Artaud on Western experimental theater since the late 1950s, with the revival of theater semiotics and its poststructuralist modifications,[5] the body, common to both performance and theater, marks a crucial point of division. Certain formulations are by now axiomatic and have been superseded by crossover connections between theater and performance art. Still, to contextuate Churchill it will be useful to recall them.[6] Theater is governed by the logos of the playwright's text; actors represent fictional entities of that text to produce a unique temporal and spatial framework or dramatic 'world.' Theater spectators are encouraged in pleasurable narrativity: prompted to identify with the psychological conflicts of individual subjects, to respond to the lure of suspense, reversal, and deferral, to decode gestural and spectacular effects.[7] Performance, on the other hand, dismantles textual authority, illusionism, and the canonical actor in favor of the 'polymorphous thinking body' of the performer,[8] a sexual, permeable, tactile body, a 'semiotic bundle of drives'[9] that scourges audience narrativity. In performance, linear fictional time gives way to spatial intensities or projections of the performer's thought, gesture, movement, and voice. Theater, the art of *representation*, transforms this polymorphous, drive-ridden, repressed, instinctual – can we call it an 'orificial?' – body into what Roland Barthes calls an 'emphatic formal body, frozen by its function as an artificial object.'[10]

Simple binaries like 'orificial–artificial' are of course dangerous; the performer's body in a performance piece is arguably no less artificial than an actor's body in a production of *The Wild Duck*; neither body escapes semiosis. My interest here is not to uphold an opposition but to suggest that the distinction helps us understand the ideological nature of representation. In theater the sexual and historical specificity of the actor's body is absorbed into a representation of the body of a character, as defined and delimited by the author's text. This absorption, as Brecht pointed out repeatedly, is one of theater's most destructive mystifications since it produces a seamless (i.e. ahistorical, apolitical) illusionism. Though an art constructed from (among other elements) human bodies, theater demands a certain distance in order for the truth of its illusions to be believed.[11] At the most basic perceptual level, the body transforms into a sign of a character only when its bodily markers are erased, when facial lines, the veins in the hand, the wrinkled stocking, all the boundaries between body and adornment, body and history, are made invisible.

This seeing from a distance has profound implications for feminism. In theater studies, feminism has moved from an empirical concern with images of women in plays to a critique, fueled by deconstruction and psychoanalytic theory of the phallic economy that underlies representation and perspectival space. With its apparatus of curtains, colored gels, follow spots, trapdoors, exits, and entrances, theater exists in a perpetual dialectic of the visible and invisible, of appearance and disappearance.[12] In psychoanalytic theory, seeing is never neutral; scopic desire is directed toward substitute objects and images that compensate for the (repressed) loss of the breast, the absence of the penis on the mother's body, and, more complicatedly at the oedipal moment, the lack the child feels in its own body image.[13] Representation, the making visible (again) of what is lacking or what has disappeared, has been called 'phallomorphic'[14] because it relieves, at the unconscious level, castration anxiety and, at the cultural level, reinscribes the authority of patriarchy. As Michel Benamou put it, representation relies on 'two vanishing points: God absent in the wings, the King present in his box.'[15]

Churchill's contribution to this discussion is the burden of this essay. What I would suggest at the outset is that her texts have become increasingly attentive to the ideological nature of the seeable. Specifically, the mystification of the body in representation has come to serve as a metaphor for the concealments of human, and especially female, experience under patriarchy and capitalism. In other words the lighted stage queries the world of *permissible* visibility, what can, and more importantly, what cannot, be seen. Churchill does not sketch out performance scenarios; she works within egocentric, logocentric representation but she stretches and reconfigures its conventions. In what I consider to be Churchill's feminist project – her version of semiotic realism – there is no ecstatic 'writing the body' but rather a foregrounding of the apparatus that makes the writing impossible.[16]

Before turning to *Fen* (1982) and *A Mouthful of Birds* (1986), I want to look at earlier texts and to consider theoretical discourses that have operated powerfully on the margins of Churchill's dramaturgy since the mid-1970s. Apart from her own receptivity to socialist-feminist discourse, Churchill has been shaped by two important theoretical constructs, Brechtian alienation and historicization techniques developed in theater collectives with whom she has worked since 1976, and Michel Foucault's theory of disciplinary technology from *Discipline and Punish*, which she read in 1978. It is not my intention to demonstrate influence or continuity in Churchill's work, but rather to identify the ideological dimensions and feminist implications of her concern with the body-limits of representation.

In Churchill's *Owners* (1972), the butcher Clegg's stinking meat is a metaphor for capitalism gone putrid; but the conversion of animals into commodities has wider analogies when Lisa gives away her newborn to the childless real-estate developer Marion, and Lisa's husband Alec resumes his affair with her; in exchange, though this is not Lisa's wish, Marion allows Lisa and Alec to stay in their rented apartment. Attempts to 'own' or exchange babies or husbands are shown to be as misplaced as property manipulations. At the close of Act I, Lisa lies on a bed with pregnancy contractions while her senile mother-in-law administers to an imaginary child. The scene alludes to birth and death but also implies the irrelevance and powerlessness of female nurturance in an exchange economy. At the end of the play, Alec, whose passivity suggests a version of Eastern mysticism as an alternative to Judeo-Christian getting-and-spending, walks into their burning apartment building to save a neighbor's child. His demise is described by Worsely:

> At this point I thought myself of going back in. Fire has a terrible attraction. As it leaps and licks up, like a creature taking over, when really of course it was the house turning into fire because of the high temperature it was reaching, rather than a fire consuming the house . . . . It was very hot. I was just coming out when Alec came in through the door, walking quite calmly considering the heat. 'The other baby, you see' is what he said and set off – I would say up the stairs but I couldn't exactly see them in the flames. But he rose as if climbing the stairs. Turning into fire quite silently. We waited but of course he didn't come out and nor did the Arlingtons' baby. It was too hot.[17]

Alec is apotheosized ('he rose . . .') for the play's one nurturing act. What interests me here is that Churchill attempts through the clearest realistic diction to make us believe in excruciating heat even as she gives the lines to the perverse Worsely, whose suicide attempts and Swiftian detachment have become a running gag through the play. When seconds later, Worsely fires into his brain with a pistol, then says 'Missed' (67), the point about the limits of seeing is subtly made. The phenomenal body has an equivocal function when it is called upon to represent pain or to stop 'being there.' The actor's body is a site of experience that cannot in fact *have* experience; physical death is always a matter of a toy gun while in language the body can be immolated and resurrected. Artaud reviled the theater of representation because it cannot 'break through language in order to touch life,'[18] but as Herbert Blau notes, language, not body, 'has the amplitude we long for, and the indeterminacy in its precisions.'[19] In this finely wrought, quick-paced farce, Churchill encodes a mistrust of the very illusionism that makes theatrical farce effective.

This mistrust is thematized in *Traps* (1977), perhaps Churchill's least-admired play, which she describes as:

an impossible object, like an Escher drawing, where things can exist on paper, but would be impossible in life . . . . In [*Traps*], the time, the place, the characters' motives and relationships cannot all be reconciled – they can happen on stage but there is no other reality for them.[20]

The play refers only to itself. This is of course true of any written text, but the relation to referentiality in *Traps* is unusual. Characters are completely recognizable; what they do is not surprising, narrativity seems absolutely appropriate, yet nothing coheres. The clock on the wall tells 'real time'; time presses inexorably forward, but characters move backward and forward temporally with no transition or justification. At the beginning of Act II Albert is discussed as dead but later enters to no remarks: like illusionism itself, impossible but true. The magic of the card trick fails, but not Jack's telepathic powers when he summons his sister and she arrives, like the actor summoned by the script, on cue. Lacking the moral resonance of absurdism and the serious playfulness of surrealism *Traps* is an exercise, a self-reflexive parable of theater logic.

However, in the closing image Churchill raises the stakes. She invokes the possibility of a 'polymorphous thinking body' or at least a phenomenal 'lived body' in Merleau-Ponty's sense, existentially present, orificial, and conscious.[21] With perhaps a sly glance at another self-reflexive theater artist, Churchill revises the 'real' pond where the child 'dies' at the end of *Six Characters in Search of an Author* and calls for a tub of water to be placed on stage, its material reality asserted by the fact that naked actors climb into it, get wet, climb out, and dry themselves. The one-by-one bathing ritual injects, for the first time, an impression of temporality and focused space. Dialogue, until now unverifiable, takes on a kind of transparency as it relates to the bathing: 'Come on, out you get.' 'No it's warm.' 'Hey it's cold, I want some more water.'[22] The final bather eats and smiles in what has been described as, and what we feel surely *is*, dirty warm water. At this point the spectator might also insist that the illusionistic surface has cracked; the orificial time-bound body of the actor, not merely the character, has become accessible, a marker for what Blau calls 'the one inalienable and arcane truth of theater, that the living person performing there may die in front of your eyes and is in fact doing so.'[23] Such 'arcane truths' are intrinsic to performance art when serial repetitions, devoid of motive, produce a kind of spatial intensity whose only referent seems to be the death drive. In this sequence, Churchill choreographs a small performance using bodies who have 'characters' only in a fragmentary sense. The smiling inertia of the final bather seems to gesture beyond the pleasure principle to the 'absolute response of the inorganic.'[24] But of course this is just another sleight of hand. Our belief in an orificial non-illusionistic body is *produced* by a representational system. The 'body' we see is perceivable not only because of its presence, but because the water which 'frames' the body has taken on a character, a narrative, of its own.

Churchill's work after *Traps* contains versions of that play's obsessions but *Light Shining in Buckinghamshire* and *Vinegar Tom*, written the same year (1976),

mark a political and epistemological shift. Simply the actor's body became, for
Churchill, a thinking, laboring, socio-political reality, and her own labor
became implicated in dismantling hierarchies in the theatrical mode of production. She has frequently expressed gratitude for the working methods of
Joint Stock (with whom she wrote *Light Shining in Buckinghamshire*) and
Monstrous Regiment (*Vinegar Tom*). Both groups start with workshop cum study
periods in which the company and writer discuss central themes, read historical material, travel, talk to experts, and explore character possibilities. This is
followed by a solitary writing period, then by rehearsal and text revisions, tour-
ing, and finally a London production. While the solitary writing period and
the author-position on the published text seem to suggest that key hierarchies
have remained in place, Churchill's notes on the Joint Stock experience reveal
a complicated authorial process:

> It is hard to explain exactly the relationship between the workshop and the
> text. The play is not improvised: it is a written text and the actors did not
> make up its lines. But many of the characters and scenes were based on
> ideas that came from improvisation at the workshop and during rehearsal.
> I could give endless examples of how something said or done by one of the
> actors is directly connected to something in the text . . .[25]

At a later interview she commented: 'Though I still wanted to write alone
sometimes, my attitude to myself, my work, and others had been basically and
permanently changed.'[26]

Change is the key to Brechtian historicization and to the theme and construction of *Light Shining in Buckinghamshire*. Representing the conflicting forces
in the British Civil War not as seamless narrative but as a colloquy of texts
drawn from Winstanley's writings, the Putney debates, a Leveller newspaper,
the Bible, Churchill attends to the unique conditions that shaped the conflicts
and discourses and, through textual fragmentation and subjective commentary,
demonstrates the volatility of the period, its susceptibility to a genuinely revolutionary consciousness. Through now-familiar alienation techniques (actors
serving as on-stage audience; speaking as 'actors,' not characters; different
actors playing the same role) spectators are prevented from identifying emo-
tionally with any single action or character, but are encouraged to make connections between a previous historical moment and their own.[27]

The legacy of Brecht is not simply a series of provocative theatrical tricks
but an insistence on the link between capitalist ideology and conventional
modes of theater representation. Drawing on this critique, Churchill has tried
to foreground for discovery the gender ideology that governs sexual representation. The spectacular, theatrical elements of *Cloud Nine*, the time compres-
sion by which 'historical time' leaps a hundred years between Acts I and II,
while the Victorian colonial family has aged only twenty-five years, demonstrates causality and change in sexual politics; cross-gender and cross-racial
casting demonstrate that gender and servitude are culturally coded effects that
erase the body and its desires. Betty, the male-centered, male-subservient angel

in the house, is literally man-made (played by a man). Serving the white colonial economy, Joshua in representation takes on the color of that economy (the African is played by a white). Important for this discussion is the way in which the theater apparatus becomes a point of reference in these inversions. Each character's sexual and racial position is marked by appropriate dress and is introduced by doggerel verse, including the phrase, repeated by each character, 'as you can see.'[28] What we *see* is what, given Victorian sexual and racial politics, cannot be seen: desiring women and rebellious blacks. The signature costumes of the transhistorical dinner party in *Top Girls* function similarly. The five 'top girls,' eating and drinking together in an expensive London restaurant, have entered Western representation but at a cost. Each points to the elaborate historical text that she embodies – Nijo in geisha silks, Joan in regal papal robes – but their fragmented speeches – the effect of the words of one being spoken through and over the words of another – refer to need, violence, loss, and pain, to a body unable to signify within those texts. After much drink, Pope Joan delivers a long speech in Latin, a fragment from Book II of *De Rerum Natura* (*On the Nature of Things*) by Lucretius that begins by extolling the philosopher's detachment from human striving (the pleasure of being 'perched on an edifice constructed by the wise'), only to plummet into speculation about the 'approach of death.'[29] Joan forgets her text toward the end ('Quod si ridicula – something something on and on and on,' 17), and though the passage she quotes concludes that 'terrors . . . fears and anxieties' are like children's nightmares and can be 'dissipate[d] . . . [by] . . . the rational study of nature,'[30] Joan stumbles on the word 'terrorem,' then *'gets up and is sick in a corner'* (17). For the irreligious Epicurean Lucretius knowledge was rooted in sense perception. Pope Joan's vomiting (the representation of her vomiting) is a sentient *gestus* announcing the female body's revulsion at the mystification and misogyny of Western religion – whose authority Joan nevertheless impersonates.

How theatrical concealment or mystification relates to *sexual* oppression is suggested by a short scene in Churchill's play about poverty, religious superstition, and 'witch'-hunting. In scene 13 of *Vinegar Tom*, Alice avenges her sexual loneliness by constructing a mudman representation of a lover who has abandoned her, and as her friend Susan watches, Alice pricks between its legs 'so he can't get on with his lady.'[31] Then Jack, a married neighbor who has tried unsuccessfully to seduce Alice, arrives and accuses her of bewitching him, removing his penis. He chokes her until she *'puts her hand between his thighs.'* Alice: 'There. It's back.' Jack: 'It is back. Thank you, Alice. I wasn't sure you were a witch till then'\ (164). This *gestus* demonstrates the crude double-blind logic by which innocent women were condemned as witches. But it also reveals the male terror that fuels such logic. The psychic economy of sight, we recall, is a phallic economy based upon the disavowal of a feared absence. The female shores up that economy by functioning as a lack (absence) in relation to phallic presence; as both complement and opposite women act as guarantor against the fear of castration. Jack endows Alice with the power of the phallus in order to repossess his organ, but then, newly authorized and empowered, he must subdue her by 'seeing' her as, labeling her, a witch. If Jack hardly seems in a phallic position of knowledge and authority, Susan as spectator believes that he is. He authorizes the truth that condemns Alice to demonic power and persecution. In this parable of female oppression, the lie is a truth if it is believed, which is another way of describing the theater apparatus itself. The theater wants us all to believe – or at least accept – its representations, and in doing so we ratify the power that authorizes them. In this case Jack stands in for Christian doctrine whose institutionalized misogyny, especially virulent in the Malleus Malificarum (on which Churchill drew for the Kramer–Sprenger duet) condemns not only women but difference itself:

> If you complain you're a witch
> Or you're lame you're a witch
> Any marks or deviations count for more.
> Got big tits you're a witch
> Fall to bits you're a witch
> He likes them young, concupiscent and poor.
>
> (170)

The referent for 'he' is unnamed and like the devil invisible. But 'he,' the authorizer of all violent binaries, whether in gender, in politics, or in religion is shored up by every pricking and hanging. In scene 19, Alice's outspoken old mother and a woman healer are hanged on stage and Margery, Jack's wife, prays to 'dear God' whose power is rearticulated precisely by this 'destroying [of] the wicked' (174).

The power of unseen systems to control human thought and behavior, the use of ritual spectacles of punishment to regulate, govern, eliminate resistance, the conception of the body as a site of disciplinary control for a turbulent population – all this and more Churchill would have found in Michel Foucault's *Discipline and Punish*, on which she bases *Softcops* (1978). Foucault's concept of 'docile bodies,' those objects of 'useful trainings' capable of being 'manipulated by authority'[32] produces a long series of chain reactions in her post-1978 work. The subject of Foucault's study is not simply the genealogy of the prison system, but of discipline as a type of power with a particular set of instruments, techniques, procedures, levels of application – a 'technology' of the body, essential for the operations of modern society. Foucault begins in the pre-classical era with the 'spectacle of the scaffold': public torture, mutilation, and spectacular confessions that rearticulate the power of the sovereign. A period of reform follows when punishment becomes a matter of highly skilled 'penalty-representations' (114), staged events using scenery, *trompe l'oeil* and other optical effects for the moral instruction of spectators. Finally, there is the decisive shift in discipline symbolized by Benthem's panopticon, a means of incarceration and confinement for mass control whereby one man centrally placed can observe many. For this latter stage and throughout *Discipline and Punish* Foucault's tropes are theatrical. In the panopticon, the cells are backlit like 'so many small theaters, in which each actor is alone, perfectly individualized and constantly visible' (200). The panopticon becomes a polyvalent disciplinary tool applied 'to reform prisoners . . . to treat patients, to instruct schoolchildren, to confine the insane, to supervise workers' (205); the goal always is to turn human beings into 'docile' – and productive – bodies. Though this feature doesn't form the basis of Foucault's argument, disciplinary control, the making and manipulating of docile bodies, is inextricable from the rise of capitalism. Power relations 'invest [the body], mark it, train it, torture it, force it to carry out tasks, to perform ceremonies, to emit signs' (25).

Foucault has been taken to task for his account of power as a vast network to which the subject can never be exterior,[33] for this account eliminates dialectical and historical analysis, class struggle and gender as explicit categories of power relations. Yet Foucaultian formulations on exclusion and sexual legitimation are suggestive for feminist criticism,[34] and I would guess *Discipline and Punish* 'excited' Churchill because it gave her evocative ways of understanding gender oppression as the production of 'docile bodies' in the family that, by extension, buttresses the schools, the military, and other branches of state power.[35] *Softcops* is a reductive but respectful gloss of Foucault's study; but *Cloud Nine*, written the same year, explores more fully the disciplinary methods of gender as a multivalent form of body control. The male playing Betty, the female playing her son Edward foreground the ways in which culture, through its custodians in the family, discipline the body, force it to 'emit signs' of clear masculinity and femininity. The notion of body discipline in the theater has been part of our argument from the outset: the transformation of a sentient, thinking – what I have been calling an orificial – body into an artificial sign or representation of a fiction. The relationship of the female body to appearance takes on specific political resonance in *Fen*, *A Mouthful of Birds*, and *The Skriker*; indeed the link between representation and the processes of social discipline will be my concern for the remainder of this chapter.

FEN

Named for the once-wild swamp land of East Anglia, *Fen* is divided into twenty-one brief scenes, each bearing the scars of social and familial discipline. The fen women's body-wrecking labor (potato-picking, onion-grading), combined with their housekeeping, rearing, and feeding chores, create a closed system of repetition and self-defeat. The love affair between Val and Frank bogs down on its own repetitions, Val attempting to leave her husband and daughters only to leave her lover because she can't live without her children; and in near-monosyllabic exchanges between the generations of women in Val's family, birth and blood create an ongoing cycle of denial, guilt, and rage. Churchill's interest in inertia, both political and emotional, goes back to *Objections to Sex and Violence*, *Owners*, *Traps*, and *Top Girls*, but early in the play *Fen* brings stasis and defeat to the very edge of representational truth. Frank, alone on stage, monologues an imagined conversation with the landowner Tewson, and as he works up to the fantasy of hitting him, he hits himself. This self-hitting, this self-discipline, marks a new point in Churchill's writing. Now the body enters decisively, the body that can be hurt. I do not mean that the actor gives himself actual pain, rather that in the *gestus* of the slap his body has become an explicit site of his character's struggle and suffering: into that slap is concentrated the historical and political pain of life in the fens.

Fen grows out of a particularly depressing moment in British politics. The Falklands war of 1982 brought unprecedented popularity to the Thatcher government, which in 1983 was returned to power with a landslide majority. In bitter homage to Thatcherite economic policies, *Fen* opened in January 1983 with a speech by a 'Japanese businessman' who praises the 'beautiful English countryside' and the fens' 'beautiful black earth' and all the multinationals (Esso, Equitable Life, Imperial Tobacco, etc.) that own a piece of them. With this unequivocal reference to global capital fresh in our minds, we meet the fen women '*working in a row, potato picking down a field,*'[36] an immemorial image of peasant labor. The ironic juxtaposition of businessmen and laboring women, multinational financing and a cash crop of potatoes, is a *gestus* for the double alienation of the women. Tewson, on whom they rely for minimal day wages, is bought out by a multinational and becomes a tenant himself.

Fen might best be compared to *Vinegar Tom*. Set in the 1970s and the 1640s respectively, each play investigates economic subjugation and female oppression: each shows the impossibility of heterosexual love (Alice–Man in *Vinegar Tom*; Val–Frank in *Fen*); each condemns religion as destructive ideology (Christian doxa reinterpreted through Kramer and Sprenger in *Vinegar Tom*; the evangelical Mrs. Finch in *Fen*). However, while *Vinegar Tom* shows the possibility of growing consciousness and possible change (Alice: 'I'm not a witch. But I wish I was . . . . I should have learnt [from the cunning women],' 175), the *Fen* women are studies in abjection. Nell, the 'witch' and 'morphrodite,' is utterly isolated in her objections to the exploitative conditions under which the women labor. At the play's midpoint, she narrates a long story about a runaway boy (her grandfather), a living corpse, and a vengeful farmer who skewers an adulterous couple with a pitchfork as they lie naked together in bed, then axes them to death. The story's gothic details – the boy's terror, the old man rising from a coffin, the gruesome central image ('suddenly he raised the pitchfork and brung it down as hard as he could directly over their bare stomachs, so they were sort of stitched together,' 13) – strike Nell as 'funny' and her listeners as evidence of Nell's eccentricity.

However, the narrative has an important correlative in the enacted play; the axe murder is carried out on Val, the adulteress, by her lover Frank, and her murder produces not just another good story but access to a new, if tenuous, representational space which alters our perspective on the play's 'world.' Frank places Val's 'dead' body in a wardrobe and then suddenly, unexpectedly, she walks back onstage from the other side and begins talking. On the night *Fen* opened in New York, her reappearance caused several spectators to scream – an understandable reaction. In an episodic but coherent text concerned with mimetic accuracy in diction, gestures, referents, what is the purpose of raising the dead?

The answer lies I think in the analogies Churchill has set up between cyclical economic exploitation, the erasure of female desire, and the regime of permissible visibility in theatrical representation. Unable to 'write' her body in the sense of figuring its desires, Val can only mark her chest with a pen indicating where her lover should stab her. However, Churchill rejects a romanticized closure which would require the body to represent itself as dead. She also rejects the foregrounding of theatrical illusionism, as in Worsely's shooting himself with a prop gun in *Owners*. Rather she *extends* the boundaries of what can be seen and said as representation. In an extraordinary feminist *gestus*, Churchill in effect moves the vanishing point. She decisively alters the logic of the illusion-apparatus in which women's desires cannot appear. The 'point' in infinity where parallel lines appear to converge, the vanishing point in perspectival space corresponds to the spectator's view; as the viewer's eye takes pleasure in a fictional space that *appears* to be perfectly ordered and measured, her 'I' is instantiated as a see-er/knower – a position that in psychoanalysis, as in Western philosophy, is gendered male. It is precisely this acceptance of an illusory order that keeps capitalism and patriarchy running smoothly. To tamper with this space – and with the fictional dramatic world in which the dead stay dead – is to insist on a different way of seeing, a different order.

Thus Val re-emerges not as a prophetic ghost or a misty mystified body but as a consciousness that instantiates a new theater space ('There's so much happening . . . ,' 23). In what I'll call her 'death-space' Val ventriloquizes the stories of other dead, but more importantly *by her bodily presence* she creates a space for her fellow laborers to explore and change their suffering. Val summons Becky by speaking her nightmare – another episode of the stepmother's sadistic abuse – and when both appear, Churchill comments on two modalities of representation.

> ANGELA   Becky, do you feel it? I don't, not yet. There's a pain somewhere.
> I can see so far and nothing's coming . . . . Let me burn you. I have to
> hurt you worse. I think I can feel something. It's my own pain. I must
> be *here* if it hurts.
> BECKY   You can't, I won't, I'm not playing. You're not *here*.
> *ANGELA goes*
>
> (24) (my italics)

Angela's 'here' is self-consciousness arrived at by inflicting pain while Becky's 'here,' in the heightened context of Val's death-space, refers both to the dream fiction which they are both enacting and to the theater whose illusionism has become an extended *gestus*, an explicit datum of the play's epistemology.

Angela banished, '*Nell crosses on stilts.*' A visual echo of the seventeenth-century fen dwellers who used stilts to cross the swampy earth. Nell converses with her own inveterate enemy:

> NELL   I was walking out on the fen. The sun spoke to me. It said, 'Turn
> back, turn back.' I said, 'I won't turn back for you or anyone.'
>
> (24)

The sun's earthly cycle figures a constant process of turning back, but human beings as historical agents can change their conditions. Equally hopeful is the final sequence that begins Val's announcement, 'My mother wanted to be a singer. That's why she'd never sing.' Suddenly *'May is there. She sings.'* (24). Characters appear like the return of the repressed, and in this liminal death-space a nightmare is redreamed, a life rerouted, an old woman's voice freed for expression. The death-space permits a representation of the unrepresentable, what Cixous has called the 'unheard songs' of the libidinal and revolutionary female body.[37] Yet in the affirmative power of these new expressions, there is no simple triumph, but rather a dialectical awareness of the conditions that prevent their singing. Nell's political self-consciousness has no projection outside this death-space. Walking on stilts she merely echoes the fen dwellers' historical defiance of – and failure to halt – exploitation that goes back to Charles II's scheme to drain the fens for grazing land. If the spectator loses track of spatial–temporal markers, *Fen* is not a dream play – no Strindbergian chrysanthemum blooms; in fact Frank sits gloomily throughout these summonings and denies any transcendence to his actions:

> FRANK   I've killed the only person I love.
> VAL   It's what I wanted.
> FRANK   You should have wanted something else.

$$(24)$$

The female bodies in Val's death-space reach across the play to a nameless female ghost in scene 9, a witness to 150 years of working women's suffering who appears to reproach the landowner Tewson. As with the appearances in the death-space, this ancient ghostly voice does not rupture representation, but marks a signifying space, the marginality of which bears witness to the ideology of permissible visibility – and audibility. The capitalist has always refused to see this woman, to hear this voice. In scene 16, the actors gather to sing in unison an excerpt from Rilke's *Duino Elegies*, which provides a gloss on the unarticulated despair of the fen-dwellers and on the logic of Val's death-space. Less Brechtian intervention than communal dirge, Rilke's elegy is another 'unheard song,' a portion of which I cite below:

> Who, if I cried would hear me among the angelic orders? And even if one of them suddenly pressed me against his heart, I should fade in the strength of his stronger existence . . . . And so I express myself, and swallow the call-note of depth-dark sobbing. Alas, who is there we can make use of?

$$(19)$$

If we judge this play for its ability to alienate and historicize the fen women's material and political pain, *Fen* is a provisional success, not because a redemptive socialism is asserted, but because the representation apparatus has been suggestively implicated as a tool of social oppression *and* as a means of resistance. The partial visibility of the death-space in which women's bodies are reinvested with stories, secrets, and mythic powers alludes to – and attempts to correct – the violent repression in the visible world (in and out of the theater) where their bodies and others like them are disciplined into silence.

A MOUTHFUL OF BIRDS

A Mouthful of Birds makes space for the body's 'unheard songs' in a register of pain and suffering that Foucault might see as the revolution of the docile and Cixous as a rupture of patriarchal constraints. Seven characters, identified specifically by social and professional roles (a Switchboard Operator, a Mother, an Acupuncturist, a Vicar, a Businessman, an Unemployed [man]) over thirty-two short scenes find themselves overtaken by passion, obsession, habit, such that law, sovereign reason, strict regulation of gender roles – all the ballasts of patriarchy – are dislodged in a violent release of psychic and sexual energy. The pre-text for *A Mouthful of Birds* is Euripides' *The Bacchae*, which Churchill and her collaborator David Lan allow to overtake their own text. Scenes marked 'Possession' intercalated with the monologues and enactments of violent behavior give all actors double identities drawn from the Euripides text. Structurally *The Bacchae* becomes a source of momentum and expectation; when Derek is possessed by Pentheus and puts on women's clothes; when the women gradually become possessed by the Bacchae, we know that the violent dismembering of Pentheus is inevitable. *The Bacchae* also supplies a reference point for a kind of historicizing of the psyche:

> We could have left the play as the seven stories without including anything from *The Bacchae* itself, but would have missed the presence of the horrific murder and possession, something not invented by us or by Euripides, so we kept it as something that bursts from the past into these people open to possession, first the voice of an unquiet spirit telling of a murder, finally the murder itself happening as the climax to all their stories.[38]

This violent 'burst from the past' suggests the libidinal and psychic turmoil within each docile social entity; more importantly Churchill inscribes this overtaking of the body through the nonrepresentational, nonlogocentric alterity of dance. Thus the common action of eating a piece of fruit produces a 'Fruit ballet' whose movements invoke what will become the ecstasy and horror of Pentheus: '*sensuous pleasures of eating and the terrors of being torn up.*'[39] At the end of Act II the actors, '*as their main character,*' dance their '*memories of moments of extreme happiness*'; this dance develops into '*a moment of severe physical pleasure*' (49). The transformation of 'characters' into 'dancers' suggests an attempt to intrude the orificial into the artificial, to overthrow the repressiveness of a representational system (the characters lose themselves in the dance). To what extent these dances 'read' to the audience is less important than the startling range of physical signification Churchill and Lan make visible. They also attempt what Freud (in *Civilization and Its Discontents*) calls the 'past of the mind.'[40] In the contemporary secretary lurks the memory of 'severe physical pleasure' which connects her to the killing ecstasies of Dionysian maenads. The final lines of the excerpt from Rilke's *Duino Elegies* seem to offer appropriate metaphors for how Churchill and Lan have imagined these turbulent bodies: 'Fling the emptiness out of your arms to broaden the spaces we breathe – maybe – the birds will feel the extended air in more fervent flight' (19).

But even the 'extended air' has a politics. No sooner imagined (or recovered) it will immediately reveal its own boundaries and rules. The beauty of this text's conception lies in the semiotic density of the 'characters.' They are inhabited as much by discourses of class politics and race as by gender. Thus we understand why the moment of possession and ecstasy for the businessman Paul, who traffics in pork in international markets, will be the discovery that the commodity he fetishizes has a history and temperament of its own: a beautiful shape 'cut in the air' (46). For the Trinidadian Marcia, possession means a fall from spiritual grace. A switchboard operator in a London office, she also operates a psychic switchboard as medium to her Trinidadian gods. But postcolonial Britain lames her powers: a spirit in the shape of a white upper-class woman appropriately named Sybil (for the Greek prophetess or sibyl), inhabits her, steals her West Indian accent and rejects her gods. Marcia's Baron Sunday has become barren and Marcia has 'lost myself. I don't know where' (36).

At different moments in scene 15, the androgynous Dionysos dances to nameless men and women: '*This dance is precisely the dance that the woman in the chair longs for. Watching it she dies of pleasure*' (37). Simultaneously, two prison guards use a ludicrously inadequate institutional discourse to try to account for a body that cannot be clearly gendered.

MALE PRISON OFFICER   It was him when we admitted her. I can guarantee that.
FEMALE PRISON OFFICER   Guarantee?

(37)

These moments preface the play's central agon, when the intrusion of the orificial into the artificial becomes a pointed gender critique. Derek's social identity is 'unemployed'; he rejects his father's own form of identification – 'He thought he wasn't a man without a job' (20, 51) – but Derek's scene of possession is an ambitious and self-reflexive comment on the processes of representation. Having revealed a susceptibility to possession by Pentheus, Derek is then possessed by the language and desires of a nineteenth-century hermaphrodite, Herculine/Abel Barbin. In other words, his double identity is doubled and strikingly divisive, for sexual confusion is precisely what Pentheus struggles to eradicate.[41] The orificial body, despite its gender discipline, retains the unconscious memory of and a yearning for the plenum of androgyny, what Lacan calls the 'real lack' that occurs at the moment of sexual differentiation in the womb, when 'the living being is subject to sex'[42] and separated from originary, primordial wholeness. The Herculine Barbin passage, spoken by a woman dressed as a man, records the physical and emotional agony of separation from the plenum of androgyny ('Sara's body, my girl's body, all lost, couldn't you have stayed?' 52) as well as the social torture it has brought her/him: 'Hermaphrodite, the doctors were fascinated how to define this body, does it fascinate you, it doesn't fascinate me, let it die' (51). We noted earlier that representation, in its function of bringing *back*, or compensating for the threat of disappearance, participates in a phallic economy. It is also a form of ideological control. Indeed Pentheus in the Euripides text reviles the Dionysian Bacchantes until the disguised god offers him the chance to be a voyeur, that is to tame and eviscerate the women's ecstatic rites by transforming them into a spectacle for his pleasure. With the Pentheus/Derek/Herculine/Abel Barbin layering comes the implication that Pentheus's attack on the Bacchae signifies the repression of a lost female nature that he himself parodies by putting on a dress. For Pentheus the girlish god and the sexual confusion he represents will produce civil anarchy but the contemporary play suggests that repression of ambivalence, self-division and difference is also violent, and tragic. Civilization, Freud notes, requires that

> there shall be a single kind of sexual life for everyone, disregards the dissimilarities, whether innate or acquired, in the sexual constitution of human beings; it cuts off a fair number of them from sexual enjoyment, and so becomes the source of serious injustice.[43]

Abel the cursed male who has lost his unsocializable, uncivilized 'girl's body' dies inhaling gas; Pentheus, whose name (we are twice told by Euripides) means 'grief', is torn to pieces.

The scene between Derek and Herculine/Abel extends the body's representational limits more definitively than ever before in the Churchill canon. The fragmented history of Herculine's hermaphroditism is delivered by an actress dressed as a man. Considering Churchill's interest in the effects of cross-dressing, the choice is predictable. What is new is that the male actor playing Derek, while he takes the objects that signify Herculine's life, does not make the image symmetrical – does not dress himself as a female. Yet he repeats her monologue verbatim and upon reaching the rhetorical question which closes the speech – 'Sara's body, my girl's body, all lost, couldn't you have stayed?' – the actress playing Herculine turns back and, standing behind him, kisses him on the neck. The image (reproduced as a photograph in the playtext) startlingly resembles a two-headed hermaphroditic body, an 'impossible object' like a Mobius strip, a Medusa's head, or an unheard song.[44]

In Part III of *A Mouthful of Birds*, the characters speak from the moment of post-possession and mark what Freud refers to as their 'expedient accommodation'[45] to the rigors of civilized representation. Lena the mother who has drowned her child struggles with her remembered pleasure in killing as well as giving birth. Paul, having lost his beloved pig, becomes a destitute alcoholic ('Days are quite long when you sit in the street but it's important not to do anything . . . . I stay ready,' 71). But Derek/Pentheus who has been torn apart celebrates here his surgical tearing, his transsexual body: 'My breasts aren't big but I like them. My waist isn't small but it makes me smile. My shoulders are

still strong . . . . My skin used to wrap me up, now it lets the world in . . . .
Every day I wake up, I'm comfortable' (71). This body ruins representation.
It undermines a patriarchy that disciplines the body into gender opposition; it
dismantles the phallomorphic economy that denies visibility to the female
(except as opposite or complement to the male). The hermaphroditic body is
excessive to itself – there is no 'self' but selves, the other in the one – orificial,
literally: 'My skin used to wrap me up, now it lets the world in.'

Derek's narcissism and his 'comfort' must be seen as part of a dialectic; he
does not have the last word. The character Doreen, a secretary, and also
Agave (the mother of Pentheus who in frenzy tears off his head), closes the
monologues and opens again the question of the untenable discipline, the ideological repression which is representation. We might look at a major trope
common to the texts in our discussion. 'Flying is woman's gesture,' Cixous
claims, pairing women with birds and robbers (*voler* in French means to fly and
to steal):

> [Women] fly the coop, take pleasure in jumbling the order of space, in dis-
> orienting it, in changing around the furniture, dislocating things and values,
> breaking them all up, emptying structures, and turning propriety upside
> down.[46]

The bird/robber trope is central to Euripides' description of the Bacchae:

> Then like birds, skimming the ground as they ran, they scoured the plain
> which stretches by the river Asopus and produces a rich harvest for Thebes;
> and like an enemy army they bore down on the villages of Hysiae and
> Erythrae . . . and ransacked them. They snatched children out of the houses;
> all the plunder they laid on their shoulders . . .[47]

Doreen has been violent; she has summoned powers to make objects fly
around the room (scene 23) but the flying/robbing have produced trauma and
further repression:

> I find no rest. My head is filled with horrible images. I can't say I actually
> see them, it's more that I feel them. It seems that my mouth is full of birds
> which I crunch between my teeth. Their feathers, their blood and broken
> bones are choking me. I carry on my work as a secretary.

(71)

The woman's bird-body, freed into murderous choreography, now stands in
repose and swallows itself, or tries to, in order to 'carry on.' When Doreen
finishes her speech, Dionysos dances again, libidinally, ferally, but she, docile,
productive, capitalized, does not. The cracks and fissures in the representational surface have been explored in *A Mouthful of Birds*, but the structure of
disciplinary control remains. Ecstatic, dying, dancing, screaming, possessed
bodies attempt to represent the release from representation, and in the futility
of that endeavor a feminist politics is made visible.

EPILOGUE: *MAD FOREST* AND *THE SKRIKER*

From gestic invisibility to gestic temporality

Churchill's recent plays, *Mad Forest* (1989) and *The Skriker* (1994) form a dip-tych of elements she has worked with since the beginning – historical mean-ing and theatrical magic – but now the gestic moment of insight gives way to the productive interconnections of Val's death-space: dramatic worlds have become worldly. *Mad Forest* self-reflexively 'represents' events in Romania before and after the overthrow of Nicolae Ceauşescu. Interweaving the lives of two fictional families (proletarian and middle-class) with 'eye-witness' accounts of what happened in December 1989 (based on interviews by English drama students with a variety of Romanian citizens), Churchill uses theatrical representation as a metaphor for how historical truth is produced. What the interviews reveal is that Romanian citizens themselves are agonizingly unable to put their revolution in perspective. Most watched 'it' on TV. So was it real or staged, 'a revolution or a putsch?'⁴⁸ Joining the human world are a talking dog, an archangel and a vampire – the play's real vanishing point. The vam-pire speaks terror's logic: 'You begin to want blood;' and its spatio-temporal con-fusion: 'you have to keep moving faster and faster' (91).

'Postmodernism,' Jameson notes, 'is what you have when . . . nature is gone for good.'⁴⁹ With *The Skriker*, Churchill's ecological millennial parable, blood-seeking fairies come screaming out of British folklore and up (through a trap-door) from the underworld, because they too need blood. When nature dies, the play tells us, we get the Skriker, 'ancient and damaged.'⁵⁰ In a sense *The Skriker* extends the possibilities of the death-space by letting Churchill bring back her own familiars: Lily, the pregnant innocent (*Owners*), Josie, the baby-killer (*Mouthful of Birds*), random encounters in the park (*Cloud Nine*). But now cross-dressing has become shapeshifting, and the device of overlapping lines metamorphoses into the Skriker's virtual doubletalk, a Joycean cacophony of associational and literary puns, rhymes, and mid-line logic switching:

Revengeance is gold mine, sweet. Fe fi fo fumbledown cottage pie curst my heart and hope to die. My mother she killed me and put me in pies for sale away and home and awayday. Peck out her eyes. I'll give you three wishy washy . . .

(5)

Mid-play the Skriker has to ask how the television works, but soon she/he/it is swimming in mediatized postmodern culture, using language that sounds appropriately in Jameson's terms 'skitzophrenic':

So the Skriker sought fame and fortune telling, celebrity knockout drops, TV stardomination, chat showdown and market farces, see if I carefree, and completely forgetmenot.

(36)

Back in her underworld the Skriker woos the mortal Josie with transnational glibness that never conceals Churchill's horror:

> Don't you want to feel global warm and happy every after? Warm the cackles of your heartless. Make you brave and rave.
>
> (30)

In *The Skriker* the tricks from *Traps* are back, now fully justified by fairy logic: toads come popping out of mouths, and giants, piglike men, and dismembered hags come and go in temporalities defying linear logic. Indeed it's the *temporal* distortion of the fairy world that interests Churchill:

> I got very taken with . . . fairy stories [in which] two different things happen with time when fairies take people off to the underworld. One is where you go off and you think you've spent years and years and it's actually the same second. And the other is . . . where you think . . . you've only been away a second and when you come home it's 100 years later and everyone is dead.[51]

Dead and dead again. When Lily, our representative human, goes off and returns, 'everybody . . . back on earth . . . was dead years and tears ago,'[52] and her future, in the shape of an '*Old Woman and a Deformed Girl*' (51), rages at her. But when the Old Woman (another Skriker?) offers Lily some food, 'Lily [again] bit off more than she could choose. And she was dustbin' (52). Images of maternity grow dark in *The Skriker*, as Churchill, like Walter Benjamin, historicizes nature and the natural. At the play's end, children are snatched from mothers not by fairies but by a dying nature: 'rockabye baby gone the treetop' (51).

But when did this 'happen'? If Romanians had their revolution, when was it? Amnesia is, Jameson argues, a postmodern condition. I think Churchill would agree. In these powerful plays, the representational frame has repositioned itself in other spaces so that temporality itself becomes a *gestus*, even as it slips past the vanishing point.

Part III

Toward a feminist postmodern

Introduction:
Mimesis in syncopated time

However unfeasible and inefficient it may sound, I see no way to avoid insisting there has to be a simultaneous other focus: not merely who am I but who is the other woman? How am I naming her? How does she name me? Is this part of the problematic I discuss?

Gayatri Spivak

As she describes it in her lecture, 'Plays,' Gertrude Stein was 'nervous' at the theater:

> The thing that is fundamental about plays is that the scene depicted on the stage is more often than not one might say it is almost always in syncopated time in relation to the emotion of anybody in the audience . . . [T]he thing seen and the thing felt . . . not going on at the same tempo is what makes the being at the theatre something that makes anybody nervous.[1]

No one could interpellate Gertrude Stein, hail her into identifications with characters through whose specular wholeness she could imagine completion. Still, syncopation made her nervous. Dramatic time conflicted with the temporality of her spectator's emotions. Her solution, in her 'landscape' plays, was to spatialize the temporal, to refuse the aggregation and accumulation by which the subject/spectator makes meanings. Syncopation, from the Greek *syncoptain*, means to strike, chop off; in musical terms it refers to the placing of an accent or accents on parts of a bar that are not usually accented. If a syncopated rhythm is continued for more than a bar it has the effect of a displaced meter superimposed on the basic meter. Jazz and blues are unimaginable without syncopation; for Stein conventional theater was intolerable because of it. The bracketed time of representation accented rhythms in disturbing syncopation to her own. Stein experienced (borrowing Gayatri Spivak's phrase above) a 'simultaneous other focus' that brought home, uncomfortably, the otherness of the stage object.

Stein wished to end or circumvent syncopation, but in considering the relation of feminism to postmodernism I am not eager to do so. In a sense, this book has thematized the syncopatedness of feminism and postmodernism from the outset. The decentering of the cogito, the deferral of the referent, the refusal of unitary or totalizing meaning, of disembodied universals, of the god's eye view, of textual authority – these commonly cited features of postmodernist cultural practice have been filtered through feminist questions about gender, history, patriarchy, and the theater apparatus in every discussion of this book. To discuss, for example, the 'new woman'/hysteric/criminal in *Alan's Wife* as one who not only fuels late Victorian patriarchal anxieties (she likes sex and kills her male child), but who takes center stage as an intentional actor even as she refuses positioning in perspectival space; who, most importantly, infects the 'objectivity' of the critic – all of this suggests a feminist critique with a post-modern bias.

These points raise other questions. However amusing it is to mock the dis-tressed Victorian reviewer of *Alan's Wife*, my activities in Chapter 1 differed from his only in degree not in kind; that is, my criticism was no less mimetic – in a classical sense. As I suggested in my opening remarks, mimesis is and always has been more than a morphological issue of likenesses between made objects and their real or natural counterparts. Mimesis is also epistemological, a way of knowing and therefore valuing. Any critical modeling posits the struc-ture of the Platonic 'self-same' – a universal knower and method for knowing that imposes rules of inclusion and exclusion by which a text, be it the text of a play or the text of someone's behavior, is judged. Mimetic criticism – in this classical sense – posits a relation of resemblance between object and model and, more insidiously, between subject and object, between I who write and the object I write on – which turns that object into a projection, the image into one of my imagoes. When I approach the plays and performances of Robins, Behn, or Churchill, Kennedy, Shaw, McCauley, and Margolin, am I not interpellating their texts with my models, making them ideologically com-fortable to deal with? But (*pace* Spivak) who are these other women/texts? How am I naming them?

The brilliance of Brecht's theater theory, and the importance, I hope, of gestic feminist criticism, is that syncopatedness, the visceral and cognitive sense of temporal otherness, becomes methodological, a praxis of seeing/knowing and performing/writing in which the object belongs not to me but to a historical force-field which is never fully knowable. In this sense Brecht begins to dislodge, to some extent, seeing from knowing. He urges us to lift the ide-ological veil to know the object but he doesn't believe it will sit still for scrutiny. In my reading the gestic body is inevitably 'located,' tangled in a dialectic of social–sexual–historical articulations and determinations; meaning-laden, part of the perspectival space, but also temporal and ephemeral.

Caryl Churchill's work belongs fully to the postmodern moment. Not only has she worked performance art into her *mises-en-scène*, she is almost unique in contemporary theater (excepting María Irene Fornes) in attempting to repre-sent multinational capitalism's effect on women. It is impossible to see her plays and not feel that irreversible changes in economic production have altered traditional social and symbolic structures. Hence her deliberate manipulation of the vanishing point in *Fen*, creating a productive 'death space,' which is echoed in the spatial overlays of *A Mouthful of Birds*. In these plays the dialectic of appearance/disappearance, the political question of permissible visibility in perspectival space, begins to make room for the temporal. In her recent plays, as I suggested in the Epilogue of the last chapter, she has grown interested in *temporal* cacophony or what I'm calling syncopated representations – mimesis in syncopated time. In which temporalities does revolution happen? At what point does nature die? Churchill's work tells us that feminist postmodernism is not merely 'pleasure in the play of surfaces; a rejection of history,'[2] but rather an intensification and critique of the theater of knowledge that we inherit from the Enlightenment. As the editors of *Chronotypes* describe the 'postmodern turn: our present does not leave modernity behind, but rather aggravates its difficulties, intensifies its concerns.'[3]

The work of Part III carries on this project, yet there is a distinction to be made between Part III and Part II. Churchill's work invites our 'naming'; she maintains enough of the apparatus of humanist representation to permit, however ephemerally, Brechtian distance on the object. Adrienne Kennedy's plays, with their multivocal and multiply identifying speakers, their disturbing indeed unrepresentable *mises-en-scène*, finally sever knowing from seeing. We cannot 'know' the Kennedy character apart from her identifications, nor can we travel through her psychic networks. Yet this doesn't, as Jameson thinks, cast us adrift without history. Rather her plays cause us to rethink historicization. To historicize in Kennedy is to uncover irreconcilable discontinuities in what Homi Bhabha calls the 'non-synchronous temporality of global and national cultures.'[4] In Chapter 6, performance art spaces become 'spaces of time,' sites of cultural memory reconceived, or as Benjamin says, 'redeemed' in the now-time of performance.[5] If my own critical writing remains mimetic, in the classical sense of interpreting objects according to my prior truths, the works of this section go far beyond me, suggesting a mimesis not of nomination but of relation, a relation whose politics emerge the more intensely in the frictions and dissonances of syncopated time.

5 Identification and mimesis
The theater of Adrienne Kennedy

[My Great-Aunt Ella] was a little touched in the head, Aunt Mary told me once. What's 'touched in the head?' I asked. 'Oh,' she said, 'she used to sit up in the trees and sing. You're the spitting image of her.' Why, I wondered, did I have to look like someone dead who was 'touched in the head'?

It is clear now that it was Jane Eyre (the child) I identified with, and the growing young woman's dilemmas of the Bette Davis character in *Now, Voyager*.

Adrienne Kennedy, *People Who Led to My Plays*

Identity. Identification. Sharing the Latin root, *idem*, for 'same,' few terms in contemporary theory are so mutually vexing. Consider the famous opening statement by the Combahee River Collective from 1974 – 'The most profound and politically most radical politics come directly out of our own identity' – a statement which confronts the decentered postmodern subject of the 1990s with the self-authorizing voice of liberation struggle. The statement's essentialism is explicit and unabashed: identity is proposed as a solid core of beliefs, images, discourses *out* of which a set of practices and coalitions emerge. 'Profound' (internal) ideas model or precede an (external) effective politics. Indeed all identity claims are propped on the hierarchical structure of classical mimesis: identity is imagined to be the truthful origin or model that grounds the subject, shapes the subject, and endows her with a continuous sense of self-sameness or being. In the case of the Combahee women, African American and lesbian, whose claims to selfhood have been and continue to be questioned in the dominant logic of race and gender, 'identity' becomes a believable and mobilizing fiction capable of binding each individual into a collective empowering 'our' which is felt to be unique, unified, and consistent.

Identification, on the other hand, is a passionate mimesis, a fantasy assimilation not locatable in time or responsive to political ethics. Identifications can only be 'recognized' and narrated from a temporal distance, as in Kennedy's mature autobiographical voice in the epigraph above: 'it's clear *now* that it was Jane Eyre (the child) I identified with' (my italics). Drawing another into oneself, projecting oneself onto another, identification *creates* sameness not with the self but another: you are (like) me, I am (like) you. Aggressivity, rivalry, and alienation are braided into identification. 'A little boy,' says Freud, wants to 'grow like his father, be like him, and take his place everywhere.'¹ Whereas identity operates through a logic of exclusion – my being or consciousness affirms its self-sameness by *not being* you – identification is trespass, denying the other's difference by assimilating her behavior, taking her place, killing her off. Art provides repeated access to such psychic thrills. As Hélène Cixous puts it:

> One never reads except by identification. But . . . [w]hen I say identification I do not say loss of self. I become. I inhabit. I enter. Inhabiting someone at that moment I can feel myself traversed by that person's initiatives and actions.²

There are disturbing consequences to such pleasures, as Cixous notes parenthetically: '(Actually, that [feeling of being traversed by the other] disturbed me. When I was younger I was afraid because I realized I was capable of mimicry) . . .' (148). To be the other *is* a loss of self, identification violates identity, even as, paradoxically, identifications produce the identity we come to recognize.

No contemporary US playwright has theatricalized the disturbances of identification with the acuity of Adrienne Kennedy. No one has underscored with her tenacity the imbrication of identity and identification. Early in his formulations, Freud linked identification with the mimicry of hysterics; later he came to understand the ego's identifications as those which form and transform the subject's identity. Freud theorized identification as a relation to an object outside the subject, but he could not, ultimately, elaborate that relation: identification in Freud (as in Lacan) imbricates the psyche and the social only in tenuous, albeit in provocative, ways. As Jacqueline Rose observes, the 'question of identity – how it is constituted and maintained – is the central issue through which psychoanalysis enters the political field.'³ Indeed to read Adrienne Kennedy with Lacan and Freud (or with her playful 'Dr. Freudenburger') is not to place her or her drama in an analysand position. On the contrary, it is to press psychoanalysis (as Frantz Fanon and Homi Bhabha have done) on political questions: what social and cultural meanings are produced in identification? What are their implications for race and gender? How does identification function in our understanding of historical experience?

It will be one of my arguments in this chapter that Adrienne Kennedy's postmodern plays (postmodern here meaning less a turn from, than an intensification of, modernity's questions) repudiate the charge of political vapidity and ahistoricism most often heard from critics on the left. Against realism's mimesis of depth and discovery, its symptomatically presented and cathartically revealed secrets, against modernism's self-reflexive fragmentations, postmodern artifacts exhibit, in Fredric Jameson's well-circulated words, only depthlessness, pastiche, a spatialized 'cultural logic' in which the artist can no longer 'gaze on some putative real world . . . a past history which was once itself a present . . . [but instead gives us] ideas and stereotypes' about the past – a 'pop history.'⁴ But what is a pop history? As Fanon notes, stereotypes circulating in the cultural marketplace generate pop histories that operate with the force of historical tradition. From the 'thousand details, anecdotes, stories' a racial history is written, or more specifically, a 'historico-racial schema,' that produces not just subjects but morphologies, 'physiological' selves.⁵ Adrienne Kennedy's texts, with their troubled physiologies, their mass culture and racial identifications, limn a 'pop history' that is also a psychic history. Her intro-verted *mises-en-scène* never lose the social referent but rather transfigure it relentlessly; 'ideas and stereotypes' are not parts of a dialectic to be rationally overcome but are determinants as material (and illusory) as ideology, class, or the economic base. Kennedy's major texts of the 1960s–1990s produce an impossible identity – a hybridity – whose social and historical identifications resonate with what Paul Gilroy has called a 'black Atlantic' project. In his cri-tique of the 'fatal junction of nationality and culture,' Gilroy analyzes the expe-rience of (following Du Bois) double consciousness or ambivalence, 'the con-stitutive force . . . [of] black experience in the modern world.'⁶ Citing few women's texts, *The Black Atlantic* suggests paradigms that Kennedy's work use-fully elaborates – and anticipates – both in its tense relation to black nation-alist discourses of the 1960s and in its postmodern querying of how, in what discursive and imaginary sites, the historical is experienced. In effect Kennedy channels the flow of commoditized images and styles associated with post-modernity into an exploration of what she and Gilroy consider to be moder-nity's historical brutalities – as he puts it: the 'encounters between Europeans and those they conquered, slaughtered, and enslaved [. . . as well as . . .] sci-entific racism (one of modernity's more durable intellectual products)' (44).

If registering 'historical brutality' involves the problematics of identification, and I think it does, Kennedy's plays ask troubling questions of Brechtian theory. Through his three decades of theorizing, Brecht placed identification (which he also called empathy, with all its feminine implications) at the nega-tive center of his argument. Identification in the theater must be deflected because it violates the necessary distance between spectator and image – a dis-tance that permits a spectator to historicize, that is, to see the other *as* other, and thus situate the play's characters and events in a usefully comparative way to the spectator's own history. Brecht's addendum to his 'Short Organum' is justifiably famous:

> When our theaters perform plays of other periods they like to annihilate distance, fill in the gap, gloss over differences. But what comes then of our delight in comparisons, in distance, in dissimilarity – which at the same time is a delight in what is close and proper to ourselves?⁷

Brecht was scornful about identity, which merely reinforced the myth of a unitary bourgeois ego, but he was happy to shore up the *fiction* of a coherent identity as a prelude to political agency. He encouraged his spectators to be 'historians' by freeing them from the thralldom of identification, keeping them from feeling 'the same as . . . .' With the *Verfremdungseffekt*, Brecht's technique for defamiliarizing any construction that has come to seem natural, he rein-forced the spectator's difference from the actor, the actor's difference from the character. Only when identification reinforced the alienation-effect did he approve of it:

> The performer's . . . act of self-alienation stop[s] the spectator from losing himself [*sic*] in the character. Yet the spectator's empathy is not entirely rejected. The audience identifies itself with the actor *as being an observer*, and accordingly develops his [self-conscious] attitude of observing or looking on.[8]

As noted in Chapter 2, historicization means that the spectator, too, is historicized, in motion and at risk. In Stephen Heath's words, the Brechtian spectator finds 'his own position [to be] critical, contradictory . . . he is *pulled out of his fixity*' (my italics).[9]

While Kennedy's work bears no resemblance to Brecht's practice or commitments, her plays, I will argue, are no less promising as invitations to political self-consciousness. Her ability to weave identification into historical temporality, to imbricate the psychic and the social, suggests that identification is not only a private psychic act: rather identifications have histories and thus permit access to subjective, cultural, and political meanings. Brechtian historicization invites spectators to see through ideological mystification to the 'truth' of historical contradiction, but identification forces us to acknowledge mimetic desire (to be the other) into the margins of our perception. If historicization posits a subject who delights in making comparisons, identification posits an unconscious wish to transgress the boundaries of social and sexual identity. In the following section, I want very much to keep identification in the proximity of historicization, to argue that processes of identification do not preclude a relation to history, but in fact permit greater access to subjective, cultural, finally political meanings – to precisely those processes and effects that are, as Brecht would say, 'close and proper to ourselves.' In other words, Kennedy offers us a vital revision of Brechtian historicization: the historicizing power of identification.[10]

FIXITY AND TRANSFORMATION: FREUD AND OTHERS

Let me trace a brief trajectory through some psychoanalytic texts relevant to identification in Kennedy's oeuvre.

Hélène Cixous's identificatory performance of entering, becoming, and inhabiting, only to suffer from her own ability to mimic, recalls Freud's early writings on identification in *The Interpretation of Dreams* (1900):

> Identification is a highly important factor in the mechanism of hysterical symptoms. It enables patients to express in their symptoms not only their own experiences but those of a large number of other people. It enables them, as it were, to suffer on behalf of a whole crowd of people and to act all the parts in a play singlehanded.[11]

The tendency to 'play all the parts' produces an obvious threat to identity. The subject's pleasurable assimilation/usurpation of the other, a tendency found not only in hysterical fantasies, but in daydreams and literary fictions, creates in Borch-Jacobsen's words, an 'indistinction of the "I" and the "s/he"'. Thus 'the subject in all sorts of identificatory roles and figures is a fundamentally *improbable* subject.'[12]

In 'On Narcissism' (1914), as Freud tries to account for the move from self-love ('ego-libido') to love of others ('object-libido'), identification exhibits both modalities. In primary narcissism the infantile ego, which 'from the start' lacks 'unity' (14:77), exists only in a mimetic dyad, indistinct from its mother. Secondary narcissism assumes an ego that is modified or 'disturbed' by 'the admonitions of others' and by its own 'awakening critical judgments.' Pleasure, Freud frequently reminds us, is never given up. In an effort to recoup the dyadic perfection of infancy, the subject identifies with an external ideal. 'What [the subject] projects before him as his ideal is the substitute for the lost narcissism of his childhood, in which he was his own ideal' (14:94).

Lacan makes that external ideal the infant's own mirror image and fixes the ego permanently in a narcissistic and alienated relation to it. A 6–18-month-old infant, barely able to sit or stand without tipping, a *'corps morcelé'* (a body in bits and pieces), glimpses itself (or a caretaker) in a mirror as a unified body-image and promptly identifies itself with, or rather misrecognizes itself as, that seductively coherent image.[13] While Freud touches on the power of images in various texts, Lacan's imaginary order gives prominence to specularity. For Lacan no ego pre-exists the specular relation: 'I' is irreducibly an I-image, or I-Other; the 'subject's relation to his own body will always be in terms of an imago.'[14] Thus the mirror stage is a source of both jubilation and alienation since the 'salutary' *imago* represents an ideal of unity not now, but in the always deferred future: the ego 'will only rejoin . . . the subject asymptotically'; 'I' will never be one, will never resolve a fundamental 'discordance with [my] own reality.'[15] Identification with the imago – with the Other – situates the subject in a condition of self-alienation, even before s/he enters language (before her 'social determination'). Frantz Fanon has no trouble recontextualizing Lacan's mirror stage. In *Black Skin, White Masks*, he equates the Other with the system of colonial supremacy. Gazing into the cultural mirror the black subject identifies with/introjects the 'frightened, trembling Negro, abased before the white overlord' (61) – a fixation that alienates, ultimately annihilates the black subject and makes of his body *a corps morcelé*.[16] (More on Fanon in a moment.)

For Borch-Jacobsen, the narcissistic relation is always a mimetic relation, a relation of resemblance in which the 'otherness of the other *as such* is not respected'; in which the recognition 'that I resemble the other [is] tantamount to admitting the inadmissible: that I am not myself and that my proper being is over there. in that double who enrages me.'[17] Freud's 'Mourning and Melancholia' (1917) binds the torment of object loss to the self-torment implicit in narcissism: the loss of a loved one (particularly when love has been ambivalent) provokes 'an identification with the abandoned object,' the effect being that 'the shadow of the object [falls] upon the ego' (14:249). Now – and this is the cruelty of melancholia – 'hate comes into operation, abusing [the ego], debasing it, making it suffer and deriving satisfaction from its suffering' (14: 251).

We learn more about this critical introjected other in 'Group Psychology and the Analysis of the Ego' (1921), the text in which identification is established as part of the affective history of every subject: 'Identification is known . . . as the earliest expression of an emotional tie with another person' (18:105). Freud will soon reiterate that identification is ambivalent, a source of rivalry and aggression, but at this point he distinguishes identification from desire and stresses the mimetic process by which identification substitutes for a lost object – as when, having lost a kitten, a child declares that she has become the kitten and crawls about on all fours. Further, the ego, having introduced the lost object, is transformed by it: the ego has 'enriched' itself by imitating the properties of the object. Enrichment, however, is achieved at a price, for the transformed part of the ego divides off from the rest, and the remainder, enraged at the transformation, is designated as the ego ideal, that which observes, corrects, censors.

This agon between the transformed ego and the ego ideal/censor reaches a peak in 'The Ego and the Id' (1923), which remaps the topography of the psyche: libido is stored in the id, ego ideal becomes the superego, while the ego 'represents what may be called reason and common sense' (19:25). As in 'Mourning and Melancholia,' Freud considers the process whereby the lost object is 'set up' inside the ego, but in this text setting up goes beyond the special condition of melancholia to become constitutive of psychic development.

> It may be that identification is the sole condition under which the id can give up its objects. At any rate, the process, especially in the early phases of development is a very frequent one, and it makes it possible to suppose that the character of the ego is a precipitate of abandoned object cathexes and that it contains the history of those object choices.
>
> (19:29)

The ego is not just a mimetic construct or 'character' but a precipitate of abandoned objects that have been introjected and assimilated. Freud's statement opens the door, as I suggested at the outset, to understanding identification as both a social and a psychical relation. Certainly Brecht's claim that identification precludes the historicizing effort of the spectator has to be reexamined. In Freud's account, it would seem that subjects are constituted by the (psychical) history of the cathected (social) objects that have transformed them. The humanist notion of identity as a stable model that the self enacts over time, that is unique, unified, and consistent, is belied by the occluded (never remembered) historicity of identificatory relations. The subject's identity is no more, or less, than the accumulated history of her identifications. Indeed 'identity' is the illusorily stable representation of that turbulent history and no less powerful (in fact far more powerful) for being imaginary.

Of course identifications are never random, any more than they are fully achieved.[18] Yet parental ego ideals never fully disappear. Now the historical,

cultural, even biological determinism of the superego – along with its patriarchal bias – emerges clearly: 'the superego reflects the "phylogenetic acquisi-
tion" of each individual' (19:36); 'as a substitute for a longing for the father,
it contains the germ from which all religions have evolved' (19:37). 'As a child
grows up, the role of the father is carried on by teachers and others in authority' (18:37). Finally, 'by giving permanent expression to the influence of the
parents it perpetuates the existence of the factors to which it owes its origins'
(18:34). Driven by the superego, we repeat and therefore validate those cultural proscriptions that derive from our earliest identifications.[19]

If I have seemed to collapse the psychic and the social, unconscious processes of identification with a subject's contingent empirical history, the Freudian
superego suggests the possibility of such connections. As Teresa Brennan notes,
'identifications of the ego-ideal drag the subject into diverse social currents'; in
fact 'a contemporary social identification of the [mature subject's] ego-ideal
with another could offset the more traditional superego.'[20] Hence the possibility of 'multiple identifications' bearing the traces of both 'predictable' psychic
patterns *and* 'flexible' social relations (11). However, lest this sound too salutary, we need to recall that identification in Freud is a sedimented concept;
the primordial (devouring, introjecting) narcissism of identification co-exists
with an 'emotional tie,' which co-exists with the regulatory grid of oedipal
relations. Annihilation of the other abuts self-annihilation, and aggressivity is
a permanent condition of being the other. Identifications produce and simultaneously destabilize identity: as Plato feared, in assimilating the other, the
subject doubles (and annihilates) herself.

Adrienne Kennedy's texts provide access to identifications that are decid-
edly double, even multiple, wherein traces of hysterical mimicry (of playing all
the parts), of narcissistic rage, ambivalence, and rivalry, of the punishing constraints of parental ego-ideals are all in evidence. She has described her work
as 'autobiographical,' her work processes as 'unconscious,' driven by dreams
and images: 'I see my writing as a growth of images.'[21] Like the writings of the
Martiniquan psychiatrist Frantz Fanon, the identificatory performances of
Kennedy's personae bring to view psyches brutalized by racism. Like Fanon
she characterizes racist culture as a 'zone of nonbeing'; and her fictional selves
as 'object[s] in the midst of other objects, sealed into objecthood.'[22] Unlike
Fanon, however, Kennedy lives fully in the visual field, particularly the photograph and the cinematic image. She is 'enriched,' profoundly, by cultural
objects – these are the psychic *and* historical stuff of her existence.

What of the relation of mimesis to identification? In Borch-Jacobsen's
deconstructive logic the terms are inseparable, the first fulfilling the second.
The identificatory wish springs to life in the theater of fantasy 'where I am the
other . . . *before seeing him.*'[23] That is, mimesis, 'the coalescence of self and other'
(42) is prior to 'the order of the specular, the visible, the theoretical-theatrical
. . . it is not mimesis as mimesis has been understood since Plato and Aristotle'
(39). Precisely. Classical mimesis cannot divorce itself from complicity with
truth telling – underneath the mask is (perhaps) a true identity, one which

depends on a logic of visual differentiation from the identities it is not. The truth-seeing Enlightenment subject whom Borch-Jacobsen is deconstructing instantiates selfhood, reason, and the continuity of identity through acts of self-mirroring and self-reflection that, of necessity, suppress prespecular identifications. It is classical mimesis within psychoanalysis that gives us, as Irigaray puts it, 'mimesis imposed'[24] – the imposition of the 'one of form' (phallomorphic modeling) and of the oedipus, in which identifications are deemed correct or abnormal. Fanon expands 'mimesis imposed' to 'cultural imposition' (193) whereby racist societies stratify their citizens according to a model of a bioethnic superiority, a model which is nothing more than mimetic fantasy, a set of 'prejudices, myths, collective attitudes' (188) that make humanness an attribute only of whites. Mimesis (as we saw with Plato) cooperates in the making of an autonomous subject, a racially pure 'I' whose truth separates it from the contaminants of the other. But (as we also saw with Plato) mimesis unmakes what it upholds.

Identification is itself double. On the one hand, identification doubles the ego at its origins – in Lacan's influential formulation, 'I' is fixed as an other; on the other hand, identification produces ego-ideals that change and transform the 'I.' The bicameral nature of identification, fixity and transformation, goes to the heart of features we associate with modernity. To be fixed is to be transfixed by the truths of the past, by the political arrangements – the hegemonies – of old aristocratic elites; by social-religious models (the chain of being; providential design) that deny individuality. Modernity means the new – a new concept of subjectivity (produced by the cogito, not God), an ardent belief in scientific method, a belief in progress and democracy, and, thus, an implicit mandate for social struggle. To transform is, in the Hegelian sense, to be part of the great historical unfolding of human reason.[25] But from the 'black Atlantic' perspective, fixity versus transformation is only one part of the Enlightenment story. Rationality has a twin, scientific racism, which, in Gilroy's words, amounts to no less than 'the repudiation of the ideology of progress by the racially subordinated who have lubricated its wheels with their unfree labor.'[26] One race is fixed, the other transforms. 'What I am asserting,' writes Fanon, 'is that the European has a fixed concept of the Negro . . . . I move slowly in the world, I am fixed . . .' (116).

In Lacanian psychoanalysis the break from imaginary fixations, the domain of identification, is achieved only by accession to the symbolic (language) which gets us out of the imaginary theater where I am another, am doubled and annihilated, and where I annihilate the other. But no subject ever forecloses the imaginary; the 'bodily ego' formed in the mirror stage continues to shape the relations of inside/outside. Identification with the ideal imago, Boothby writes, 'installs at the most fundamental level of psychic life a profound libidinal equivalence of ego, others and objects in the world – an equivalence that remains inchoatively present in all subsequent experience.'[27] *All subsequent experience.* The fixity of the mirror stage is marked in Lacan's metaphor of the imago as (erect) 'statue' which makes the ego, in Borch-Jacobsen's words, similarly 'immobile, frozen, "statuefied."[28] It is this immobility at the core of 'all subsequent experience,' all future object relations, that Teresa Brennan and Mikkel Borch-Jacobsen attempt, in different ways, to *qualify*.

Against the regressive specular fixity of identification in Lacan, Brennan poses the possibility of 'thinking past fixed ideas' – even as 'the ego needs its fix' (its imaginary coherence: its identity). As a feminist and psychoanalyst, Brennan wants to tease out a more flexible reading of the superego:

> a contemporary social identification of the ego-ideal with another could offset the more traditional superego; which might explain how it was ever possible to think outside patriarchy . . . . We can postulate that an ego-ideal identification with feminism, in the form of a person, a people, or a body of writing, suspends the ego-ideal's existing prohibitions, that it *permits* different thinking.[29]

Which is not to say that identification itself is transformative. Regressive, narcissistic, identification continually rejects the differentiations on which rational thought is based. Still, Brennan argues, 'multiple identifications' may produce, at a *later* point, a point of recollection and revaluation, a way of 'coming to terms with *images one receives from others*,' a way of moving past our fixities, including our imaginary, illusory sense of coherence (11, 13). 'The fact is,' writes Brennan, 'we move. But how?' (14).

Is it too glib to say: at the theater? And yet theater is the site of appearances taken as truth. The visual logic that governs the theater is a logic that theater can expose. For producers of a discourse on the 'black aesthetic' in the 1960s and 1970s, smashing representational 'fixity' for a 'modal' fluidity was designed precisely to alter spectatorial passivity. Aware of this discourse but independent of it, Kennedy situates her theater in a 'growth of images.' She brings forth not a new truth, nor even, in a Brechtian sense, a foregrounding of the ideological ('funnyhouse') mirrors into which we fixedly gaze. When Kennedy writes out the 'images fiercely pounding in my head,'[30] she interpellates her spectator not as see-er/knower but as a witness to imagoes that generate the racialized subjects she places on stage. Her characters belie the representation apparatus whose function is to deliver up a unitary ego, a self. Pardoxically, the Kennedy spectator is one who cannot know what she sees.

In this sense her plays carry forward an implication that Borch-Jacobsen has teased out in contrasting the specularity of Lacanian identification with Freud's 'affective identification.' In the former, we recall that the imago not only fixes the ego, (it) makes of every object 'a decoy, a trap in which the ego pursues its own image.'[31] Borch-Jacobsen concedes that Freud also talks of identification as an image taken as a model, but emphasizes Freud's other formulation: '[I]dentification is the earliest and original form of emotional tie [with an object]' (18:107). As an emotional tie, identification is not initially specular, nor a fixation, but rather of a 'corporeal-affective mimesis.' This produces, in turn, not the 'statue man' of the mirror phase, but an 'ecstasy of alienation: I *am* the other . . . .'[32] Such a mimesis is untheorizable. unseeable.

unrepresentable. The mirror stage is an objectification, a theatricalization of that earliest affective mimesis, not the other way around. The Freudian subject, for Borch-Jacobsen, is a mime, effectively an other in the unviewable scene of the unconscious. And

> who says that the stakes for the actor are knowledge, self-knowledge via (the gaze of) the other that freezes him into a statue, an idol? Isn't his joy (or his anguish) above all to *play* his role, to move *inside* the pathetic scene that he incarnates. And why, after all, should true life always be elsewhere, in front of me, in that double who augurs my death? . . . 'Only later' will I run up against that hard, frozen 'object' that I am and am not, that I am not all the while I am ravished in it. So yes, I will be able to meet myself, run into myself in mirrors, struggle with my doubles, love myself in them while hating myself, project myself into them while losing myself.
>
> But then I will no longer be what 'I am,' in the invisible and untheorizable affect of my identification.
>
> (70, 71)

Kennedy, I am arguing, makes visible (theater from) that invisible mimesis and in that making brings forth intimations not of self-same truths but of affective ties, the historical emotional ties that fix and transform her. Identifications may never 'take place,' but they have material effects – in the imaginary coherences that smooth over the racism of everyday modes of thought, and in the 'abraded' bodies we choose not to see.

READING ADRIENNE KENNEDY'S THEATER – I

> The dilemma of the 'negro' artist is that he makes assumptions based on the wrong models. He makes assumptions based on white models. These assumptions are not only wrong, they are even antithetical to his existence. The black artist must construct models which correspond to his own reality. The models must be non-white.
>
> James T. Stewart, *Black Fire*

> I write poetry filling white page after white page with imitations of Edith Sitwell . . . . Queen Victoria is my idol.
>
> Adrienne Kennedy, *Funnyhouse of a Negro*

> The ideology of blackness [and nationalist ideology] sprang out of . . . a reaction to a racist language and imagery that had made blackness a thing of evil.
>
> Larry Neal

> Black man, black man, I never should have let a black man put his hands on me. The wild black beast raped me and now my skull is shining.
>
> Adrienne Kennedy, *Funnyhouse of a Negro*

Most black writing of the last few years . . . has been aimed at the destruction of the double-consciousness. It has aimed at consolidating the African-American personality.

Larry Neal

'She who is Clara Passmore who is the Virgin Mary who is the Bastard who is the Owl'

Adrienne Kennedy, *The Owl Answers*

In the 1960s, in the crucible of black nationalist self-fashioning, a year before Willie Ricks and Stokely Carmichael yelled 'black power' to marchers in Mississippi and gave a label to a complex revolutionary struggle, Adrienne Kennedy's *Funnyhouse of a Negro* (1964) and *The Owl Answers* (1965) addressed audiences with black subjectivities for whom double consciousness was a kind of infinite metaphor; whose mimetic doubling not only foreclosed the possibility of a unified self, but, in 'an extasy of alienation,' so embraced the depradations of assimilation and colonialism as to make the perspective of black revolutionary critique seem impossible. 'The Revolutionary Theatre must EXPOSE,' wrote Amiri Baraka in his groundbreaking manifesto of 1964,[33] but Kennedy's *Funnyhouse*, which opened the same season as Baraka's world-famous *Dutchman* (and won the same award – an Obie), exposed hairless skulls, bloody faces, flying birds, nightmarish sound and light, in short a concatenation of jarring images and rhythms, a discourse that mingled private fantasy and colonial history in an ever-unraveling tale of family miscegenation. In her identifications and obsessions Kennedy seemed hellbent on *de*consolidating the African American personality.

This is undoubtedly why Larry Neal, in a celebratory genealogy of the Black Arts movement, 'Into Nationalism, Out of Parochialism,' leaves Kennedy out of consideration although *Funnyhouse of a Negro*, even more than Baraka's *Dutchman*, 'break[s] with the social realism which dominated the forties and fifties.'[34] But as many critics have noted, not only was Kennedy producing incorrect images of black identity, as a woman writer she like many women artists and activists was disadvantaged by what bell hooks calls the 'narrow nationalism [of the 1960s and 1970s] with its concomitant support of patriarchy and male domination.'[35] In a politicized atmosphere dramatists suffer special scrutiny, not only because an activist theater is always struggling to find and consolidate its audience, but because image production and consumption in a white supremacist culture are precisely what a black insurgency movement was determined to contest and influence. As Lance Ermatinger wrote in 1969, both black and white audiences reacted with 'confused anger'; white liberals were given none of the usual clichés, and black militants heard no 'sizzling slogans.'[36]

African American feminists, in solidarity with the liberatory aims of those vital years, have also carefully critiqued the sexism of the black arts/nationalist movements. As Barbara Christian puts it, 'when the ideologues of the 1960s said *black*, they meant *black male.*'[37] What I want to suggest in the comparatively thin political climate of the 1990s, but without apology, is that Kennedy's is a theater not of identity but of identification, and as such it interrogates the fixities of racism precisely by avoiding positivities of form or ideation. In this Kennedy resembles Fanon who, in Homi Bhabha's suggestive words

> is the purveyor of the transgressive and transitional truth; [she] may yearn for a complete transformation of society, but speaks most effectively from *uncertain interstices* of historical change; from the area of *ambivalence* between race and sexuality . . . from deep within the struggle of psychic representation and social reality.[38]

In the uncertain interstices from which Kennedy's images grow, we glimpse a fractured representation of what Althusser calls 'ideological state apparatuses'[39] – family, church, school, nation – that interpellate individuals as correct social subjects. With Harold Cruse, an early nationalist who considered African American existence to be a condition of colonial dependence, Kennedy finds the obscene abuses of Jim Crow to be 'a built-in component of the American social structure.'[40] In the oedipal family configuration (Kennedy: 'I am always writing about my family'[41]) allusions to a guilty secret are always refractions of racial-historical crimes. In this theater of identification, not only is Her Majesty the Ego dethroned, but also the 'bodily ego' is phantasmatically reimagined in the form of rats, owls, dogs, white birds, dwarfs, and Nazis. Her first five plays, *Funnyhouse of a Negro*, *The Owl Answers*, *A Rat's Mass* (1966), *A Beast's Story* (1969), *A Lesson in Dead Language* (1970) are Kennedy's Bataillan zoo stories. Like Bataille's serious revelry with animalism, Kennedy explores a definitive detour from Enlightenment myths of progress, particularly the rationalism of Darwinian evolution. Kennedy's Negroes are doubled, split by the Other, but that is only the beginning of the nightmare.

FUNNYHOUSE OF A NEGRO, THE OWL ANSWERS

The Negro is not. Any more than the white man.
                                       Frantz Fanon, *Black Skin, White Masks*

SARAH   I want not to be.
                                       Funnyhouse of a Negro

Before the 'Scene' there is the guilty 'Beginning.'

> *Before the closed Curtain A WOMAN dressed in a white nightgown walks across the Stage carrying before her a bald head. She moves as one in a trance and is mumbling something inaudible to herself. Her hair is wild, straight and black and falls to her waist . . . . Before she has barely vanished the CURTAIN opens. It is a white satin . . . of a cheap material and a ghastly white . . . [like] the interior of a cheap casket, parts of it are frayed [as though] gnawed by rats.*[42]

Here is trauma imagined as grand guignol (how else?): a mumbling mad-woman, mother of Sarah's personal prehistory, whose light skin speaks the 'racial-corporeal' schema of centuries of colonial 'encounters' with African peoples. Out of this beginning, 'Negro-Sarah' is not, that is, not an 'I' but always an I-as-other. We recall that in the annihilating frame of (narcissistic) identification, every object or other is a 'a decoy, a trap in which the ego pur-sues its own image' – an image that never satisfies but rather alienates, since it demonstrates me that 'I' will never be whole, will never resolve a funda-mental 'discordance with [my] own reality.'[43] Sarah's imagoes, her internalized images, leave the mirror and join her on stage; discordance and alienation become *mise-en-scène*. As Kennedy designates a 'Negro-Sarah' so her imagoes are cultural–familial: two royal women of imperialist regimes, the Duchess of Hapsburg and Queen Victoria; two male martyrs, the Congolese liberator Patrice Lumumba and a hunchbacked Jesus – each her image, that is, bear-ing some version of her own 'head of frizzy hair, unmistakably Negro kinky hair' that is now, in imitation of her mother, falling out. Singly or in chorus the 'selves' recite a story/her story of rape and miscegenation. Introjected models they punish and betray her even as they speak her history. And like one of Freud's hysterics Sarah plays all the parts – or they play her – amid ebony masks, chandeliers, bald heads that drop from above, bagsful of human hair, and a huge bust of Queen Victoria, a figure of '*astonishing repulsive white-ness*' (22).

In Sarah's first monologue comes the ambivalence and rage of identifica-tion with a powerful Other:

> Victoria always wants me to tell her of whiteness. She wants me to tell her of a royal world where everything and everyone is white and there are no unfortunate black ones. For as we of royal blood know, black is evil and has been from the beginning. Even before my mother's hair started to fall out. Before she was raped by a wild black beast. Black was evil:
>
> (22)

Here are what Etienne Balibar calls the 'affective stereotypes'[44] that produce Fanon's 'massive psychoexistential complex' (12) – the 'negro enslaved by his inferiority, the white man by his superiority,' (60) both needing the other to affirm their truth. But Fanon quickly denies the Hegelian symmetry of his for-mulation as barely containing the repression that upholds it:

> For not only must the black man be black; he must be black in relation to the white man. Some critics will remind us that this proposition has a con-verse. I say this is false. The black man has no ontological resistance in the eyes of the white man.
>
> (110)[45]

Fanon's masculinist preoccupations are distracting, but in Sarah's encounter with herself-as-Victoria, in whose name much of the African world was colo-nized, he is constantly suggestive. On 'the day' when '[my] corporeal schema crumbled [and] I took myself far off from my own presence . . . what else could it be for me but an amputation, an excision, a hemorrhage that spattered my whole body with black blood?' (112). Sarah enters the performance space with '*a hangman's rope around her neck and red blood on the part that would be her face*' (4) and like Fanon's colonized persona she has no ontological resistance against the Victorian imaginary or against the post-Enlightenment race theory that flourished throughout the Victorian period. Not only has she internalized the fetishization of skin hue as visible evidence of racial hierarchies, she sees her own 'yellow skin' (6) as, to use Etienne Balibar's phrase, 'bodily stigmata':[46] '[My] father is the darkest of us all, my mother was the fairest, I am in between' (17). And in between, she is 'not,' as Fanon puts it: 'an object in the midst of other objects . . . abraded into nonbeing' (109).

The light-skinned mother-selves pull her toward European imperialists but from her religious father, who never appears, Sarah has internalized the impossible contradictions in black consciousness from the time of her parents' generation to her own. This is the question of whether redemption of the race will come from Christian teaching or from pan-African political struggle (when Kennedy was writing this play, the conflict was embodied in the complicated estrangement of black nationalist militancy from non-violent civil rights practice). Sarah's masculine selves are mimetic doubles of her father – his missionary zeal (the deformed Jesus) and his identification with pan-African liberation (Lumumba) – and these identifications are rivalrous to the point of murder. Jesus/Sarah: 'I am going to Africa and kill this black man named Patrice Lumumba. Why? Because all my life I believed my Holy Father to be God, but now I know that my father is a black man' (19). This father, this guilty failed Jesus-like 'nigger of torment' (21) is the imago that most torments Negro-Sarah. Having hanged himself in one story fragment when he learned Lumumba was murdered, the black father 'keeps returning . . . . Yet he is dead, but dead he comes knocking at my door' (21).

And like the return of the repressed, this line keeps returning, ruining, as does all constant repetition, the discourse of individual identity, the fantasy of linear progress.[47] Like Fanon's colonized Negro, Kennedy's split Sarah has no ontological resistance; she is 'overdetermined from without'[48] – not only mimicking her mother's trauma and her father's suicide but also playing in a family romance that points allegorically to the struggle of new African states against colonialism. Repeated references to straight hair (her mother's), kinky hair (her own) and hair falling out (all her selves) are Fanonian 'racial-epidermal' symptoms of sexual torment and of a diasporic condition that embraces both the old biologistic models of racial hierarchy and the continuing sense of cultural difference. Speaking as Lumumba, Sarah needs her white friends 'as an embankment to keep me from reflecting too much upon the fact that I am Patrice Lumumba who haunted my mother's conception. They are necessary for me to maintain recognition against myself' (13).

This line can be read doubly, and a certain reading of Kennedy depends on the difference. Recognition 'against myself' might suggest an authentic blackness, a true identity, that internalized racism and the company of whites conjoin in repressing – a reading based in modernity's self-doubting (hence self-affirming) cogito. But the line might also be read as 'recognition against myself-as-*other*,' as in-identification with cultural models, some dangerously repressive, which divide me and send me on an asymptotic trajectory of (futile) self-recovery – a postmodern ecstasy of alienation. Only the black–white 'embankment,' the culture of racism, maintains the comforting facticity of identity. That is, the Other-imago of white supremacy fixes black and white each in a 'neurotic orientation'[49] precisely by occluding the comfortlessness but potential transformability of social existence with others. Patricia Williams notes: 'I think that the hard work of a nonracist sensibility is the boundary crossing, from safe circle into wilderness . . . .'[50] The dead mimeticism of racism, the prophylactic habits of othering what isn't me, repress a transgressive transformative mimeticism, which might be, *pace* Brennan's formulations, how we 'move' out of fixities.

Interrogating the dialectic of movement and fixity *The Owl Answers* joins *Funnyhouse of a Negro* (1965) to produce Kennedy's revision of the Middle Passage, a fantasy journey by a Georgia black woman 'back' to England, even as she is/becomes/has always been a West African owl. Kennedy's autobiography provides a context.

> The owls in the trees outside the Achimota Guest House [in Accra] were close and at night, because we slept underneath gigantic mosquito nets, I felt enclosed in their sound. In the mornings I would try to find the owls in the trees but could never see them. Yet at night in the shuttered room . . . they sounded as if they were in the very center of the room . . . . In a few months I would create a character who would turn into an owl.[51]

The Owl Answers is also an homage to Kennedy's childhood bestiary of 'zombies, mummies, the Cat woman, vampires . . . and Lon Chaney, the Wolf Man [whose metamorphoses] held a power over me.'[52] Performed first in a double bill, *Cities in Bezique*, along with *The Beast Story* (an intrafamily dirge of rape and murder in which characters were to be covered with fur), *The Owl Answers* has characters 'change slowly back and forth into and out of themselves,'[53] a *mise-en-scène* less of narcissistic projection than of multiple identification. With her composite protagonist, 'She who is Clara Passmore who is the Virgin Mary who is the Bastard who is the Owl,' Kennedy dramatizes both an illusory ego *and* its cultural and historical specificity – her protagonist's particular set of abandoned objects. Clara, the bastard daughter of a poor black mother and the 'Richest White Man in Town,' is adopted by the Reverend Passmore but though she bears her mother's color she idolizes her father's culture, the 'England . . . of dear Chaucer, Dickens and dearest Shakespeare' (31), whose works she reads as a child in the Passmore library, and later disseminates as a 'plain, pallid' (26) schoolteacher in Savannah. The great white fathers of literary history merge with those of Christian myth, as God's white dove (associated with Reverend Passmore's preaching) replaces the black ravens in

Funnyhouse's jungle. With her mother labeled a 'whore,' Clara, a 'pass more,' identifies with the Virgin Mary. But on a fantasized visit to England the white fathers refuse her access to St. Paul's and lock her in the Tower of London: having colonized her desire, they deny her white ancestry. Rejected by her father, but unable to repress or bury him, She who is Clara is imprisoned in her history – the tower – which, in the play's nightmare logic, is simultaneously a screeching New York subway car. Here the 'real' She, guilty and enraged, picks up a Negro man, introduces herself as Mary, addresses him as God and tries to stab him.

Despite her temporal and spatial drift, Clara like Sarah is overdetermined from without and in *The Owl Answers* these determinations are violently oedipal. The parental imago as seductive Other is not the lightskinned mother but the 'Goddam Father who is the Richest White Man in the Town who is the Dead White Father who is Reverend Passmore,' a 'figure' whose political–religious proscriptions produce the gender positioning of the dutiful daughter and the concomitant destruction of her sexual agency. Hence the hysterical dropping and gathering of papers and the quasi-religious roleplaying in her interlude with the Negro man (the only character not multiply represented – an essentialism the play will not explore). In both *Funnyhouse of a Negro* and *The Owl Answers* Kennedy's daughter figures are traversed and displaced by the very identifications that constitute their subjectivity. But the latter play racializes and distorts heterosexual desire, thereby foregrounding the daughter's ambivalent relation to femininity and the maternal body. In *People Who Led to My Plays* (1987), the writer credits her mother's anecdotes and dreams with supplying the voice of her characters (33), yet her mother's body is a seductive but impossible source of identification:

> My mother looked to me to be a combination of Lena Horne and Ingrid Bergman. I thought she was the prettiest person I'd ever seen. But I couldn't look forward to growing up and looking like her . . . everyone said we looked nothing alike . . . . My face as an adult will always seem to be lacking because it is not my mother's face.
>
> (50–51)

In *Funnyhouse* and *The Owl Answers* Sarah and Clara (whose names are explained in *People*, p. 35) take on the look and the lack of their mothers. Sarah's selves lose their kinky hair in skewed mimesis of her mother's loss of 'her straight black hair' (15). But more importantly, the 'mass' of black hair on the pillow that travels from hand to hand is what Julia Kristeva calls the 'abject,' that which is 'rejected from [the body] but from which one does not part, [. . . which . . .] beckons to us and ends up engulfing us [. . . disturbing . . .] identity, system, order.'[54] In the subject's formation, abjection signifies the inability to separate from the mother's body. In Kennedy's texts, abjection is enacted in both corporeal identification and psychic torture. Sister Rat's 'rat's belly' from an incestuous conception is the abject synecdoche for the maternal body (*A Rat's Mass*), so too are the menstrual bloodstains on the pupils' white dresses (*Lesson in Dead Language*), marking their guilty 'conspiracy' as females. In *The Owl Answers*, the Black Bastard's Mother appears with 'owl feathers about her' (37), and in the play's closing moments Clara 'suddenly looks like an owl' (45). While the white bird laughs, Clara speaks: 'Ow . . . oow' (45). As in Fanon, Kennedy's symptomatic bodies 'speak' of cultural as well as psychic oppression, but if he modifies the ego's 'corporeal schema' to include the 'historico-racial schema,'[55] she modifies his schema to include gender – to insist that a black woman's subjectivity – her most intimate identifications – is forged, inevitably, in the funnyhouse of white patriarchy. bell hooks notes that Kennedy's image of femininity 'subverts traditional paradigms,'[56] including the mythoi of familial memory. The black bastard cannot be an ancestor or have one, hence the text confuses 'ancestor' with 'descendent.' 'Owl in the fig tree, owl under the house, owl in outhouse . . . . Why be confused?' asks the Black Bastard's Mother, 'The Owl was your beginning, Mary' (35).

It would be as mistaken to reduce the 'extasy of alienation' of these plays to sentimental suffering as it would be to trust to interpretations that tame their affective violations. Put another way, the political – the historico-racial-gendered – schema in these plays becomes clear only if we respond to the identificatory rage of the protagonists and their alienating and annihilating imagoes. Only then do we understand that the mimesis of bestiality on Kennedy's stage constitutes the inhuman *mise-en-scène* of racism. As Bataille's pineal eye at the top of the skull 'opens itself and blinds itself . . . to the incandescent sun,'[57] so Kennedy's Sarah and Clara and the others are destroyed by, but also *explore*, indeed, embrace, their '*sense of exploding imprisonment*' (35).

Wanting only to write about her family, Kennedy tried and failed to write realism. In the 1950s, self-apprenticed to powerful modernists, she found liberation in Tennessee Williams's expressionistic use of music and color and in Garcia Lorca's violent families and spare symbolism. She was enabled by and contributed to the post-Artaudian context of New York experimental theater, the transformation and psychophysical techniques that disengaged actors, directors, and writers from conventional representation. But what released her to write *Funnyhouse of a Negro* and the plays that followed was a trip to West Africa, 1960–61. From this we can trace a move from modernism to a black Atlantic sensibility:

> A few years before, Picasso's work had inspired me to exaggerate the physical appearances of my characters, but not until I bought a great African mask from a vendor on the streets of Accra, of a woman with a bird flying through her forehead, did I totally break from realistic-looking characters. I would soon create a character with a shattered, bludgeoned head. *And that was his fixed surreal appearance.*[58]

(my italics)

This fixed image/imago of Sarah/Lumumba/father is certainly surrealist, and like most self-conscious surrealist work, aligned with psychoanalysis's privileging of dreamwork as an authentic mode of expression. But Kennedy was simultaneously claimed by Paul Carter Harrison, one of the formulators of the black aesthetic who anthologized a Kennedy play (*The Owl Answers*) and considered her, along with Baraka, Aimé Césaire, and others, to be smashing representational 'fixity' through a 'modal' fluidity, 'potent enough to excavate the surface of reality . . . heightening the apperception of black reality.'[59]

Yet Kennedy is hardly celebrating a pan-African aesthetic any more than she can be strictly annexed to the modernism that exoticized and abstracted the African mask. In *Funnyhouse* the mask is a murder instrument. Kennedy's work, to use Paul Gilroy's phrase, is 'unashamedly hybrid,' deliberately 'confound[ing] any simplistic understanding of the relationship between racial identity and racial non-identity.'[60] We cannot, in other words, see her contributing to what Kimberly Benston has called the 'vast genealogical poem that attempts to restore continuity to the ruptures or discontinuities imposed by the history of black presence in America.'[61] Or rather to read Kennedy this way is to place emphasis on a fragmented but incipiently whole identity and ignore the duplicitous pleasures and rages of identification. Negro-Sarah's 'psychoexistential' torment is indeed modernist; her signature line, 'I want not to be' instantiates the cogito/subject ('*I* want' – subject of desire) even in the act of self-cancellation. But the texts (and this is their postmodern feature) complicate the turbulent egoic struggles of the modernist subject, precisely by magnifying them, extending their referential range. As one of the protagonist's imagoes, the bludgeoned face in *Funnyhouse* is simultaneously private and cultural, emotional and political.

Ironically it is in these dangerous relations, these overlappings of private and cultural objects, that a route to recognition and political self-reflection might be traced. Sarah and Clara's horrifying slide into nonidentity foregrounds precisely what identity tends to conceal: the allurement and violation of identificatory relations. Because the spectator's identificatory desires are not fixed on a heroic ego, because the Kennedy 'character' is always an effect of, a precipate of, contradictory racial and cultural identifications, the dramatist signals the possibility of a critical discourse on reception of which even Brecht might approve: a rethinking of identification for political ends. Teresa Brennan reminds us that 'points of identification'[62] can become points of recognition. In Kennedy's *mise-en-scène* which immerses spectators in subway screeches, rat gnawings, batting wings, funnyhouse guffaws, a '*RED SUN, FLYING THINGS,*' and burning beds, it's possible that points of identification are the *only* form of recognition; not a means of being lulled to passivity, but a means of exploring the affective assault, the bestializing effects of racism.

Consider, for example, *Funnyhouse of a Negro*, a play whose dominant trope is the mirror. Amidst Sarah's mimetic doubles, her 'selves,' there are two white characters, one a landlady with the resonant name of Mrs. Conrad, and the other Raymond, the Jewish boyfriend, also designated 'Funnyhouse Man.' Dressed in Hamletic black this funnyman, not Sarah, is the artist, a trafficker in mimetic arts. The walls of his room, behind the blinds, are all mirrors that reflect and split Sarah into distorted fragments while he, like God the Father, remains coherent and consistent. Sarah and her selves lose their hair but Raymond questions, admonishes, judges, and, at the end, '*observing*' the hanged woman, puts closure to her torment, giving, at least in its position in the play, the final version of her story: 'Her father never hung himself in a Harlem hotel when Patrice Lumumba was murdered. I know the man' (23).

Do I know Raymond? In a play about *his* funnyhouse, *he* might be the one losing his hair. But in a text that investigates the multiple identities of a young black woman, he becomes a discomfiting object. If the vestiges of my psychic history propel me toward Sarah's perverse family romance, her fascination with a mother's raving, such identifications have to circulate through Raymond as well. Because Raymond, Sarah tells her audience, is 'very interested in Negroes' (6). I can historicize Raymond, situate him in the context of Jewish liberalism of the 1950s and 1960s which enlisted early in civil rights struggles; I can recall that among New York beat poets, musicians, and artists, racial/cultural lines, especially between blacks and Jews, were complexly intertwined. I can, in Brecht's words, take delight in (recognize, learn from) such comparisons. But historicizing Raymond presses a nerve. It invites me to recognize what I can't remember – early powerful identifications with 'being a Jew' – and to inhabit, across gender, his space. Do I find myself implicated in the funnyhouse images by which African American women are discordantly constructed (and do I know what those images have done to me?)? Do I find myself any less implicated in the disastrous fundamentalism that currently dominates the notion of 'being' a Jew?

In *The Owl Answers* another trajectory of identification might be explored, one that extends beyond Clara's tortured self-transformations to the university community that has kept Kennedy's texts alive on syllabi if not in theaters. With the schoolteacher Clara's references to her 'blood father,' the 'Richest White Man in Town,' commingled with the noble white fathers of Western literature ('dear Chaucer, Dickens, and dearest Shakespeare,' 31), Kennedy's readers/spectators are challenged to identify themselves, however ironically, as professors in a university system dominated by post-Enlightenment models of disciplinary specialization, most notably the English department, devoted in name if not in current practices to perpetuating traditions still being felt in the postcolonial world. If, through private symbols, Clara manages to displace the greatest white Father ('I call God and the Owl answers,' 43), she is also in the Shylockian position of loving dominant culture when it doesn't love her. Entering the network of Clara's identifications brings us into disturbing proximity with her white fathers, her ego-ideals of the canons that we teach. In other words, this text asks its teachers to historicize the canon from the vulnerable position of our identifications with it. Teaching *The Owl Answers*, then, becomes performative, a way of producing and querying the very questions it raises.

Such ideas and interrogations are in the nature of a Brechtian auto-critique, but they become accessible only by transgressing Brecht's injunction to rise above, or to suppress, spectatorial identifications. Given Kennedy's theater of identification, given her experimental daring, her narcissistic freefall, we might also rethink Brecht's *Verfremdungseffekt*. Perhaps this amount of perceptual alienation from a naturalized given, this moment of re-cognition, is propped on an earlier, more inchoate moment of mimeticism, an assimilative encounter between psychic trauma and politico-cultural formation that is restaged in the private/public space of performance reception. If such moments are retrieved and historicized in retrospect – when Adrienne Kennedy recollects her identificatory desire to be Bette Davis (see below), as opposed to when, in fantasy, she *was* Bette Davis – no matter. The process of becoming aware of and politicizing one's identifications, like the process of identification itself, is potentially transformative.

A MOVIE STAR HAS TO STAR IN BLACK AND WHITE

> I cannot go to a film without seeing myself. I wait for me. In the interval, just before the film starts, I wait for me. The people in the theater are watching me, examining me, waiting for me. A Negro groom is going to appear. My heart makes my head swim.
>
> Frantz Fanon, *Black Skin, White Masks*

> As long as I can remember I've wanted to be Bette Davis. [Pause] I still want to be Bette Davis.
>
> Adrienne Kennedy

The second epigraph is a quotation from Adrienne Kennedy, at least I think it is. On the printed page in epigraph position, these words have perhaps an unwarranted certainty. For in her public interview at my university in 1989 – an oddly voyeuristic format that Kennedy prefers over speech-making – I had not thought to bring a tape recorder, the machine that would play back to me, in a space far from the seductions of presence, Kennedy's true utterance. Then, too, the epigraph makes univocal what were in fact multiple (and perhaps divergent) utterances. At a conference several months after the interview, I appropriated Kennedy's pronominal before an audience of feminists and theater scholars. Hence two performances of a line about Bette Davis, one authorized by a celebrated black dramatist, the other impersonated by a white critic, both recollected for a chapter that attempts to rethink the issues of identification and mimesis.

If her precise words during the interview elude me, I remember that the university audience laughed awkwardly at the comparison she playfully invited. Attired in a dark suit and white frilly blouse, she called to our collective mind the star image of Bette Davis and in that moment foregrounded the racism inscribed in classical mimesis. For the subject of the enunciation not only did not resemble her model, it was unacceptable, in the cultural discourses through which we think, speak, and most of all see, that she could represent her. In her impromptu performance Kennedy laid bare as well the problematics of identity. Insofar as identity implies a stable and continuous model – call it blackness, whiteness, womanness – that the subject imitates or enacts over time, identity limits the workings of fantasy, of transformation.

Yet another inference might be drawn from Kennedy's statement: the radical power of identification to override the constraints of identity. Dropping the comparative 'like' of Freud's exemplary little boy, who wants to be 'like his father and take his place everywhere,' bypassing the model-copy relation that can be observed and evaluated, Kennedy speaks introjection, projection, incorporation – 'I want to *be* Bette Davis' (and take her place everywhere?). A film theorist might argue that Kennedy presents an obvious case of cinematic colonization. The camera of Hollywood narrative film, typically overvaluing the female star, enthralled and captured Kennedy in its dreamy image. Undoubtedly this is true. And yet the fact that she specifies that particular lure – offers as public narrative what she unconsciously performed in a movie theater as identificatory wish – reveals to us, and to Kennedy, the history of her object-choices and her emotional ties. The passivity and masochism of the female viewing position is persuasively discussed by film scholars.[63] What Kennedy contributes is the pleasurable possibility of (to paraphrase Cixous) becoming, inhabiting, entering, as well as the particular historicity of that process. Kennedy's identifications *are* her history, the 'character of [her] ego is [not only] a precipitate of her abandoned object-cathexes' but '*the history of those object choices*' (my italics).[64] Introjecting Bette Davis as a new ego ideal, sneaking her in past the censorious superego that enforces cultural (racial) proscriptions, *situates* Kennedy in a place and time – in Saturday afternoon movie theaters in the 1940s in the Cleveland of her youth, or later in the 1950s at the Thalia in New York. For a young girl growing up in the Midwest, for a struggling writer raising a child in New York while her husband was busy in graduate school, harried by racism as well as an intimidating cultural marketplace, there is no delight in attributing referential power to whiteness or for that matter to blackness.

'I have always wanted to be Bette Davis' is perhaps different from 'I want not to be' only in tone. Each is an evasion of ontology. But the former self-consciously promotes the other scene of being, a scene of identification, of fantasy reinscription which is theatricalized differently from the invaded rooms of *Funnyhouse of a Negro* and *The Owl Answers*. In *A Movie Star Has to Star in Black and White* (1976), Kennedy produces hybridity. The reflexive decentering of suffering 'protagonists' is replaced by reflexive spatialization, a *mise-en-scène* of writing with and against the conservative mythoi of mass culture. Indeed Kennedy's movie star fandom seems to inoculate her against Fanon's Sartrean nausée and masculine vanity as he anxiously anticipates his *inevitable* and humiliating identification with the Negro actor playing a groom. At such moments Fanon writes out of a kind of heroic existentialism, representing political oppression as the extirpation of an essential self. Unlike the black nationalists who were her contemporaries, who used precisely this Fanon for nation-building, Kennedy follows that 'other' Fanon who locates political demand in desire, who describes human agency, in Bhabha's words, through image and fantasy – 'those orders that figure transgressively on the borders of history and the unconscious . . . .'[65]

Indeed the political import of Kennedy's text is understandable only through its play of image and identification. *A Movie Star Has to Star in Black and White* refers both to the technology of film-making in the great period of Hollywood narrative cinema and to the racial semiotics Kennedy constructs for the play's spectators/readers. While the text demonstrates the way mass culture narratives shape our lives ('*[Clara's] movie stars speak for her*'[66]), Kennedy co-opts the cinematic image. Her white movie stars, retaining the appearance, rhythms, and gestures of their roles in three classic Hollywood films (*Now Voyager* 1942, *Viva Zapata!* 1952, *A Place in the Sun* 1951), utter lines not from their movie scripts but from black Clara's life. Moreover, as the movie stars recount and enact events from the summer of 1955 (when Clara and her husband Eddie moved to New York) and summer 1963 (when she and her divorced parents reunite at the hospital beside of her comatose brother Wally), Clara, a more explicit Kennedy surrogate, wanders among them writing in her notebook. '*Totally preoccupied*,' she occasionally reads out lines from *The Owl Answers*, refers to *A Lesson in Dead Language*, and comments on her anxieties with theater producers and directors. Repetition, Kennedy's signature device, shapes the interconnections between movie stars (playing 'leading roles') and family members (playing 'supporting roles'). Thus the parents' estrangement and the child's inability to redeem them overlap with Clara's alienation from Eddie; similarly, Wally's near-fatal accident parallels Clara's horror about her pregnancies:

> When I have the baby I wonder will I turn into a river of blood and die? My mother almost died when I was born. I've always felt sad that I couldn't have been an angel of mercy to my father and mother and saved them from their torment.
>
> (83)

That these lines are spoken by 'Bette Davis' to 'Paul Henreid' in a simulation of the shipboard scene from *Now Voyager* reveals the textual and performative blurring of memory, history, fantasy, and mass culture iconography. The stage of *A Movie Star* resembles the 'displaced stage . . . [Freud's] *andere Schauplatz*' of identificatory fantasy where, as Borch-Jacobsen puts it, '"I" is always another' and 'resembling is equivalent to being and affinity is instantly transformed into identity.'[67] Indeed Kennedy makes the issue of iconicity, visual resemblance to a model, a theatrical joke. The actor's performative 'being' on stage is entirely subsumed by manufactured images: Kennedy's 'movie stars' are actors 'who look exactly like' Bette Davis, Paul Henreid, Jean Peters, Marlon Brando, Shelley Winters, and Montgomery Clift; family members 'look like photographs Clara keeps of them' (80). And neither group has ontological presence beyond the text of 'Clara's thought.' They interact momentarily then 'fade' to the strains of 'movie music' (82).

Which does not mean that Clara's choice of identificatory objects isn't thematically suggestive. As I have read Freudian theory, her identifications necessarily arise from previous identifications, parental ones particularly but not exclusively, which are imbricated in her history, which become part of the process of historicization. Hence within seconds of the romantic yearning invoked by Davis–Henreid (shipboard scene), Peters–Brando (wedding night/'teach-me-to-read' scene), and even Winters–Clift (rowboat scene) – comes Mother's recollection of the racist demographics of southern life in the 1920s, a speech that both describes and indicts the racial semiotics of the play's *mise-en-scène*:

> MOTHER   (*Sitting down in a deck chair, takes a cigarette out of a beaded purse and smokes nervously. She speaks bitterly in a voice with a strong Georgia accent.*) In our Georgia town the white people lived on one side. It had pavement on the streets and sidewalks and mail was delivered. The Negroes lived on the other side and the roads were dirt and had no sidewalk and you had to go to the post office to pick up your mail . . . . When a Negro bought something in a store he couldn't try it on. A Negro couldn't sit down at the soda fountain in the drug store but had to take his drink out. In the movies at Montefore you had to go in the side and up the stairs and sit in the last four rows . . .
> (*She is facing Paul Henreid and Bette Davis.*)

(84)

'Facing' these movie stars in their delicious black and white celluloid simulations is, for the spectator of Kennedy's *Movie Star*, to face as a *Verfremdungseffekt* the black woman's exclusion.

In effect, Kennedy reworks the mimetic operation of identification to historicize and politicize her *mise-en-scène*. 'The *lexis* of fantasy is *mimesis* [in the Platonic sense of impersonation]'[68] – an identification grounded in resemblance. On Kennedy's stage the question of resemblance registers the historical struggle that film images and the industry that disseminates them elide. The white spectator might expect the iconic disjunction between movie image and theatrical performance but the whiteness of the performers enters into consciousness when, and only when, they speak the life of the *visible* black woman. Colonized by these glamorous images, Clara/Kennedy in turn remakes and re-presents them in a context that bears the materiality of her consciousness (her language), if not her color – which is precisely the point. To identify with 'whiteness' or 'blackness' is to identify with an image; to see whiteness as an image, and not an origin, is vital alienation effect. In this text, the political is marked in spectatorial consciousness when identification-as-*racial* resemblance breaks down. Clara's movie stars are proximate and continuous with her psychic life but their mimetic relation creates, rather than mystifies, cultural, social, and racial difference. In *Movie Star*, more than any other Kennedy text, the imbrication of identification and identity becomes full-scale collision.

Consequently, the spectator's pleasures are mediated by her cognition of, for example, the racist history of a powerful culture industry that traditionally excludes or stereotypes black performers (why Kennedy's 'movie star *has to* star in *black* [as well as] white').[69] More subtly, Kennedy retrieves a spectatorial position that early feminist film theory had nearly abandoned. Two of the female roles, Bette Davis as Charlotte Vale (*Now Voyager*) and Jean Peters as Josepha Espejo (*Viva Zapata!*) are classical invitations to masculine visual plea- sure and fetishization. After treatment by her male psychiatrist, Bette Davis leans over the ship railing with Jerry (Henreid), the signs of her sexual repres- sion – dowdy dress, thick eyebrows, overweight body, glasses – transformed into the glamorous face and wardrobe of Hollywood perfection. Peters's Josepha, sexually glamorized on her wedding night, teaches a suddenly vul- nerable Zapata/Brando to read. Lifted from their contexts, speaking the life of an ordinary woman, these 'characters' are returned to me as social not cinematic constructs, as culturally hybrid not transcendently coherent.

Moreover, building on such hybrid images, I 'see' that Clara projects her ambivalence about pregnancy by identifying with movie roles in which female sexuality is marred by repression (Bette Davis); or displaced onto reading (Jean Peters/Josepha); or repellently represented (the whining pregnant Shelly Winters). Mother, we recall, addresses the opaque screen image with her Jim Crow Georgia story – the usually occluded apparatus, the time and place of production and reception, is laid bare. But Clara historicizes through *identifi- cation*: the time of her pregnancy (and her fears about bleeding), as it conflicts with her desire to become a writer, is registered and recognized by her 'being' Jean Peters, who in turn not only speaks Clara's life but bleeds for Clara into black sheets which she and Brando 'continually . . . change' (92). Needless to say Elia Kazan never directed this scene in *Viva Zapata!*

[The unconscious] represents nothing, but it produces.
Gilles Deleuze and Félix Guattari, *The Anti-Oedipus*

Identification doesn't 'take place.' As Borch-Jacobsen insists, '[t]here is . . . a cleavage between the stage where one is playing – the "other stage" [*andere Schauplatz*] . . . and the stage one sees, about which one speaks.'[70] The first, the unconscious 'scene' of mimesis where I-am-another is nonreflexive, non- specular, in effect blind; the second, where one sees oneself, represents oneself to consciousness, is already a scene of interpretation, of theater. Kennedy's writing works in the interstices of this neat cleavage – or rather, her work must, like any representation, be situated in the latter scene, while her specif- ic representations, unrooted, cross-hatched by repetition and unnamed desires, constantly invoke the former, the unseeable 'other scene' in which the subject- in-identification, as an other, as an imago, never sees herself. Identificatory fantasy is not a proscenium stage with the subject on stage *and* in the audi- ence. Rather '[identification] is (en)acted by the "subject" who executes its sce- nario *blindly* – at the risk of bumping into all those "others" that he is playing on the other stage.'[71] What better suggestion of the *mise-en-scène* of *A Movie Star Has to Star in Black and White*? Writing in her notebook Clara walks blindly among her imagoes, the celluloid and photographic images of her movie stars and parents: '*She pays attention to no one* . . .' (87) at the risk of bumping into all those others who are playing her. To make her 'other stage' our stage is, in Brecht's sense, to alienate both, to demonstrate their mutual exclusivity and their profound imbrication, each/both racialized, gendered, dangerous in their projective violence. Each is carefully choreographed *as a conjuncture* of the familial and the political, the personal and the historical.

Perhaps this suggests a reduced quotient of identificatory pleasure for the spectator. But the brilliance of this text lies in its marking both the transformative possibilities of identification *and the inaccessibility of such identifications except as cognitive restagings*. Here Brecht's theater of alienation intersects with Kennedy's theater of identification. Both challenge the 'present tense' of bourgeois production, both insist that repetition and reproduction can be palpable, disturbing: *the* data of spectatorial reception. Watching Clara's Bette Davis on Kennedy's stage I am prompted not to identify but to *remember* identifying with Bette Davis – who was, of course, not Bette Davis, but sensuous cinematic images, manipulated by a specific technology, of a female performer of that name.

MIMETIC NETWORKS: FROM FREUD TO FREUDENBERGER TO FANON IN *THE ALEXANDER PLAYS*

> . . . resembling is equivalent to being and affinity is instantly transformed into identity.
>
> Mikkel Borch-Jacobsen

> I'd often stare at the statue of Beethoven I kept on the left-hand side of my desk. I felt it contained a 'secret.' I'd do the same with the photograph of Queen Hatshepsut that was on the wall. I did *not* understand that I felt torn between these forces of my ancestry . . . European and African . . . a fact that would one day explode in my work.
>
> Adrienne Kennedy, *People Who Led to My Plays*

> Despite the enchantment there was a subplot in England that I couldn't perceive.
>
> Adrienne Kennedy, *A Theater Journal*

In *The Alexander Plays* (1992), the appropriative violence of identification has softened, yet the identificatory moves are so familiar that we are not surprised when the writer-protagonist Suzanne Alexander frames bitter memories of racist dormitory life at Ohio State (*Ohio State Murders*) through evocations of literature and film – Thomas Hardy's *Tess of the D'Urbervilles*, Sergei Eisenstein's *Potemkin* – and that these texts in turn shape the young writer's consciousness. Nor is it surprising that an obsession with Beethoven's musical career becomes identified with the writer's own career (*She Talks to Beethoven*), or that she writes her sadness over her missing husband into the plot of a Bette

Davis movie (*The Film Club*) or speaks to her absent husband through Napoleon's love letters to Josephine (*The Dramatic Circle*). Except for *She Talks to Beethoven*, *The Alexander Plays* have characters who are also narrators, so that the space of action is temporally doubled, the theatrical 'present' sucked into a historical 'past.' Unlike the earlier plays, in which subway cars *were* bedrooms, the narrative framing of distinct times and places becomes the datum of perception. Moreover, in these new plays, scenes of identificatory transformation are explained rather than enacted. The retrospective tone of Kennedy's autobiography (second epigraph above) anticipates the odd insularity of *The Alexander Plays*. In *The Dramatic Circle*, Alice Alexander, speaking of events in 1961, discusses Suzanne's identificatory symptoms with a narrator's authority:

> In the past my brother had written me when he had been traveling with Frantz Fanon, the famous psychiatrist and revolutionary from Martinique. He'd written about the psychiatric cases they had encountered in Algeria. I realized now [the now of 1961] some of the symptoms of Fanon's patients were like Suzanne's symptoms. She had always missed David when he traveled to do research.[72]

But in these writerly plays the identity of authority is also impugned, or rather hidden, secreted, woven into discourses that deny theater's truth–illusion nexus and draw us toward the unknown, the unknowable – the un-dead. Sarah (*Funnyhouse of a Negro*) could identify the steady knocking in the candlelit chamber of her Duchess of Hapsburg. In the more banal rooms of the Alexander texts signs and symbols proliferate, disappear, transmogrify, reappear with the cadence of certain dread, growing paranoia. Instead of the exuberant surrealism of a father's head smashed by an African mask, Kennedy offers us a mystery melodrama of vanished loved ones, strange messages, odd reprieves, anxiety, and illness. 'Despite the enchantment, there was a subplot in England that I couldn't perceive,' Kennedy writes in her *Theatre Journal*.[73] She echoes the young Suzanne Alexander's encounter with her dormmates' impenetrable racism, which Suzanne experiences as 'danger' (*Ohio State Murders*, 59).

In *The Alexander Plays*, the unbearable fact of multiple identification transforms into the ironic facticity of multiple inscription. Fragments of diaries, histories, monologues, radio programming, storytelling become spatio-temporal points of a mimetic network connecting cities (Accra, Columbus, OH, London, Washington) to battlefields, hospitals, and to dark campus walkways. Family members are 'like' political figures, teachers, writers, and fictional characters in prose and film. Rather than draw the spectator's eye to an abjected body part like the traveling mass of hair, the signifier announces its own spectacular trajectory from Hardy to Fanon to Bram Stroker to Leopold Senghor to Kennedy to unnamed 'actual sources.' Kennedy's mimetic network is a relay of resemblances, in which 'affinity is instantly transformed into identity' and 'character' dissolves and reforms as an other (scene), condensing textual spaces, geographical places, and diverse temporalities. Within these shifting scenes of inscription the writer, or rather the figure of the writer, achieves a pressing corporeality. Suzanne Alexander, now a famous writer married to a famous poet/scholar who is writing on and with Fanon, is, in both her European and African sites, sick. Her body is not erupting in owl feathers, but stands passive to scientific scrutiny. At the opening of *She Talks to Beethoven*, Suzanne gazes not at the silver screen but at her own X-rays, an unreadable image of an 'unspecified illness.' The hysterical body returns in *The Film Club* and *The Dramatic Circle* in the narrative of the mysterious and comically named Dr. Freudenberger, 'a London doctor' who diagnoses Suzanne's breathlessness, makes repeated inquiries into her past, and invites her to his dramatic circle for readings of Bram Stoker's *Dracula*.

In the mimetic network of these plays, Freud–Freudenberger connects us to that other psychiatrist Frantz Fanon. As poet and filmmaker Alice Alexander tells us, Suzanne's symptoms mimic those observed by the Martiniquan doctor in his hospital work in Blida, Algeria. Like the body of Lucy Westenra in *Dracula*, Suzanne's body, with its 'pale white wound' (16), serves as a relay point, not just between two psychiatrists, but between two sites of psychic and corporeal trauma: Suzanne's painful vigil in the English capital and the revolutionary struggles of new African states in the death throes of colonial rule. Indeed Stoker's *Dracula* and Fanon's *Wretched of the Earth* are the dominant relay stations in Kennedy's mimetic network, sites of extremity, passion, and violence that produce, by affinity and resemblance, the shape and meanings of the London-based plays. These texts allow Kennedy's identificatory theater to develop its earliest obsessions. For Lucy Westenra does more than connect two doctors or even two cultures: she links two realities, the rationalist scientism that was late nineteenth-century positivism with its obsessive taxonimizing of nature and its aberrations, and the primitive world of shifting matter embodied by the Transylvanian Other, Count Dracula, and his dark children. The question posed by the racial semiotics of *The Alexander Plays* is not which reality is living, which dead, or even which is moving and which fixed, but how does the subject live in both?

Suzanne Alexander lives in many rooms, but the symptomatic body she exhibits in London is unique to Kennedy's oeuvre. *The Film Club* and *The Dramatic Circle* cover three weeks in 1961, in which Suzanne and Alice await the arrival of David Alexander who is researching Fanon's life, and seeking the 'secret' of Fanon's illness. Possibly poisoned, possibly imprisoned, David is two weeks late, during which time the pregnant Suzanne haunts American Express and journeys with Alice to sites famous for Queens Victoria and Elizabeth. She identifies herself with Josephine and Napoleon whose love letters of anxiety and separation she recites; recalls moments of dread from an earlier separation in Accra (*She Talks to Beethoven*); and attends the dramatic circle where she and Alice recite excerpts from *Dracula*. Kennedy leaves no doubt that her plays are 'bitten' by the Stoker novel. The overdetermined Freudenberger, complete with German wife, recalls Freud (whose *Studies on Hysteria* 1895, with Jacob Breuer, was published two years before *Dracula*) as well as Stoker's foreign Dr. Van Helsing and the alienist Dr. Seward (called 'Stewart' in the play). As Seward secretly loves Lucy Westenra, Freudenberger admits to loving Suzanne whom he asks to read the part of Lucy in the dramatic circle. Like Freud, Seward and Van Helsing are students of the French neurologist, Charcot. But like the metamorphosing Dracula, Freudenberger appears 'as an apparition,' feigns a limp and prowls the Alexander women's house between midnight and dawn, his white hair an echo of Dracula's own hair and moustache before he grows younger in the course of the Stoker tale. The latter, like Kennedy's text, weaves multiple discourses – Jonathan Harker's secret diary; Dr. Seward's diary cum case notes; Lucy and Mina's letters to one another; and long sections from Mina's journal. Not only does Kennedy's text speak through a myriad of texts (Napoleon's and Josephine's letters, Senghor's and Diop's poetry, Fanon's polemic, Stoker's prose), Kennedy's 'narrator' Alice Alexander is asked by Freudenberger to play the part of Mina Harker.

To historicize Stoker's novel, published in the same year (1897) as Queen Victoria's Diamond Jubilee, is to read both its celebration of the rational imperialist state – Van Helsing and company eventually hunt down and destroy the eastern European monster – and its symptomatic anxieties. As David Glover observes, in 1897 Britain was recovering from the Great Depression (1873–96) and would soon face the political uncertainties of the Boer War. Moreover, Glover notes, during the 1890s, while Stoker was drafting *Dracula*, the 'ruling paradigm in the human sciences, running across medicine and biology into psychology and social theory, was concerned with the pathologies of natural selection, what we might call Darwinism and its discontents, particularly the slide back down the evolutionary chain.'[74] Max Nordau and Cesare Lombroso are mentioned by name in *Dracula*. Their extemely popular *Degeneration* (Nordau, 1893, 1895) and *Criminal Man* (Lombroso, 1875) 'scientifically' linked late nineteenth-century social crises to sexual and racial deviancy. Lombrosian criminology sought in particular to 'distinguish the body of truly authentic citizens from those Others,'[75] the born criminals, who drained society of its productive powers. Such discourses grew out of phrenology in the 1820s and later craniometry and prognathism (a measure of the protrusion of the jaw), the latter used by Darwin's cousin, Francis Galton, founder of eugenics and statistics in Britain, to link Negroes through facial angles and jawlines to apes, which in turn became a measure for the inferiority of women, criminals, idiots, foreigners – that growing yet fixed category of social degenerates.[76] Foucault dates this lunatic positivism, what he calls the 'heredity-perversion system,' from the end of the eighteenth century and cautions:

> let it not be imagined that [this system] was nothing more than a medical theory which was scientifically lacking and improperly moralistic. Its application was widespread and its implantation went deep – [into] psychiatry, to be sure, but also jurisprudence, legal medicine, agencies of social control, the surveillance of dangerous or endangered children . . . .[77]

Indeed the implantation of the heredity-perversion system yields its foul fruit in the 'double consciousness,' the 'black Atlantic' ambivalence, that Kennedy explores in her theater. As Mina Harker diagnoses Dracula as a Lombrosian 'criminal type,' whose noseshape, nostrils, and earsize indicate a sensual, impulsive character, an 'imperfectly formed mind,'[78] Sarah, a weary physiognomist, diagnoses her own heredity-perversions: 'In appearance I am good-looking in a boring way, no glaring Negroid features, medium nose, medium mouth and pale yellow skin. My own defect is that I have a head of frizzy hair, unmistakably Negro kinky hair' (*Funnyhouse of a Negro*, 6). All discourses employing racial stigmata stem from this (per)version of Enlightenment science, or perhaps represent its truest manifestation: an empirical 'method' based on visual 'evidence' designed to exclude and criminalize those others (of color, of mixed race) whose mere presence brings infection, contamination to rational European selfhood. Fanon's diagnosis of the effects of this positivist 'rationalism' was the black man's inability to 'construct a physiological self.' Instead, his 'corporeal scheme' concealed a 'historico-racial scheme . . . that *had been provided for me* . . . not by residual sensations, but by the other, the white man, who had woven me out of a thousand details, anecdotes, stories' (111) (my italics). For the colonized subject/object, such 'popular history' is a story of cultural eugenics whose political arm would become state terrorism and annihilation: 'the systematic negation of the other person . . . a furious determination to deny the other person all human attributes,'[79] which Fanon observed in colonized Algeria during the seven-year war of independence.

The violent Manichean fixities of Enlightenment pseudoscience versus Fanonian description drive *The Film Club* and *The Dramatic Circle*, but Kennedy's mimetic networking of *Dracula* and *The Wretched of the Earth* belies their binary logic. Instead she borrows the shape-changing logic of the seductive Dracula, particularly his 'shifting affinities' with nonhuman others – wolves, bats, dogs, lizards – a bestiary not unlike Kennedy's own. The vampire is of course mimesis 'personified,' identification corporealized: his bite transforms the other into a double, gathers her, undead, into a dark inhuman family that mimcs, preys upon, and subverts the human one. A Kennedyesque composite, Stoker's Dracula is, in Glover's words, simultaneously 'rake and mother, a patriarch who gives birth to monsters'; Stoker inverts Victorian convention: 'men become sexually quiescent, women [become] sexual predators who cannibalize children, madness . . . overwhelm[s] reason, and all of this is charged by a ceaselessly fluctuating economy of blood and desire' (70, 71).[80]

Such inversions are precisely what Kennedy welcomes. For Suzanne Alexander is her revision of Stoker's Lucy Westenra ('light of the west'). Suffering from Lucy's breathlessness, Suzanne, like all Kennedy females, has been vampirized by colonialism. Her body bearing the miscegenistic stigmata, an unhealed 'pale white' wound, Suzanne/Lucy roams London, but rather than hunt for a child she carries one, feeding it with her blood. The geography of Ohio State University in 1949 made the young Suzanne 'anxious' (*Ohio State Murders*, 27). For Kennedy, London in 1961 has a Transylvanian feel, a site of confused temporalities in which ancient horrors wind around daily actions:

[In 1961] after leaving Africa I stayed the entire time in a room I found through American Express, on Old Brompton Road. It overlooked a dark square fenced in by an iron gate. You lit the fire with shillings. The city in February, the early darkness, walks in the rain excited me. It made me feel that just beyond that darkness was a completed person, a completed writer, a completed life. I felt the city held a key to my psyche. And apart from literature and my constant interest in British writers, I felt too [that] these were the people who had colonized my West African ancestors. What were these people like?[81]

Like her? How like? A completed life is of course that life's fulfillment but also perhaps that life's death. The Lucy sections in *The Dramatic Circle* review the vampire's first 'kiss' and then cite directly rather dense passages from Chapter 15 of *Dracula*, describing Lucy, now undead, as the 'bloofer lady' who prays on children. As he and Van Helsing gaze upon Lucy's undead blood-glutted body in the crypt, Steward comments (and Kennedy quotes): 'There lay Lucy, seemingly just as we had seen her that night before the funeral. She was, if possible, more radiantly beautiful than ever and I could not believe that she was dead.'[82] As she and Suzanne read these lines, Alice (a sensible Mina) wonders whether Freudenberger isn't preparing Suzanne for her death. But the passage deserves an even more mimetic reading. At this point in the novel Lucy is not the English virgin but a deceptive, treacherous monster; she has drunk blood and will soon kill. In Kennedy's mimetic network the breathless, fragile, intellectual Suzanne 'completes her life' by impersonating a monstrous double which, to extend the fantasy, transforms her into one of Dracula's monster children, and links her to a powerful family line that makes 'the Hapsburgs and the Romanoffs [look like mere] mushroom growths.' Dracula and his family cast no reflection in the mirror, thus cannot be split by the Other. Indeed the old Count so successfully passes for human that he turns up one afternoon in Piccadilly to survey the soft necks of passers-by. In brief Dracula loans Suzanne and her creator the possibility of a triumphal snarling embrace with otherness in all its irrationality and murderousness. In *The Film Club*, the *Washington Post* informs us that Suzanne's infant daughter died 'an accidental death' (77) – a bromide worthy of the Count's own secret treacheries. The same text reports that David Alexander was poisoned by filicin – a coded way perhaps of sending us to the dictionary where we discover nothing on filicin, but are reminded that a filicide is a childkiller. More secrets. Paranoia suffuses the mimetic network.

A less guignol reading of Suzanne's identification with the undead lies in citations from Jonathan Harker's diaries. As in the Lucy texts, Kennedy provides a summary sketch of Harker's horrific experiences in Castle Dracula, then cites specific lines from the end of Chapter 1 as Harker's coach with its mysterious driver nears the castle:

All at once the wolves began to howl . . . . The horses . . . reared and looked helplessly round with eyes that rolled in a way painful to see; but the living ring of terror encompassed them on every side . . .[83]

As Castle Dracula signifies the Englishman's encounter with the subhuman world, London, the heart of imperial England and center of the civilized world, is, for the modern African American woman, a heart of darkness – or, at the very least, a city with 'a subplot.' As she travels up the Thames to admire the birthplace of Queen Elizabeth, Suzanne 'carries . . . records of slave ships. Slaves quarters, slaves crouching below the stern of the ship' (*Dramatic Circle*, 102), a guilty conjuncture of historical horror and her own desire. As a port of call on the slavers' triangular route, London may indeed hold 'a key to [her] psyche,'[84] but the discourse of keys and locks belongs to the early Freud and to Stokerian gothic. Both are too static to be a description of 'black Atlantic' ambivalence. Better to understand Kennedy's London as a site of enchantment and of uncanny presentiments, of glorious conquests and of unknown, unquiet victims, of 'ancestors' who are unrememberd and yet not quite dead.

Fanon, however, mercilessly analyzes his ambivalence. In his texts images of colonial atrocities spring to lurid life. At the close of both *The Film Club* and *The Dramatic Circle*, Kennedy cites the first paragraph of the last chapter of *The Wretched of the Earth*, 'Colonial War and Mental Disorders,' which leaves no doubt about who is biting whom: 'But the war goes on; and we will have to bind up for years to come the many, sometimes ineffaceable, wounds that the colonialist onslaught has inflicted on our people.'[85] Child of the very Enlightenment scientism that has devastated native cultures, Fanon, as psychiatrist/clinician, attempts to put order to the myriad symptoms he encounters – and Kennedy's mimetic network produces further relays. The 'bloodthirsty and pitiless atmosphere, the generalization of inhuman practices'[86] could describe Castle Dracula, yet this is Fanon's description of the world in which mental disorders resist cure. The wolf-ring that surrounds the terrified horses of Harker's journal is echoed in a fragmented citation about a 'mass attack' that Suzanne borrows from Fanon (*Film Club*, 66). Fanon's text reads:

> We here refer to brutal methods which are directed toward getting prisoners to speak, rather than to actual torture . . . . There is no finicking about. There is a mass attack taking several forms: several policemen striking the prisoner at the same time; four policemen standing around the prisoner and hitting him backward and forward to each other . . .[87]

Other symptoms that Suzanne cites and partially enacts – 'states of agitation, rages, immobility, many attempted suicides, tears, lamentations, and appeals for mercy' (*Film Club*, 69) – are drawn from Fanon's observations of pregnant Algerian women (*Wretched*, 279). David's 'idiopathic tremors, hair turning white . . .' (*Film Club*, 78) are the 'psychosomatic disorders' Fanon encounters in young Algerians who manifest 'a refusal with regard to colonial authority' (*Wretched*, 291).

But around Fanon there is 'danger.' In *The Ohio State Murders*, David Alexander is said to 'look like' Frantz Fanon (28), but in *The Dramatic Circle*,

Kennedy identifies him with Harker, suggesting that Fanon is himself a version of Dracula, and that David's inflamed nationalist rhetoric – 'We only need to march and charge. We have mobilized furious cohorts, loving combat, eager to work. We have Africa with us' (*Dramatic Circle*, 84) – is a kind of infection by a force capable of destroying those whom it seduces. Likening David to Napoleon, whose letters to Josephine are written during a French imperialist venture in Egypt, Kennedy underscores the unstable doublings of the mimetic network. As 'African music' blends with Beethoven, Chopin, and Wagner, the signifiers 'prisons' and 'secrets' unite Fanon to Harker to Senghor, and Suzanne to Diop to Beethoven to Lucy Westenra, and, across the Atlantic, to Suzanne and Robert Hampshire, the seeming ur-couple of murderous, racialized sexual seduction in *The Alexander Plays*.

In *The Ohio State Murders*, revolution is marked by the young Suzanne's fascination with Eisenstein's *Potemkin* and romantic love by Hardy's *Tess*, but perhaps more resonantly, the Ohio State girls' dormitory is the young Suzanne's Castle Dracula, a structure of many doors, most of them locked to the Negro girls, a place of secrets, privation, pain, and telltale drops of blood. The murder of her twin daughters, immediately secreted, is posited as the 'main source' of the writer's 'violent imagery' but the white girls' racism in the college dormitory, however typical it seems and is, is this text's real secret, a secret that has no 'source' or logic but that bites into the consciousness of Suzanne: 'I felt such danger from them' (53).

Frantz Fanon died in 1961 in Washington D.C., the same year Lumumba was murdered (and a year before Algeria achieved independence), and in keeping with the atmospherics of the Alexander plays, Kennedy makes Fanon's death (of cancer) as mysterious as Lumumba's, or, for that matter, Dracula's. Like the husbandly Harker (but without, it seems, Harker's moment of sexual seduction), David survives his quest and returns, not just 'haunted' by Blida (93) but 'changed' (106) – changed in ways both predicted and documented by the European and Martiniquan psychiatrists. How do we read this change? We've noted that the vampire's terrible and tempting kiss, the bloodsucking that mingles identities and cultures, lets Kennedy explore the historical circuits of identificatory fantasy: 'I' and 's/he' meld and travel between sites and times. Yet not all circuits are equally charged. Her two psychiatrists are reading similar symptoms for different ends. Suzanne's tale of personal deprivation is produced in Freudenberger's and Stoker's Gothic cityscape, but Fanon's story of vampirism, the colonialist's bite into the psyche and the flesh of Africans, is reproduced on the bodies of the African American couple. Wandering between Western and African capitals, Washington D.C., Accra, London, at the eruptive conjuncture of decolonization and late capitalism, multiply configured across time and space, Suzanne and David demonstrate, as a bodily *gestus*, that hybridity hurts, and that racism in all its mirrorings and secrets remains the undead of global culture. To paraphrase Kennedy, this story *must* be told in 'black and white.'

At the penultimate meeting of the London dramatic circle (a circle that 'a man from Budapest' and 'a Trinidadian painter' have just joined), the ersatz Dr. Freudenberger attempts to treat Suzanne's breathlessness by having her recite 'the sequences of Lucy's life' (181). After each line, the circle responds 'yes' – a brief imitation of the call-and-response form embedded in the earliest black music traditions. Suzanne is brought to tears by the ritual but the text refuses to sentimentalize the moment. It is yet another instance of what Gilroy might call the 'diaspora multiplicity' of her texts, her contribution to a black Atlantic perspective that complicates the 'exceptionalist narrative' (black victimization) fostered by nationalists of all stripes.[88] Kennedy offers theatrically what Gilroy celebrates in Du Bois, complex images of the 'interconnections between Africa, Europe, and the Americas.' Producing mimetic figurations of the rational/historical *as* the private, the emotional, the embodied, the writerly, Kennedy's identificatory theater addresses the promises and disappointments of modernity, making palpable the author's own rage, hope and complicity.

PEOPLE WHO LED TO MY PLAYS

> I am completely enamoured of *People Who Led to My Plays* . . . . To read the fragments – to look at the pictures – there is something very infinite about this work.
>
> bell hooks

People Who Led to My Plays (1987) is autobiography that speaks to the subjective complexities and desires of postmodernity. In violation of the 'self'-construction of generic autobiography wherein the authorial 'I' succeeds or fails to invoke the fullness of its authentic 'I-in-the-world'; departing too from the presumptive subject position in Barthes' *Roland Barthes by Roland Barthes* and Derrida's *The Post Card*, Kennedy's 'I' eschews not only the narrative fullness of a self but also the arch poststructuralist reflexiveness of a subject presumed to know. A chronological collage of language, drawings, and, most of all, photographs, *People Who Led to My Plays* disperses *and* produces Kennedy's 'I' amidst a disparate array of personal and mass cultural simulacra. 'Orson Welles,' 'My Mother,' 'T.S. Eliot,' 'Jesus,' 'Lena Horne,' 'Hitler,' 'My Father,' 'Julius Caesar,' 'Old Maid Playing Cards,' 'Myself,' and countless other signifiers precede a colon mark, followed by brief lines of description or commentary. No distinction is made between the style of each entry, or between things and humans, or between races: all are objects 'mingling in my life, my thoughts and my imagination' (110). The conceptual brilliance of this text lies in Kennedy's historicization of her cross-gendered, multiple identifications – the ways in which familial, political, and mass cultural ties situate her, during the post-Depression and World War II years, in the middle-class environment of Cleveland, a city of integrated schools and progressive Negro families, the parents often, like Kennedy's, southern born and graduates of revered black colleges who came north to work as teachers, social workers, and doctors. Kennedy's identifications further disclose her years at Ohio State University, then in New York City, newly married with a young son, years spent trying to become a published writer, ending with a life-changing trip to West Africa. My narration is a list, and the list chronological, but the overwhelming impression the text makes is of nonlinear space – space between lines, between photos, space even after a colon, where in defiance of the rules of punctuation, silence, not explanation, is forthcoming, as in

Our son Joe . . . his birth:

(79)

Faded newspaper photos look across the page at Hollywood studio glossies; family snapshots sit near magazine photodocuments. Fred and Ginger are caught in a whirling embrace, his tuxedoed leg flying, while opposite, flanked by grimfaced brethren in full Nazi dress, Hitler strides stiffbooted, his hands crossed tightly over his crotch. Given Kennedy's lifelong love of 'people in the movies' the studio glossies reproduced here are especially poignant, for the photos, unlike the text, were first accumulated by a precocious child, and it's through those photos (the implied labor of cutting, taping, storing, saving) that the child's desires are remembered.

And yet this autobiography is not a re-membering, an attempt to endow wholeness and coherence to the bits of self, nor does it perform, as de Man would have it, the necessarily disfiguring task of enacting the impossibility of becoming present to oneself.[89] While her autobiography is certainly a performance in the postmodern sense of defying a stable referent for the self, the point rather is that the 'referent' is never the anchor for a *self*, but for a *temporality* that is no more fixed than last month's *Silver Screen* sensations. In a text so reliant on images of people now dead, fading or lost, memory lists dangerously toward nostalgia. What is powerful for Kennedy, then, is not the referent in all its mortality, or even the delicious memory of Bette Davis's image on the screen. What beckons and holds her is the object itself, whether photographic or textual, and its careful arrangement on the page. Her autobiography will not 'add up' to a life, nor will it refuse to do so. Rather it performs with each 'entry' an affective relation between objects on either side of the colons. Here is a typical sequence from the section labeled 'junior high':

Freddy Jamison:
I was still secretly in love with him, but my mother didn't approve of him. I wrote about him in the autograph books I hid under the mattress.

Miss McCreary:
I did well in our journalism class and informed Miss McCreary, our teacher, that I wanted to be a journalist. She said she didn't think, because of my color, that it was realistic for me to pursue that thought.

Louis Jordan, Nat King Cole, Billy Eckstine, Frank Sinatra:
Said romance and joy awaited me.

Elizabeth Taylor (in *Jane Eyre*):
She was Jane Eyre's best friend, Helen, and as a child died of pneumonia
because cruel Mr. Brocklehurst punished her and made her walk in the rain
after he had cut off her hair.

My mother and her hair:
When my mother cut her hair I used to beg her to let me keep the strands.

(45)

The unapproachable boyfriend, the racist teacher, the sexy masculine croon-
ers, the book and film and life of two favorite imagoes, Jane Eyre and her
mother, and the familiar obsession with hair. Familiar, yet not predictable, for
in its temporal elasticity this consciousness, like its objects, is heterogeneous,
heterotopic. While Kennedy set up the book to look like her mother's red
scrapbook (recall the red playbooks in *The Dramatic Circle*, the red bags of hair
in *Funnyhouse*), her readers are interpellated by their own desires. bell hooks
gazes at a photo of Kennedy's mother and comments, 'you can read the image
in your own way comparing your response to Kennedy's';[90] Diane Johnson is
'charmed' by the possibility of shared memories 'from the people on the Old
Maid's cards to the young Marlon Brando.'[91]

In psychoanalysis, identification is linked to the loss of an object. A lost
loved one produces an identification with that other, an assimilation that is as
tortuous as it is 'enriching.' One can never live up to, complete oneself in, the
imago. The infant rapt in its image/other is not, and never will be, 'it.'
Kennedy's *People Who Led to My Plays* enacts the fort/da of object-love and
object-loss in the dialectic of its design; the space that is empty, the space that
is filled. Into this unresolvable dialectic the reader is beckoned, for not only
are the objects (photo and text) redolent of cultural histories, the spaces
between are both private and common sites of interpretive pleasure – spaces
of temporal drift in which to dream or pause, in which to mingle one's own
objects/memories in another's, and a culture's, imaginary. The object,
Kennedy tells us repeatedly, has a secret, but she is not thereby trying to create an illusion of reality. She is instead marking what is mysterious and also,
simply, other.

In this sense, Kennedy's partner in pleasure is Walter Benjamin, the
collector, the lover of objects that carry mysterious historical secrets. Such
objects can be displayed, arranged, but never dominated, exchanged, or
reduced to an extension of the self. Kennedy's objects are the key to her
subjectivity; they are the material residue of her object choices, and in Freud's
resonant phrase 'contain the history of those object choices.'[92] This subject-in-
relation is of course how we have described identification all along, but,
fittingly for an autobiography, the *mise-en-scène* of this identification is not a

candlelit space with flapping wings, burning altars, screams and vile laughter. Nor do we have – or not only – the vaunted spatialized subject, dispersed and decentered. In her autobiography Kennedy presents us with a mimetic subject – a subject in relation – who sees herself and enriches herself in her objects, but who also preserves them. Who, instead of being lacerated by remembered objects (as her protagonists so often are), simply shows them. They are the beginning of meaning-making, but they are not those meanings.

6 Performance and temporality
Feminism, experience, and mimetic transformation

History not remembered gets told anyway.

Robbie McCauley

My mother said, 'Every word you speak is forever in the air, it will never go away.'

Peggy Shaw

I can feel the raw movement of time, rubbing against my nipples as it passes; time blubbering with life and all its waste products and its night light.

Deb Margolin

The murmur of time is the essence of the theater space, mantic, coded by history . . .

Herbert Blau

To articulate the past historically does not mean to recognize it 'the way it really was.' It means to seize hold of a memory as it flashes up at a moment of danger.

Walter Benjamin

Cultural criticism at its best should offer a remedial course in imagining the present.

Barbara Johnson

In current feminist performance art the challenge is to transform performance time into temporality. By temporality I mean a shifting time-sense, a receptivity both to the contingency of the present and to mimetic figurations of what we might call historical experience. In the previous chapter, we read Adrienne Kennedy's *People Who Led to My Plays* as a performative autobiography in which subjectivity emerged as a sedimented history of identifications. Kennedy's text/photo scrapbook format, we noted, produced a temporal play of objects and memory. Is it possible to generate this complex temporality in live performance? Can we give the performative 'present' the sense of the historical without invoking teleology (linearity, fulfillment)? And if memory gives us a temporal flexibility, how does *historical* memory 'appear' when we have not only a solo woman performer in view, but a female body that seems once again to claim what performance art in the 1970s and 1980s tried to displace: the performer's 'aura' – Walter Benjamin's term for the esoteric presence and authority of the artwork before technologies of reproduction. In Peggy Shaw's *You're Just Like My Father* (first performed 1993); in Robbie McCauley's *Indian Blood* (first performed 1987); in Deb Margolin's *Carthieves! Joyrides!* (first performed 1995), the body is carefully lit, even spotlighted, music syncopates but also enhances, there is minimal but emphatic costuming and transformation, in short – theater. But to suggest that auratic elements should be read as valorizing a 'self' and a 'story beyond any rupture,' as in Josette Féral's recent critique of contemporary performance, would be mistaken.[1] The performance work named above belies the continuist narrative, the self-reflective modeling, that underpin the stability of 'self' and identity. What is innovative and politically resonant in this performance work is the practice of mimetic thinking – what Benjamin calls thinking in 'similarities,' in sensuous relation. Through mimetically constructed 'dialectical images,' these performers *temporalize* perception, producing new means of imbricating the psychic and the historical – of externalizing the private interior through images of collective fantasy. Deploying the auratic in order to destroy its uniqueness, they allow us to read, and experience, recent US history 'against the grain.'[2]

TIME OUT, TIME IN

Questions of temporality that invoke 'real' historical time seem peculiar in relation to theater and even to much performance art. In articulating the fundamental phenomenology of theater, Bert States reminds us of the moment of 'opening' in which the 'lights dim' and the process begins which 'radically shifts the ground and conditions of our perception of the world.' States borrows catharsis from tragedy as the 'best word for what takes place at large in the theater. It is precisely a purging: what is purged . . . is time – the menace of successiveness, of all life falling haphazardly through time into accident and repetition.'[3] Certainly classical mimesis abets this purgation. Aristotelian mimesis of an action implies the selection – and employment – of those materials that produce order, the *other* order of aesthetic time. 'The play,' States observes, 'imitates the timely, in order to remove it from time, to give time a shape' (50). Gertrude Stein introduces a spectator's protest at the tyranny of aesthetic time, insisting that 'the thing seen and the thing felt about the thing seen not going on at the same tempo is what makes the being at the theater something that makes anybody nervous.'[4] Alternative theater and performance since the happenings of the 1960s have increased our nervousness, not only by moving performance to unconventional sites but – more importantly – by unbinding aesthetic time, and the narrativizing it invites. In one of the landmark performance pieces of the 1980s, *Rt 1 & 9, The Last Act*, a wall clock prominently in view was set to 'real' time, and its slow time intervals were duly noted during 'live' telephone calls made during the performance to order food for the performers. The effect of this temporal incongruity was to bring space acutely to consciousness – not the extensions and contractions of stage space in its measured coordination with stage time, not the signifying space of a 'dramatic world,' but rather a depthless space in which no pocket of illusionistic time or meaning could hide. Pushing beyond the self-reflexiveness of Beckett's temporal repetitions and spatial constrictions, performance art attempts, futilely of course, the uncoupling of aesthetic space-time; space is what performers inhabit as time simply continues.[5]

The intensive indexing of space – a performance space that hides nothing and reveals nothing – was born in modernism and has become a fundament of the postmodern. It is space, Edward Soja reminds us, that is the perceptual modality of postmodernity, temporality being the trope of experience and history wherein even the Marxian revolutionary moment must await its arrival in the evolution of productive forces.[6] Spatiality, as those frequenting cyberspace well know, means the delicious possibility of 'sidetrack[ing]' from 'a sequential flow . . . into simultaneities.'[7] In Fredric Jameson's dour rendition, the postmodern body is 'bereft of spatial coordinates,' although for many this is a condition to celebrate.[8] As is often the case in discussions of the postmodern, feminism is Janus-faced. Committed to ideology critique and material change in society, but with a profound (and postmodern) skepticism of historical narratives that reproduce patriarchal relations of power, feminists have been exploring what Gertrude Stein called, in her own performance poetics, the 'space of time.' Metaphors like 'parenthesis,' the 'interstitial,' are space-of-time tropes that attempt to imbricate phenomenal experience and historical articulation. Poststructuralist feminism has given us compelling spatial tropes – Kristeva's 'chora,' Irigaray's 'hystera,' the 'two lips' (about which more later), that stress nearness and nonhierarchical contiguity, all ways of refusing the binaries of mind and body, knowledge and experience.[9] But feminism's queries and practices also require context, and are strongly shaped by the desire to remember, to represent, and, as Barbara Johnson puts it above, to 'imagin[e] the present.' The question remains, how to *perform* Stein's 'space of time,' and how understand performance time as the 'space' of subjectivity, embodiment, and history?

BRECHT, BENJAMIN, AND DIALECTICAL IMAGES

As we saw in Chapter 2, the theorist most concerned with history as a space of performance time is Brecht. Rejecting aesthetic experience as the 'beauty cult' precisely because it purges time, Brechtian techniques of 'historicization' and the *gestus* charge objects and episodic stories with dialectical tension, widening the spectator's gaze to include historical determinants and contradictions. To think historically, however, does not mean, as in Leopold von Ranke's famous formula, to recover the past 'the way it really was.'[10] Fetishizing the authentic historical moment is for Brecht profoundly unhistorical; it implies that the past, enshrined in its own truth, waits to be discovered. This feeds the mythic belief in a continuity between past and present, so that (in Brecht's words) 'social structures of past periods . . . look more or less like our own,' and 'unique and transitory' incidents acquire an air of 'having been there all along . . . of permanence.'[11] For Brecht, historicism's aesthetic correlate is the purportedly timeless present of art perception, which encourages our imagined discovery of the 'eternally human' in '"universal" situations that allow Man with a capital M to express himself' (96–97). Because bourgeois aesthetics enshrines the object (hero, event), it keeps us from seeing its social determinations, and by extension, from seeking reasons for the human misery and expropriation that capitalist ideology has naturalized. Indeed the political tension in Brecht's practice depends on positing an *identity* between aesthetic time and bourgeois historical time. This in turn lends urgency to his estrangement devices. To the relaxed (cigar-smoking) spectator, placards and song encourage extra-theatrical acts of ideology critique; the understanding that 'reality' and its history are produced, like theatrical illusion, by economic, political, and (I must add) gender effects that only appear to be fixed and eternal. Pleasure for the Brechtian spectator lies in noting *differences* between past and present and within our contemporary moment. As noted in the Introduction, Brecht wanted more mimesis not less, more revealing of reality's relational workings, not aesthetic escapes therefrom. The *gestus* is the stage sign (verbal and/or gestural) that reveals historical relations – the personal/social contradictions implied in the play's fable. To read the sign or image against bourgeois myths of historical continuity is to see, as a transformative act of cognition, the possibilities emerging of another reality, what is not there, but could be.

Walter Benjamin, Brecht's friend and critic, also said early on that 'humanity has not woken up to the persistent consciousness of its historical existence,' and he too rejected the givenness of the past and what he called the 'hollow continuum' of empirical time under capitalism.[12] For Benjamin historicism, including literary and art history, as well as the idealist strain of Marxist historiography with its Enlightenment vision of progress, all accommodated/glossed over the depredations of commodity culture – routinization, conformism, unrelieved human suffering – and thus contributed to the rise of fascism and Nazism in the 1920s and 1930s: 'One reason why Fascism has a chance is that in the name of progress its opponents treat it as a historical norm.'[13]

While rejecting the mystifications of historical progress, Benjamin was, after the 'Artwork' essay (1936), more ambivalent than Brecht about the meaning and uses of the auratic object. In 'On Some Motifs in Baudelaire' (1939), Benjamin links the 'experience of the aura' with a complex temporality; traditional auratic art is not just a reactionary 'cultic' component of bourgeois life but a repository of past experiences which might serve as a stimulus to change.[14] Moreover, the phantasmagoria of commodity culture was also auratic, worthy of philosophical attention.[15] Benjamin reconceived Max Weber's notion of 'disenchantment' – the progressive rationalization of social forms of life – as 're-enchantment.'[16] With its profusion of commodity production – each commodity a lifeless but seductive reproduction of the last – the fiercely churning machines of industrial capitalism produced a wonderland of consumption that turned urban populations of the West into 'dreaming collectives.' In these mercantilist fairylands, particularly in the detritus of last year's novelty items, Benjamin, like the surrealists of the 1920s, read their 'original utopian potential.'[17] Borrowing Freud's notion that dreams are disguised wishes, Benjamin saw the phantasmagoric commodity as potential wish image which, if resuscitated in a new 'constellation' (of non-identical terms, concepts) might contribute to collective awakening.

Despite his and Brecht's masculinism,[18] it is Benjamin's engagement with mass culture and consumerism that makes him interesting for feminist theorizing. Women have long been associated with the superficialities and duplicities of fashion, advertising, consumerism, and fantasy. Typically, an image of idealized or abjected 'woman' is circulated in order to sell goods, affirm the patriarchal family, prop up masculine sexual prowess – usually a combination of the three. These 'all-consuming images,' pleasurable to both genders, are of course constitutive of capitalist culture – commodities unto themselves.[19] To jam the machinery of image reproduction, critics have articulated strategies of reiteration or reinscription to mark the specificity of what is elided – in the above case, the complexity and differences of women's experiences and desires. What I want to add to our critical arsenal is a strategy I've learned from the performance artists discussed in this chapter: a strategic reimagining of the images themselves. Images, they show us, can be torqued from within, thrown into new relations, shocked into dialectical contradiction. Dialectical images . . .

Benjamin developed the 'dialectical image' as he worked on his unfinished Arcades project (*Passagen-Werk*), from 1927 to his suicide in 1940, after a failed attempt to flee Nazi-occupied France. All his major essays of the 1930s were drawn from the voluminous notes he made for this 'ur-history of the 19th century.'[20] The presentation of the Arcades project was to be graphic, concrete, with images constructed directly from the 'trash' of history, the phantasmagoria of nineteenth-century Paris: the catacombs, department stores, wax figures, souvenirs, arcades, flaneurs, prostitutes, etc.[21] 'History decomposes into images, not narratives,' wrote Benjamin. 'I have nothing to say, only to show.'[22] The *Passagen-Werk*, in Susan Buck-Morss's words, sought to 'juxtapose the original utopian potential of modernity [with] its catastrophic and barbaric present reality . . . [it] relies on the shock of these juxtaposed images to compel revolutionary awakening' (251).

The *dialectical* image, then, doesn't stand in for an absent real (woman, man, toaster, Chevy), nor is it internally harmonious. A version of the demystifying *gestus*, the dialectical image is a montage construction of forgotten objects or pieces of commodity culture that are 'blasted' out of history's continuum. In the moment of reading, Benjamin theorizes, the past and the now 'come together in a flash as a constellation,' shocking us into 'redemption' (recognition) of the object, and simultaneously awakening us from the dreamstory of historical progress under capitalism.[23] This moment of reading – Benjamin called it a 'now-time' (*Jetztzeit*) – is sentient, dynamic, philosophically crucial. For dialectical images challenge the myths of historical progress not because they exist ontologically, but because we *perform* that challenge in the disjunctive '*Jetztzeit*' or now-time of our reading.[24]

Now-time is key to Benjamin's Messianic Marxism – his visioning of revolution not as the logical result of class struggle in all its stages, but as the perpendicular collision of linear historical time with Messianic time, when, suddenly, history becomes 'citable [meaningful] in all its moments'.[25] Because history is too enamoured of its progress-myths, the historical continuum must be 'explode[d] and in that "flash" of insight, not only are we awakened from the fantasy of progress but the historical object is freed of its esoteric aura – its illusory authority and autonomy, its embeddedness in the historical continuum.' To destroy the aura is to *release experiences* – emotions, understandings, correspondences – for *esoteric* use in the present.[26] When, as we'll see, Peggy Shaw and Robbie McCauley don military gear from World War II, their dialectical images not only 'shock' the myth of military glory in the name of historical progress, they also release unsorted experiences of childhood, memories of sexual pleasure and terror, of political awakening. In other words, now-time is a 'space of time' of recognition and transformation. It doesn't carry us to a utopian or paradisal beyond, or to the 'remove' of aesthetic contemplation. Rather in now-time we are palpably, mimetically immersed in the unrecorded history of our social existence – in the conflicting loops, freeze-frames, vanishings, fragmented memories, in the very 'accident and repetition' (as States puts it) that aesthetic time banishes.[27]

For Benjamin, Baudelaire was the first modern poet not only because he renounced the aestheticist pretensions of *l'art pour l'art* but because he incorporated the physical shock effects of city life into his poetry. In *Les Fleurs du Mal*, Benjamin finds more than esoteric symbolist excursions into longing and despair. He finds the *exoteric* experience of being jostled and shocked by anonymous crowds pouring down Haussman's boulevards and through the newly built Parisian arcades, those temples of consumerism and prototypes of our shopping malls. Benjamin writes: 'Moving through this traffic involves the individual in a series of shocks and collisions. At dangerous crossings, nervous impulses flow through him in rapid succession, like energy in a battery.'[28] Social alienation is experientially (mimetically) likened to neuronal shocks generated by a mass-produced object of industrial technology. Benjamin constructs not a sentimental representation of the 'once upon a time' of early bourgeois experience but *a dialectical image of modern subjectivity* at the 'dangerous crossings' of two historical eras (pre- and post-industrialization). While the relation of body to machine is typically modernist, and the evocation of a pre-shock era seems almost nostalgic, the relevance to our postmodern notions of the subject is also clear. As Irigaray might say, the Baudelairean 'individual' is 'one who is not one' – whose experience of embodiment is not private, inner, esoteric but permeable, exoteric, formed in the crucible of conflicting tempor[e]alities.[29]

But what do these temporalities mean now?

With a real millennium approaching and a large community of Jews believing that the Messiah has *already* come, with the numbing down of intellectual discourse and much journalism in the wake of perpetual global crises, the bourgeois dreamstory of progress, and the creative political resistance to it imagined by Benjamin and Brecht, are harder and harder to engage. Postmodernity, Sue-Ellen Case has recently suggested, means the 'fad[ing] away' of 'agonistic positions' in both 'performance traditions and critical reception.'[30] In technoculture's screenings, the 'distinction among erstwhile interior processes and exterior effects has been subsumed by morphing, traveling, simultaneously appearing . . .' Case consigns interiority 'to a prior capitalist project' and celebrates a lesbian body that 'exteriorizes the internal' (339). And yet it's Gertrude Stein's *cubistic* spatial disruptions of the linear text that help her model the 'cyberlesbian.' In other words, Case wonderfully retains and recontextualizes the most powerful strain of resistant modernism: its all-out critique of a bourgeois interiority that masquerades as enlightened individualism. She enlists '*exteriority*' to erase the traces of private subjectivity. Lingering in New York's 'poor theater' sites in the 1990s, I find the notion of 'exoteric experience' equally compelling. A way perhaps of revisioning experience itself.

EXOTERIC EXPERIENCE AND THE PERFORMANCE APPARATUS

Mention of experience 'itself' recalls us to a thorny debate in feminist theory, between radical feminist visions of the irreducibility of embodied female experience and the poststructuralist critique of experience as a self-authenticating, stable marker of knowledge and truth. Alice Jardine notes that experience met its 'demise' in poststructuralism, but immediately adds that 'feminism, while infinite in its variations, is finally rooted in the belief that women's truth-in-experience-and-reality is and has always been different from men's.'[31] Still, she argues, correctly I think, that it is precisely these hyphenated connectives that need to be queried. One problem lies in the disjunction of experience and discourse.

Commonsensically, we understand experience to be the uncontestable stable ground of being and knowing, what we conceptualize and speak *from*. But experience comes to consciousness *through* discourse, making it impossible to attach to a secure interiority or 'self.' The linguistic sign is, for Derrida, infinitely citational, movable from any given context, thus incapable of stable referentiality. To believe that subjecthood is produced by experience which can then be narrativized as identity is to be infected, so this argument goes, with the delusions of 'presence,' the fantasy that one is fully present (transparent) to oneself, free of the divisions of the signifier and unconscious desire. Autobiography, the genre wherein past experience is made to testify to the subject's self-consciousness, meets a similar critique in Paul De Man's 'Autobiography as De-Facement'; the past 'self' adumbrated is a fictional construct, not an index of truth to validate present consciousness.[32] Another problem with 'truth-in-experience-and-reality' is its political conservatism, the tendency, as Diana Fuss notes, to convert what seems 'real and immediate' into universal truth. Against this tendency, Fuss cites Althusser's notion that 'lived experience' is only the 'lived experience of ideology': social and political structures produce the experience we imagine to be real and truthful.[33] And yet, as Donna Haraway notes, 'through the politically explosive terrain of linked experience feminists make connections and enter into movement.'[34]

Teresa de Lauretis suggests that we stop relating experience to authentic subjecthood but view it instead as the 'interaction' of the 'real and immediate' with specific political and social realities. Eschewing the empirical meaning of experience as sense data and the behaviorist sense of experience as an aggregation of skills and competences; rejecting, too, the 'individualistic, idiosyncratic sense of something belonging to one and exclusively her own,' de Lauretis links experience to subjectivity *exoterically*, as

> a *process* by which, for all social beings, subjectivity is constructed. Through that process one places oneself or is placed in social reality, and so perceives and comprehends as subjective (referring to, even originating in oneself) those relations – material, economic, and interpersonal – which are in fact social and, in a larger perspective, historical . . . . The subject in social reality [must be] rearticulated from the historical experience of women.[35]

What is useful here is the intrication of ideology, subjectivity, and history. Experience, de Lauretis suggests, is always a sleight of hand; what is perceived as subjective is 'in fact' a set of objective conditions. But *contra* Althusser, and *contra* the sexual 'in-difference' of psychoanalytic theory that can only speak of 'woman,' not 'women,' de Lauretis uses experience to argue for *both* the provisionality of the subject ('subjectivity is an ongoing construction, not a fixed point of departure or arrival,' 159), *and* the specificity of that subject's gendered experience in the world. That experience, de Lauretis insists, will be simultaneously *mediated and embodied, public and private, political and personal*, and its articulations need to be historicized.

The performance art of Robbie McCauley, Peggy Shaw, and Deb Margolin is extraordinary in precisely this articulation of social/personal experience; its historicization, however, is not carried out discursively but *imaged exoterically* in a force-field of conflicting temporalities marked by the detritus of consumer culture. Using dialectical images to bring past and present into collision, these feminist artists turn performance time into a now-time of insight and transformation. For Benjamin, the historico-epistemological frame was the mid-nineteenth-century phantasmagoria of industrial capitalism and the ruin of its utopian potential in World War I and after. When technology became a branch of capitalism's deadly division of labor, society was sent backward not forward into the mythic thinking that prepared the way for fascism.

For McCauley, Shaw, and Margolin the frame shifts to US society and culture of the 1940s and 1950s, when the culture of consumption expanded exponentially, marking the beginning of what Jameson (citing Mandel) calls the 'long wave' of late capitalism: '[L]ate capitalism began in the 1950s, after the wartime shortages of consumer goods and spare parts had been made up, and new products and new technologies (not least those of the media) could be pioneered.'[36] The media were happy to ignore the fact that even with higher paychecks and easy credit, 'not everyone could afford a new car, new house, TV set, or high fidelity sound' – middle-class staples of the 1950s and testimony to the enduring power of mythic (dream) thinking.[37] US capitalism's division of labor was happily installed in the ideal (white) middle-class home, with ideal Dad, war memories tucked away, underwriting family affluence, and ideal Mom, forced out of wartime employment, securing the borders of the nuclear family. Daughters of very different class and racial versions of this scenario, McCauley, Shaw, and Margolin conjure the family as a force-field of strict (if inconsistent) gendering, shot through with virulent strains of the misogyny, racism, and homophobia that we perpetuate and contest today. While their pieces address 'Dad,' personal fathers are remembered and sought for in exoteric spaces, primarily amidst the patriarchal erotica of the 1940s and 1950s – the starched, romantic soldier image, the metallic 'gorp'-laden, wide-bodied family car, – mnemic signposts of private subjectivity and public memory.

'Where there is experience,' writes Benjamin, ' . . . certain contents of the individual past combine with materials of the collective past.'[38] Because the 'materials' of a collective past are no longer accessible they have to be read out of the detritus of what remains; the faint auratic glow of the wish image in the discarded commodity needs to be fanned in order to renew our political energies, to deepen our experience of/in the present. The performance art discussed below interrelates both these elements: first, a recovery of the contradictory energies of popular culture – military mythology, car fetishism – as a strategy for reflection, resistance, and comedy; second, an embodied troping on temporality through which we grasp what is innovative and politically resonant in these practices: a subtle refunctioning of experience. What makes their performance work feminist is not that it is 'by and about' women, or that it validates a woman's way of feeling and knowing (although both are important), but that it enacts a tension between auratic body and dialectical image, between private recollection and cultural memory. Women's experiences, these performances suggest, exist not just in a 'space of time,' but in colliding temporalities. The body's emphatic ('live') presence is offered as a momentary habitus of what is not present – the forgotten objects and cultural detritus that constitute a piece of the 'historical experience of women.'

The postmodern performance apparatus – its regime of seeing/knowing – needs to be factored into this argument. Henry Sayre speaks of the 'contingency, multiplicity, and polyvocality' of performance art of the 1970s and 1980s, not as features of a suspect or fashionable pluralism, but as connected to the 'other' side of modernism – cubist collage, assemblages, Dada, and futurist performance.[39] Postmodern performances, he argues, evacuate the 'wholly manifest, self-present' modernist art object, replacing it with, as Michael Fried put it, the 'theatrical': art dependent upon staging and upon 'conspicuous manipulation' of its audience.[40] Of course this 'theatrical' virulence rarely infects most theater audiences, who are pleased enough to reverence the auratic object. Indeed Benjamin saw the film actor as dispersed and divided by technologies of reproduction, while the stage actor's 'aura is tied to his presence; there can be no replica of it.'[41]

Performance art of the 1970s and early 1980s, using new video technologies, attacked that auratic body – cutting it up, distributing it, recomposing it as a coded body, 'inscribed in and through technology.'[42] As part of its intensive indexing of space, performance art affirmed postmodern subjectivity as a precarious assumption of an 'I-place,' a coded blip in a network of language games and social discourses. 'As for spoken language, there are many different voices and positions in the performance . . . the authority of this language breaks down . . . classifie[d] and overcode[d] in repetition.'[43] In its signifying operations language splits the speaker from the presence of her own words; at the moment of utterance the signifier is, as noted above, always traveling to another context, arriving from still another. Presence, then, is never simply present. The 'auratic' uniqueness of the performer's body, its apparent 'unity' as logical and experiential home of the subject, is dispersed by its 'own' discourse, the discourse it cannot own.[44] 'When you name yourself,' said Brecht, 'you always name another.'[45]

In another sense, presence is 'ghosted' (as Herbert Blau puts it) by an absence it never completely conceals.[46] When the performer 'plunges into visibility' (in Peggy Phelan's fine phrase),[47] s/he enters a space that, since the 1970s, feminist theory has described as socially, culturally, and psychically predicated on sexual difference. In this discourse the female subject is 'seen' as both different and inferior (castrated). Conventional theater as a 'seeing place,' particularly the proscenium space with its hidden lights, its illusionary magic, its techniques of illuminating and obscuring the body, reactivates these psychic mechanisms. If, for the male spectator, the female body is a particularly potent threat and lure, an invitation to fetishistic fantasy and pleasure, the appearance–disappearance matrix of theatrical vision incites both genders to replay the anxious and pleasurable fort/da relation to the mother's body/presence: the site/threat of lack.

For the pyschoanalytic subject, conceived as it were in lack, seeing is always desiring: seeking for what cannot be found, the lost object, the lost breast, the plenitude of wholeness. 'Seeing,' writes Phelan, 'is hooded with loss . . . . In looking at the other, the subject seeks to see itself' (16). For years Herbert Blau has explored the psychic duplicities of seeing as a metaphor for thought. Seeing cues reflexive thinking; the actor's body, abraded in the act of being seen and by its own libidinal flows, is less a substitute object than a relay point in the trajectory of Blau's deracinated reflections.[48] Both Blau and Phelan take disappearance to be a phenomenological given of all performance. In Phelan's 'ontology,' performance is unrecuperable, nonreproductive, only in the performative now. Blau's phenomenology is deeply invested in temporality and history. The time of performance, he suggests, is amortized: borrowing time from life, performance is the payback on a loan that cannot be repaid, which is why performance is always already a site of death. As we watch, the performer is dying before our eyes, even as s/he struggles to appear.[49]

I find this last phrase beautifully counter-intuitive and entirely apt. Historically women, especially lesbians and women of color, have struggled to appear, to speak, be heard, be seen. In the history of Western metaphysics, the female body is figured as both crude materiality and irreparable lack. The essence of her 'being,' then, is appearance/disappearance: a dangerous form of her fabled duplicity. In postmodern theory, duplicity is endemic to all subjects who disavow lack or difference and pretend to wholeness behind the unitary 'I.' Subjectivity is performance, at best, and performance with its improvisational traces showing. Socially and culturally, however, all performances are not equal. In their *historical experience*, women are burdened with an extra duplicity. Doubling the appearance of every woman, whether in a bar, a MUD, or a performance space, is some version of the heterosexist fantasy of Woman – lure and prop to masculine mastery.

STORIES AND MIMESIS

When Shaw, McCauley, and Margolin enter the performance space they are as female performers, as postmodern speakers, 'struggling to appear,' to take up an 'I,' propped up by the auratic authority that illusorily accrues to those who address us from the stage. The narrative 'I' has been a staple of feminist performance art since the 1970s, a means of inciting the expectation of narrativity only to displace it.[50] Feminist theater of the 1980s offered self-consciously nominated 'texts from elsewhere' to provoke a connection to authoritative narratives of history.[51] In juxtaposed fragments of multivocal narrative the stage space became a scene of desire in which women were incitements to speech, never subjects of discourse. In the visual regime of Marguerite Duras's *India Song* (1982), for example, Anne-Marie Stretter's semi-nude stage presence marks her absence; 'she' is the effect of the desire of disembodied voices, 'situated' in different space/times. Body/presence with all its humanist implications of ego and consciousness is decisively severed from the spoken 'I' of subjectivity. Carolee Schneemann's *Interior Scroll* (1975) makes the female 'I' a conceptual joke: in the performance Schneemann stripped, applied paint to the contours of her body, then read from a scroll (a jargon-filled structuralist riposte addressed to a male artist) that she unraveled, 'inch by inch,' from her vagina.[52] As arresting, in *Micropolis* (1982) sculptor Theodora Skipitares stood by her 28-inch-high likeness as it/she decomposed in an illuminated jar of formaldehyde. If we recall de Lauretis's dialectical categories – public and private, mediated and embodied – for describing phenomenal experience, we can see that much feminist theater and performance in the 1970s and 1980s made common cause with the theoretical suspicion of any *mise-en-scène* that implied the ontological presence of the female body and the ability of language to speak of it.[53]

This makes all the more intriguing the seeming dependence on the 'I-word' in the performance art of the late 1980s and 1990s. Certainly this movement to narrative retains the performative skepticism of the 1970s and 1980s; the referents of the signifiers 'my mother,' 'my father,' are unstable markers, pieces of the speaker's memory and fantasy. And yet, undeniably, that speaker is a woman, before us, saying 'I' – and more. She is, like Benjamin's long-vanished 'Storyteller,' attempting to speak of experiences and, by extension, of history.[54] Does this mean the subject is no longer subjected, no longer an effect of discourse? Is the body in performance, as Phelan puts it, metonymically implying a self? (150). The short answer, by way of Benjamin's notion of mimesis, would be yes, but a 'self-in-relation, a self in time.'

Mimesis for Benjamin is not about the visual economies of Platonic modeling that promote true–false, model–copy, real–imaginary divisions and judgments, but about sensuous thinking and similar – that is, contiguous – relations. Mimesis is not a means of ordering experience, but a 'faculty' that enables alienated subjects to experience the other/the world. To rethink experience from within the divisions of subjectivity, we need to think mimetically, to let correspondence back into thought.

In his account of 'the mimetic faculty,' Benjamin identifies the 'powerful compulsion to become and behave like something else,' the ability – now in decline – to recognize and generate similarities.[55] Becoming the other, or inventing similarities, might seem perilously close to Irigaray's critique of Platonic mimesis, an expropriation of, or subsumption of, the other by the Same. But for Benjamin oddly, queerly, it was the opposite. The truth mimesis produces is not in the model (Platonic Form or My Ego) but in the social object. In Adorno's words, 'Benjamin's thought . . . presses close to its object, [as if through] touch . . . smell . . . taste, [it could] transform itself' – note that the *thought* is transformed, not the object.[56] Whether he was writing on Baudelaire, Proust, the gambler, or hashish, the mimetic procedure of a Benjamin essay is to break down metaphysical hierarchies of subject and object – this is what Michael Taussig calls 'a yielding,' an 'involvement of the perceiver in the image.'[57]

The dialectical image depends on mimetic thinking, thinking in relation (in the Baudelaire image: shoppers to shock effects; body to battery; busy intersection to historical eras) while never collapsing one element into another. The body is mimesis's force-field; mimetic acts shift 'from the eye to the lip, taking a detour across the entire body.'[58] Benjamin posits a 'phylogenetic' origin to the mimetic faculty in the 'natural correspondences [between] microcosm and macrocosm, [expressed] in dances, whose oldest function . . . was to produce similarities, and also recognize them.'[59] These 'origins' are unrecuperable, the faculty itself in decay. Nature is no longer a terrifying Other that must be appeased through mimicry, but rather a fully rationalized piece of the capitalist economy. However, the 'ontogenetic' aspect of mimesis is alive and well in the behavior of children whose mimetic play is not limited to iconic models. 'The child,' notes Benjamin, 'not only plays shopkeeper or teacher but also windmill and railroad train' (333). As Susan Buck-Morss puts it, children intuit 'secret affinities' in widely differing materials; their cognition has 'revolutionary power' because it 'links perception and action; laying hold of an object releases new possibilities of meaning.'[60]

This sensuous relation to objects is, for Benjamin, present in language. Indeed 'language may be seen as the highest level of mimetic behavior.'[61] Sensuous correspondence to nature has faded, but 'nonsensuous (figurative, not literal) correspondences' (335) are still accessible in words and writing. Rejecting the Saussurean system of the arbitrary and conventional sign as yet another totalizing metaphysics, Benjamin discerned a link between 'the spoken [and the written] word and the signified' that recalled a primordial connection of body to word (335). This primordial connection – what Benjamin calls 'the name' – is a trope of kabbalistic mysticism, yet, typically, Benjamin gives it a materialist and, for our purposes, a usable turn.[62] When he insists on traces of embodiment, of experiential life, in the word, it is to make the word *act* against the grain of historical crisis.[63] Semiotic psychoanalysis tells us that we leave the instinctual body behind when we enter language. But for Benjamin the 'semiotic' (the Saussurean sign) functions as a 'bearer' of forgotten experiences – 'like a flash, similarity appears' (335). Like Artaud's hieroglyph and Stein's 'lively words,' the mimetic trace in language constitutes a kind of hyper-essentialist materialism. But unlike the first two, Benjamin's project was dialectical, an effort to illuminate contradictions in the collision between present and past.

Similar to theater and performance artists of the 1970s and 1980s, Shaw, McCauley, and Margolin use storytelling to tell history, to change aesthetic time to a temporality that, metaphorically at least, makes 'space' for women's experience. They assume the 'I,' not to assert that they speak from personal experience, nor to claim a unitary self-presence, but to produce exoteric experiences from which new performative I-positions can 'struggle to appear.' Their stories (paraphrasing Benjamin) decompose into dialectical images,[64] complex mimetic productions that help us read history against the grain – and read the body against the grain . . . recovering its transgressiveness. By inhabiting not a character, nor a narrative 'I,' but a dialectical image, the auratic body with all its cultic power is instantiated and destroyed. Instantiated because its 'presence' generates, like all auratic objects, a whole series of pleasurable identifications, fantasies, and 'natural' correspondences (indeed Shaw and Margolin trope the goddess themes that inspired 1970s feminism). Destroyed because that body-image is suddenly apprehended as constellated pieces of disparate experience belonging not to the performer but to our cultural junkheap, our collective memory.

PEGGY SHAW, *YOU'RE JUST LIKE MY FATHER*[65]

I want to produce new images not old lies.

Peggy Shaw

Peggy Shaw launches *You're Just Like My Father* from recollections of growing up butch in the 1950s. She charges her fictional batteries with the erotic energies of Elvis ('He taught me to pay attention to my lips'), the soul music of James Brown ('It's a *man*'s world . . .'), and the spectacular macho of a 1962 Corvette ('with a beautiful woman next to me').[66] In the accents of a working-class tough, Shaw produces sensuous mnemic images that work subversively against the gender proscriptions of the 1950s – and the 1990s. The 'shock' experience in her story fragments is not the press of the dead-faced urban crowds in Benjamin's version of Baudelaire, but the dead hand of gender structuration in a religion-soaked working-class 1950s household, dominated by a frightened, damaged, but intriguing mother who, out of acuity and love, captioned ('recognized') the identifications the young Shaw was discovering, concealing, performing. '"You look just like your father," my mother would say,' says Shaw, miming her mother's snarl (2). This statement of classical mimesis (fidelity to a model), suggests the conventional oedipal triangulation, in which the daughter, having inherited her mother's 'castration,' transfers her desire to her father, whilst the mother's desire is simultaneously acknowledged and written out. In the images of her storytelling Shaw wrenches the oedipal story, turning resemblance into identification, identification into mimesis. 'My father . . . had a heart condition; he had to count to ten before he hit us. I have the same heart condition simply because I knew him so well. He had big hands. I have his big hands' (2).

But even as she describes (with a coy eyebrow ripple) flirting with her mother's friends ('Their husbands seemed so old. And I was so full of desire . . . '5) and her first attempts to love girls, *You're Just Like My Father* is more than butch autobiography rooted in a refunctioning of the oedipal scenario. After a speech of rapid-fire sexual puns on the heteronormative missionary position, on keeping it up, on the impossible but disturbing mimesis between dildos, real dicks, and the 'dolphin' shape of her own father's organ, Shaw closes the riff with a biff on the chin to her interpreters, 'I don't want to be like my parents / In any way / Unless, of course I can't help it. / You should never take your parents personally' (4–5). Tossed off as she turns upstage, this witty quip both embraces and mocks psychoanalysis: what one 'wants' versus the desires one can't 'help' begs for a reading of desire that feminist theory has long struggled with. On the other hand, not taking one's parents *personally* urges us to take them *socially*, in connection to the marketplace of gendered American imagery.

Shaw begins the piece in dadlike faded boxer shorts, bare-breasted and barefoot. Standing in profile to her audience she unravels a medical ace bandage and slowly wraps her breasts. Although a prelude to passing, the anticipated auratic moment of female 'becoming male' is deflected by the performer's careful labor, her face working in concentration, in an imaginary mirror. Indeed an *imaginary* mirror. Unlike Lacan's, however, in which a fantasy image of masterful wholeness is internalized and reproduced, here a fantasy is carefully and critically constructed in the context of social norms – norms brought into the performance space through the looks of knowing and baffled spectators alike. The breast-wrapping becomes a *gestus*. Who is 'caught' not just looking at, but understanding, this mirror ritual?

As Shaw dons a dadlike World War II soldier's uniform and then a tailored man's suit from the period; as she sings and resignifies such male croon-tunes as James Brown's 'It's a Man's, Man's, Man's World' and Julio Iglesias's 'To All the Girls I Loved Before,' she demonstrates not only the theatricality of drag, but also the drag of the gender binary: 'I have these big hands. These are the butch queer feminine parts of me' (4). Shaw's persona is an explicit performative, an iteration of style and desire that defies, as Sue-Ellen Case has shown so well, ontological readings.[67] Yet, as important as Shaw's nonontological queerness is the 'uptake' of her performatives. The context in which her saying becomes a doing is, palpably, the sedimented history of homophobia – a context of prohibition that she resists and mocks and mimes. The dust of gender binaries never settles. Even an imaginary mirror hanging in a make-believe room reflects back to Shaw more than what she herself constructs: the gender structuring whose iterations are as binding as her ace bandages. Hence her next act of binding is of her hands, in boxer's gauze, an action that culminates in fast feints and head rolls. When she ventriloquizes her mother – 'You look just like your father' (2) – she clenches bound fists defensively to her chest, but launches a clean right hook to affirm her genealogy: 'My father told me that his father knocked out Joe Louis with his bare hands' (2). Ultimately Shaw mimes receiving more hits than she dishes out, less from feminists who want her to abandon her dildo, than from the phallic Other whose regulations for 'perverts' might send her to 'sex jail' (12).

So the fighter needs help. While her muscles glimmer auratically in chiaroscuro light, Shaw displays a more complex arsenal of butch resistance: dialectical images that release in the still-lethal homophobia of the 1990s wish images of the 1940s, whose very commodification increases their value as stimulants to collective memory. Shaw walks to her suitcase and removes the uniform of an army-enlisted man from World War II. Pressed in cleaner's cardboard, the uniform and the act of dressing provoke a very different monologue:

> My mother used to make me things from cardboard all taped together like houses. She used the cardboard from my father's Sunday shirts from the Chinese laundry.
>
> (5)

Eroticized in their starched stiffness, the father's clothes are talismanic pieces of pleasure exchanged between daughter and mother, and as Shaw dons the remembered shirt, she narrates/ventriloquizes her mother:

She caught me at the kitchen table at 5 years old drawing a picture of a woman tied to a tree with her hands behind her and her breasts were naked and I drew a woman kissing her breasts. My mother watched me closely from then on and made sure I didn't have girlfriends for too long . . . [puts her dukes up]. She said I'd go to hell if I didn't get married.

(5)

The audience laughs through these lines, as mother's attempts at passing down gender norms are delivered while Shaw calmly buttons the paternal army shirt. As she shakes out the starched military pants and draws our eyes to her boxer shorts and her private's privates, she comments drolly, 'I liked other people's mothers . . .' (5), and so on, confiding in and playfully titillating the audience, until finishing with the soft triangular army hat, she stands in what might have been anyone's father's uniform whilst articulating her mother's lines and life.

In the dialectical image of the soldier, Shaw brings camp theatricality and butch stylistics into mimetic relation with a romanticized image of state power. The romanticization is surely undeniable. World War II was the USA's happiest war, immortalized in scores of war movies, musicals, and famous photographs, not to mention untold numbers of black-and-white family snapshots in the drawers of our ageing parents. After the Depression, World War II was the defining moment of Shaw's parents' generation, even as the baby boomers of Shaw's generation ushered in the conspicuous consumption and cold-war conservatism of the 1950s. In the soft glow of theatrical lighting, with hands thrust in pockets and head cocked jauntily, Shaw moves from drag embodiment to auratic image, exuding the magical cult-value Benjamin found in the artwork before mechanical reproduction: its unapproachableness, its distance, its experiential density. With the laser accuracy of the practiced drag performer Shaw lovingly inhabits, and mockingly frames for critique, her GI-typical guy.[68]

Dialectical images are not nostalgic, nor are they one more addition to the fetish-commodity junkheap. If Shaw's drag is deliciously successful, we never forget the ace-bandage wrapping underneath, the signifier of a certain kind of lesbian desire whose meanings are created not by the heteronormative gaze, but by the recognition of another lesbian – a femme – who, as Joan Nestle puts it, appreciates a butch's 'willingness to announce [herself] as a tabooed woman by wearing clothes that symbolize the taking of responsibility . . . [of] sexual expertise.'[69] Nestle goes on, 'in the 1950s this courage to feel comfortable with arousing another woman became a political act . . .' (101). In Shaw's lesbian address, and in the intensity of its reception by those who recognize its meanings, the auratic image of the soldier is both displaced and powerfully enhanced. That is, while we see Peggy Shaw appropriating the icons of male mastery and power, the same appropriation dialectically releases the opposite, *political* story. It's when Shaw eases her frame into pressed and starched Army khaki that the brutality of homophobia emerges as clearly as the earsplitting bells that punctuate sections of the performance. Symbol and index of state power, the uniform marks the military's forced conformity ('Don't ask. Don't tell') through which homophobia is not simply tolerated, but protected.

But that the state is homophobic comes as no surprise. The politics in the style is released when, as she stands 'at ease,' it's her mother's homophobic and fearful pronouncements, not a sergeant's orders, that Shaw barks out:

> My mother said, 'You'll go to hell if you keep this up.'
> My mother said, 'You'll die if you run into the street.'
> My mother said, 'If you bowl on Sunday, you'll go to hell.'

(6)

Reading the dialectical image is never simple or unambiguous. The 'bandages' underneath the softly lit army shirt speak not just to Shaw's willed resignifications but to the wounding of the gender binary – and this reaches beyond the persona of Peggy Shaw to embrace her mother and 'the historical experience of women.' As the phallic aura of the soldier is smashed, given a shock through its lesbian embodiment and the remembered fragments of her mother's language, its romantic and repressive history collide and flash before our eyes, exposing the historical continuum of patriarchy and gender normativity that continues unabated, if more intensively contested, today. In dialectical images, Benjamin's historical materialist (here Peggy Shaw) takes a 'tiger's leap into the past' (to her 'pre-history' in the 1940s) to blast open the continuist narrative that drives our sense of the present.[70] Had she chosen to be Rosie the Riveter, she would have given us bourgeois historicism in a feminist key: dispossessed female, past and present. By filling out to airbrushed perfection the contours of the manly hero, s/he foregrounds instead her own impossibility – and not just in military culture.

The uniform, a metaphoric border crossing, takes Shaw, in story, to a 'real' border at which gender logics are hollowed out and reaffirmed through classic drag impersonations. Shaw and her drag queen companion have to cross 'back' to cross over – the male queen, dressing butch, borrows Shaw's suitcase filled with suits, ties, letters to girls; Shaw, dressing femme, borrows the friend's dresses, high heels, and poems to boys: 'they passed us through as normal' (6). But Shaw pushes the border in a different sense, raising the stakes in sexual transgression: 'I didn't have my gun. And I didn't have my dildo. Packing, I call it, in both cases' (6). But with deliberate and witty perversity, she carries the gun but 'keep[s] the dildo in my drawers with my neatly folded white boxer shorts . . . I don't use it. I'm not dangerous . . . . You could even trust me with your wife if you wanted to [eyebrow ripple]' (6). In expropriating (smashing) the male soldier's aura, Shaw opens all erotic channels, diverting the energies of countless pulp fictions about soldiers and lonely women into 'unspeakable' lesbian scenes. The 'historical experience' of many women suddenly gets spoken, experienced – albeit in a much mediated way.

Still in uniform Shaw adds another auratic memory to her image-constellation: an anecdote about a health worker who told Shaw she had a 'beautiful cervix' in spite of fibroids ('barnacles, as I call them,' 7) covering it. Putting in relation the memory of the feminist health movement of the 1970s (few women of a certain age have not discussed their cervix in an alternative clinic somewhere in the US) and the masculine pride of the US army, Shaw gestures toward her mother. She tenderly, without explanation, makes sugar bundles out of kleenex as her mother once did. Health worker, mother, Shaw – is this female community being remade across the body? If so, this isn't quite the mythic pre-symbolic body championed by so-called 'cultural feminism.'[71] Shaw's nonidentical similars – barnacles/fibroids; 'beautiful cervix'/male erotics; mother/sugar bundles; lesbian/mother/GI/health worker – produce a dialectical image based in private recollection and *exoteric* experience across different temporalities. The ambivalence of the soldier image (both homophobic and empowering) is answered by the multivalence of the image of female community, especially when, in another story-fragment, Shaw constellates herself with Pele the volcano goddess – her one image drawn from 'mother nature.' This mimesis is deliberately comic. Woman and volcano share not transcendent female power, but high blood pressure.

'You're Just Like My Father' is a citation: what disgruntled co-workers told Shaw when she was too assertive. 'So I decided to explore that and ended up writing about my mother.'[72] Walter Benjamin, a 'normal' heterosexual fetishist, cannot help us with Shaw's mother, but Shaw's amazing performance piece, with a little help from Teresa de Lauretis, will lead us back to dialectical images in a powerful way. Moving through father to end up with mother seems a comfortable feminist narrative, but performance theory (not to mention Shaw's sexuality) helpfully constructs obstacles. Performance, we noted, operates in a visual field that historically and culturally has been dominated by the phallic gaze – that is, from infancy we are trained to look through the lens of sexual difference; parents, teachers, and especially the media reinforce the familiar binarisms masculine–feminine, active–passive, penis–lack of penis.

Where is the mother ('s desire) in this schema? Deeply repressed . . . therefore 'spectral,' always returning.[73] In the visual regime described by psychoanalysis, all female bodies are sites of lack, but the mother's body is the originary, terrifying site, inspiring in the little boy horror, but also desire. Representation itself, this story goes, follows from lack; re-presentation is the desire to *see* (what was missing) and brings the concomitant alluring frustration that, in Lacan's words, 'what I look at is never what I wish to see.'[74] Feminist theater and performance art have worked to displace the see-er/knower position engrailed in the realist plot and in the conventional proscenium-view *mise-en-scène*.[75] Feminist psychoanalytic theory, in its turn, has sought to rescue the pre-oedipal mother–child dyad, on whose elision, in both Freud and Lacan, psychic health depends. In a much-cited debate in film theory, the entire structure of castration, hence representation, is called into question, 'inverted,' with the suggestion that the mother, instead of being the object of the boy's look, looks back.[76] As we noted in Chapter 2, one of the uses of Brechtian theory for feminist theory is precisely this return of gaze: the actor looking back at the spectator dispels the fetish structure in phallic representation. Speaking of the mother, Barbara Freedman argues that her return of gaze

> in essence reconstruct[s] the woman's gaze. The mother's body is [after all] at once the material out of which a spectacle is constructed, the spectacle itself, and the means by which a spectator is constructed. To return the look in this context is to break up performance space . . . subvert the classical organization of showing and seeing, revision spectatorship . . . .
>
> (69)

In Shaw's performance piece, the mother is hardly a passive object: 'my mother who loved me in the house. . . . My mother used to watch me getting dressed. I used to let myself take forever getting dressed' (2, 13). If the mother ventriloquizes patriarchal theology ('You're going to hell because of the way you dress,' 17), if she acts the role of crazy 1950s housewife ('. . . this was my mother before they destroyed her,' 2) and was too working class for Betty Friedan's feminism to reclaim, she is also Shaw's companion in discovery: 'My mother loved me, she *recognized* me' (14). In effect Shaw's persona and her mother rewrite feminine lack and produce a different kind of looking – a looking that has left the house for the exoteric arena of theatrical performance. Shaw's contribution to feminist theory is her configuring of desire through and with her mother while avoiding the fantasy of a pre-oedipal – and thus asexual – mother–child dyad – a problematic formulation for many feminists since it reduces female sexuality to the maternal function and erases women's very different political histories and struggles.[77]

What de Lauretis dislikes about the mother–child dyad as a basis of lesbian sexuality is that while it circumvents phallic law, it is *for that reason*, not sexual – not adult, active, genital. This, she reasons, is no improvement on psychoanalytic doxa that says lesbian desire is merely imitative of heterosexual models, and that lesbians suffer from a 'masculinity complex.'[78] Taking Freudian theory as still the best means of theorizing 'perverse desire,' de Lauretis refuses the tactic of many feminists, to discount the Oedipus complex and the theory of castration. Castration alone, de Lauretis argues, triggers desire.[79] To disavow castration is to lose the psychic mechanisms of active adult sexuality, not to mention access to subjectivity. In Freudian doxa, however, the castration complex results in awarding desire only to the boy (with the penis that's threatened); the girl 'already castrated' can, in Mary Ann Doane's terms, only 'desire to desire.'[80] So de Lauretis gives the girl her very own castration wound – loss of erotic attachment to the mother – and thus gives the grown-up girl a desire stemming from her disavowal of that wound, a desire that, like masculine desire, is enhanced and displaced by a fetish.[81] Again de Lauretis must intervene, since in classical Freudian theory fetishes are penis-substitutes. De Lauretis argues that the lesbian fetish is not a substitute penis, but a substitutive fantasy. Lesbian desire, de Lauretis hypothesizes, 'is sustained on fantasy scenarios that restage [through fetish objects] the loss and recovery of the female body' (265).

De Lauretis's argument, the complexity of which I can hardly do justice to in a paragraph, provides an intertext to Shaw's piece – and I mean intertext seriously: I understand de Lauretis's theorizing and Shaw's performance as cultural 'texts' whose significations are mutually suggestive. Certainly de Lauretis's description of the fetish helps account for the auratic beauty of Shaw's incarnations as GI and crooner-seducer, and as libidinal singer of James Brown, Elvis, Julio Iglesias, and Fats Domino songs. The reason (if I may say so) that one of her reviewers gushed, 'Shaw seems to transcend gender,'[82] is that her mimesis (making herself similar) so thoroughly upstages the One (identity) of phallic law. The clothes, songs, styles of Shaw's persona are her fetishes – fantasy signs that announce *her* mode of active desiring, not a replication of a model-male. That she borrows masculine signifiers is, for de Lauretis, perfectly logical: 'in a cultural tradition pervasively homophobic, [signs of] masculinity carr[y] a strong connotation of sexual desire for the female body' (243).

What Shaw adds to de Lauretis is the persistence of an always-eccentric maternal function in the schema of fantasy and representation. In Shaw's performance, each favorite fetish is related back to the mother's desire – not to reclaim an imaginary dyadic plenitude, but as further stimulus to her own desire. This in turn draws out the complexity of the mother's sexual agency: in her daughter she 'recognize(s)' a (per)version of the phallus that she can both reject and adore. Shaw describes the triangulation that galvanized their erotic pairing:

> My mother used to watch me getting dressed.
> I used to let myself take forever getting dressed.
> My mother watched me.
> She loved me, my mother
> She recognized me.
> 'You look just like your father,' she said.
> I put on a starched shirt
> And I was my father.

> (13–14)

The fetish power of the father's shirt ('stiff and rectangular'; 'I put on my starched shirt / And I *was* my father') is activated by the mother's watching (which in turn cues the daughter's slow sartorial performance). Indeed Shaw *animates* the mother's desiring gaze by situating it, carefully and consistently, in the spectator's position. Throughout the performance Shaw dresses to an imaginary mirror, showing the audience her profile as if we, too, were lingering disapprovingly but captivatedly at the daughter's bedroom door. 'I dressed in my mother's memories' (17), says Shaw, and in the now-time of performance we are constellated with the mother, mingling our (nonidentical) memories with hers. Indeed our looking (Shaw claims us as 'witness' to her 'truth,' 10) becomes performative and politically charged: a dialectical image constructed by spectators and performer that brings into collision a profusion of personal temporalities, and brings into dialectical tension the mother's look and the masculine gaze historically inscribed in the performance apparatus. In this moment of shared looking we do not perhaps jam the machinery of representation but we do, momentarily, release the energies of a repressed 'maternal gaze.' And what is this gaze (like)? Certainly nothing like the purported dyadic bliss of pre-oedipal bonding. It is horrifying, familiar, perverse, and cruel. Through the artistry of Peggy Shaw we participate in an irrational bond of loyalty, of enraged desire and love.

INTERLUDE: AUTOEROTICISM[83]

. . . with their Dynaflow pushbutton transmissions, their power brakes, automatic windows, vacuum ashtrays, retractable roofs, and wraparound windshields, the feelings they aroused in driver/owners were straightforward; after the privations of the Depression, after the hardships and the shortages of the war . . . victorious Americans deserved nothing but the best. . . .

Behind the wheel of a 1955 Ford, so the catchphrase went, 'you become a new man.' Buicks were often shown gliding among the planets like garish spacecraft . . . . 'Driving a Buick,' read one memorable line of copy, 'makes you feel like the man you are.'

Karal Ann Marling

The manly symbiosis car and driver is a staple of American mythology. Becoming a 'new man' is the birthright of American citizenship and nothing certified that new identity better (in the 1950s and now) than buying and being seen in a new car. But 'being seen,' the projection of a new image, as important as that was in the language of 'status symbols,' was undergirded by something more authentic and experiential: the transformative power of the touch and feel of 'Dynaflow pushbutton transmissions' and 'retractable roofs.' This is what Karal Ann Marling calls '*emotional* symbiosis,' a concentrated mixture of sexual exultation and social power, that turns a functional commodity into an auratic wish-image.

Of course these automobiles were never merely functional nor were their messages uncomplicated. 'Autoeroticism' in the 1950s was fueled both by fantasies of power and thrust and by the androgynous fetishistic 'gorp' (superfluous embellishments) protruding from the body. 'After 1953, all Cadillac bumpers were finished off with factory-fresh "gorp" . . . in the form of "bombs" or "Dagmars" – protruding breasts that were utterly devoid of utility' but long on fantasy potential.[84] Female in front the Dagmars (named after a 'TV bombshell,' 141) were compared to the look of women's breasts in

Maidenform bras, another favorite 1950s item. The back ends, with their enhanced tail fins, were distinctly male. Indeed by 1959 'the Cadillac tail fin towered three and one-half feet above the pavement and terminated in multiple taillights, nasty fearsome red things, shaped like frozen bursts of flame from the afterburner of a jet engine' (141).[85] These kinds of accoutrements help make sense of Peggy Shaw's fantasy:

> Every time someone hurts me, I want to become famous
> And buy a 1962 Corvette and get all dressed up with a beautiful woman
> Next to me, and drive past them on the street.
> Just so they can catch a glimpse of me and see how happy and successful
> I am.
>
> (12)

Not discounting the importance of a beautiful woman, this fantasy is zip without the car. The car heals. The car transforms. The car defeats the enemy. Moreover, Shaw's transgressive sexuality is powerfully signified – no, flaunted – in her appropriation of the Corvette as fetish. Touted as 'America's sports car,' the 1962 Chevy Corvette was a fast, relatively sleek, convertible two-seater; hence (it announced) *not* for the suburban family.

But whether a sporty cruiser or a gorp-laden behemoth 'larded with primal symbols of war and lust' (147), the American dream car signified more social sexual potency. In it was concentrated the typically American utopian wish of classlessness. Of course the dream car belonged to Jim and Margaret Anderson, in their 'Father Knows Best' TV suburbia, but it also inhabited the worlds of anxious eroto-intellectuals like Nabokov's Humbert Humbert and rock-and-rollers like Chuck Berry – who, while motivatin' over the hill, saw Maybellene in a (Cadillac) Coupe de Ville . . . and pursued her confidently in his V-8 Ford. American 1950s car dealers noticed that members of minority groups who 'were denied the satisfactions of housing and other property commensurate with their incomes, always bought Cadillacs.'[86] Says Robbie McCauley about her father and his love of 'male mythology': 'He wanted a Cadillac more than anything in the world.'[87] And Deb Margolin recalls the moment her father unveiled the '1948 spanking new Plymouth, curving from roof to rear like someone's fat ass, making [my mother] scream. She screamed with happiness.'[88] One kind of feminist critique is easy to anticipate: from the 1949 Motoramas, with dancing showgirls pointing ecstatically at the Cadillac fin, to the advertisements we'll see on television tonight, women's bodies sell the car (metonymically, they *are* the phallus) to men who want the car (metaphorically, they *have* the phallus). Shaw, McCauley, and Margolin choose instead to release the utopian energies of these consummate commodities, albeit in contradictory directions. On the one hand, they annex American automophilia for a *female* imaginary, refiguring the lives of girls and women not in private spaces, but on the erotic dream highways usually reserved for males.[89] On the other hand, their dialectical images (McCauley and Margolin particularly) reconnect 1940s and 1950s American automophilia to fathers, militarism, racism, and capitalism, not just to critique the past but to reveal, in the now-time of performance, the persistent crises of the present.

ROBBIE McCAULEY, *INDIAN BLOOD*⁹⁰

> History not remembered gets told anyway . . .
>
> Robbie McCauley

In Robbie McCauley's *Indian Blood*, the dream highway of upward mobility encounters the geography of racism and dispossession. Her narrative fragments cast back to a father's and grandfather's military service in various US wars and a daughter's effort to rethink the psychic and political costs. Like Shaw's piece, though on a different terrain, *Indian Blood* is a work of historical and political memory. The auratic images of a 'father who was always in some-body's army, navy, air force, national guard' and who 'longed to be a police-man' (18) are given a dialectical 'shock' in the daughter's stories. McCauley moves us back and forth across a landscape of personal memory, which is also, as Benjamin puts it, 'a persistent consciousness of [her] historical existence.'⁹¹ And this experience is inseparable from the bitter aporias of contradiction that are the legacy of race in the US. The father's and grandfather's devotion to and participation in the US military gave them a public means of expressing citizenship, of supporting their families, of achieving a social status otherwise denied them, even as, by their very participation, they helped reproduce the institutional apartheid of the military they served. Charging up San Juan Hill with Teddy Roosevelt's Rough Riders, McCauley Senior served in the All Black Regiment in the Spanish–American war – a war that produced defini-tive US hegemony in Central and South America, and intensified the killing and the expropriation of the culture and land of indigenous populations. 'And always there were the Indian Wars' (2): her grandfather helped ambush Native Americans returning from Canada. While McCauley sees these mili-tary triumphs as service to the racist white supremacy that has destroyed African American life during and since slavery, these accomplishments, duly recorded in her grandfather's discharge papers, save his son's family (barely) from racist attacks in 1950s America. Most excruciating, with the military honors accorded her patriarchs for helping to annihilate the Indians, comes McCauley's recognition that she and her forebears on her paternal grand-mother's side, have 'Indian blood.' Annihilation of the Indians is self-annihi-lation. The shedding of 'Indian blood' signifies not only the brutality of capi-talist expansionism in US history and in McCauley's family history but also the inevitable self-destruction that racism produces, and always disavows.⁹²

I have been arguing that the feminist performance art discussed in this chapter presents an exoteric subjectivity, produced in the discourses of history and sexuality. Feminist performance makes those discourses sentient, palpable, fueled by the desire to alienate, thus to *imagine anew* our present moment. Again, I am assuming a postmodern feminism, by which I mean that the truth of women's experiences is mediated by the discourses that give it voice, discourses not only of unstable signification but that contain multiple identifications and multiple temporalities, all complicating the subject's position. I noted that storytelling in performance 'decomposes' into dialectical images, embodied constructions that allow glimmers of 'historical experience' to emerge. The dialectical images of feminist performers engage with dominant cultural ephemera; they are complex mimetic productions because the unique otherness – the auratic presence – of the performer is engaged in their creation. This means that the shock of the image is precisely the sexual or political transgression that that embodiment produces. I said that the auratic body is both instantiated and displaced in the production of the image; instantiated because in its unicity and otherness it generates a whole series of interrelations and correspondences; displaced because that body-image is suddenly apprehended as constellated pieces of disparate experience whose temporary cohesion brings to view, for a moment, a world of inaccessible past experiences. These unleashed experiences provoke us to break through 'the illusory appearance [under capitalism] of the always-the-same [eternal same],' to read our own moments with heightened awareness, renewed vigor.[93]

The multiple temporalities of memory, history, and embodiment are laid bare in McCauley's opening moments of *Indian Blood*, an 'opening' that, in the traditions of experimental theater since the 1960s, she makes spatially indeterminate. As the audience take their seats, the McCauley persona is in our walkway cutting apples, munching a sandwich, watching us, nodding, being watched. The musicians, a pianist/singer, a clarinetist/saxophonist, and a guitarist, who will improvise on a score ranging from free jazz to soul to banjo picking, begin to play and McCauley removes the apples. She stretches and, almost as an afterthought, as though the mode of address between herself and her spectators had not yet been settled, announces:

> Sometimes I think that if I could get my body free, I could be free. 'Course that's not the way it is. A regular old socialist can tell you that one can't be free till all are free.
>
> (1)

This wishful mimesis between the one and the all, the promise of American democracy, and its inevitable disappointment in American life, generates mimetic correspondences throughout *Indian Blood*, between fragments of McCauley's life and patterns of social and political oppression. The young Robbie's journey into 'white people's territory' in rural Georgia to buy some coveted strawberry bubblegum is a replay of her grandparents' forced migration from Fort Bening, Georgia, and her own family's migration from Georgia to Washington DC. These journeys mime each other, particularly in the encounter of white and black – the strangeness of these encounters, and the strangeness of their strangeness. This is marked specifically when McCauley invokes a child's voice to recall the mutuality of poverty and constraint suffered by both races in the early 1950s.

> Po' white folks we automatically called crackers and they us niggers. They
> lived down past Mr. Reddick's store. We automatically got along for what
> was necessary. Me and my sister would take notes to Mr. Reddick and read
> 'em to him since he couldn't read and Grandma Willie said it was just
> 'cause po' white people wasn't educated. I played with his daughter Sheila
> and Martha Faye when I was real small. I even taught Martha Faye how
> to read. But after we got to be ten, everybody knew you just said how d'ya
> do to the white folks, do business, or nothing.
>
>   (6)

The 'eternal same' for Benjamin of commoditized, routinized experience is
here the eternal same of racism. Both are dependent upon mythic thinking:
'we *automatically* called them crackers'; and '*everybody knew* . . .' (my italics). This
is the cultural discourse that precedes, surrounds, and awaits the girls Robbie
and Martha Faye, who spend a few uncoerced moments in early childhood
bent over the same book.

It is the routinization of racism, its sedimented history that *shocks* McCauley:
the 'big invisible thing, tight people, tiny streams of light and hidden terror.'[94]
Racism produces 'shock' experience for McCauley no less forcefully than the
jostling urban masses did for Benjamin's Baudelaire. In its obsession with history
and experience McCauley's work in fact recalls that of a cultural other, Walter
Benjamin. Linked in broad strokes by their Marxist critique of capitalism, it's in
their elaborations – the notion of shock experience, for example – that the links
are palpable. Benjamin has been criticized for an interpretation of history wed-
ded to an idea of perpetual catastrophe: 'Catastrophe is not what threatens to
occur at any given moment but what is given at any given moment.'[95] Yet no
statement more clearly speaks to the devastations of racism for McCauley. Its
'hidden terror,' as much as overt attack, is our American catastrophe, which only
habit, disavowal, and life-preserving instincts prevent us from naming as such.

Materialist analysis is one such life-preserving instinct. For McCauley, the
historical systemic roots of racism breed the ubiquitous wars her military patriarchs fought (wars – and honorable service that did nothing to alter racism
either in or out of the service). For the Marxist McCauley all wars are imperialist, especially the Indian wars, whose expropriations of land and life mark
her life experiences ('It took me years to figure out reasons for Daddy's anger,'
13), and extend beyond her conscious experience, as in this dialectical image
of linear time and perpetual catastrophe:

> I was born in 1942 when the war was very new
> and now the war is over I am four years old . . .
> I was born in 1952 when the war was very new
> and now the war is over I am ten years old . . .
> I was born in 1962 when the war was very new
> and now the war is over I am twenty years old . . .

I was born in 1972 when the war was very new
and now the war is over I am thirty years old . . .
I was born in 1982 when the war was very new
and now the war is over I am forty years old . . .
I was born in 1992 when the war was very new
and now the war is over I am fifty years old . . .
I was born in 2002 when the war was very new . . .

(1)

McCauley's life history is splayed across a bloody calendar whose blood never dries. Her life history exceeds her life, and that too has been a guiding principle: 'I wanted to do a kind of theater I felt I remembered from before I was born.'[96] As noted earlier, Benjamin thought of the now-diminished mimetic faculty in human beings in reference to an archaic world governed by 'the law of similarity . . . in macrocosm and microcosm,' in which correspondences were newly inscribed in the moment of every child's birth: 'it is not difficult to imagine that the newborn child was thought to be in full possession of this gift [of seeing correspondences], and to be molded on the structure of cosmic being.'[97] For McCauley, the mold of the late twentieth-century cosmos is set by war-times and her decades are locked into correspondence with them. Like Benjamin's storyteller, McCauley tells stories and tells history as interwoven exercises. But what stories and how to tell them?

I told you about San Juan Hill like Grandfather was some kind of hero. I said he went up that hill and talked it over with his Indian brothers, that he apologized for taking their land to give to the Americans . . . that Grandfather and 'em were just doing their job in order to survive. Well history not remembered gets told anyway.

(4)

'History not remembered . . . .' McCauley rejects the historical continuum as vehemently as Walter Benjamin does. It's the history not remembered or consciously experienced, one that emanates from another kind of memory, that McCauley summons/performs. In 'On Some Motifs in Baudelaire,' Benjamin called this memory, after Proust, '*mémoire involuntaire*' (160). Benjamin drew on Freud's distinction between memory and consciousness in *Beyond the Pleasure Principle*, in which memory traces are 'often most powerful and most endurable when the incident which left them behind was one that never entered consciousness' (160). Consciousness, then, 'receives no memory traces' but serves rather to protect against stimuli (161). Shock effects, the *experience* of racist encounters, for example, are not captured in consciously recorded incidents – or not solely. As Benjamin puts it:

The greater the share of the shock factor in particular impressions, the more constantly consciousness has to be alert as a screen against stimuli; the more efficiently it does so, the less do these impressions enter experience (*Erfahrung*), tending to remain in the sphere of a certain hour in one's life (*Erlebnis*).

(163)

In her 'history not remembered,' McCauley follows Benjamin and Proust in demonstrating that voluntary memory – memory at the service of consciousness or intellect, whose function is to filter out disturbing memory traces – always falls short. It is only experience as it arises *involuntarily*, through mimetic associations, through unguarded correspondences, that can deliver the meaning of unremembered shocks. It's the historical richness of experience, of history *as* experience, that McCauley longs for. Certainly she depends on conscious memory to parry the shocks of racist encounters ('I should get a more material perspective on this'[98]), but more often her performance text prowls the warzone of memory traces, recording 'memories' that will not sit still 'in a certain hour of one's life' but break into her present moment, producing a *Jetzeit.*

Africa! My Father! Memory of chains!

(11)

I remember seeing chain gang trucks down in Georgia. Black men in prison clothes huddled down. White men standing with a gun. I remember the [military] convoy trucks too. Black men in fatigues up inside. I used to get the chain gang trucks and the convoy trucks mixed up. I used to run 'longside looking for my Daddy. Everyone said he was off in somebody's war when I was born.

(19)

In Freud's text, Benjamin finds that a 'sensation of fright . . . confirms the failure of the shock defense' (163). Invoking a complex loved father is, for McCauley, a destructive act; to seize hold of his memory is to find herself again in a moment of danger. A disciplined performer, McCauley pushes her voice into dissonant scat-singing, clutches her head, wrings her hands, explodes in rage, whirls, collapses. In the rush of images above, truck miming truck, 'Daddy' is not the performer's madeleine but rather seeking him (again and again) is. And in this angry memorial, she, like all desirers, seeks him ('run[ing] 'longside') where she can never find him: in his 'male mythology' of hard-drinking, chainsmoking homosocial heroism, his world of uniforms, guns, honorable discharge papers, and American pride. 'He loved America!' she shouts (13).

To redeem that love (as his legacy) is to *recognize* its dialectical pain: the strength and self-betrayal that underpin loyalty to America's government and institutions. It also means, with the fluid mimetic connection between word and body, to assume that pain:

Heavy breathing, quick breath just like my father . . .
I'm obsessing just like my father. If Daddy could've obsessed in public who knows? . . . I was never quite sure if it was myself or him who judged the

world so, so determined to fix it. But I am sure it was him. He was here
first. I would have loved to have been more carefree . . .

(11)

To redeem, to recognize, her father also means to explore his pain in images
that, as Benjamin puts it in his 'Theses on the Philosophy of History,' 'wrest
tradition away from a conformism that is about to overpower it' (255). Here
the conformism lies not in military protocol but in the exemplary narrative of
African American service and sacrifice to the United States (which, like the
chain gangs, another form of unfree labor, continues the structures of slavery
by other means). Exemplary narratives, instead of offering pieces of usable
exoteric experience, occur in the 'homogeneous, empty time' (261) of the
historical continuum in which the oppressors never change. McCauley wants
to wrest nonbourgeois traditions of black survival – visionary politics, ingenuity, wit, artmaking, spirituality, community awareness – away from the
old/new modes of mythic thinking. She like Benjamin refuses to endorse a
progress fantasy that tolerates so much suffering. Her particular dialectical
pain is that such black traditions are also home traditions, and for McCauley
that hollow narrative of progress is also parental, part of the home history
lessons of a daddy who drew heroic maps for his children across the bedcov-
ers. Like the historical materialist in Benjamin's 'Theses,' she needs to 'make
the continuum of history explode' (261), to insist on telling the story differently, not to preserve the traditions, but to transform them.

McCauley's techniques of transformation – images and music – display the
history of experimental theater in the twentieth century. Full-sized projections
are expanded images from historical documents, private and public – of the
Middle Passage, of meetings between early American colonists and Indian
tribes; of her father in uniform, of the black regiment under Teddy Roosevelt,
of the young McCauley and Daddy leaning against the family Buick.
'For every image of the past that is not recognized by the present as one of
its own concerns,' wrote Benjamin in his 'Theses,' 'threatens to disappear irretrievably' (255). The images of public and private documents, evanescently
projected, document McCauley's effort to expand experience through historical memory – through memories that we cannot consciously remember. The
projections, then, are also projections in the psychic sense, flickering pieces of
internal trauma that await their redemption: 'I turn around,' says McCauley,
'and there they are' (11) (a daguerrotype of the black regiment suddenly
appears).

McCauley's performance makes clear that her redemption of these unsung
heroes has nothing to do with what is officially remembered; she will not and
cannot narrativize the fragments of memory that these images convey. Instead
she offers us glimpses and tries to catch us off guard. Moving between two
microphones that establish the key playing spaces, McCauley's words, both
spoken and scat-sung, pointedly mime the dissonance of one of the musicians'
jazz phrasing –

When we moved *up*-south-to *D-C* it was the stran-*gest* a-part-*theid town* . . .

– a syncopation that, as Brecht wanted, alienates the line's disturbing content. Such A-effects in turn open the spectator to the social vista of black culture's (particularly jazz's) commodification as well as its continuity as a source of communal inspiration. To give it the appropriate dialectical turn, a Marxist homily needs to be sung *and* swung:

Ra-ci-sm is based on class, is *caste* biased, *is* class, *is* class, *is* cla-ss biased . . .

But in this instance she can't keep up her part in a jazz improvisation. She speeds up, blurs the words till one of the musicians summons her back. Far from sugarcoating the message, the music intensifies its strangeness.

In the black political and cultural traditions of the twentieth century, deepened in the post-civil rights era, the counterhegemonic story to systemic racism has been that of race-based identity – a position that has been as community binding as it has been contested and divisive. If McCauley would reject the concept of essential blackness as ahistorical, she would also find unhelpful any formalism in which an artwork's value as symbolic form is held to be distinct from theme and political resonances. And she would want to query the root cause of 'blackness' – not simply attributing it to racial pride but to what Sandra Richards has called the 'radioactive terrain' of the racialized gaze for both blacks and whites, both in the theater and in the streets.[99] Richards observes that when philosopher Anthony Appiah enlisted W.E.B. Du Bois to discuss race as a socio-historical not a biological category, the protest of black critics reflected personal hurt: 'it [was] as though a family member ha[d] dared to desecrate the lines of lineage' (45–46).[100] Further, Richards argues, for both black and white critics, deconstructing the 'metaphysics of substance' seems to stall around race, or 'more properly stated . . . [around] visible difference in skin color' (47).

McCauley's contribution to these issues is expressly to solicit and bring into mimetic relation the 'radioactivity' of the racialized gaze *and* the pained reactivity of 'family' discourse in order to lay bare and transform them. To do this she summons the auratic power of the performer's body to create a dialectical image of extraordinary complexity. Having established from the outset an experimental Brechtian style for her piece, she, like Peggy Shaw, dons army gear and comments on the problematic of survival. Miming her grandfather, she stands at attention with her gun-prop raised:

The blood was everywhere
Grandfather took a deep breath.
He'd got one more Indian
Now he was alone with his thoughts and a smoking gun
[Speaking loudly in the voice of her grandfather]
'To be on guard like this is a great opportunity for a colored man.'
[Returns to her own voice]

Grandfather was a Father Courage with the paradoxes of parents who
lead their tribe through the wars.
[She sits and slowly removes the Army coat from her shoulders and
resumes her narrative tone]:
It was my grandmother P's grandmother who had Indian blood. Actually
they said she was half Indian. That's what they said when one of the parents was a full blooded Indian and one was real black . . . she was a full
blooded half-blood [McCauley rolls her eyes] . . . and they said that everyone down that line on that side was 1/2 Indian. They used to tell me *I* had
Indian blood [she opens her arms to audience], that I had orange under-
tones to my skin, that I looked good in green . . . [audience laughs ner-
vously].

(9)

Gently mocking family and folk rhetoric on bloodlines, McCauley helps us
produce her dialectical image. Having gazed with detached interest at old photographic reproductions of Indian tribes, our eyes are suddenly riveted on the
body that brings those images 'to life,' a body no longer instantiating the racial
'substance' we had taken for granted. What really do we see? orange under-
tones? 'mixed' blood? Is this a 'black' woman?

The transformation of auratic body into dialectical image shocks our
consciousness. Just as Peggy Shaw positions us to be her desiring mother
(thereby producing a witness to her performance as lesbian), McCauley, by dis-
playing her body as auratic object, subtly causes us to racialize her, to identify
(and *fail* to identify her) by race. Which means we all take a tiger's leap into
the past. We suddenly glimpse the performer's body not as unique, separate,
esoteric, but constellated with an unknown black woman on an auction block,
a site where blood and skin once spoke with perfect clarity to those invested
in maintaining racial markings.[101] It's that one drop of 'black blood' in seven
that seals the fate of Dion Boucicault's *Octoroon* (1859), and indeed blood and
skin are still speaking, are still being 'told' -- as our spontaneous attempt to
'really' *see* this performer's 'blackness' or lack of it, proves -- though the history is not 'remembered.' As a performer McCauley makes this knowledge possible: she *reveals* it as an image. In Irving Wohlfarth's words, 'it is only when
the self-identical subject opens up that the non-identical image arises.'[102]

By constructing the body through gesture and language as a dialectical
image McCauley announces the lie of bloodlines. As the video monitors
explain and scramble a story of the Middle Passage she announces, 'these confessions are . . . a kind of mourning for the lost connections' (9). But if *Indian
Blood* destroys the notion of lineal purity, its dialectical images forge other connections. They release the utopian energies contained in the very mythogra-
phy she critiques. In one of the 'teacher' narratives on a video monitor, those
energies cluster around a utopian fantasy of nonhierarchical community. 'The
first settlement,' says the teacher with comic self-importance, 'was *not* in 1620,
but in 1526 . . . . It was made up of runaway slaves and Indians who moved

into the interior of South Carolina and started the first settlement.' McCauley is limning a complex history. As racial others in the new America, Africans, enslaved and free, and Indians suffered similar oppressions, if not similar fates. Numerous accounts describe runaway slaves in the company of Indians.[103] And in the 1960s, McCauley's own moment of political and artistic awakening, a black–Indian alliance was forged in the crucible of racism when the American Indian Movement (AIM) and the Black Panthers both become targets of FBI surveillance.

McCauley yearns for communities forged in suffering and historical-political consciousness. 'Blood-lineage' narratives too easily redound to myth, and like any idealist historiography must be 'read against the grain.' In her dialectical images McCauley redeems African American suffering within the complex weave of historical experience. In the closing moments of the performance, McCauley opens for the first time that battered suitcase that has come to signify her 'full-blooded half-blood' great-grandmother. As the music grows loud and cacophonous she reads from a sheaf of yellowed government documents the official commendation to her grandfather for helping to exterminate the Indians. The soldier's achievement is dialectically intertwined with the extinction of his ancestral family. In a reprise of the moment described above, McCauley shouts: 'They say I have Indian blood, well I think I have it on my hands!' (22). Shaking her head the performer reaches out for the catharsis. But for the spectator the transformation of auratic body into dialectical image has offered another pleasure, that of experiencing 'historical existence': the relief of awakening.

DEB MARGOLIN, *CARTHIEVES! JOYRIDES!*[104]

> Adventure stows away inside of failure.
>
> Deb Margolin

In Irigaray's theorizing, submission to the masculine imaginary is the structural fate of women. This is mimesis on the phallic model of the 'one of form,' in which woman, as mirror, reflects an image not only of constitutive lack but of envy of his penile authority. Irigaray calls this 'mimesis imposed' and answers this harsh imposition in two ways, both of which relate interestingly to Benjamin and to the performance artist Deb Margolin. The first Irigarayan response is, famously, the 'two lips' (in '*Quand nos lèvres se parlent*') – an image of contiguity and similarity that is constitutively nonhierarchical and nonviolent:

> How can I say it differently? We exist only as two? We live by twos beyond all mirages, images, and mirrors. Between us, one is not the 'real' and the other her imitation; one is not the original and the other her copy. Although we can dissimulate perfectly within their [masculine] economy, we relate to one another without simulacrum. Our resemblance does without semblances . . .[105]

What Irigaray calls the patriarchal symbolic would be, for Benjamin, the rule of the abstract concept that casts its net over the world of experiential particulars. Benjamin's version of mimesis, as we have noted, unmakes, completely alters the self-mirroring Platonic 'I' of 'mimesis imposed.' To press close to the object, stripping it of the effects of its commodified shell, is not to master or subsume, but to transform and be transformed. Irigaray's 'our resemblance does without semblances' recalls Benjamin's insistence that mimetic acts are not limited to visual resemblance, but 'pass from eye to lip and take a detour across the entire body'[106] as when children imitate windmills and trains. The 'similar' in Benjamin suggests the possibility of 'liv[ing] by twos, beyond mirages, images, mirrors.'

Irigaray's second response to 'mimesis imposed' is articulated in 'The Powers of Discourse' in which she proposes a '*mimétisme*,' an act of deliberate submission to phallic-symbolic categories in order to expose them:

> To play with mimesis is thus, for a woman, to try to recover the place of her exploitation by discourse, without allowing her to be simply reduced to it. It means to resubmit herself – inasmuch as she is on the side of the 'perceptible,' of 'matter' – to 'ideas,' in particular to ideas about herself, that are elaborated in/by a masculine logic, but so as to make 'visible,' by an effect of playful repetition [mimicry, *mimétisme*] what was supposed to remain invisible: the cover-up of a possible operation of the feminine in language. It also means to 'unveil' the fact that, if women are such good mimics it is because they are not simply resorbed in this function. *They also remain elsewhere.*[107]

Like the neoromantic traces in Benjamin's notion of the natural correspondences, which draw charges of mysticism, Irigaray's 'feminine in language' draws the charge of ahistorical essentialism. Like Benjamin's *Jetztzeit*, Irigaray's roughly analogous 'elsewhere' has been labeled negatively as utopian, rather than politically engaged, thinking. These criticisms are understandable but I think beside the point. Whatever their provenance (Jewish Messianism; 'the divine') I read *Jetztzeit* and 'elsewhere,' as productive metaphors: image-constructions designed to 'jam the machinery' of patriarchal reproduction (Irigaray), of the continuum of bourgeois history (Benjamin), in order to image what we cannot as yet perform given political and social mechanisms at hand. Marxism's mystification of 'progress' (Benjamin), Marxist 'monosexual' economic paradigms (Irigaray), reproduce the very constraints that make real contestation impossible. This doesn't mean, however, that change is impossible. Indeed Irigaray's 'elsewhere,' which seemed so apolitical in the 1970s, makes sense if we read it in connection with Benjamin's now-time: as an anti-historicist image *that requires historical agents to fulfill.* That is, both Irigaray and Benjamin share the belief that, as Susan Buck-Morss so eloquently puts it, the 'present course of events does not exhaust reality's potential.'[108]

Irigaray's *mimétisme* has been annexed rather reductively to parody, a kind of subversive copying. Judith Butler shrewdly defuses this presumptive subversion: to mime is to participate in what is mimed. Irigaray's 'possible operation of the feminine in language' thus becomes 'radically implicated in the very terms of a phallogocentrism it seeks to rework.'[109] Benjaminian dialectics might contribute here. First, it would embrace Butler's 'radical implication'; there is always a 'dialectical intertwinement' in any critical operation, an inter-implication of terms or positions that appear to be antithetical. Second, Benjamin would tease out what Butler takes for granted; in Irigaray's '*possible* operation of the feminine' one reads an invitation to consider the socio-symbolic processes that prevent its emergence. If we place Irigaray's *mimétisme* near to Benjamin's mimesis, the latter working as the experiential mortar in the production of shock-producing dialectical images, the subversive element in *mimétisme* can be understood. '[T]o recover the place of her exploitation by discourse, without [being] simply reduced to it'[110] is to display a *nonidentical* similarity to the other, whereas patriarchal culture sees only 'the one of form.'

Conversely, Irigaray interrupts the conventional gender assumptions in Benjamin's texts with a powerful network of sexually specific tropes and images – of which the 'possible operation of the feminine in language' resonates most interestingly. As noted earlier, Benjamin imagined a prelapsarian language rooted in nature and fundamentally mimetic; experience was inseparable from the human capacity to produce and recognize similarities – between humans and natural others, between words and things. In its 'fallen' state, the linguistic sign, albeit 'nonsensuous,' retains the sensuous (embodied) trace of those imagined natural correspondences: the semiotic is the 'bearer' of forgotten experiences. Like the dialectical image itself, the mimetic element of the word 'flashes up' in the now-time of perception. To borrow Margolin's figure, the sensuous trace 'stows away' inside the word, which is not unlike Irigaray's figure of the 'maternal-feminine' which stows away inside the patriarchal symbolic. Benjamin's 'trace' is similar to Irigaray's 'residue,' the experiential, embodied remainder of what is extruded in our conceptualizing, and thus (for Irigaray at least) that which makes our conceptualizing possible.[111]

The trace, the residue are implied in Naomi Schor's discussion of Irigaray, which will help to frame the novelty of Deb Margolin's performance work. We noted in Chapter 1 the way in which Irigaray's mimesis-mimicry tropes the phallic mirror by calling on the material apparatus of the theater – and used this to challenge the summary dismissal of her work as essentialist. On the question of mimesis Naomi Schor extends those possibilities. There is mimesis and mimesis-mimicry, and then, what she calls (in a Nietzschean vein) 'the third meaning of mimesis,' which is 'difference as a positivity, a joyful reappropriation of attributes of the other that is not in any way to be confused with a mere reversal of the existing phallocentric distribution of power.' This mimesis 'lies beyond masquerade and mimicry' and signifies 'an emergence of the feminine . . . from [the specular patriarchal] femininity within which it lies buried.'[112]

In Deb Margolin's witty, linguistically dense performance pieces, the 'playful repetitions' in her dialectical images are geared to explore not just the 'discourse that exploits her,' but also an 'emergence of the feminine' – of 'a possible operation of the feminine in language.' Language for Margolin is mimetic behavior of a most vertiginous sort, producing a network of correspondences or rather an unmapped intersection where comedy and politics, running at very high speeds, collide. If Robbie McCauley and Peggy Shaw show us the dialectical image's shock value with all its critical and utopian potential, Deb Margolin shows us how these dialectical images are made, the thinking through similars, and through past and present, that creates the image and in turn allows us a view of what female experience – not is, but might be. Unquestionably the Margolin persona is fissured by the signifier, the signifier that cannot fully speak her desire. But her end-run around this problem is to *work* the word, massage it, explode it, indeed to *insist* upon her linguistic being. In performance linguistic being becomes linguistic behavior, a way of imbricating word and body.

In 'N,' an early performance piece, Margolin demonstrates her own style of messianic reading, an unwitting satire of Benjamin's notion of onomatopoesis as primordial source of language. In Margolin's version, the secret origin of the letter 'N' is a horny woman imprisoned in words like 'condemn' and 'goddamn.' To N's great irritation, she is also called to service in 'dislimnable' – by a pretentious cad trying to pick up a woman at a museum. Benjamin's modernist interest in the pictorial hieroglyph lies in its mimetic material similarity to the referent which, he insists, persists in a 'fallen' language of arbitrary signification. Margolin, no less pictorial, recasts (and voices) Benjamin's mystical anthropomorphism in a comic femiNist key:

> You know, when letters meet in words it's not a simple thing . . . a word is a whole show made up of active letters . . . and the energy between letters is . . . physical, you know . . . like actors on a stage. When you say a word you see it, don't you . . . you like it . . . and when you write a word down you paint portraits of these actors . . . for example, the word MISOGYNIST is like a Chekhov play because all the letters just stand around wondering how to relate to each other, the Greek roots stick out all over the place, and when it's said and done, the meaning is very sad.[113]

In *Carthieves! Joyrides!* a series of interwoven monologues about time, sex, and mortality, the mimetic object is not the human face in a letter, but that supreme commodity fetish of western capitalism and patriarchy: the family car (and its simulacra). Like Shaw and McCauley, Margolin links private memory to this powerful wish image of commodity culture, recalling Benjamin's motto for Baudelaire, 'Where there is experience . . . certain contents of the individual past combine with material of the collective past.'[114] Benjamin saw that combinative material in rituals, ceremonies, and festivals in a preindustrial age while for Margolin, as for Shaw, all meaningful experiences in her life are rituals centered around or associated with cars. A family story of her father's success and mother's (barely concealed sexual) pleasure features a shiny new 1948 Buick that was 'black as hope and shiny as death' (18). Constellated with this ur-story are memories of virile ice-cream truck jockeys whose behavior just escapes pre-teen comprehension; sexual initiation rituals ('A '76 Chevy pulls up. It's his parents' car. I love him,' 16) and death ('Clark Page was killed by a car,' 22). Cars are the madeleine of this performance piece, a way not simply to remember past time, but to experience it in the ironic crucible of the present – in Margolin's case, an embodied present yearning to be a Benjaminian *Jetzeit*, a time of decoding, of recognition, of, as Schor puts it, 'emergence.'

Margolin's persona emerges, calculatedly and spontaneously, from language. She talks about making images, arouses herself through images. But in this piece, while the image pools are as deep and strange as in previous works, language is also an Irigarayan minefield, commoditized and reekingly phallic, an alien social mesh that clings to the body and must be clawed off and restitched with female hands. 'Emergence' in *Carthieves!* skids quickly into emergency.

In the opening monologue – a parody of comedy-club gambits – about the pain and humiliation of going to the dentist, Margolin's images are dehiscent, drawn from the tabloids –

> My teeth have just completely rotted in my head. OK, my teeth were never terrific but all of a sudden the empire just collapsed . . . like a solid working class neighborhood that suddenly went to seed with no sociological explanation.
>
> (1)

– and mortality:

> teeth [remind me of] tombstones . . . . Where else does bone show in the human body but when you smile?
>
> (1)

Mortality segues to sex – her dentist excites her by talking 'dirty dental,' the professional jargon of 'mesial' and 'distal.' Later in the piece, completing the image-tryptich of sex and mortality, is the car:

> The Toyota Motor Corporation is proud to introduce its all new compact/sport/utility Recreational Active Vehicle (RAV4) . . . . This model features 15 by 8's made by Sendal . . . a Hypertech chip, K&N air filter, Doug Thorley Tri-Y headers, a Pete Gibson 3-inch cat-back exhaust system . . .
>
> (26)

Toward this orgy of parts-fetishism Margolin has two mimetic responses. One is to offer a mordant Irigarayan repetition, reminding us to what uses, historically, high-tech fetishism has led us:

> an electric fan, a Bergen Belsen modified transmission for firmer shifts and kickdown . . . . Phew! This is a real hunk! It's a lot of car! You can feel it on the body and smell it in the rear!
>
> (26)

The second is to imbricate car body and female body.

> Men say cars are like women, and they're right. Me? I'm like the 1995 Riviera. In almost every way. I'm Jewish and the Riviera is a Buick. Look at this steel arc. That's my line too.
>
> (6)

This piece of mimetic correspondence has one foot in anthropological mimicry (animals and humans conforming to a superior 'nature') and one foot in feminist rage at human reification. With oddball assonance (Buick, Jewish) Margolin finds the scratch in the auratic surface from which to emerge. Her ageing body lines resemble the car's hard sleek line in *almost* every way, a quiet qualifier that shouts volumes about sexism, ageism, youth worship, and the degradation of female experience in capitalist culture.

In the 1920s, Marxist culture critics, following Lukacs, gave the mid-nineteenth-century phantasmagoria of industrial commodities (railroads, department stores, exhibition halls, boulevards) the ironic label of 'second nature' in order to criticize technology's assumption of the role of nature or the natural. Writing on Benjamin, Buck-Morss adopts the term 'new nature,' by which she means 'not just industrial technology but the entire world of matter (including human beings) as it has been transformed by that technology.'[115] In *Le Paysan de Paris* (1926), Benjamin's favorite book on Paris, the Surrealist Aragon describes Paris as an enchanted forest of commodity fetishes: the Eiffel Tower as a giraffe, Sacre Coeur as an icthyosaurus and gas tanks at filling stations as 'the great red gods, the great yellow gods, the great green gods . . . O Texaco motor oil, Esso, Shell! Noble inscriptions of human potential!'[116] Thirty years later, in the post-World War II dreamscape of American automophilia, 1950s Buick advertisements, we recall, not only promised that the car would create a 'new man,' but that in our new Buicks we could go 'gliding among the planets like garish spacecraft.' Not yet so phallic and futuristic, the Buick her father brings home in 1948 makes Margolin's mother scream with happiness. In a dialectical image, this shimmering black high-octane status symbol from 1948 collides with Margolin's new 1993 Honda and releases in a flash both the dream image and its disintegration:

> It's black also. I'm surprised too. This car isn't curved like that, like someone's ass; it's boxed, like the shape of someone's head . . . . Automatic transmission and power this and that, power everything, yet driving it is very physical somehow, you work up a sweat, in fact it's like the Flintstone's car. Just makes me want to blast a hole through the floor, stick my feet through and run for my fucking life.
>
> (18)

Wish images grown dim, Buicks no longer take us on interplanetary journeys or produce a classless utopia where Chuck Berry and Jim Anderson become brothers through the shared love of gorp and speed. The new Hondas hardly even beckon with the visceral bodiedness of the 'new nature,' but rather testify to the persistent amnesia of commodity culture. As Benjamin puts it, 'the sensation of the newest, the most modern, is in fact just as much a dream form of events as the eternal return of the same.'[117]

But Benjamin also insists on historicizing new nature. By the end of the nineteenth century the original Parisian arcades had failed, become obsolete, 'fossilized.' Dialectical images show us that this year's exciting commodity always has contradictory 'faces': fetish and fossil, wish image and ruin.[118] Drawing on our culture's cartoon primitives, Margolin transforms her new Honda into the Flintstone's car which, as she experiences it, runs on panic.

'Adventure stows away inside of failure.' If the car is a prime representative of new nature, it is historically time-bound *and* timeless, a piece of Bergen Belsen and a piece of paradise. As she strains away from numbness, psychic and physical, Margolin tells of writing a college essay for a beloved eccentric roommate in which she investigates experimental psychologist Achter Ahsen's 'eidetic images' – 'a sort of dreamlike mental image that appears to the dreamer, on the deepest, most magical, most repeatable level, an image that [one] can call up at will . . . whenever [one] needs it' (10). Margolin herself keeps an eidetic image locked away in a kind of Cartesian creation myth. The story begins with a vision; she is a disembodied consciousness living in an orbitless 'cool medium.' Then she accepts an offer to 'come into the body.' With the body comes experience – desire, lust, the agony of beauty, mortality – and the eidetic image is of her re-entry:

> I see myself from very far off, young and luscious, coming out of a tunnel blasted into a mountain, coming round a curve from inside the mountain, sleeveless white shirt, drenched in youth and desire, in a sleek white car. This car (*holds up toy car, [kisses it, drops it into her bosom]*).

> (11)

Like Pele, the hungry goddess of a living volcano that Peggy Shaw mimes and writes into a lesbian imaginary, this mountain, blasted open by Margolin's sheer sexy vitality, is her ironic, yet empowering, homage to woman-as-nature. Described in cinematic tracking-shot prose, Margolin gives herself cinematic technology's contribution to new nature: star quality – Bonnie before Clyde. Ironizing her timeless eidetic image, she turns it into a fetish object – a 79-cent toy – which she kisses reverentially and places close to her breasts.

But Margolin moves beyond irony, blasting her eidetic image with a feminist dialectical one. The lights go down momentarily and come up on Margolin standing next to, and dressed exactly like, a lifesized cardboard female fetish from *Car and Driver*. To a pop tune she heard in her dentist's office, 'All I wanna do is have some fun,' she turns her back to us and dances a grotesque ass-jiggling go-go, transforming her audience momentarily into *Car and Driver* readers, increasing our discomfort (and, of course, laughter) by turning anxiously to see how we are judging the performance of her behind. A very downmarket version of Julia Meade, the spokeswoman in evening gown for Lincoln in the 1950s, who ran her manicured hands over the car upholstery for millions of rapt television viewers,[119] Margolin's fun-girl in cut-offs and halter top introduces the newest Toyota 'Recreational Active Vehicle (RAV4),' then mimes stroking its smooth seats:

> This car is power itself! It's got a 2.0 liter 16-valve engine with double ended rear suspended dual overhead cam and monocoque body construction . . . . And Jesus and his friends is this car fun! Look at it! Look at the body! . . . . It's got a dark interior. The leatherized custom work is all a sabled silver, and the carpet is ebony and the roof is black and the lights have dark gels over them . . .
>
> (27)

Where is the feminist critique in this abjection of the woman's body, this servicing of masculine fetishism? Dialectical images are constructed precisely in order to arrest the flow of dreamlike images, to give them a shock. Margolin's method of arresting the flow of advertising images is, appropriately enough, torquing – a car term, she tells us with eyes popping, for 'twisting force.' What she narrates in performance is a violent mimetic torquing, which like McCauley's head-shaking and cries, is registered in breakdown, bodily innervations. This trembling body in turn generates more images. Furiously rubbing (instead of stroking) the imaginary 'sabled silver' seats, she sputters:

> . . . and the whole [car interior] is black as pitch and you know what, the truth is you can't see a thing! I knew this man, he died at the racetrack one day. He said, You've got no business driving where you can't see! He said that! And he was right! And in my community they have corners where you have to turn left or right onto a two way street but cars are parked along the sides so you don't know if another car is coming or not! You have to turn without knowing! You have to glide out into the stream of traffic and hope!
>
> (27)

Her dialectical image is produced by torquing the image of Toyota's new RAV with its soft leatherized surfaces, twisting it until we see its other 'face,' that of a ruin: Margolin as an old man who hesitates at corners and drives blind into traffic. Suffering stows away inside of glitz.

In the penultimate monologue, she constellates a pyramid-scheme salesman whose wing-door Lamborghini is a triumph of commodity wish-imagery, and a Bosnian woman murdered by a sniper while shopping. She captions this constellation 'Dexter Yaeger and the Dead Woman.' In interwoven narrative pieces, the capitalist con man grows a gigantic body: 'Every person [whom Dexter Yaeger cons into buying] toilet paper by computer . . . is called your leg! And under Dexter Yaeger's leg are so many people he is a millionaire . . . . And we are so close to him, we are, so to speak between his legs' (34). Implicitly so is the dead woman, a potential consumer of Dexter Yaeger's goods as they reach into every shopping thoroughfare of our so-called 'global village.' The well-dressed woman ten thousand miles away was killed on her way to buy bread, but Margolin torques again to caption her caption, to force a correspondence: 'Two different ways of shopping I guess. Hope her chariot had wings' (34).

Margolin's last story-image is about high-school girls on a joy ride in the 1960s. The steering wheel comes loose in the driver's hand and is hilariously tossed out of the window. Margolin tosses away the hula hoop that has served as her steering wheel. The gesture and verbal image of the rudderless car are shocking, liberating. It's one of those moments when time stands still. But Margolin can no more discard this piece of new nature than Robbie McCauley can drain the traces of guilt from her Indian blood, than Peggy Shaw can stop invisible fists from pummeling her too-handsome face. Failure stows away inside adventure . . .

CONCLUSION

. . . Yet this 'failure' attests to performance's deepest pleasures, the incommensurability that lies at the heart of mimesis. The body is never fully subsumed in impersonation. Experience is never captured in the words and gestures we use to speak of it. The object in view is never what we desire. Theater of all kinds, with its playful, disturbing dialectic of appearance/disappearance, stages our desire to look and keep looking.

What is extraordinary in the feminist performance art discussed in this chapter is that the yearning eye joins the 'I' of the performer's private fictions and arrives, as it were, at a third site: the junkheap of cultural memory. Spectator and performer find themselves looking not at each other (or not only), nor at an object of desire, but at a dialectical image. And here the sign-referent gap of 'classical' mimesis is overwritten by the relational inventiveness of Benjaminian mimesis. In a moment of mimetic apprehension, the commoditized images embodied and destroyed by these women performers suddenly illuminate the crises of the present. Old habits of thinking/judging/performing are temporarily cast aside. The present of aesthetic contemplation becomes 'the present' – a particular temporality, a space of 'now-time' with no comforting historical narratives to limit meanings.

What we might experience at such moments is our 'historical existence' and its dialectical pain. The dead objects shocked into life by Shaw, Margolin, and McCauley – a GI from World War II, a 1948 Buick, daguerreotypes of Indian chiefs, among others – reveal the powerful utopian desires in US culture and, simultaneously, the social ideologies that prevent their fulfillment. We are still a society unable to waken from what Benjamin called capitalism's (now transnational) dream state, with its inevitable diversion of technology and its profits from democratic uses. We are still a culture invested in the racist, homophobic annihilation of anyone deemed 'other,' as though identity were not a necessary but always performative construction. We are still a culture mired in the loathing and fear of women's experiences and desires, still addicted to the female body as fetish-commodity.

Dialectical images remind us, again and again of failure, but *this* failure, as Michel de Certeau says, is ethical. It defines 'a distance between what is and what ought to be. [A] distance [that] designates a space where we have something to do.'[120] *Unmaking Mimesis* has explored a certain number of such doings across specific times and locations. Playwrights and performers as varied as Aphra Behn, Elizabeth Robins, Caryl Churchill, Adrienne Kennedy, Peggy Shaw, Robbie McCauley, and Deb Margolin have put their feminist thinking and their dangerous bodies into spaces of representation precisely to challenge reigning notions of mimetic doing, to imagine differently the dominant cultural norms of representation, embodiment, and pleasure. A *gestus* or dialectical image may not deliver us, but each reminds us that the present is not owned by the past. Rather, as Benjamin would have it, the past becomes readable only through the *present* image that transforms it, the present understandable only through that transformative reading.

Perhaps Benjaminian mimesis, his 'concept' of the nonidentical similar, offers an affective stimulus to still-fractious debates over identity politics. For Benjamin the similarities unleashed in mimesis release us from, in Wohlfarth's words, the 'dumb, closed self, the A=A of formal identity. [T]he similar would "itself" be without self-identity . . . it would both underlie and undermine identity.'[121] But the undermining of identity, everyone's favorite postmodern project, does not make difference or differences suddenly understandable or meaningful. Difference may redound to the very subject/object, insider/outsider dualisms responsible for the social violence we deplore. In 'Not You/Like You: Post-Colonial Women and the Interlocking Questions of Identity and Difference,' Trinh T. Minh-ha offers a vision of the non-identical similar that moves beyond current obsessions with identity and difference. 'Not quite the same, not quite the other' creates a 'ground,' she argues, that 'belongs to no one.'[122] Though this is not her brief, Trinh outlines how one might in the 1990s pursue the ever-urgent calls for coalition politics. 'Not you/like you' describes a subjectivity that seeks rigorously to explore relatedness while refusing the easy assumption of analogous or common reference points. Practical goals may supply the occasion for coalitions but only mimetic thinking, in which the 'I' is performed as a 'not you/like you,' will make them work.

As for the images created by the gestures, voices, and words of the performers discussed here . . . surely Robbie McCauley's thick army coat is not equivalent to Peggy Shaw's GI regalia and Deb Margolin's Buick is not McCauley's Cadillac, and neither parks in the same lot as Shaw's 1962 Corvette. What makes these images and performers 'similar' in my mimetic thinking is their rejection of the 'I' as 'dumb closed self,' their production of experience as a wild collision of past and present, as embodied and socially mediated, always private and public, esoteric *and* exoteric. Such experiences will not be remembered in official US histories, but in small theater spaces in the last decade of this century, with wit and political passion, they are being performed.

Notes

INTRODUCTION

1 Plato, *The Republic*, trans. Richard W. Sterling and William C. Scott (New York: W.W. Norton, 1985), p. 286. All references to this edition.

2 Fritz Kramer, *The Red Fez: Art and Spirit Possession in Africa*, trans. Malcolm Green (London: Verso 1993), p. 250.

3 My definition in 'Mimesis, Mimicry, and the "True-Real,"' *Modern Drama*, 32:1 (March 1989), p. 58.

4 A.O. Rorty, 'The Psychology of Aristotelian Tragedy,' in A.O. Rorty, ed., *Essays on Aristotle's 'Poetics'* (Princeton, NJ: Princeton University Press, 1992), p. 4. See also Paul Ricoeur, *Time and Narrative*, vol. 1 (Chicago: University of Chicago Press, 1983), pp. 31–51.

5 'Representation' is closest to the 'meanings covered by the mimesis word-group in Greek. Thus a picture can represent a subject, an actor represent a character, a play represent an action, event or story' while '"imitate" has none of these senses in modern English.' Stephen Halliwell, *The 'Poetics' of Aristotle* (Chapel Hill: University of North Carolina Press, 1986), p. 71.

6 Richard McKeon, 'The Concept of Imitation in Antiquity,' in R.S. Crane, ed., *Critics and Criticism* (abridged edition) (Chicago: University of Chicago Press, 1952), p. 122. The sentence, referring to Platonic mimesis, continues: 'the likeness may be good or bad, real or apparent.' Since imitation is ubiquitous in Plato (arts, philosophy, discourse, governments, and, in a different sense, words are all imitative), the crucial distinction is between a 'maker of realities' (that are based on the Forms, therefore true) and a 'maker of images' (based on appearance, not knowledge, therefore false) (122). Images too are parsed. As Gilles Deleuze notes, the good copy (or image or icon) is 'endowed with resemblance' – not of a visual surface but of the Idea's 'internal essence.' The bad copy (or semblance, phantasm, simulacrum) abandons truth; it dissembles, producing 'wholly external' likenesses through 'entirely different means than are at work in the model.' ('Plato and the Simulacrum,' trans. Rosalind Krauss, *October* 27 (Winter 1988), p. 48.) The sophist produces simulacra, so, as we'll see, does Luce Irigaray's *hystera*. Derridean 'writing' (in relation to the Father's *logos*) is a simulacrum (see Jacques Derrida, *La Dissemination* [Paris: Editions du Seuil, 1972], trans. Barbara Johnson [Chicago: University of Chicago Press, 1981], p. 75ff.); and our 'age of simulation' is in thrall to the simulacrum (Jean Baudrillard, *Simulations* [New York: Semiotext(e), 1993], p. 2ff.).

7 Deleuze: 'The Platonic model is Sameness ["pure identity"], in the sense that Plato speaks of Justice as nothing other than justness.' ('Plato and the Simulacrum,' p. 40.) Aristotle, limiting the reference of mimesis to the arts, breaks with the other-

worldly Platonic Form. But, Spariosu argues, he remains committed to 'true knowledge,' intelligible only to the philosopher, which the poet simulates through the universal. See Mihai Spariosu, ed., *Mimesis in Contemporary Theory*, vol. I (Philadelphia: John Benjamins, 1984), p. viff. Halliwell rejects any link between Aristotelian mimesis and artistic idealism but concedes that in *Poetics*, Chapter 9, Aristotle's universal comes close to philosophical truth – its imitation having 'the capacity to enlarge understanding and to direct the mind from particulars to objects of higher significance.' *Aristotle's Poetics* (Chapel Hill: University of North Carolina Press, 1984), p. 136. See n. 36.

8 For a feminist critique of patriarchal modeling in the discourses of truth, see, for example, Rosi Braidotti, *Patterns of Dissonance* (London: Routledge, 1991); Donna Haraway, *Simians, Cyborgs, and Women* (New York: Routledge, 1991); Linda Alcoff and Elizabeth Potter, eds., *Feminist Epistemologies* (New York and London: Routledge, 1993); Drucilla Cornell, *Beyond Accommodation: Ethical Feminism, Deconstruction, and the Law* (New York: Routledge, 1991); Genevieve Lloyd, *The Man of Reason* (Minneapolis: University of Minnesota Press, 1993).

9 Luce Irigaray, *Speculum of the Other Woman*, trans. Gillian C. Gill (Ithaca, NY: Cornell University Press, 1974), p. 54.

10 John D. Lyons and Stephen G. Nichols, Jr., *Mimesis: From Mirror to Method, Aristotle to Descartes* (Hanover, NH: University Press of New England), p. 1.

11 See Halliwell, *'Poetics' of Aristotle*, pp. 17–26.

12 See Joel Black in 'Idolology: The Model in Artistic Practice and Critical Theory,' in Spariosu, p. 176.

13 Cited in Tzvetan Todorov, *Theories of the Symbol*, trans. Catherine Porter (Ithaca, NY: Cornell University Press, 1983), p. 117.

14 Ibid., p. 145.

15 Göran Sörbom, *Mimesis and Art: Studies in the Origin and Early Development of an Aesthetic Vocabulary* (Uppsala, Sweden: Svenska Bokforlaget, 1966), pp. 12–13.

16 See Philipe Lacoue-Labarthe, *Typography: Mimesis, Philosophy, Politics* (Cambridge: Harvard University Press, p. 124ff.), and Irigaray's *Speculum* (pp. 298–302ff.), and Derrida's elaboration (through Kant) of mimesis as/in *oikonomia*: 'Economimesis,' *Diacritics* 11 (June 1981), pp. 3–25.

17 Jacques Derrida, *Of Gramatology*, trans. Gayatri Chakravorty Spivak (Baltimore, MD: Johns Hopkins University Press, 1976), p. 36.

18 Derrida's mime epitomizes intransitivity: 'a mimicry imitating nothing . . . a double that doubles no simple . . . there is no simple reference.' *Dissemination*, p. 206. See also Lacoue-Labarthe: Since the essence of mimesis is that it has no essence (116), or rather since 'the essence of mimesis [is] absolute vicariousness, carried to the limit . . . endless and groundless – something like an infinity of substitution and circulation' (116), the question 'what is mimesis?' puts us back in the 'old ruse': 'One can then speak of what is seen and of what is not seen, of what appears and of what does not appear . . . . In short we can be installed within the visible realm: we do *theory*' (91). Put another way, 'the mirror game in Book X is to correct mimesis with mimesis: put the mimetic in the mirror, make it the object of contemplation' (101). To recall how often Nietzschean notions of primordial mimesis, primordial repetition (i.e. prior to representation) circulated in the French theory scene of the 1970s is to be reminded of the originality and importance of Irigaray's *Speculum* as *gendered* intervention.

19 Sue-Ellen Case, *Feminism and Theatre* (London: Routledge, 1988), p. 15.

20 Froma I. Zeitlin, 'Playing the Other: Theater, Theatricality, and the Feminine in Greek Drama,' *Representations* 11 (1985), p. 79.

21 Ibid., p. 85.

22 Lacoue-Labarthe, pp. 125, 128.

23 For arguments for and against this position, see *Feminism/Postmodernism*, ed. Linda

J. Nicholson (New York: Routledge, 1990), and Gayatri Chakravorty Spivak, *In Other Worlds: Essays in Cultural Politics* (New York: Methuen, 1987).

24 Elizabeth Robins, *Ibsen and the Actress* (London: Hogarth Press, 1928), p. 18.

25 A.W. Schlegel in *Die Kunstlehre* (1805), cited in Todorov, p. 151; Karl Philip Moritz, *Über die bildende Nachahmung das Schönen* (1788), in Todorov, p. 153. However, by 1710 the Earl of Shaftesbury was already situating mimesis between Creator and creator: '[the] poet is a second Maker: a just Prometheus under Jove.' Cited in M.H. Abrams, *The Mirror and the Lamp* (New York: W.W. Norton, 1953), p. 280. See also Helga Madland, 'Imitation to Creation: The Changing Concept of Mimesis from Bodmer and Breitinger to Lenz,' in *Eighteenth-Century German Authors and their Aesthetic Theories*, eds. Richard Critchfield and Wulf Koepke (Columbia, SC: Camden House, 1988), pp. 29–43.

26 In 'On Form and Subject Matter,' in *Brecht on Theatre: The Development of an Aesthetic*, ed. John Willett (New York: Hill and Wang, 1964), p. 29. In such statements Brecht crosses paths with a virtual contemporary Erich Auerbach, in his monumental *Mimesis: The History of Representation of Reality in Western Literature*, trans. Willard R. Trask (Princeton: Princeton University Press, 1953). Auerbach's sly use of random details over abstract concepts, his passion for the 'ordinary,' the 'down-to-earth,' the 'creatural,' his praise for a 'problematic' realism that, like Flaubert's, 'penetrate[s] to the existence of things' (505); his disapproval of writers like Voltaire for whom 'the social milieu is an established frame of reference, which is accepted as it happens to be' (401), all resonate in Brecht's own discourse. But Auerbach's Hegelian depiction of literary history's inexorable move toward realism (namely Balzac) and his distrust (with Lukács) of modernist experimentation divide him completely from Brecht, whose Marxist-inspired *gestus* (see Chapters 2 and 6) ruins the creatural individuality of characters. For Brecht reality 'in all its multifariousness' could never be and should never be 'comprehended as a whole' (Auerbach, p. 473).

27 Adorno announces that Aristotelian catharsis 'makes common cause with repression.' Theodor W. Adorno, *Aesthetic Theory*, trans. C. Lenhardt (London: Routledge and Kegan Paul, 1970), p. 338. He theorizes

> the mimetic taboo [as] a central part of bourgeois ontology . . . . Tagging along behind its reification, the subject limits that reification through the mimetic vestige, the plenipotentiary of an integral life amid a damaged life where the subject is being reduced to an ideology.
>
> (170, 171)

As behavior, mimesis is making oneself similar to the object: an identification with, not an identification of. Hence its importance in the critique of Enlightenment domination of nature in M. Horkheimer and T. Adorno, *Dialectic of Enlightenment*, trans. John Cumming (New York: Continuum, 1987), pp. 3–42. Mimetic behavior is also the capacity to 'thrill' (Adorno, p. 30) or 'shudder' (455) before the artwork. See Michael Taussig's imaginative weaving of mimesis into the discourses of modernity and anthropology in *Mimesis and Alterity* (New York: Routledge, 1993), particularly his figuring of Benjamin's 'mimetic faculty' as the 'radical displacement of self in sentience' (39). See also Michael Cahn, 'Subversive Mimesis: Theodor W. Adorno and the Modern Impasse of Critique,' in Spariosu, pp. 27–64. By contrast, René Girard's version of mimesis refers to 'mimetic desire,' a rivalrous, appropriative, inevitably violent behavior in which subjects desire objects because of, and in imitation of, their rival/model's desire. Mimetic desire pushes societies toward self-annhilation and is containable only by ritualized sacrifice of a scapegoat. See *Violence and the Sacred* (Baltimore: Johns Hopkins University Press, 1977); '*to double-business bound*': *Essays on Literature, Mimesis, and Anthropology* (Johns Hopkins

University Press, 1978).

28 Walter Benjamin, 'On the Mimetic Faculty,' in *Reflections*, trans. Edmund Jephcott (New York: Schocken Books, 1986), p. 333.

29 In Halliwell, *'Poetics' of Aristotle*, p. 34.

30 Stephen Halliwell, 'Pleasure, Understanding, Emotion,' in Rorty, *Aristotle's 'Poetics'*, p. 247.

31 Alice Rayner, *To Act, To Do, To Perform* (Ann Arbor: University of Michigan Press, 1994), p. 15.

32 See Naomi Schor's ground-breaking article, 'This Essentialism Which Is Not One: Coming to Grips with Irigaray,' *Differences* 1:2 (Summer 1989), pp. 38–58, for which an excellent companion piece is her 'French Feminism Is a Universalism,' *Differences* 7:1 (Spring 1995), pp. 15–47, which argues that 'Irigaray is committed to reclaiming the universal for women, or rather to feminizing it by branding it with the mark of gender' (35). See also Diana Fuss's analysis of the debates surrounding Irigaray in *Essentially Speaking: Feminism, Nature, and Difference* (New York: Routledge, 1989), pp. 55–72, and Margaret Whitford's subtle discussion throughout *Luce Irigaray: Philosophy in the Feminine* (London: Routledge, 1991).

33 Sigmund Freud, 'Femininity,' in *New Introductory Lectures on Psychoanalysis*, ed. James Strachey (New York: W.W. Norton, 1965), p. 104. Cited in Irigaray, p. 26ff.

34 Irigaray comments: '. . . through her "penis-envy," she will supply anything that might be lacking in this specula(riza)tion' (54).

35 To name just a few examples, see Jill Dolan, *The Feminist Spectator as Critic* (Ann Arbor: UMI Research Press, 1988), pp. 41–42, 86–87; Jeanie Forte, 'Women's Performance Art: Feminism and Postmodernism,' in *Performing Feminisms* (Baltimore: Johns Hopkins University Press, 1990), pp. 251–269. For Sue-Ellen Case's rethinking of representation and the gaze, see 'Performing Lesbian in the Space of Technology: Part II,' *Theatre Journal* 47 (1995), pp. 331–343.

36 See Richard Rorty on Aristotle and the universal in *The Mirror of Nature* (Princeton, NJ: Princeton University Press, 1979), pp. 41ff.

37 See Irigaray, p. 48ff. See Richard Rorty for a discussion of visual metaphors for knowledge, originating in the separation, since Plato, of the eye of the body from the eye of the mind: 'The notion of "contemplation," of knowledge of universal concepts or truths . . . makes the Eye of the Mind the inescapable model for the better sort of knowledge' (39). Since, as Herbert Blau notes, 'theater' (*theatron*) and 'theory' (*theoros*) share a common Greek root (*theasthai*), meaning 'to watch, contemplate' (in *Take Up the Bodies: Theater at the Vanishing Point* [Urbana: University of Illinois Press, 1982], p. 1), it's not surprising that philosophers call knowing-as-seeing the 'spectator theory of knowledge' (R. Rorty, p. 39).

38 For a discussion of the hijacking of feminist theory by the maternal imaginary, a move that renders this form of feminist theorizing effectively heterosexual if not completely bourgeois-liberal, see Teresa de Lauretis, *The Practice of Love: Lesbian Sexuality and Perverse Desire* (Bloomington: Indiana University Press, 1994), pp. 163–175.

39 Meaghan Morris, 'The Pirate's Fiancée: Feminists and Philosophers, or maybe tonight it'll happen,' in *Feminism and Foucault: Reflections on Resistance*, eds. Irene Diamond and Lee Quimby (Boston: Northeastern University Press, 1988), p. 35.

40 See 'The Power of Discourse,' in *This Sex Which Is Not One*, trans. Gillian C. Gill (Ithaca, NY: Cornell University Press, 1994), pp. 76ff.

41 Halliwell, *'Poetics' of Aristotle*, p. 137.

1 REALISM'S HYSTERIA

1 H.E.M. Stutfield, 'The Psychology of Feminism,' *Blackwood's Magazine* 161:975 (January 1897), pp. 104–117.

2   On the education front, the foundation of Queen's and Bedford Colleges in London (1848, 1849) produced the first generation of well-qualified women teachers while the North London Collegiate (1850) and the Cheltenham Ladies' College (1854) promoted secondary education. The opening of Girton (1869) gave women a foothold at Oxford and Cambridge. Legal changes were slower. The Matrimonial Causes Act (1857) allowed for divorce although husbands were far more protected than wives. The Married Woman's Property Act of 1882 gave women the right to their own property after marriage but suffrage for all women was not law until 1928. Books on sociology and sexuality – George Drysdale's *The Elements of Social Science or Physical, Sexual and Natural Religion* (1854); J.S. Mills's *The Subjection of Women* (1869); Bradlaugh and Besant's *The Fruits of Philosophy* (1877) – paved the way for debate on female emancipation, employment, and birth control. George Meredith, Thomas Hardy, and George Gissing brought the 'new woman' into fiction as did the novelists Stutfield chastises, Mrs. Roy Devereux, George Egerton, Grant Allen, all afflicted with what *Punch* called 'Ibscenity.' On these and related issues see Gail Cunningham, *The New Woman and the Victorian Novel* (New York: Macmillan, 1978).

3   By 1891 William Archer had published a five-volume translation of Ibsen's drama, the last volume including *Rosmersholm, The Lady from the Sea,* and *Hedda Gabler,* but there were also translations by Gosse (*Hedda Gabler* 1890); Eleanor Marx-Aveling (*An Enemy of Society* [*sic*] 1888, *The Lady from the Sea, The Wild Duck* 1890); and others. See Thomas Postlewait's *Prophet of the New Drama: William Archer and the Ibsen Campaign* (Westport, Conn.: Greenwood Press, 1986), p. 139.

4   Emile Zola, *Naturalism in the Theatre* in *The Theory of Modern Drama,* ed. Eric Bentley (New York: Penguin, 1978), p. 351

5   G.B. Shaw, *The Quintessence of Ibsenism* (London: Constable, 1932), p. 144.

6   Erwin Panovsky, *Perspective as Symbolic Form* (New York: Zone Books, 1991), p. 29. This is not to say that the precise geometry of Renaissance and seventeenth-century perspective is upheld in the late nineteenth-century box sets (in which the apron – the downstage playing area that brought actors close to spectators – had been abolished). Panovsky distinguishes between the 'perspectival view of space' and actual perspectival construction (71). The former is at issue here. One important reason why theater managers were able to woo middle-class audiences back to the theater was that they offered serious – that is, scientific – that is, rational and objective treatments of social problems, and, crucially, a theater environment conducive to such treatments. In this vein, see W.B. Worthen's important analysis of the modern realist theater as a 'scene of vision,' whose 'rhetoric' is readable in the drama, productions, and audience reception (*Modern Drama and the Rhetoric of Theater* [Berkeley: University of California Press, 1992], pp. 12–53). The fascination with the realist theater apparatus may be rooted in an even more complex socio-cultural rhetoric. According to historian Judith Walkowitz, the city of London defied orderly apprehension: 'the literary construct of the metropolis as a dark, powerful, and seductive labyrinth held sway over the social imagination of educated readers [in the 1870s and 1880s] . . . . There was a "crisis" of representation . . . .' *City of Dreadful Delight: Narratives of Sexual Danger in Late-Victorian London* (Chicago: University of Chicago Press, 1992), p. 17. A city environment of threatening incoherence may account for the pleasure taken in apparently orderly mini-spectacles enacted in picture-frame sets. Perhaps it also accounts for the 'immobile eye' noted by contemporary commentators. In 1877, Henry James wrote of the London audience, 'It is well dressed, tranquil, motionless,' and Karl Marx's wife Jenny made a similar observation: '[The audience] sat in deadly silence . . . everyone sat passive and immovable.' In Andrew Davies, *Other Theatres, The Development of Alternative and Experimental Theatre in Britain* (Totowa, NJ: Barnes and Noble, 1987), p. 27.

7   See Jacob Breuer's section in Jacob Breuer and Sigmund Freud, *Studies on Hysteria*

(New York: Basic Books, reprinted 1955), p. 234. All references are to this edition.

8 See Lorraine Code, 'Taking Subjectivity into Account,' in *Feminist Epistemologies* (New York: Routledge, 1993), pp. 15–48, especially pp. 26–32. See Elaine Showalter, 'On Hysterical Narrative' (*Narrative* 1:1 [1992], pp. 24–35), for a skeptical view of the metaphorization of hysteria in feminist criticism.

9 Hélène Cixous and Catherine Clément, *The Newly Born Woman* (*La Jeune Née*, 1975), trans. Betsy Wing (Minneapolis: University of Minnesota Press, 1986).

10 Sarah Kofman, *The Enigma of Woman: Woman in Freud's Writings* (*L'Enigme de la Femme: La Femme dans les textes de Freud*, 1980), trans. Catherine Porter (Ithaca, NY: Cornell University Press, 1985), pp. 122–225.

11 Elizabeth Berg, 'The Third Woman,' *Diacritics* 12 (Summer 1982), p. 18. Berg's interest here is Nietzsche's equation of the veiled deceptive women as truth in Derrida's *Spurs*.

12 William Archer, *The Old Drama and the New: An Essay in Re-valuation* (Boston: Small, Maynard, 1923), p. 286.

13 Elizabeth Robins, *Ibsen and the Actress* (London: Hogarth Press, 1928), p. 18.

14 In J. Laplanche and J.-B. Pontalis, *The Language of Psycho-Analysis*, trans. Donald Nicholson-Smith (New York: W.W. Norton, 1973), the imago is defined as 'a prototypical figure . . . a stereotype through which . . . the subject views the other person' (211). In Lacan's imaginary register, the mother's gaze and the infant's own mirror reflection produce the first imagoes; others derive from family relations and permanently affect one's identifications in the world. In Jane Gallop's words, 'The imaginary is made up of *imagoes* . . . . In the imaginary mode, one's understanding of other people is shaped by one's own imagoes. The perceived other is actually, at least in part, a projection.' In *Reading Lacan* (Ithaca, NY: Cornell University Press, 1985), pp. 60–61. It is this combined sense of subjective projection and illusion that makes the term apt for theater reception.

15 See Walkowitz's account of the Men and Women's Club and their attendance at Ibsen's *A Doll's House* at the Novelty Theater in 1889 (along with Eleanor Marx and Olive Schreiner): 'Edith Lees who later married Havelock Ellis, [recalled that] "a few of us collected outside the theater breathless with excitement . . . . We were restive and almost savage in our arguments. What did it mean? . . . Was it life or death for women?"' (Walkowitz's ellipses), p. 166. This was the same performance (with Janet Achurch as Nora) that so profoundly affected Elizabeth Robins and her actress friend Marion Lea (see Robins, pp. 9–15ff.). See the account of Herbert Waring (who played Helmer) on the difficulty of mounting the production in Miriam Franc, *Ibsen in England* (Boston: Four Seas, 1919), pp. 81–83.

16 On the little theater movement in England, see James Woodfield, *English Theatre in Transition, 1881–1915* (Totowa, NJ: Barnes and Noble, 1984); Postlewait; Davies; Sheila Stowell, *A Stage of Their Own: Feminist Playwrights of the Suffrage Era* (Ann Arbor: University of Michigan Press, 1992). It's important to keep this movement in perspective, as it were. The audacious new drama never dominated the stage. In 1896, the year in which *Little Eyolf* ran for twenty performances, Edward Rose's version of *The Prisoner of Zenda* opened to acclaim. In the same year, Henry Arthur Jones's *Michael and his Lost Angel* failed at the Lyceum but a ridiculous nautical melodrama *True Blue* opened at the Olympic. See Michael Booth, *Prefaces to English Nineteenth Century Theatre* (Manchester: Manchester University Press), pp. 46–47, 52.

17 Jane Marcus's research has been crucial and I am indebted to her for advising me to read *Alan's Wife* a decade ago. See her edition of Robins's *The Convert* (New York: The Feminist Press, 1980), especially her informative introduction. There are two recent biographies, Joanne E. Gates, *Elizabeth Robins, 1862–1952: Actress, Novelist, Feminist* (Tuscaloosa: University of Alabama Press, 1994), and Angela V. John, *Elizabeth Robins: Staging a Life* (London: Routledge, 1995); see also Postlewait, and for the wider context of the London theatrical scene, see Nina Auerbach, *Ellen*

Terry: Player in Her Time (New York: W.W. Norton, 1987).

18 Michel Foucault, *Madness and Civilization: A History of Insanity in the Age of Reason*, trans. Richard Howard (New York: Vintage, 1965), p. 154. See Charles Bernheimer's Introduction to *In Dora's Case: Freud – Hysteria – Feminism*, eds. Charles Bernheimer and Nancy Kahane (New York: Columbia University Press, 1985), pp. 1–18.

19 Cited in Ilza Veith, *Hysteria: The History of a Disease* (Chicago: University of Chicago Press, 1965), p. 141.

20 The Harveian Society of London published their diverse opinions in the *British Medical Journal*, 25 February 1888, pp. 417–418. About malnutrition of the uterus:

> Dr. Graily Hewitt [reported that] his own experience of hysterical cases in women had taught him the fact that general malnutrition was almost invariably present, and probably the basis for the whole case. Certainly the uterus showed signs of this malnutrition in such cases, its tissues being soft and deficient in normal firmness to a remarkable degree. Probably the central nervous system was in like condition of malnutrition . . . .

(418)

21 Carroll Smith-Rosenberg, *Disorderly Conduct: Visions of Gender in Victorian America* (Oxford: Oxford University Press, 1985), p. 183. These dualities find a resonance in constructions of Victorian masculinity. See Ed Cohen, 'The Double Lives of Man: The Dehiscence of Male Subjectivity in Late Nineteenth-Century Narrative,' in Sally Ledger and Scott McCracken, eds, *Cultural Politics at the Fin de Siècle* (Cambridge: Cambridge University Press, 1995), pp. 88–114.

22 Cited in the *Lancet* 1 (1855), p. 205.

23 Cited in the *British Medical Journal*, 25 February 1888, p. 417.

24 Cited in Smith-Rosenberg, p. 203.

25 Cited in the *British Medical Journal*, 11 October 1902, p. 1140.

26 Cited in Veith, p. 211.

27 *Lady Audley's Secret* adapted from Braddon's novel by C.H. Hazlewood (London: Thames Hailes Lacy), reprinted in *Nineteenth Century Plays*, ed. George Rowell (Oxford: Oxford University Press, 1972), p. 266. All references are to this edition.

28 Cf. Elaine Showalter's comment comparing Freud's treatment of Dora to 'Victorian nerve-doctors who saw themselves locked into combat with their hysterical patients in a contest for mastery . . . .' *The Female Malady* (New York: Pantheon, 1985), p. 160.

29 See Elaine Hadley, *Melodramatic Tactics: Theatricalized Dissent in the English Marketplace, 1800–1885* (Stanford, CA: Stanford University Press, 1995) who identifies a 'melodramatic mode' in relation to private capital accumulation in diverse sites – the O.P. riots, the reaction to the New Poor Law, intellectual culture, as well as theater. For Hadley the melodramatic mode always 'hearken[s] back to a deferential society and its patriarchal grounds for identity' though it is not for that reason merely nostalgic. Rather its 'hyperbole and exaggeration, its suspicion and providential plotting . . . attest to the combative conditions [market capitalism] under which it struggled to represent deferential values in the nineteenth century' (11). Melodrama dominated English theater in the first half of the nineteenth century and though it was always stigmatized by its association with a vulgar working-class audience, its values if not its exuberance harmonized with those of the well-made bourgeois drawing-room dramas frequented by the respectable middle classes. See, for example, Booth, pp. 1–53.

30 Peter Brooks, *The Melodramatic Imagination: Balzac, Henry James, Melodrama and the Mode of Excess* (New Haven: Yale University Press, 1976), p. 20.

31 Ned Albert, *East Lynne* (New York: Samuel French, 1969), p. 97.

32 See Martha Vicinus, '"Helpless and Unfriended": Nineteenth-Century Domestic Melodrama,' *New Literary History* (Spring 1981), pp. 127–143.

> Melodrama was popular with the working class in its efforts to understand and assimilate capitalism; it appeared to offer truths not found elsewhere. Social and economic conditions were unstable during much of the nineteenth century; melodrama acknowledged this and seemed to demonstrate how difficult circumstances could be endured and even turned to victory.
>
> (131)

33 Lady Audley embodies the woman/demon's 'boundless vitality' that 'recreate[s] itself in endless freedom from time.' See Nina Auerbach, *Woman and the Demon: The Life of a Victorian Myth* (Cambridge: Harvard University Press), p. 9. Lynda Hart links the demonic in Braddon's novel to fantasies about lesbianism in *Fatal Women: Lesbian Sexuality and the Mark of Aggression* (Princeton, NJ: Princeton University Press, 1994).

34 On Trilby's transformative powers in contrast to her weak-hearted mesmerist, see Auerbach, *Woman and the Demon*, pp. 17–20.

35 Cited in Michel Foucault, *The History of Sexuality*, trans. Robert Hurley (New York: Vintage, 1980), p. 56.

36 A much-criticized maneuver when it was learned that his assistants may have been coaching the patients. Charcot was one of those physicians who believed that susceptibility to suggestion was a definitive characteristic of hysteria. See Veith, pp. 239–241.

37 Ibid., p. 235.

38 In 'General Remarks on Hysterical Attacks' (1909), Freud thought that the 'reflex mechanism of coitus-action' (156) resembled hysterical attacks for the good reason that all motor activity by the hysteric was motivated by sexual fantasy 'translated . . . and represented in pantomime' (153). 'Even the ancients called coitus a minor epilepsy' (157). Reprinted in *Dora: An Analysis of a Case History*, with an introduction by Philip Rieff (New York: Macmillan, 1963), pp. 153–157.

39 John Coleman's account from 1847 of Charlotte Cushman playing Bianca in Henry Hart Milman's *Fazio*, from Coleman, *Fifty Years of an Actor's Life*, cited in Booth, p. 19.

40 Kofman, p. 45.

41 Diana Fuss and Joel Sanders, 'Bergasse 19: Inside Freud's Office,' in Joel Sanders, ed., *Stud: Architectures of Masculinity* (New York: Princeton Architectural Press, 1996), pp. 113–137.

42 The hysteric's attacks are 'phantasies projected and translated into motor activity and represented as pantomime.' In 'Hysterical Attacks,' p. 153.

43 Sigmund Freud, 'Some Character-Types Met With in Psycho-Analytic Work: Those Wrecked by Success II,' trans. James Strachey, in *The Standard Edition of the Complete Psychological Works of Sigmund Freud* (London: Hogarth Press, 1962), vol. 14, pp. 329, 331. In his reading of *Rosmersholm*, Freud ignores references to Baeta's and Rebecca's erotic passions, which the puritan Rosmer views as sick and which conform to the popular view of hysteria as sexual degeneracy. Nor does Freud discuss Rebecca's control and manipulation, signs of her intellectual (and demonic) power. Rather, like the good scientist, he concentrates on Rebecca's resistance (repression); on Ibsen's knowing dissimulation of her secret; and on his own penetration of her secret.

In the *Enigma of Women*, Sarah Kofman argues that Frued's analysis of narcissistic woman in 'On Narcissism' (1914) acknowledges male nostalgia for what men have lost, their original narcissism. The narcissistic woman, unable to find object-love, loves only herself, and this self-sufficiency, this refusal to divulge her secrets,

Kofman suggests, is so threatening that Freud must claim that women are in fact *not* sufficiently in possession of their secret (their sexuality), but *ignorant* of it, in need of the analyst to unveil their truth. Kofman suggests that Freud's friendship with the intellectual, self-sufficient Lou Andreas-Salome helped inspire 'On Narcissism.' Written two years after that essay, Freud's analysis of Ibsen's Rebecca West (self-sufficient intellectual and possible criminal) may have been similarly inspired.

44 Michell Clarke, 'Review of Breuer and Freud's *Studien uber Hysterie*,' *Brain* 17:19 (1894), p. 401.

45 Charles D. Fox, *The Psychopathology of Hysteria* (Boston, R.G. Badger, 1913), p. 34.

46 Frau Emmy von N. 'gave us an example of how hysteria is compatible with an unblemished character and a well-governed life' (103), but in casting about for the correct etiology of Frau Emmy's hysteria, Freud names 'the natural helplessness of women' (102), sending us back to biological destiny. Both Breuer and Freud feel the need to vouch for the moral credentials of their hysterics, as though to combat their own tendency to view them as 'natural' victims or deceitful perpetrators of their illness: 'But I always found [Anna O.] entirely truthful and trustworthy' (43). Near the end of *Studies* Freud vouches for himself: 'I cannot imagine bringing myself to delve into the psychical mechanism of a hysteria in anyone who struck me as low-minded and repellent, and who, on closer acquaintance, would not be capable of arousing human sympathy' (265).

47 Henry Arthur Jones, 'The Delineation of Character in Drama,' in *The Foundations of a National Drama* (New York: Books for Libraries Press, 1967), p. 191.

48 As in Breuer's account: '[Anna O.] created a hypnoid state for which she had amnesia. This was repeated on different occasions and its ideational content gradually became richer and richer; but it continued *to alternate with* states of completely normal waking thought' (235).

49 This claim only confirms Georg Lukàcs's early analysis of the modern drama as a bourgeois drama in which 'what was once destiny becomes character'; and 'motivations . . . wholly based upon character . . . will drive the character relentlessly to the limits of pathology.' See excerpt of 'The Sociology of Modern Drama,' trans. Lee Baxandall in Eric Bentley (ed.), *The Theory of the Modern Stage* (New York: Penguin, 1979), p. 448.

50 Alexandre Dumas, *La Dame Aux Camélias* (Oxford, Oxford University Press, 1972), p. 144. 'There are times when I forget what I've been, and the Marguerite of old and the Marguerite of today seem to be two separate women, the second barely remembering the first' (my translation).

51 In his *The Old Drama and the New*, Archer celebrates the best of English realism, Henry Arthur Jones and Arthur Wing Pinero. Archer's favorite of the two was Pinero ('Insofar as any man may be called the regenerator of English drama, that man is Arthur Pinero . . . he was the brilliant and even daring pioneer of a great movement,' 286), but he considered Henry Arthur Jones a 'born dramatist,' cites Matthew Arnold's praise of Jones's 'literary' ear as proof of his talents, and avoids mentioning (as Jones did most of his life) *Breaking the Butterfly*, Jones's idiotic adaptation of Ibsen's *A Doll's House*, in which Torvald takes on Nora's sins and she falls happily into his arms. Jones frequently changed the endings of his potboilers if he thought the public would be offended.

52 Henry Arthur Jones, *Mrs Dane's Defence*, in *Representative Plays* (Boston: Little, Brown, 1925), pp. 252–253. All references are to this edition.

53 A.W. Pinero, *The Second Mrs. Tanqueray* (London: Methuen, 1985), p. 85. All references are to this edition.

54 Austin Quigley's analysis of *The Second Mrs. Tanqueray* convincingly elaborates the shock, ultimately the impossibility, of Paula's entry into a society in which there are 'pluralistic divisions, and pluralistic lived values, but . . . only one set of publicly acknowledged values' (89). While Quigley allots every character his or her

world ('The truth of the matter is that Ellean, Aubrey, Paula . . . all come from separate worlds,' 89), I am suggesting that the exploitation of hysteria as type, trope, and plot device in this and other plays of late nineteenth-century realism, undermines the spectator's perception of individual worlds. See Quigley's *The Modern Stage and Other Worlds* (New York: Methuen, 1985).

55 W.B. Worthen links 'paint and dye' to theatrical make-up and to Paula's imitative skills throughout the play, not only as commentary on the character but to make a larger point about the gendered epistemology of late Victorian theater. See *Modern Drama and the Rhetoric of Theater*, p. 41.

56 All references to Ibsen's notes are from Toby Cole, ed., *Playwrights on Playwriting* (New York: Hill and Wang, 1964), pp. 156–170.

57 Henrik Ibsen, *Hedda Gabler*, in *Ibsen: The Complete Major Prose Plays*, trans. Rolf Fjelde (New York: NAL), p. 773.

58 Bert O. States, *Great Reckonings in Little Rooms: On the Phenomenology of Theater* (Berkeley: University of California Press, 1985), p. 62.

59 Henrik Ibsen, *Letters and Speeches*, ed. Evert Sprinchorn (New York: Hill and Wang, 1964), p. 298. In some ways the idea for this chapter came from Herbert Blau's comment about directing *Hedda Gabler*: '[There is a] wilder life secreted in the parlor, the trolls grinning in the corners . . . . The bourgeois parlor can't contain such power.' In *The Impossible Theater: A Manifesto* (New York: Collier, 1964), p. 149.

60 Sigmund Freud, 'Hysterical Phantasies and Their Relation to Bisexuality' (1908), in *Dora: An Analysis of a Case of Hysteria* (New York: Macmillan, 1963), p. 151.

61 For Kofman, the difference between the 'path to normal femininity . . . differs from the neurotic path only by a difference in the degree of repression.' Kofman, p. 203.

62 Cole, p. 166. See also Gail Finney, *Women in Modern Drama* (Ithaca: Cornell University Press, 1989), pp. 149–165.

63 See Miriam Alice Franc, *Ibsen in England* (Boston: Four Seas, 1919), pp. 25–26.

64 Archer, p. 286.

65 Cited in Franc, p. 40.

66 Shaw in fact said that Robins was 'intensely self-conscious' in temperament and was only convincing 'in parts that . . . enable her to let herself loose in this, her natural way.' In Bernard Shaw, *Our Theatres in the Nineties*, vol. 2 (London: Constable, 1954), p. 262.

67 Robins, p. 22.

68 Cited in William B. Worthen, *The Idea of the Actor: Drama and the Ethics of Performance* (Princeton, NJ: Princeton University Press, 1984), p. 145.

69 Cited in Gay Gibson Cima's review/analysis of acting style and Ibsenite realism, 'Discovering Signs: The Emergence of the Critical Actor in Ibsen,' *Theatre Journal* 35:1 (March 1983), pp. 5–40. Cima finds change from melodrama to realism a change in kind, not degree, and certainly the retrospective acting, the intellectual preparation, the sense of actors collaborating and creating with the playwright, creates changes. But is Harry Siddons's gesture manual really overhauled when Robins explains the gesture's narrative?

70 Stuart Schneiderman, 'Lacan's Early Contributions to Psychoanalysis,' in *Returning to Freud* (New Haven: Yale University Press, 1983), p. 7, cited in Sharon Willis, *Marguerite Duras: Writing on the Body* (Urbana: University of Illinois Press, 1987), p. 26.

71 See Jane Gallop, *The Daughter's Seduction: Feminism and Psychoanalysis* (Ithaca, NY: Cornell University Press, 1982), p. 73.

72 Cited in Cima, p. 16.

73 Sigmund Freud, 'Psychopathic Characters on the Stage,' *Standard Edition*, vol. 7, pp. 305–310.

74 See, most helpfully, Bernheimer and Kahane.

75   When Robins saw her first Ibsen performance, Janet Achurch as Nora (*A Doll's House*), she was dazzled by the naturalness of Achurch's impersonation, but she objected to the tarantella: there was too much 'theatricalism' (Robins, p. 13). This moment of hysterical expression, of an actor's body imitating an out-of-control body, seemed to Robins 'a mistake' (12). But according to Phillipe Lacoue-Labarthe the disturbance to the spectatorial position is precisely the effect of masochism; as a concept 'it is situated at the very frontier between stage and auditorium, actor and spectator . . . ' 'Theatrum Analyticum,' in *Glyph 2: Johns Hopkins Textual Studies*, eds Samuel Weber and Henry Sussman (Baltimore: Johns Hopkins University Press, 1977), p. 134. Rebutting Jean-François Lyotard's charge that Freud remained imprisoned in the Western system of representation, Lacoue-Labarthe offers Freud's theory of masochism in modern theater reception to mark 'the "constitutive" *undecidability* of Freud's treatment of representation' (137).

76   Cited in Robins, p. 50.

77   See Jacques Lacan, 'The Meaning of the Phallus,' in *Feminine Sexuality: Jacques Lacan and the école freudienne*, trans. Jacqueline Rose, eds Juliet Mitchell and Jacqueline Rose (New York: W.W. Norton, 1982), p. 76.

78   Cited in George Rowell's Introduction to *Late Victorian Plays* (London: Oxford University Press, 1972), p. 8.

79   Cited in Cima, p. 9.

80   For Dostoevsky, the naturalist's obsession with factual detail has more to do with a mentally 'diseased condition' than with artistic vision. See *Crime and Punishment*, Part 1, Chapter 5, cited in Marshall Brown: 'The Logic of Realism: A Hegelian Approach,' *PMLA*, 96:2 (March 1981), pp. 227, 239. Similarly, but from a different and later perspective, Brecht called Balzac 'the poet of monstrosities,' his passion for detail an example of 'the fetishism of objects [over] hundreds and thousands of pages.' Cited in *Aesthetics and Politics*, trans. Ronald Taylor (London: New Left Books, 1977), p. 78.

81   Cited in *Alan's Wife: A Dramatic Study in Three Scenes*, with an introduction by William Archer (London: Heinemann, 1893), p. xii. All play references are to this edition. See Catherine Wiley, 'Staging Infanticide: The Refusal of Representation in Elizabeth Robins's *Alan's Wife*,' *Theatre Journal* 42:4 (1990), pp. 432–446. Wiley makes the important point that while Robins's performance in *Alan's Wife* received a good review in the *Atheneum* ([Robins played] 'with great feeling and force; [she] conveyed an excellent idea of a brooding woman broken down by grief and haunted by an abiding sense of wrong,' cited in Wiley, p. 435), she would never have been forgiven for also *writing* such a character (438).

82   Cited in *The Portable Nietzsche*, ed. and trans. Walter Kaufmann (New York: Viking, 1968), p. 487.

83   Glenda Dickerson, 'A Womanist African-American Theatre,' in Sue-Ellen Case, ed., *Performing Feminism: Feminist Critical Theory and Theatre* (Baltimore, MD: Johns Hopkins University Press, 1990), p. 111.

84   Simone Benmussa, Introduction to *Benmussa Directs: Portrait of Dora and The Singular Life of Albert Nobbs* (London: John Calder, 1979), p. 11. See my 'Benmussa's Adaptations: Texts from Elsewhere,' in Enoch Brater, ed., *Feminine Focus* (Oxford: Oxford University Press, 1989), pp. 64–78.

85   James Clifford coined this term at a conference, 'Realism and Representation' at Rutgers University, 1989. See also my 'Refusing the Romanticism of Identity: Narrative Interventions in Churchill, Benmussa, Duras' in *Performing Feminisms*, pp. 92–105.

2   BRECHTIAN THEORY/FEMINIST THEORY

1   This chapter both follows and revises the original article, 'Brechtian Theory/ Feminist Theory: Toward a Gestic Feminist Criticism,' in *The Drama Review* 32:1 (Spring 1988), pp. 82–94.

2   Catherine R. Stimpson, 'Stein and the Transposition of Gender,' in *The Poetics of Gender*, ed. Nancy K. Miller (New York: Columbia University Press, 1986), p. 7.

3   Laura Mulvey, 'Visual Pleasure and Narrative Cinema,' *Screen* 16:3 (Autumn 1975), pp. 6–18. See Mulvey's further thinking on the narrative cinema, 'Afterthoughts on "Visual Pleasure and Narrative Cinema" inspired by *Duel in the Sun*,' *Framework* 15–17 (Summer 1981), pp. 12–15.

4   Carl Weber, 'Brecht in Eclipse?' *The Drama Review* 24:1 (Spring 1980), p. 121.

5   Jonathan Dollimore, *Radical Tragedy: Religion, Ideology and Power in the Drama of Shakespeare and His Contemporaries* (Chicago: University of Chicago Press), pp. 1–28ff., 53–108ff.

6   Francis Barker, *The Tremulous Private Body: Essays on Subjection* (London: Methuen, 1984), pp. 18–21.

7   Terry Eagleton, 'Brecht and Rhetoric,' in *Against the Grain: Essays (1975–1985)* (London: Verso, 1986), pp. 167–172. See also Elizabeth Wright's *Postmodern Brecht: A Re-Presentation* (London: Routledge, 1989).

8   Toril Moi, *Sexual/Textual Politics: Feminist Literary Theory* (London: Methuen, 1985), p. 17.

9   Martin Esslin, *Brecht: The Man and His Work* (New York: W.W. Norton, 1971), p. 146.

10   Eric Bentley, *The Brecht Commentaries* (London: Metheun, 1981), p. 46ff.

11   Herbert Blau, *Take Up the Bodies: Theater at the Vanishing Point* (Urbana: University of Illinois Press, 1982), p. 1.

12   Bertolt Brecht, *Brecht on Theatre: The Development of an Aesthetic*, ed. John Willett (New York: Hill and Wang, 1984), p. 192.

13   Judith Butler, *Gender Trouble: Feminism and the Subversion of Identity* (New York: Routledge, 1990), p. 8.

14   Judith Butler, 'Performative Acts and Gender Constitution: An Essay in Phenomenology and Feminist Theory,' in Sue-Ellen Case, ed., *Performing Feminisms: Feminist Critical Theory and Theatre* (Baltimore, MD: Johns Hopkins University Press, 1990), pp. 270–1.

15   Caryl Churchill, *Cloud Nine* in *Plays: One* (London: Methuen, 1985), p. 251.

16   Judith Butler, *Bodies that Matter: On the Discursive Limits of 'Sex'* (New York: Routledge, 1993), pp. 1–23.

17   Ibid., p. 234.

18   Elin Diamond, Introduction to *Performance and Cultural Politics*, ed. E. Diamond (London: Routledge, 1996), p. 5.

19   Jacques Derrida, 'Signature, Event, Context,' in *Margins of Philosophy*, trans. Alan Bass (Chicago: University of Chicago Press, 1982), p. 310ff.

20   See n. 1.

21   Teresa de Lauretis, 'Feminist Studies/Critical Studies: Issues, Terms, and Contexts,' in Teresa de Lauretis, ed., *Feminist Studies/Critical Studies* (Bloomington: Indiana University Press, 1986), p. 14.

22   See Barbara Johnson in *The Critical Difference: Essays in the Contemporary Rhetoric of Reading* (Baltimore: Johns Hopkins University Press, 1980), p. 4:

> Difference . . . is not what distinguishes one identity from another. It is not a difference between . . . independent units, but a difference within. Far from constituting the text's unique identity, it is that which subverts the very idea of

identity, infinitely deferring the possibility of adding up the sum of a text's parts or meanings and reaching a totalized, integrated whole.

23 Sigmund Freud, *Civilization and Its Discontents*, in *The Standard Edition of the Complete Psychological Works of Sigmund Freud*, vol. 21 (London: Hogarth Press, 1975), p. 106, n. 3.
24 Gayle Rubin, 'The Traffic in Women: Notes on the "Political Economy" of Sex,' in *Toward an Anthropology of Women*, ed. Rayna Reiter (New York: Monthly Review Press, 1978), p. 179.
25 Brecht, *Theatre*, p. 137.
26 Bertolt Brecht, *In the Jungle of Cities*, in *Collected Plays*, vol. I, eds Ralph Manheim and John Willett (New York: Vintage, 1971), p. 140. See Wright on the dialectic, pp. 10–22, 36–48.
27 Brecht, *Theatre*, p. 190. All subsequent references are to this text.
28 Luce Irigaray, 'The Power of Discourse and the Subordination of the Feminine,' in *This Sex Which Is Not One*, trans. Catherine Porter with Carolyn Burke (Ithaca, NY: Cornell University Press, 1985), p. 76.
29 See 'Alien Nation: An Interview with [Suzan-Lori Parks] by Michele Pearce,' *American Theatre* 11:3 (March 1994), p. 26.
30 Timothy J. Wiles, *The Theater Event: Modern Theories of Performance* (Chicago: University of Chicago Press, 1980), p. 72.
31 Patrice Pavis, *Languages of the Stage: Essays on the Semiology of the Theatre* (New York: Performing Arts Journal Publications, 1982), p. 88.
32 Stephen Heath, 'Lessons from Brecht,' *Screen* 15:2 (Summer 1974), p. 112.
33 See Sandy Flitterman-Lewis, 'Psychoanalysis, Film, and Television,' in *Channels of Discourse*, ed. Robert C. Allen (Chapel Hill: University of North Carolina Press, 1987), pp. 172–210.
34 Jean-Louis Baudry, 'The Apparatus: Metapsychological Approaches to the Impression of Reality,' in *Apparatus*, ed. Theresa Hak Kyung (New York: Tanam Press, 1980), p. 56.
35 Pavis, p. 138.
36 See Cora Kaplan, 'Pandora's Box: Subjectivity, Class, and Sexuality in Socialist Feminist Criticism,' in *Sea Changes: Culture and Feminism* (London: Verso, 1986), pp. 147–176.
37 By historicity I mean the constantly negotiated interpretation of the subject's own history in relation to social and historical understandings. How performance deals with 'historical experience' will be discussed in Chapter 6.
38 Mulvey, p. 11.
39 Director John Edward McGrath told me that Ruth Maleczech grabbed the video herself one day in rehearsal, and the effect was so suggestive it became a permanent part of the show.
40 Brecht, *Theatre*, p. 198.
41 Pavis, p. 42.
42 Heath, p. 112.
43 This is fully played out in Brecht's attitude toward textual authority. As is well known, he revised constantly and cared little about definitive or authoritative versions of his plays.
44 Mulvey, p. 18.
45 Pavis, p. 42.

3 *GESTUS*, SIGNATURE, BODY IN THE THEATER OF APHRA BEHN

1 Brecht's *gestus* refers to a gesture, a word, an action, a tableau that encapsulates

the social and political attitudes in the text and beyond it. As the semiotician Patrice Pavis puts it, *gestus* is 'the key to the relationship between the play being performed and the public, [as well as] the author's attitude to the public, that of the era represented and of the time in which the play is performed . . . .' Pavis, *Languages of the Stage* (New York: Performance Art Journal Publications, 1982), p. 42. See Chapter 2.

2 Robert Gould, *Satirical Epistle to the Female Author of a Poem called 'Sylvia's Revenge'* (London, 1691) cited in Catherine Gallagher, *Nobody's Story: The Vanishing Acts of Women Writers in the Marketplace, 1670–1820* (Berkeley: University of California Press, 1994), p. 23. For other discussions of use of the prostitution metaphor in the Restoration and through the eighteenth century, see Jacqueline Pearson, *The Prostituted Muse: Images of Women and Women Dramatists, 1642–1737* (New York: St. Martin's Press, 1988), and Janet Todd, *The Sign of Angellica: Women, Writing and Fiction, 1660–1800* (New York: Columbia University Press, 1989).

3 See 'Arachnologies: The Woman, the Text, and the Critic' in *The Poetics of Gender*, ed. Nancy K. Miller (New York: Columbia University Press, 1986), p. 275.

4 See Bertolt Brecht, *Brecht on Theatre*, ed. John Willett (New York: Hill and Wang, 1964), pp. 252–265.

5 Some 'discoveries' were better than others. When Pepys had to sit in a box because the pit was full, he noted 'that from this place the Scenes do appear very fine indeed and much better than in the pit' (19 October 1667). Cited in Peter Holland, *The Ornament of Action: Text and Performance in Restoration Comedy* (Cambridge: Cambridge University Press, 1979), p. 36. I am indebted to Holland's book for its detailed discussion of Restoration theater practice.

6 Richard Flecknoe, 'A Short Discourse of the English Stage' in *Critical Essays of the Seventeenth Century*, vol. 2, ed. J.E. Spingarn (Oxford: Clarendon Press, 1908), p. 96. See Kristina Straub's discussion of the politics of theatrical gazing in the decades following Flecknoe's remarks in *Sexual Suspects: Eighteenth-Century Players and Sexual Ideology* (Princeton, NJ: Princeton University Press, 1992), pp. 3–23ff.

7 See Dryden's Prologue to *Marriage A-la-Mode* in *Four Comedies*, eds L.A. Beaurline and F. Bowers (Chicago: University of Chicago Press, 1967), p. 284. Pepys frequently comments on Scenes and costumes. On 8 March 1644, he saw *Heraclius* at Lincoln's Inn Fields (the home of the Duke's Company before Dorset Garden was built):

> But at the beginning, at the drawing up of the Curtaine, there was the finest Scene of the Emperor and his people about him, standing in their fixed and different postures in their Roman habits, above all that ever I yet saw at any of the Theatres.
>
> (*The Shorter Pepys*, ed. Robert Latham
> [Berkeley: University of California Press, 1985], p. 362)

All references to Pepys are to this edition. See also Hugh Hunt, 'Restoration Acting' in *Restoration Theatre*, eds John Russell Brown and Bernard Harris (London: E. Arnold, 1965), pp. 178–192, on competition between theater companies over spectacular displays.

8 Karl Marx, *Capital*, trans. Ben Fowkes (New York: Vintage, 1977), p. 176.

9 Cited in A.H. Avery and A.H. Scouten, 'The Audience,' in *Restoration and Eighteenth-Century Comedy*, ed. Scott McMillin (New York: W.W. Norton, 1973), p. 445.

10 Ibid., p. 442.

11 William Wycherley, *The Gentleman Dancing Master*, in *The Complete Plays of William Wycherley*, ed. W.C. Ward (London: T. Fisher Unwin, 1902), p. 242. All references to Wycherley are to this edition.

12 Dryden, p. 283. More damning are Dryden's lines to the playhouse 'gallants' (probably a mixture of country squires, London aristocrats, and young professionals) in the epilogue 'To The King And Queen, At The Opening Of Their Theatre Upon The Union Of The Two Companies In 1682' (cited in Montague Summers, *The Restoration Theatre* (London: Kegan Paul, Trench, Trubner, 1934), p. 56:

> We beg you, last, our Scene-room to forbear
> And leave our Goods and Chattels to our Care.
> Alas, Our Women are but washy Toys,
> And wholly taken up in Stage Employs:
> Poor willing Tits they are: but yet I doubt
> This double duty soon will wear them out.

13 In Dryden's play, identified by Pepys as *The Mayden Queen*, subtitle for *Secret Love*, Nell Gwynn was Florimell, a 'breeches part' in which she 'hath the motions and carriage of a spark the most that ever I saw any man have,' (Pepys, p. 735).

14 See Holland, pp. 4–18ff. He cites a letter from 1667 commenting on the assertiveness of women spectators 'to a new [play] at the King's house . . . call'd *The Custome o' th' Country* . . . which is so dam'd bawdy that the Ladyes flung their peares and fruites at the Actors' (15).

15 Ibid., p. 15.

16 Aphra Behn, *The Town Fop: Or, Sir Timothy Tawdrey* in *The Works of Aphra Behn*, ed. Montague Summers, vol. 3 (New York: Phaeton Press, 1967), p. 94.

17 Aphra Behn, *The Forc'd Marriage: or, The Jealous Bridegroom* in *Works*, vol. 3, p. 286.

18 Gallagher, p. 2. Ultimately Gallagher's argument about 'Nobody' and the 'emptiness' of the site of the author (p. 87) is similar to the revised ending of this chapter (revised from my article, 'Gestus and Signature in Aphra Behn's *The Rover*,' *ELH* 56:3 [September 1989], pp. 519–541, which Gallagher cites) but my reading is a bit more melancholy (not surprising given Walter Benjamin's contribution). That the historical woman 'vanishes,' disappears into her commodity status, is, for Gallagher, a 'sign of her success' (89).

19 See Angeline Goreau, *Reconstructing Aphra* (New York: Dial Press, 1980), p. 77ff.

20 Marx, p. 161.

21 Margaret Cavendish, cited in Hilda Smith, *Reason's Disciples: Seventeenth-Century English Feminists* (Urbana: University of Illinois Press, 1982), p. 79.

22 Because she focused on female exploitation in the marriage market, Behn's sympathy for impoverished libertines who were similarly dependent is all the more striking. Created in perhaps ironic homage to her friend, the financially desperate Earl of Rochester, are Behn's Gayman (*The Lucky Chance*), who is 'Moneyless, for six tedious weeks, without either Clothes, or Equipage to appear withal' (*Works*, vol. 3, p. 195), and Gaillard (*The Feign'd Curtezans*), who observes that 'a good handsome proper Fellow is as staple a Commodity as any's in the Nation . . .' (*Works*, vol. 2, p. 349).

23 From 'To the Ladies,' cited in Moira Ferguson, *First Feminists: British Women Writers, 1578–1799* (Bloomington: Indiana University Press, 1985), p. 237.

24 Aphra Behn, *The Second Part of The Rover*, in *Works*, vol. 1, p. 152.

25 Cited in Smith, p. 133.

26 Ibid., p. 135.

27 Frederick Engels, *The Origin of the Family, Private Property and the State* (New York: International Publishers, 1985), p. 134.

28 Aphra Behn, *The Lucky Chance: or, An Alderman's Bargain*, in *Works*, vol. 3, p. 208.

29 Gallagher separates Julia's maneuvers from the plots of Diana and Letitia, since despite all impediments, Julia 'is still somehow free to dispose of herself.' Gallagher, p. 37.

30 Behn, *Works*, vol. 3, p. 305.

31 Aphra Behn, *The Feign'd Curtezans*, in *Works*, vol. 2, p. 374. All subsequent references are to this edition.

32 Cited in Jonas Barish, *The Antitheatrical Prejudice* (Berkeley: University of California Press, 1981), p. 158. William Prynne's *Histriomastix*, closer to Behn's time, also rails against 'the common *accursed hellish art of face-painting [which] sophisticates and perverts the workes of God . . . .*' Cited in Barish, p. 93.

33 Ibid., p. 86.

34 Ibid. pp. 166–167.

35 Thomas Hobbes, *Leviathan*, ed. Michael Oakeshott (New York: Collier, 1962), p. 125.

36 Ibid.

37 Christopher Pye, 'The Sovereign, the Theater, and the Kingdome of Darknesse: Hobbes and the Spectacle of Power,' *Representations* 8 (Fall 1984), p. 91.

38 Cited in Norman Holland, *The First Modern Comedies* (Bloomington: Indiana University Press, 1959), pp. 48–49.

39 Jacques Derrida, *Of Grammatology*, trans. Gayatri Chakravorty Spivak (Baltimore: Johns Hopkins University Press, 1984), p. 36.

40 Aphra Behn, *The Rover*, ed. Frederick M. Link (Lincoln: University of Nebraska Press, 1967), p. 7.

41 Aphra Behn, *The Dutch Lover*, in *Works*, vol. 1, pp. 221–225. Until Act V of *Sir Patient Fancy*, the prevailing view of the learned Lady Knowall is expressed by Sir Patient: 'that Lady of eternal Noise and hard Words . . . she's a Fop; and has Vanity and Tongue enough to debauch any Nation under civil Government.' (In *Works*, vol. 4, p. 32.) Indeed like the old senex Lady Knowall pursues her daughter's lover. Act V, however, reveals her 'design'; she has been testing the lovers and scheming to wrest from Sir Patient a fabulous jointure for them. The satirical signs of Lady Knowall's learning, such as abstruse vocabulary, remain in place to the end but are rendered benign by her assumption of her proper gender role.

42 Cited in Smith, p. 63.

43 Jacqueline Rose, 'Introduction II,' in *Feminine Sexuality: Jacques Lacan and the école freudienne*, trans. J. Rose, eds J. Rose and J. Mitchell (New York: W.W. Norton, 1982, p. 48.

44 Jacques Lacan: 'when one is a man, one sees in one's partner what can serve, narcissistically, to act as one's own support.' Ibid., p. 157.

45 Derrida, p. 36.

46 'J.H. Wilson estimates that of the 375 new plays written between 1660 and 1700, 89 contained at least one breeches role.' Cited in P. Holland, p. 184.

47 Aphra Behn, *The Widow Ranter*, in *Works*, vol. 4, p. 295.

48 Aphra Behn, 'The Golden Age,' in *Works*, vol. 4, p. 141.

49 See 'Contestations of Nature: Aphra Behn's "The Golden Age" and the Sexualizing of Politics' (in *Rereading Aphra Behn: History, Theory, and Criticism*, ed. Heidi Hutner [Charlottesville: University Press of Virginia, 1993], pp. 301–321), in which Robert Markley and Molly Rothenberg argue that Behn's desire for an 'autonomous, self-sufficient realm of nature' (301) is consistently compromised by the incommensurability of her strategies; the 'eternal state of nature' will not conflate easily with the historical-political realm (304). But see Catherine Gallagher's notion of the way in which 'autonomy' works as a crucial trope in the critical strategies of Tory feminists, in 'Embracing the Absolute: The Politics of the Female Subject in Seventeenth Century England,' *Genders* 1 (Spring 1988), pp. 24–39.

50 Hobbes, p. 21.

51 Behn, *Dutch Lover*, p. 255. This song occasioned masturbatory praise from Behn's young friend Thomas Creech in 'To the Author, on her Voyage to the Island of Love' (*Works*, vol. 4, pp. 121–123), but also calumny that lasts well into the fol-

lowing century. Pope's couplet is often cited: 'The stage how loosely does Astrea tread / Who fairly puts all characters to bed!' in Alexander Pope, 'First Epistle of the Second Book of Horace. To Augustus,' in *Collected Poems*, ed. Bonamy Dobree (London: J.M. Dent, 1987), p. 300.

52 P. Holland, pp. 41–42.
53 Thomas Killigrew, *Thomaso, or the Wanderer*, parts 1 and 2, in *Comedies and Tragedies* (London: Henry Herringman, 1663), p. 333. All references are to this edition.
54 Goreau, pp. 173–174.
55 Marx, p. 138.
56 See Walter Benjamin, *Understanding Brecht*, trans. Anna Bostok (London: Verso, 1973), pp. 17–18: '[There is an] important but badly marked road . . . [which] ran in the Middle Ages, via Hroswitha and the Mysteries; in the age of the baroque, via Gryphius and Calderon. Later we find it in Lenz and Grabbe, and finally in Strindberg . . . [and] the plays of Brecht.'
57 Brecht, p. 201.
58 Walter Benjamin, *The Origin of German Tragic Drama*, trans. John Osborne (London: NLB, 1977), p. 185.
59 See Max Pensky, *Melancholy Dialectics: Walter Benjamin and the Play of Mourning* (Amherst: University of Massachusetts Press, 1993), p. 199.
60 See Charles Rosen, 'The Ruins of Walter Benjamin,' in *On Walter Benjamin: Critical Essays and Recollections*, ed. Gary Smith (Cambridge, MA: MIT Press, 1991), p. 149.
61 Benjamin, *German Tragic Drama*, pp. 118, 209. Yet see Richard W. F. Kroll's reading of Restoration frontispieces, emblems and hieroglyphics in relation to neo-Epicurean atomism and Lucretius's belief, in *De Rarum Natura*, in the embodied origins of language (*The Material World: Literate Culture in the Restoration and Early Eighteenth Century* (Baltimore: Johns Hopkins University Press, 1991), p. 191ff).
62 Rosen's translation, in Rosen, p. 144.
63 Benjamin, *German Tragic Drama*, p. 175.
64 Terry Eagleton, *The Ideology of the Aesthetic* (Oxford: Blackwell, 1990), pp. 334–335.
65 Benjamin, *German Tragic Drama*, p. 166.
66 See Wycherley's obscene satire, 'To the Sappho of the Age, Supposed to Lye-In of Love-Distemper, or a Play,' cited in Goreau, pp. 231–232.
67 See Goreau's account of 'The Apotheosis of Milton,' 'a literary fantasy' published fifty years after Behn's death in the popular *Gentleman's Magazine*, vol. 8 (September, 1738), p. 469. In the narrative Behn crashes the party celebrating Milton's induction into the society of 'Great Writers.' Wearing a 'loose robe de chambre with her neck and breasts bare,' she is told 'that none of her sex has a right to a seat there.' In Goreau, pp. 14–15.
68 Behn, Preface to *The Lucky Chance*, p. 186.
69 Aphra Behn, *Sir Patient Fancy*, in *Works*, vol. 4, p. 8.
70 Behn, Preface to *The Lucky Chance*, p. 187.
71 Miller, p. 275.
72 Benjamin, *German Tragic Drama*, p. 233.
73 Brecht, pp. 35, 39–42ff.
74 Marx, p. 161.

4 CARYL CHURCHILL'S PLAYS

1 Hélène Cixous, 'The Laugh of the Medusa,' *New French Feminisms*, eds E. Marks and I. de Courtivron (New York: Schocken Books), p. 245. First published as 'Le rire de la méduse,' *L'Arc* (1975), pp. 39–54.
2 See Jacques Lacan on the symbolic (language) as a function of the 'name of the father,' hence 'the patriarchal symbolic,' *Ecrits*, trans. Alan Sheridan (New York:

Norton, 1979), pp. 67ff., 199ff. Cixous believes that the subversion of the law of meaning is possible only if a woman 'blazes *her* trail in the symbolic . . . [making] of it a chaosmos of the "personal,"' by writing from her otherness, her body. Cixous, p. 258. For objections to Cixous's position, see n. 3.

3 One of the earliest and best rebuttals to *l'écriture féminine* was Monique Wittig's 'One is Not Born a Woman,' *Feminist Issues* 1:2 (1981), pp. 47–54, a Marxist-feminist attack (pp. 50–51). See also Wittig, *The Straight Mind* (Boston: Beacon Press, 1992), which reprints 'One is Not Born a Woman. For a discussion of the ways in which *l'écriture féminine* might still prove an enabling myth for feminism, see Ann Rosalind Jones, 'Writing the Body: Toward an Understanding of *l'écriture féminine*,' in *Feminist Criticism and Social Change: Sex, Class, and Race in Literature and Culture*, eds J. Newton and D. Rosenfelt (London: Methuen, 1985), pp. 86–101. For an analysis of body-writing via the late 1980s disputes over essentialism, see Diana Fuss, *Essentially Speaking: Feminism, Nature, Difference* (New York: Routledge, 1989), pp. 39–72ff.

4 See discussions of Churchill's socialist-feminism in Michelene Wandor's *Carry On, Understudies: Theatre and Sexual Politics* (London: Routledge and Kegan Paul, 1986); Amelia Howe Kritzer, *The Plays of Caryl Churchill: Theatre of Empowerment* (New York: St. Martin's Press, 1991); and Janelle Reinelt, *After Brecht: British Epic Theater* (Ann Arbor: University of Michigan Press, 1994).

5 See especially the work of Patrice Pavis in *Languages of the Stage: Essays in the Semiology of the Theatre* (New York: Performing Arts Journal Publications, 1982), which breaks away from both systematic communication models and exclusive focus on *mise-en-scène* to consider problems of ideology and desire in performance and reception.

6 See my Introduction to *Performance and Cultural Politics* (London: Routledge, 1966), p. 3ff. See Chapter 7.

7 In the anti-realist tradition of expressionism, surrealism, and absurdism, narrativity is challenged, spacial and temporal referents are confused but, with the possible exception of Brecht and Artaud, the dominance of the text as antecedent to performance is accepted. As in much modernist writing, the conventions and centrality of representation are reaffirmed by their seeming violation.

8 Herbert Blau, 'Precipitations of Theater: Words, Presence, Time Out of Mind,' in *Blooded Thought: Occasions of Theater* (New York: Performing Arts Journal Publications, 1982), p. 30.

9 Josette Féral, 'Performance and Theatricality: The Subject Demystified,' *Modern Drama* 25:1 (1982), p. 177.

10 Roland Barthes, 'Baudelaire's Theater,' in *Critical Essays*, trans. Richard Howard (Evanston: Northwestern University Press), pp. 27–28.

11 Brecht also demands distance – he preferred conventional proscenium stages to allow some space for reflection and analysis. See Walter Benjamin on 'astonishment' and 'abyss,' in epic theater, in *Understanding Brecht* (London: Verso, 1983), pp. 12–13, 22. See Herbert Blau: 'Brecht . . . tries to dispel the mystery in performance by looking at it from a distance, while not at all depreciating just how stubborn the mystery is.' 'Universals of Performance,' in his *The Eye of Prey: Subversions of the Postmodern* (Bloomington: University of Indiana Press, 1987), p. 176ff.

12 Michael Goldman helpfully broaches these same issues but draws different conclusions in *The Actor's Freedom* (New York: Viking, 1975), pp. 35ff., 113ff.

13 I am not proposing symmetry in the male and female experience of the oedipus but since split subjectivity applies to both sexes so too does unconscious longing for originary wholeness. The discussion of whether castration is one of many separations human beings undergo on the road to subjectivity or *the* complex which may refer back to other separations is beyond the scope of this chapter. See Juliet Mitchell's discussion in *Feminine Sexuality: Jacques Lacan and the école freudienne*, trans.

Jacqueline Rose, eds J. Mitchell and J. Rose (New York: Pantheon, 1977), pp. 13–26. See also Madelon Sprengnether, *The Spectral Mother: Freud, Feminism, and Psychoanalysis* (Ithaca, NY: Cornell University Press, 1990), pp. 144–153.

14 Luce Irigaray, 'This Sex Which Is Not One,' in *This Sex Which Is Not One*, trans. Catherine Porter with Carolyn Burke (Ithaca, NY: Cornell University Press, 1977), p. 26.

15 Michel Benamou, 'Presence and Play,' in *Performance in Postmodern Culture*, eds M. Benamou and C. Caramello (Madison, WI: Coda Press, 1977), p. 6. For a feminist view of nonphallomorphic representation see Jill Dolan, 'The Dynamics of Desire: Sexuality and Gender in Pornography and Performance,' *Theatre Journal* 39:2 (1987), pp. 156–174.

16 In an interesting reading of Churchill with Irigaray, '"Make Us the Women We Can't Be": Cloud Nine and the Female Imaginary' (*Journal of Dramatic Theory and Criticism*, 8:2 (Spring 1994), pp. 7–22, Mark Silverstein takes up my argument in an earlier version of this chapter, '(In)Visible Bodies in Churchill's Theatre,' *Theatre Journal* 40:2 (June 1988), pp. 189–205, but disagrees with this position: Churchill, he insists, aims for reinscription. Silverstein follows Margaret Whitford's wonderful development of the Irigarayan imaginary, in which she defends Irigaray against charges of essentialism: Irigaray, Whitford claims, never places the body beyond semiosis, rather she wants to accord the body 'its own specific symbolization' (cited in Silverstein, p. 8). Silverstein's argument is helpful in figuring what I have called Churchill's 'death-space' in *Fen* and in *The Skriker*.

17 Caryl Churchill, *Owners*, in *Plays: One* (London: Methuen, 1985), p. 66.

18 Antonin Artaud, *The Theater and Its Double*, trans. Mary Caroline Richards (New York: Grove Press, 1958), p. 13.

19 Herbert Blau, 'Flights of Angels, Scattered Seeds,' in *Blooded Thought*, p. 149.

20 Caryl Churchill, *Traps*, in *Plays: One*, p. 71.

21 See Maurice Merleau-Ponty, *The Phenomenology of Perception*, trans. Colin Smith (London: Routledge and Kegan Paul, 1962), pp. 71ff. See also Stanton Garner's extensive and impressive treatment of modern theater through phenomenology in *Bodied Spaces: Phenomenology and Performance in Contemporary Drama* (Ithaca, NY: Cornell University Press, 1994).

22 *Traps*, p. 122.

23 Blau, 'Precipitations,' p. 105.

24 See J. Laplanche and J.-B. Pontallis, *The Language of Psycho-Analysis*, trans. Donald Nicholson-Smith (New York: W.W. Norton, 1973) p. 103.

25 Churchill, in *Plays: One*, p. 184.

26 Ibid., p. 131. See Kritzer, pp. 83–100.

27 Brecht discusses historicization throughout his theoretical writings. See especially 'On the Use of Music in an Epic Theatre' (84–90); 'Alienation Effects in Chinese Acting' (91–99); 'A Short Organum for the Theatre,' nos 33–40 (189–191) in Bertolt Brecht, *Brecht on Theatre: The Development of an Aesthetic*, ed. John Willett (New York: Hill and Wang, 1965). See Reinelt, pp. 81–107.

28 Caryl Churchill, *Cloud Nine*, in *Plays: One*, pp. 251–252. For a fuller discussion of *Cloud Nine*, see my 'Refusing the Romanticism of Identity: Narrative Interventions in Churchill, Benmussa, Duras,' in *Performing Feminisms: Feminist Critical Theory and Theatre*, ed. Sue-Ellen Case (Baltimore: Johns Hopkins University Press, 1990), pp. 92–105.

29 Caryl Churchill, *Top Girls* (London: Methuen, 1982), pp. 16–17.

30 Lucretius, *De Rerum Natura*, trans. C. H. Sisson (Portsmouth, England: Eyre and Spottiswoode, 1976), pp. 44, 45.

31 Caryl Churchill, *Vinegar Tom*, in *Plays: One*, p. 162.

32 Michel Foucault, *Discipline and Punish*, trans. Alan Sheridan (New York: Vintage, 1979), p. 155.

33 For Foucault's synthesis of the 'power network' see Michel Foucault, *The History of Sexuality*, vol. 1 (New York: Vintage, 1980), pp. 92–96. See also H.L. Dreyfus and P. Rabinow, *Michel Foucault: Beyond Stucturalism and Hermeneutics*, 2nd edition (Chicago: University of Chicago Press, 1983), pp. 126–226.

34 See, for example, *Feminism and Foucault: Reflections on Resistance*, eds I. Diamond and L. Quimby (Boston: Northeastern University Press, 1988), especially the editors' Introduction, pp. ix–xx.

35 See Churchill's brief account of censorship by the state-subsidized BBC in *Plays: One*, p. xxii.

36 Caryl Churchill, *Fen* (London: Methuen, 1983), p. 5.

37 Cixous, p. 246.

38 Caryl Churchill, 'Author's Notes,' in *Mouthful of Birds* (London: Methuen, 1986), p. 5.

39 Churchill, *Mouthful of Birds*, p. 28.

40 Sigmund Freud, *Civilization and Its Discontents*, in *The Standard Edition of the Complete Psychological Works of Sigmund Freud* (London: Hogarth Press, 1975), vol. 21, p. 71.

41 Though the Methuen text of *A Mouthful of Birds* never mentions this source, Churchill and Lan probably made use of the memoirs and dossier on Herculine Barbin, first published in 1978 as *Herculine Barbin, dite Alexina B.* by Gallimard, then in 1980 as *Herculine Barbin: Being the Recently Discovered Memoirs of a Nineteenth-Century French Hermaphrodite*, introduced by Michel Foucault, trans. Richard McDougall (New York: Pantheon Books). For Foucault, the case of Herculine/Abel Barbin illustrates juridical attempts to regulate sexual identity in the 1860s and 1870s after centuries of relative tolerance for hermaphroditism. The nineteenth-century concept of a 'true sex' supports a medical–ethical discourse across diverse cultural practices, from biological science to religious confession to psychiatry; thus Herculine's doctors and judges force her to leave the 'happy limbo of . . . nonidentity' and become 'himself' (Introduction, p. xiii). Churchill and Lan pare down Herculine's effusive prose to narrative fragments and unanswered questions, suggesting the unbridgeable gap between nonidentity and a medically acceptable, legally 'true' sex/self.
    That such issues fascinate Churchill is evident from her radio play *Schreber's Nervous Illness* (first performed 1972), which deals with Freud's case history of Judge Schreber, whose physical sufferings stemmed from his belief that God planned to turn him into a woman and impregnate him in order to produce a new race of men.

42 Jacques Lacan, *The Four Fundamental Concepts of Psycho-Analysis*, trans. Alan Sheridan (New York: Norton, 1978), pp 204–205, cited in Kaja Silverman, *The Subject of Semiotics* (Oxford: Oxford University Press, 1983), p. 152.

43 Freud, p. 104.

44 The two-headed but divided figure has a parallel in the divisions of this co-authored text. Compare Churchill's introduction to Lan's on the fate of Agave. *Mouthful of Birds*, pp. 5–6.

45 Freud, p. 96.

46 Cixous, p. 258.

47 Euripides, *The Bacchae*, in *The Bacchae and Other Plays*, trans. Philip Vellacott (Baltimore: Penguin, 1967), p. 204.

48 Caryl Churchill, *Mad Forest: A Play from Romania* (London: Nick Hern Books, 1990), p. 54.

49 Fredric Jameson, *Postmodernism, or The Cultural Logic of Late Capitalism* (Durham NC: Duke University Press, 1992), p. ix.

50 Caryl Churchill, *The Skriker* (London: Nick Hern Books, 1994), p. 1.

51 Caryl Churchill in interview with Nicholas Wright, excerpted from 'The Platform Discussion at the Royal National Theater of Great Britain,' in *Public Access*,

Program of the Public Theater, 2:7 (May 1996), p. 40.
52   Churchill, *Skriker*, p. 51.

INTRODUCTION TO PART III

1   Gertrude Stein, 'Plays,' in *Gertrude Stein: Writings and Lectures 1909–1945*, ed. Patricia Meyerowitz (Baltimore, MD: Penguin, 1967), pp. 60–61.
2   Todd Gitlin, 'Postmodern Roots and Politics,' in Ian Angus and Sut Jhally, eds, *Cultural Politics in Contemporary America* (New York: Routledge, 1989), p. 347; cited in Philip Auslander, *Presence and Resistance* (Ann Arbor: University of Michigan Press, 1992), p. 9.
3   John Bender and David E. Wellbery, eds, *Chronotypes: The Construction of Time* (Stanford, CA: Stanford University Press, 1991), p. 2.
4   Homi Bhabha, 'How Newness Enters the World,' in *The Location of Culture* (London: Routledge, 1994), p. 218.
5   For Benjamin's use of the concept of redemption, see 'Theses on the Philosophy of History,' in *Illuminations*, ed. Hannah Arendt, trans. Harry Zohn (New York: Schocken Books, 1969), pp. 253–264.

5   IDENTIFICATION AND MIMESIS: ADRIENNE KENNEDY

1   Sigmund Freud, *The Standard Edition of Complete Psychological Works*, trans. and ed. James Strachey (London: Hogarth Press, 1971), vol. 28, p. 105. Unless otherwise stated, all references to Freud, giving volume and page no., are to this edition.
2   Hélène Cixous and Catherine Clément, *The Newly Born Woman (La Jeune Née)*, trans. Betsy Wing (Minneapolis: University of Minnesota Press, 1975), p. 148.
3   Jacqueline Rose, *Sexuality in the Field of Vision* (London: Verso, 1988), p. 5.
4   Fredric Jameson, 'The Cultural Logic of Late Capitalism,' in *Postmodernism, or the Cultural Logic of Late Capitalism* (Durham, NC: Duke University Press, 1992), p. 25ff.
5   Frantz Fanon, *Black Skin, White Masks*, trans. Charles Lam Markmann (New York: Grove Weidenfeld, 1967), p. 111. Unless otherwise stated, all Fanon references are to this text.
6   Paul Gilroy, *The Black Atlantic: Modernity and Double Consciousness* (Cambridge: Harvard University Press, 1993), pp. 2, 38.
7   Bertolt Brecht, *Brecht on Theatre: The Development of an Aesthetic*, ed. John Willett (New York: Hill and Wang, 1964), p. 276.
8   Ibid., pp. 92–93.
9   Stephen Heath, 'Lessons from Brecht,' *Screen*, 15:2 (1974), p. 112.
10 These formulations and those that follow were developed in shorter form in my 'Rethinking Identification: Kennedy, Freud, Brecht,' *Kenyon Review* 15:2 (Spring 1993), pp. 86–99. Since then Diana Fuss's luminous *Identification Papers* (New York: Routledge, 1995) has appeared, greatly clarifying the metaphorics and the historical and political implications of Freud's, and later Fanon's, stances on identification.
11 Sigmund Freud, *The Interpretation of Dreams* (1900), trans. James Strachey (New York: Avon, 1965), p. 149. See Fuss for earlier references, pp. 21–27.
12 Mikkel Borch-Jacobsen, *The Freudian Subject*, trans. Catherine Porter (Stanford, CA: Stanford University Press, 1988), pp. 20, 54.
13 Jacques Lacan, 'The Mirror Stage,' in *Ecrits*, trans. Alan Sheridan (New York: W.W. Norton, 1977), p. 4. *Corps morcelé* is translated as 'fragmented body.'
14 Richard Boothby, *Death and Desire: Psychoanalytic Theory in Lacan's Return to Freud* (New York: Routledge, 1991), p. 31.

15 Lacan, 'Mirror Stage,' p. 4, except the word 'salutary' from 'Aggressivity in Psychoanalysis,' *Ecrits*, p. 19.

16 On p. 161, n. 25, Fanon explores what the translator calls Lacan's 'mirror period.' Fanon comments that for the white, the black man is 'absolutely . . . the not-self [while] for the black man . . . historical and economic realities come into the picture.' Which means, as he puts it earlier, that the black man 'has no ontological resistance in the eyes of the white man' (110). Hailed on the street ('Dirty Nigger' or 'Look, a Negro'), '[I am] sealed into that crushing objecthood . . . [and] the glances of the other fixed me there . . . I burst apart. Now the fragments have been put back together by another self' (109). When Fanon first explicates Lacan's mirror stage he claims that 'the real Other for the white man is and will continue to be the black man. And conversely' (161, n. 25). This would suggest that there is reciprocity, but then Fanon qualifies: for the white, the black is other 'on the level of the body image – [he is] the unidentifiable, unassimilable' (161), whereas for the black man reality's mirror is historically distorted. Kennedy would call it a funnyhouse mirror. To look in is to see, already, an inferiority. In the sub-chapter, 'The Negro and Hegel,' Fanon demonstrates that the self–other dialectic which makes subjectivity possible – a dialectic based on mutual recognition – is impossible in racist societies: 'What [the master] wants from the slave is not recognition but work' (220, n. 8). Racism pathologizes reality. '[W]hen we assert that European culture has an *imago* of the Negro . . . [which] the Negro faithfully reproduces . . . we do not go beyond reality' (169). But as many have noted, Fanon's analysis in *Black Skin, White Masks*, gives only a crude description of black women's reality.

17 Borch-Jacobsen, p. 95.

18 See Judith Butler on this important point in *Bodies That Matter: On the Discursive Limits of 'Sex'* (New York: Routledge, 1993, p. 106ff).

19 See Judith Butler's vital work on this point: 'Identifications are never fully and finally made; they are incessantly reconstituted and, as such, are subject to the volatile logic of iterability.' *Bodies That Matter: On the Discursive Limits of 'Sex'* (New York: Routledge, 1993), p. 105. That is, every (re)iteration of gender 'law' introduces 'instabilities [and] possibilities for rematerialization . . . that call into question the hegemonic force of that . . . regulatory law' (2). Yet resistance to the law, Butler insists, does not change it: 'the law . . . cannot itself be reworked or recalled by the kind of resistances that it generates' (105)

20 Theresa Brennan, Introduction to *Between Feminism and Psychoanalysis*, ed. T. Brennan (New York: Routledge, 1989), p. 10.

21 Adrienne Kennedy, 'A Growth of Images,' interview transcribed and edited by Lisa Lehman, *The Drama Review* 21:4 (December 1977), p. 42.

22 Fanon, pp. 8, 109.

23 Borch-Jacobsen, p. 45.

24 Luce Irigaray, *Speculum of the Other Woman*, trans. Gillian C. Gill (Ithaca, NY: Cornell University Press, 1974), p. 54.

25 Feminists have long understood that the Enlightenment concept of the 'social contract' – which was to sweep away the abuses of aristocratic hegemony and patriarchalism in the historical march toward freedom – had little or nothing to do, in its conceptualizing, with liberating women. See Carole Pateman, *The Sexual Contract* (Stanford, CA: Stanford University Press, 1988), p. 19ff.

26 Gilroy, p. 215.

27 Boothby, p. 32.

28 Mikkel Borch-Jacobsen, *Lacan: The Absolute Master*, trans. Douglas Brick (Stanford, CA: Stanford University Press, 1991), p. 52.

29 Brennan, p. 13.

30 Adrienne Kennedy, Preface to *In One Act* (Minneapolis: University of Minnesota

Press, 1988), p. ix.

31 Borch-Jacobsen, *Lacan*, p. 49. See Ruth Leys's gendering of Borch-Jacobsen's non-specular mimesis-that-precedes-subjectivity; Leys revises 'the Freudian subject' with her 'mimesis-suggestion paradigm' (175) in 'The Real Miss Beauchamp: Gender and the Subject of Imitation,' in *Feminists Theorize the Political*, eds Judith Butler and Joan W. Scott (New York: Routledge, 1992), pp. 167–214. That Leys's example is a case of multiple personality makes this essay interesting in relation to Kennedy's representation of multiple identification.

32 Borch-Jacobsen, *Lacan*, pp. 70–71. 'Thus the spectacle of the imaginary was only the projection, on the world's stage, of the mime that the "ego" initially is. Why did Lacan forget that so quickly?' (70).

33 Amiri Baraka (LeRoi Jones), 'The Revolutionary Theatre,' in *Home* (New York: William Morrow, 1965), p. 210. Also cited in Kimberly W. Benston, 'The Aesthetic of Modern Black Drama: From Mimesis to Methexis,' in Errol Hill, ed., *The Theatre of Black Americans* (New York: Applause Theatre Book Publishers, 1987), p. 65.

34 Larry Neal, 'Into Nationalism, Out of Parochialism,' in Hill, p. 296. See also *The Drama Review* 12:4 (Summer 1968), pp. 29–39, for Neal's 'The Black Arts Movement,' among other important essays from this period. In her article, 'Black Theater' on theater in the 1960s (in *Black Expression*, ed. Addison Gayle [New York: Weybright and Talley, 1969], pp. 134–143), Toni Cade Bambara (writing as Toni Cade), while naming dozens of others, also omits mention of Kennedy's work. As Bambara's strong sympathy for writers and her acute analysis of black women's oppression in the black nationalist movement are well known (see *The Black Woman* [New York: Random House, 1970]), this omission is all the more telling.

Foreigners were less nervous about linking Kennedy to her peers. In a review of the first Paris production in 1968, Jean Paget wrote that Kennedy's theater 'has a power to attack that is, finally, as sure as that of LeRoi Jones.' Cited in Lois More Overbeck, 'The Life of the Work: A Preliminary Sketch,' in *Intersecting Boundaries: The Theatre of Adrienne Kennedy*, eds P. Bryant-Jackson and L.O. Overbeck (Minneapolis: University of Minnesota Press, 1992), p. 26.

35 bell hooks, 'The Chitlin Circuit,' in *Yearning: Race, Gender, and Cultural Politics* (Boston: South End Press, 1990), p. 36.

36 Cited in Overbeck, in *Intersecting Boundaries*, p. 28. In this volume see also Billie Allen (the first Sarah of *Funnyhouse of a Negro*):

> What interests me is that some people got very angry about this play . . . especially some black people because they felt it was denigrating of blacks . . . .
> [T]he words say . . . 'niggers' this and 'niggers' that, but it was [Sarah's] psychotic anger. What [the play is] so clearly about [is] the depth of the damage of institutionalized racism.

(219)

37 Barbara Christian, 'The Race for Theory,' reprinted in *Making Face/Making Soul: Creative and Critical Perspectives by Feminists of Color*, ed, Gloria Anzaldúa (San Francisco: Aunt Lute Books, 1990), p. 342.

38 See Homi K. Bhabha's brilliant essay, 'Interrogating Identity: The Postcolonial Prerogative,' in *The Anatomy of Racism*, ed. David Theo Goldberg (Minneapolis: University of Minnesota Press, 1990), p. 183.

39 Louis Althusser, *Lenin and Philosophy*, trans. Ben Brewster (New York: Monthly Review Press, 1971), p. 140ff.

40 Harold Cruse, 'Revolutionary Nationalism and the Afro-American,' in *Black Fire*, eds LeRoi Jones [Amiri Baraka] and Larry Neal (New York: William Morrow,

1968), p. 62. Cruse adds, 'Moreover there is no organized force at present, capable of altering the structural form of American society' (62).

41 Adrienne Kennedy in a telephone call to me, December 1990.

42 Adrienne Kennedy, *Funnyhouse of a Negro*, in *In One Act*, p. 2.

43 Lacan, 'Mirror Stage,' p. 2. See also René Girard on mimetic desire: 'Once his basic needs are satisfied . . . [man] desires *being*, something he lacks and which some other person seems to possess.' *Violence and the Sacred* (Baltimore: Johns Hopkins University Press, 1972), p. 146. If mimetic desire in Kennedy produces the 'monstrous' doubling that Girard describes, she goes far beyond him in historicizing that process.

44 Etienne Balibar, *Masses, Classes, Ideas: Studies on Politics and Philosophy Before and After Marx*, trans. James Swenson (New York: Routledge, 1994), p. 17.

45 See Fanon, p. 220, n. 8: 'For Hegel there is reciprocity; here the master laughs at the consciousness of the slave – what he really wants from the slave is not recognition but work.' See also Gilroy's reading of Hegel's master–slave allegory, (Gilroy, pp. 50–51, 54ff., 63–71), via Frederick Douglass's *My Bondage* and the Margaret Garner story (source material for Toni Morrison's *Beloved*), in which the slave's 'turn towards death' (63) means the

> refusal to concede legitimacy to slavery and thereby initiate the dialectic of intersubjective interdependency and recognition that Hegel's allegory presents as modernity's precondition . . . . The repeated choice of death rather than bondage . . . helps to define this primal history of modernity . . . the moment of jubilee that has the upper hand over the pursuit of utopia by rational means.
> (68)

While Kennedy's subject is a subject-in-relation, the operations of identification are anti-Hegelian since they preclude the stable appropriation of what is not-self or other. In Gilroy's argument the Hegelian model is important for other black intellectuals (Du Bois, Wright, Baraka), whose work suggests that the subject-in-relation, typified in the master–slave allegory, must be revisited since it 'correctly places slavery at the natal core of modern sociality' (63).

46 Balibar, p. 18.

47 But for the performer, repetition can mean more opportunity for exploration. In actress Billie Allen's words (about performing *Funnyhouse*): 'The repetition allows you to go deeper and find another place.' In Bryant-Jackson and Overbeck, *Intersecting Boundaries*, p. 221. See Suzan-Lori Parks on 'rep and rev,' in Steven Druckman, 'Suzan-Lori Parks and Liz Diamond: Doo-a-diddly-dit-dit. An Interview,' *The Drama Review* 39:3 (Fall 1995), pp. 56–57.

48 Fanon, p. 116.

49 Ibid., p. 60.

50 Patricia Williams, *The Alchemy of Race and Rights* (Cambridge: Harvard University Press, 1991), p. 129.

51 Adrienne Kennedy, *People Who Led To My Plays* (New York: Alfred A. Knopf, 1987), pp. 121–122.

52 Ibid., p. 16.

53 Adrienne Kennedy, *The Owl Answers*, in *In One Act*, p. 25.

54 Julia Kristeva, *Powers of Horror: An Essay on Abjection*, trans. Leon S. Roudiez (New York: Columbia University Press, 1982), p. 4. I thank Beth Loffreda for her fine insights on this point.

55 Fanon, p. 21.

56 bell hooks in her witty (self-)interview with Gloria Watkins, 'Critical Reflections: Adrienne Kennedy, the Writer, the Work,' in Bryant-Jackson and Overbeck, *Intersecting Boundaries*, p. 181.

57 George Bataille, 'The Pineal Eye,' in *Visions of Excess: Selected Writings, 1927–1936,* ed. Allan Stoekl, trans. A. Stoekl with C.R. Lovitt and D.M. Leslie, Jr. (Minneapolis: University of Minnesota Press), p. 82.

58 Kennedy, *People,* p. 121.

59 Paul Carter Harrison, *Kuntu Drama: Plays of the African Continuum* (New York: Grove Press, 1974), p. 10.

60 Gilroy, p. 99.

61 Kimberley Benston, 'I Yam what I Yam: The Tropes of Un(naming) in Afro-American Literature,' in Henry Louis Gates, Jr., ed., *Black Literature and Literary Theory* (New York: Methuen, 1984), p. 152. Cited in Rosemary Curb, '(Hetero)Sexual Terrors in Adrienne Kennedy's Early Plays,' in Bryant-Jackson and Overbeck, *Intersecting Boundaries,* p. 151. See Robert L. Tener's 'Theatre of Identity: Adrienne Kennedy's Portrait of the Black Woman,' *Studies in Black Literature* 6:2 (Summer 1975), pp. 1–5, for an early discussion of *The Owl Answers* and the impossibility of 'transcendental spiritual identity' (5).

62 Brennan, pp. 9, 11ff.

63 See, for example, Mary Ann Doane's discussion of female masochism in relation to female consumerism in *The Desire to Desire: The Woman's Film of the 1940s* (Bloomington: Indiana University Press, 1987), pp. 7–37.

64 Freud, 'The Ego and the Id,' *Standard Edition,* 19:29.

65 Bhabha, p. 220.

66 Adrienne Kennedy, *A Movie Star Has to Star in Black and White,* in *In One Act,* p. 32.

67 Borch-Jacobsen, p. 23.

68 Ibid., pp. 22–23.

69 On cultural coercion, the media, and black American drama, see Timothy Murray's 'Screening the Camera's Eye: Black and White Configurations of Technological Representation,' *Modern Drama* 28:1 (March 1985), pp. 110–124. Recently Kennedy has commented that she never saw her movie stars through a racial 'filter':

> Remember, the 30s were different. We didn't have the tools to question. Film was the common language in my immigrant elementary high school. All of us – Jewish, Italian, Negro – talked about Tyrone Power and Ginger Rogers . . . . I don't recall any of my Negro friends questioning our marginal relationship to what we saw.
> (In Lisa Jones, 'Beyond the Funnyhouse: A Conversation with Playwright Adrienne Kennedy,' *The Villlage Voice,* 16 April 1996, p. 42)

70 Borch-Jacobsen, *Freudian Subject,* p. 40

71 Ibid., p. 44.

72 Adrienne Kennedy, *The Alexander Plays* (Minneapolis: University of Minnesota Press, 1992), p. 83. All further citations from *She Talks to Beethoven, The Ohio State Murders, The Film Club,* and *The Dramatic Circle* are from this edition.

73 Adrienne Kennedy, *Deadly Triplets: A Theatre Mystery and Journal* (Minneapolis: University of Minnesota Press, 1990), p. 124.

74 David Glover, *Vampires, Mummies, and Liberals: Bram Stoker and the Politics of Popular Fiction* (Durham: Duke University Press, 1996), p. 65.

75 Degeneracy was a pressing social question precisely because of imperialism's ravages. The question for the positivist anthropologist was whether an advanced civilization could, in Glover's words, 'continue to produce the heroes it needs,' or was Britain '"being assailed by diseased and vicious children"' (ibid., p. 98) – the latter phrase a citation from John Buchan, *Memory Hold-the-Door* (London: Hodder and Stoughton, 1940), p. 286 (see Glover, p. 177, n. 90).

76 See Nancy Leys Stepan, 'Race and Gender: The Role of Analogy in Science' in Goldberg, *Anatomy of Racism,* pp. 38–49ff.

77 Michel Foucault, *The History of Sexuality*, vol. 1, trans. Robert Hurley (New York: Vintage, 1980), pp. 119–120.

78 Bram Stoker, *Dracula*, in *The Annotated Dracula*, ed. Leonard Wolf (New York: Clarkson N. Potter, 1975), p. 300.

79 Frantz Fanon, *The Wretched of the Earth*, trans. Constance Farrington (New York: Grove Press, 1963), p. 250.

80 Glover, p. 15 9ms)

81 Kennedy, *Theatre Journal*, p. 105.

82 Stoker, p. 81.

83 Stoker, p. 16; Kennedy, *Film Club* and *Dramatic Circle*, p. 70.

84 Kennedy, *Theatre Journal*, p. 105.

85 Fanon, *Wretched of the Earth*, p. 249.

86 Ibid., p. 251.

87 Ibid., p. 280.

88 Gilroy, pp. 122, 121.

89 See Kimberley W. Benston's brilliant article, 'Locating Adrienne Kennedy' (in Bryant-Jackson and Overbeck): 'Autobiography, of the flesh and its inscriptions, is the very signature of Adrienne Kennedy's impossible though endless quest for a clarifying and stabilizing source' (115). Particularly powerful is Benston's testimony as reader: '. . . I experienced instead the frustration of any sure conceptual grasp as Kennedy's play continuously displaced my schema by its own ceaseless self-interrogation' (114).

90 hooks, 'Critical Reflections,' p. 184.

91 Diane Johnson, jacket blurb for *People Who Led To My Plays*.

92 Freud, 19:25.

6 PERFORMANCE AND TEMPORALITY

1 Josette Féral, 'What is Left of Performance Art? Autopsy of a Function, Birth of a Genre,' *Discourse* (Spring 1992), p. 154. Féral's argument is, as usual, clear and stimulating, but the sense that there are no longer coherent ideologies against which performance can fashion its subversion seems to deny continuing effects of global capitalism, the manifestations of ethnic cleansing and racism – which spanned the 1980s and are present, quite coherently, today.

2 Walter Benjamin, 'On the Mimetic Faculty,' in *Reflections*, ed. Peter Demetz, trans. Edmund Jephcott (New York: Schocken Books, 1986), p. 333ff. Dialectical images will be explained shortly. The phrase 'against the grain' comes from 'Theses on the Philosophy of History' in *Illuminations*, ed. Hannah Arendt, trans. Harry Zohn (New York: Schocken Books, 1969), p. 257: '[The historical materialist] regards it as his task to brush history against the grain.'

3 Bert O. States, *Great Reckonings in Little Rooms: On the Phenomenology of Theater* (Berkeley: University of California Press, 1985), pp. 49, 50.

4 Gertrude Stein, 'Plays,' in *Gertrude Stein: Writings and Lectures 1909–1945*, ed. Patricia Meyerowitz (Baltimore: Penguin, 1967), p. 59.

5 The futility lies in what Herbert Blau calls the 'agitation over . . . temporality': 'Whether prescribed or felt out, the determining of time is a universal of performance. It determines in turn the relations between what seems . . . familiar and what strange, the artificial and the natural, the sense of just being or being someone . . . .' Herbert Blau, 'Universals of Performance,' in *The Eye of Prey: Subversions of the Postmodern* (Bloomington: Indiana University Press, 1987), pp. 163–64. I don't want to suggest that performance art in the 1970s wasn't insistent on temporality. John Cage's I Ching-inspired *4'33"*, Yvonne Rainer's *Continuous Project* in dance, Nicholas Nixon's serial photographs – see Henry Sayre's *The Object of Performance: The American Avant-Garde since 1970* (Chicago: University of Chicago

Press, 1989) for these and scores of other examples – are explorations of temporality, although not in the sense I will be discussing.

6 See Edward Soja, *Postmodern Geographies: The Reassertion of Space in Critical Social
Theory* (New York: Verso, 1989), p. 1ff. In a reading of the Introduction to the
Grundisse, Terry Eagleton works to counter the 'genetic-evolutionist' *narrative* in
Marxism but concedes that the effort runs aground on Marx's own organic-evo-
lutionist metaphors. In Terry Eagleton, *Walter Benjamin, or Towards a Revolutionary
Criticism* (London: Verso, 1981), p. 64ff.

7 Ibid., p. 2.

8 Fredric Jameson, 'The Cultural Logic of Late Capitalism,' in *Postmodernism, or, The
Cultural Logic of Late Capitalism* (Durham: Duke University Press, 1991), p. 43. See
Sue-Ellen Case, 'Performing Lesbian in the Space of Technology,' Parts I and
II, *Theatre Journal* 47:1 (March 1995), pp. 1–18, and 47:3 (October 1995), pp.
329–343, who celebrates 'lesbian as embedded in spatial ecryption' and, in a
witty turn, finds 'Sappho, reconstructed as scrim interpenetrated by communal
messages, traveling through the inter-net . . .' (339). For Case the cyberlesbian is
the latest figuration of a sexuality resisting capitalist patriarchy, linear time, and
heterosexism: 'Homosexual, a consideration of sameness, may lend itself better to
notions of space than time' (I, p. 18).

9 See also Catherine Stimpson's notion that Stein's poetry suggests a female
expansion into space: 'a tribute to woman's being, and being in space,' along
with Jessica Benjamin's 'what is experientially female is the association of
desire with a space, a place within the self.' Cited in Lidia Curti 'What is Real
and What is Not: Female Fabulations in Cultural Analysis,' *Cultural Studies*,
eds L. Grossberg, C. Nelson and P. Treichler (New York: Routledge, 1992),
p. 146.

10 Cited in Benjamin's 'Theses on the Philosophy of History,' in *Illuminations*, p. 255.
All Benjamins scholars discuss his loathing of historicism. For one lucid account
see Michael W. Jennings, *Dialectical Images: Walter Benjamin's Theory of Literary
Criticism* (Ithaca, NY: Cornell University Press, 1987), pp. 42–81.

11 Bertolt Brecht, *Brecht on Theatre: The Development of an Aesthetic*, ed. John Willett
(New York: Hill and Wang, 1964), pp. 140, 190.

12 Walter Benjamin, *Gesammelte Schriften* (Frankfurt am Main: Suhrkamp, 1980), vol.
2.1, pp. 56–57, cited in Rainer Nägele, 'Introduction: Reading Benjamin,' in
Benjamin's Ground, ed. Rainer Nägele (Detroit: Wayne State University Press,
1988), p. 10. The 'hollow continuum' comes from Benjamin's 'Theses,' p. 261.

13 Benjamin, 'Theses,' p. 257.

14 Walter Benjamin, 'On Some Motifs in Baudelaire,' in *Illuminations*, p. 188ff.

15 As Susan Buck-Morss puts it:

> Within advertising, a new dissimulating aura is injected into the commodity,
> easing its passage into the dream world of the private consumer . . . .
> Advertising images attempt to 'humanize' products in order to deny their com-
> modity character; consumers continue in this effort when they provide cases
> and covers for the possessions, sentimentally providing them with a 'home'.
>   (*The Dialectics of Seeing* [Cambridge, MA: MIT Press, 1991], p. 184)

16 Ibid., p. 253ff.

17 Ibid., pp. 254–262ff., 116–117ff.

18 Like many male modernists Brecht and Benjamin fetishized the prostitute. See
Rebecca Schneider, 'After Us the Savage Goddess . . . ,' in *Performance and Cultural
Politics*, ed. E. Diamond (London: Routledge, 1996), pp. 158–159, on the prostitute as one of Benjamin's dialectical images (158); see Brecht's *Drums in The Night*
and *In the Jungle of Cities*, in *Collected Plays*, eds Ralph Manheim and John Willett

(New York: Vintage, 1971) for unreconstructed representations of the beloved as whore.

19 On the female character of postmodern image-culture see Lidia Curti's discussion in 'Female Fabulations,' p. 140ff. Sounding like a latter-day Tertullian, Jean Baudrillard moves his longstanding indictment of hyper-reality to the sphere of 'models, fashion, simulation' in which the 'power' of woman derives from 'her triumphant in-difference, her triumphant lack of subjectivity.' In *Les stratégies fatales* (Paris: Editions Grasset et Pasqualle, 1983), pp. 9ff., 113ff., cited in Curti, p. 140. See also Susan Bordo, 'Reading the Slender Body,' in *Body/Politics*, eds Mary Jacobus, Evelyn Fox Keller, and Sally Shuttleworth (New York: Routledge, 1990), pp. 83–112; and Kate Davy, 'Buying and Selling the Look,' *Parachute* (Fall 1985), pp. 22–24. For a more general discussion, see Stuart Ewen, *All Consuming Images* (New York: Basic Books, 1988), and Ian Angus and Sut Jhally, eds, *Cultural Politics in Contemporary America* (New York: Routledge, 1989).

20 Cited in Buck-Morss, p. 251.

21 Buck-Morss, pp. 93, 33.

22 Cited in Buck-Morss, pp. 220, 73.

23 The full passage reads:

> The past does not throw its light on the present, nor does the present illumine the past but an image is formed when that which has been and the Now come together in a flash as a constellation. In other words, image is dialectic at a standstill . . . . Only dialectical images are genuinely historical.
>
>   (*Gesammelte Schriften*, vol. 5, N3, 1, cited in Jennings, p. 36)

Another related elaboration:

> In the dialectical image, the past of a particular epoch . . . appears before the eyes of [. . . a particular, present epoch] in which humanity, rubbing its eyes, recognizes precisely this dream *as a dream*. It is in this moment that the historian takes upon himself the task of dream interpretation.
>
>   (*Gesammelte Schriften*, vol. 5, p. 580, cited in Buck-Morss, p. 261)

24 See Mirian Hansen, 'Benjamin, Cinema and Experience: "The Blue Flower in the Land of Technology",' *New German Critique* 40 (Winter 1987), pp. 194–195ff.

25 Benjamin, 'Theses,' p. 254.

26 See Jürgen Habermas, 'Walter Benjamin: Consciousness-Raising or Rescuing Critique,' reprinted in Gary Smith, ed., *On Walter Benjamin: Critical Essays and Recollections* (Cambridge, MA: MIT Press, 1991), p. 95: 'In a succession of discrete shocks, the art work deprived of its aura releases experiences that used to be enclosed within an esoteric style.'

27 This refusal of teleology distinguishes Benjamin's (and Adorno's) notion of dialectics from the Hegelian process of opposition, synthesis, sublation, leading to, ultimately, a harmonious reconciliation – the transcendence of alienation of subject and object – indeed the identity of subject and object. For Adorno and Benjamin, both committed modernists, there could be no harmonious reconciliation, no 'universal history' that might grasp the 'whole of social development,' and certainly no (as Adorno puts it) 'hypostasized . . . mind or vantage point that could comprehend the totality' (cited in David Held, *Introduction to Critical Theory* [Berkeley: University of California Press], p. 204). For Benjamin, the universal is graspable, if at all, only in concrete individual phenomena. Dialectical thinking never arrives at abstract truth but tries *to uncover or recover the truth of the particular*. This means not resolving but rather maintaining the tension – and the inter-implication – of antithetical elements. For example, while Benjamin praised the Surrealists for attempting 'to win the energies of intoxication for the revolu-

tion,' he criticized them for their 'inadequate, undialectical conception of the nature of intoxication,' which he felt was 'enmeshed in a number of pernicious romantic prejudices.' He goes on:

> A serious exploration of occult . . . phenomena presupposes a *dialectical intertwinement* to which a romantic turn of mind is impervious. For histrionic or fanatical stress on the mysterious side of the mysterious takes us no further; we penetrate the mystery only to the degree that we recognize it in the everyday world, by virtue of a *dialectical optic* that perceives *the everyday as impenetrable, the impenetrable as everyday* . . . . The reader, the thinker, the loiterer, the flaneur, are types of illuminati just as much as the opium eater, the dreamer, the ecstatic.
>
> ('Surrealism,' in *Reflections*, pp. 189–190)

Benjamin's 'dialectical intertwinement,' while it rests on contradiction, is not, I think, completely out of line with Rosi Braidotti's notion of current feminist critique: 'feminists have evolved towards a non-dialectical view of alterity, affirming positive differences so as to posit new parameters for the definition of female subjectivity.' *Patterns of Dissonance* (New York: Routledge, 1991), p. 277. Braidotti would get rid of the Hegelian 'system' of penetrating and sublating (the other, the object). Benjamin put faith in alterity – in modes of reasoning and being, not penetrated by knowledge. He considered Hegel an 'intellectual brute' – see Buck-Morss, p. 9.

28 Walter Benjamin, *Charles Baudelaire: A Lyric Poet in the Era of High Capitalism*, trans. Harry Zohn (London: New Left Books, 1973), p. 132.

29 It may seem eccentric to annex the dialectical image to a performance medium. Yet though he never wrote for the theater, Benjamin wrote superbly about the theater in *The Origin of German Tragic Drama* and in *Understanding Brecht*. In fact the former work, Benjamin acknowledged, was impelled by an 'accidental alienation-effect': 'the skewed crown on the king's head marked an imbalance of power' in a production of *El Cid* which he saw in Geneva in 1916. In Carrie Asman, 'Return of the Sign to the Body: Benjamin and Gesture in the Age of Retheatricalization,' *Discourse* (Spring 1994), p. 47. In the Arcades project, as we've seen, he had (like any theater worker) 'nothing to say, only to show.' Most tellingly, in his 'Konvolut N,' Benjamin identifies 'dialectic at a standstill' as his method for the Arcades project (*Philosophical Forum* 15:1–2 [Fall–Winter 1983–84], p. 8), the very term he used to describe the Brechtian *gestus*, where the historicity of the play and the character is made readable via a complex image. (See *Understanding Brecht*, trans. Anna Bostock (London: Verso, 1983], p. 12, and 'Short Organum for the Theatre,' no. 39, in Brecht, *Brecht on Theatre*, p. 191.)

30 Case, I, pp. 12–13.

31 Alice A. Jardine, *Gynesis: Configurations of Woman and Modernity* (Ithaca, NY: Cornell University Press, 1985), p. 147.

32 Paul De Man, 'Autobiography as De-Facement,' in *the Rhetoric of Romanticism* (New York: Columbia University Press, 1984), p. 70. See also Joan W. Scott's 'The Evidence of Experience,' *Critical Inquiry* 17 (Summer 1991), pp. 773–797, which argues that experience is not a prediscursive category but rather 'always already an interpretation *and* something that needs to be interpreted' (797).

33 Diana Fuss, *Essentially Speaking: Feminism, Nature and Difference* (New York and London: Routledge, 1989), p. 114ff.

34 Donna Haraway, *Simians, Cyborgs, and Women: The Reinvention of Nature* (New York: Routledge 1991), p. 109.

35 Teresa de Lauretis, *Alice Doesn't: Feminism, Semiotics, Cinema* (Bloomington: Indiana University Press), pp. 159, 186.

36 Jameson, p. xx.

37 Todd Gitlin, *The Sixties: Years of Hope, Years of Rage* (New York: Bantam Books,

1987), p. 14ff.

38 Walter Benjamin, 'Motifs in Baudelaire,' p. 159.
39 Sayre, p. xii.
40 Cited in Sayre, p. 9.
41 Walter Benjamin, 'The Artwork in an Age of Mechanical Reproduction,' in *Illuminations*, p. 229.
42 Philip Monk, 'Common Carrier: Performance by Artists,' *Modern Drama* 25:1 (March 1982), p. 164. Josette Féral's excellent early piece, 'Performance and Theatricality: The Subject Demystified,' trans. Terese Lyons, *Modern Drama* 25:1 (1982), restates this coding psychoanalytically:

> The body is made conspicuous: a body in pieces, fragmented and yet one, a body perceived and rendered as a *place of desire*, displacement, fluctuation . . . . The body is cut up not in order to negate it, but in order to bring it back to life . . . [to be] enriched by all the part-objects that make it up . . .
>
> (171, 172)

43 Monk, p. 167. Monk is discussing video artist Elizabeth Chitty but one might consider Valie Export, Vito Acconci, Eleanor Antin, Martha Rosler, and of course Lariue Anderson whose highly praised, commercially successful *United States*, Parts I–IV at the Brooklyn Academy of Music in 1983 made the arcana of performance art accessible and approachable.
44 Despite a healthy rejection of poststructuralist doxa in recent performance theory, I continue to think the relation of the gendered body to discourse is a powerful source of pleasure, pain, and desire in performance, especially – as in the performances discussed in these chapters – when presence becomes implicitly temporal (i.e. partially absent to itself). See my Introduction to *Performance and Cultural Politics* (London: Routledge, 1966), p. 1ff. The debate about presence among performance theorists is too extensive and complex to summarize; I offer only a very few texts and a few pointers. Besides Henry Sayre's *The Object of Performance*, see Philip Auslander's *Presence and Resistance: Postmodern and Cultural Politics in Contemporary American Performance* (Ann Arbor: University of Michigan Press, 1992) which explores mediatized presence as political intervention, p. 21ff.; Jill Dolan's *Presence and Desire: Essays on Gender, Sexuality, and Performance* (Ann Arbor: University of Michigan Press, 1993) offers materialist explorations of the seductive presence of women performers, the self-awareness of the desiring critic. Regarding the above texts, see Sue-Ellen Case, who wants her presence and her media too (Case, I and II). See Michael Vanden Heuvel's *Performing Drama/Dramatizing Performance* (Ann Arbor: University of Michigan Press, 1991), which discusses presence via the tensions between text and performance. See Jon Erickson's description of a Heraclitean notion of presence as becoming, in 'The Body as Object of Modern Performance,' *Journal of Dramatic Theory and Criticism* (Fall 1990), pp. 241–243. As phenomenology is uniquely equipped to address the body's coming-to-presence in the performance space, see Bert O. States's *Great Reckonings in Little Rooms*, and Stanton B. Garner's *Bodied Spaces: Phenomenology and Performance in Contemporary Drama* (Ithaca, NY: Cornell University Press, 1994), which extends notions of habitation and perception to gender and history. I discuss Herbert Blau and Peggy Phelan in the text.
45 Bertolt Brecht, *A Man's A Man*, in *Collected Plays*, vol. 2, eds Ralph Manheim and John Willett (New York: Vintage, 1977), cited in Eagleton, p. 36.
46 Ghosting runs through all of Blau's work, especially *Take Up the Bodies: Theater at the Vanishing Point* (Urbana: University of Illinois Press, 1982).
47 Peggy Phelan, *Unmarked* (London: Routledge), 1993, p. 148.
48 For Benjamin, seeing was of course married to knowing, but neither could be

trusted. He came to feel that auratic contemplation, however corrupt, finally provided a remnant of integration because one had the sense of the beloved object returning the gaze. ('To perceive the aura of an object we look at means we invest it with the ability to look at us in return,' 'Some Motifs in Baudelaire,' p. 188.) Miriam Hansen cautions that this returning of the gaze is not a mirroring of the subject 'in its presence, conscious identity, but confronts us with another self, never before seen in a waking state' (Hansen, p. 188). With this in mind I wonder about a connection to Brecht. In 1938, when he read a later version of the artwork essay that contained the motif of auratic object returning the gaze, Brecht wrote in his diary: 'It is all mysticism, in a posture opposed to mysticism. It is in such a form that the materialistic concept of history is adopted! it is rather ghastly.' Cited in Susan Buck-Morss, *The Origins of Negative Dialectics* (New York: Free Press, 1977, p. 149). Is it possible that in order to retrieve the aura for his materialist philosophy of history Benjamin took the notion of returning the look from Brecht's epic theater? Benjamin describes the traditional stage actor as auratic ('The Artwork,' p. 229) and wrote contrastingly about the Brechtian actor as one who shows herself to be acting and, in the didactic play especially, who 'fills' in the abyss between stage and audience. In *Understanding Brecht*, pp. 22, 20.

49   See Blau, 'Universals of Performance,' pp. 163, 170, 181, Blau's radical phenomenology, positing the empirical body in its dying, also helps posit the body in its lived experience; this is the real 'relevance' of the performer's body; it's precisely its dying that interrupts the ordered emplotments of aesthetic time. In my reading, Benjamin's now-time intensifies the sense of lived experience, which is, in the performances I discuss below, the historically lived experience of women in their conflicting temporalities, whose articulations are set in motion by their forgotten objects.

50   See Sayre, pp. 66–100, 174–210. See also Nick Kaye, *Postmodernism and Performance* (New York: St. Martin's Press, 1994), pp. 6–143.

51   See my 'Refusing the Romanticism of Identity: Narrative Interventions in Churchill, Benmussa, Duras,' in *Performing Feminisms: Feminist Critical Theory and Theatre*, ed. Sue-Ellen Case (Baltimore: Johns Hopkins University Press), pp. 92–105, and 'Benmussa's Adaptations: Unauthorized Texts from Elsewhere,' in *Feminine Focus*, ed. Enoch Brater (New York: Oxford University Press, 1989), pp. 64–78.

52   Cited in Sayre, p. 90.

53   See Joan Driscoll Lynch, 'Theodora Skipitare's Performing Objects,' *The Drama Review* 33:2 (Summer 1989), p. 147. What this discussion leaves out is the feminist ritual theater of the 1970s, in which the 'I' of Western metaphysics is transformed, not because of poststructuralism, but because of an understanding of performance as communally based, designed to restore political and spiritual action for and with a given community. See for example the brilliant work, begun in the mid-1970s, of the Kuna-Rappahannock women of Spiderwoman Theater.

54   See Irving Wohlfarth, 'Walter Benjamin's Image of Interpretation,' *New German Critique* 17 (Spring 1979), pp. 70–98: 'The connection between telling stories and telling history [is] one of the themes of "The Storyteller" . . . ; it was itself historically woven, now it is becoming historically unwoven' (77). Yet I am suggesting that the performances to be discussed, without any of the nostalgia that Benjamin evinces, are attempting as well to tell history.

55   Benjamin, 'Mimetic Faculty,' p. 333.

56   Thedor W. Adorno, 'A Portrait of Walter Benjamin,' in *Prisms*, trans. Samuel and Shierry Weber (Cambridge, MA: MIT Press, 1982), p. 240.

57   Michael Taussig, *Mimesis and Alterity* (New York: Routledge, 1993) pp. 45, 21.

58   Benjamin, *Gesammelte Schriften*, vol. 2.3, p. 958. Cited in Carrie Asman, 'Return of the Sign to the Body: Benjamin and Gesture in the Age of Retheatricalization,'

Discourse 16:3 (Spring 1989), p. 49.

59 Benjamin, 'Mimetic Faculty,' p. 334.

60 Buck-Morss, *Dialectics of Seeing*, pp. 262, 264.

61 Benjamin, 'Mimetic Faculty,' p. 336.

62 The idea that words are onomatopoetic, that they sound like – and also look like or imitate – what they signify, goes back to Plato's *Cratylus* and is thoroughly and wittily explored in Gérard Genette's *Mimologics*, trans. Thais E. Morgan (Lincoln: University of Nebraska Press, 1994; originally *Mimologiques: Voyage en Cratylie* [Paris: Seuil, 1976]). Benjamin has a nearer influence in German Romanticism, as it tried to mend the Kantian breach of subjects and objects, man and nature. For Benjamin this meant postulating a prelapsarian Adamic language, but (here is the rescuing materialism), he also felt there could be no retrieval, no Romantic 'return.' I agree with Jennings: 'By establishing a pre-Adamic perfect language as a reference point, Benjamin makes possible the systematic study of human existence in history' (*Dialectical Images*, pp. 101ff.). For Benjamin capitalism and its reifications are analogous to linguistic reification; words are reduced to mere information-passing, unless their mimetic experiential residue is 'redeemed' by the artist or critic.

63 In Miriam Hansen's words, 'language and experience in Benjamin are intimately interlocking terms' though they 'can neither be identified with, nor hierarchically subsumed by, each other.' What Benjamin was attempting through mimesis was 'a different *use* of language, one that could mobilize the mimetic power historically concentrated in language against the "'Once upon a time'" of classical historical narrative.' In Hansen, pp. 198–199.

64 I am paraphrasing Benjamin: 'History decomposes into images . . . .' Cited in Buck-Morss, *Dialectics*, p. 220.

65 I saw this performance at La Mama ETC in New York City, 1994. I thank Peggy Shaw for providing me later with script, video, and conversation about the piece.

Peggy Shaw is co-founder of the WOW Cafe, New York City and (with Lois Weaver and Deb Margolin) co-creator of Split Britches, a lesbian feminist theater company that since 1981 has edified and wildly entertained theater scholars and everyone else with their vaudevillian satirical gender-bending performances at national conferences and universities, as well as the WOW Cafe. Their original pieces are *Split Britches* (1981), *Beauty and the Beast* (1982), *Upwardly Mobile Home* (1984), *Little Women* (1988). *Lesbians Who Kill* (1992), originally scripted by Margolin, developed and performed by Shaw and Weaver, was their last collaboration. Through the 1980s Split Britches meaningfully extended the post-1960s political theater mandate of combining art and life; they explored butch–femme stylistics, Jewish satire, and, in every piece, women's rage, desire, poverty, hope, and love. Their performances were, for me, deeply heuristic, sites of clarity, inspiration, and community.

Shaw and Weaver wrote and performed *Anniversary Waltz* (1989), and collaborated with Isabel Miller in *Patience and Sarah* (1984), with Holly Hughes in *Dress Suits to Hire* (1987), with Bloolips in *Belle Reprieve* (1991), and with James Neale-Kennerley in *Lust and Comfort* (1995). For texts and bibliography, see *Split Britches*, edited and with extensive critical introduction by Sue-Ellen Case (London: Routledge, 1996).

66 Peggy Shaw, *You're Just Like My Father*, typescript, p. 12.

67 See Sue-Ellen Case, 'Towards a Butch–Femme Aesthetic,' *Discourse* 11.1 (Fall–Winter 1988–89), pp. 55–73.

68 On the special appeal of military drag, see Margorie Garber, *Vested Interests: Cross Dressing and Cultural Anxiety* (New York: Harper, 1992), pp. 54ff. Military drag is just one component of time-honored camp traditions in gay and lesbian communities in and out of theater, in which parody is never just parody but

witty/serious commentary on how lives are lived. About *Lust and Comfort* (her recent collaboration with Peggy Shaw), in which the three storylines interweave characters and scenes from Joseph Losey's *The Servant* and Rainer Werner Fassbinder's *The Bitter Tears of Petra Von Kant*, Lois Weaver comments: '[*Lust and Comfort*] is a play about how we lesbians invent our lives out of popular hetero-sexual culture.' Cited in Nina Rabi, 'Lust, Comfort and Danger,' *Everywoman* (April 1995), p. 28.

69   Joan Nestle, 'Butch–Femme Relationships: Sexual Courage in the 1950s,' in *A Restricted Country* (Ithaca, NY: Firebrand Books, 1987), p. 100.

70   See Benjamin, 'Theses,' p. 261.

71   'Cultural feminism,' coined by Alice Echols, refers to the apolitical retrenchment among many American feminists after the radical feminism of the 1960s lost sup-port and credibility. Focusing on 'gender differences as . . . deep truths . . . argu-ing that women are more nurturant, less belligerent, and less sexually driven than men, cultural feminists have simply revalued dominant cultural assumptions about women.' *Daring to Be Bad: Radical Feminism in America, 1967–1975* (Minneapolis: University of Minnesota Press, 1989), p. 9. The attempt to dislodge 'cultural feminism' helped trigger the essentialist–constructivist debates in the 1980s. I don't dispute the argument, just the label, which reveals Echols's own monolithic sense of culture, and which, historically speaking, created a confusing contrast with the left critical practice 'cultural materialism' that came into view in the US some years earlier.

72   Phone call to me, December 1995.

73   See Madelon Sprengnether's *The Spectral Mother: Freud, Feminism, and Psychoanalysis* (Ithaca, NY: Cornell University Press, 1990).

74   Jacques Lacan, *Four Fundamental Concepts of Psycho-Analysis* (New York: Norton, 1981), p. 103. In Peggy Phelan's nice twist, representation 'conveys more than it intends,' and its supplementary excess can be refunctioned for political ends. See *Unmarked*, p. 2ff.

75   One of the early successes of Second Wave feminism, María Irene Fornes's *Fefu and Her Friends* (1977) runs the gamut of feminist themes, but most innovative is the play's form, moving spectators from one site to another, insuring that no cen-tral perspective will be instantiated, no one impersonating Clement Scott, 'gaz-ing with interest' at the hysterical object (see Chapter 1). Yet the last time I saw this play performed, each scene became a mini-panopticon. It is difficult even in experimental theater to dislodge the knowledge-hungry eye.

76   See Barbara Freedman, 'Frame-up: Feminism, Psychoanalysis, Theatre,' in Case, *Performing Feminisms*, pp. 66–69.

77   Teresa de Lauretis, *The Practice of Love: Lesbian Sexuality and Perverse Desire* (Bloomington: Indiana University Press), p. 198.

78   Ibid., pp. 30–78.

79   'If lesbianism does involve a return to the mother, it is no simple nostalgia for pre-Oedipal bliss and mother love but a complicated passage through Oedipal phallic and genital drives, and such instinctual vicissitudes as s-m, exhibitionism, voyeurism, and fetishism.' Ibid., p. 121.

80   See Mary Ann Doane, *The Desire to Desire: The Woman's Film of the 1940s* (Bloomington: Indiana University Press, 1987). Cited in de Lauretis, pp. 93–94ff.

81   This wound cannot involve body parts as does classical Freudian castration (for that would eliminate the girl from the story), but a 'wound' to her 'body-image' implanted by the mother's disapproval. It's not the loss of a penis but the loss of her body-image that must be disavowed – through a fetish object, a fetish that is not a phallic symbol, a penis substitute, but 'something that would cover over or disguise the narcissistic wound.' Ibid., pp. 241–242.

82   Robert Hurwitt, 'Peggy Shaw scores a 50-minute KO,' *San Francisco Examiner*

(August 21, 1995), p. 52.

83 From Karal Ann Marling, *As Seen on TV: The Visual Culture of Everyday Life in the 1950s* (Cambridge: Harvard University Press, 1994), pp. 129–162.

84 Ibid., p. 141.

85 Just before the end of World War II, the General Motors styling team

> were allowed – from a distance of thirty feet, under tight security – to examine the twin-tailed Lockheed P-38 Lightning pursuit plane, with its paired Allison engines (built by GM), fuselages, and stabilizing fins. According to [Harley] Earl, who recalled the event in a first-person article for *Saturday Evening Post* in 1954, automotive history was made on the spot.
>
> (Marling, p. 139)

86 Ibid., p. 137.

87 Robbie McCauley, *Indian Blood*, typescript, p. 6.

88 Deb Margolin, *Carthieves! Joyrides!*, typescript, p. 18.

89 As Marling points out, though, the sales blitzes of the 1950s also featured not just women like Julia Meade in an evening gown stroking the soft leather interiors of the newest Lincoln, but women in the driver's seat, as Detroit's planned obsolescence demanded upwardly mobile Americans learn to 'need' a second car for the little woman. But this is about class and status, never about the pleasure women take in a powerful car, the big road. Which is why there is transgressive pleasure for Shaw when the lesbian character in *Desert Heart* backs up her truck really fast; and why the 'roadie' side of *Thelma and Louise* pleased many women spectators (myself included) who were happy to dismiss the morbid unfeminist connotation of suicide at the end of this Hollywood narrative, to revel instead in the fantasy of a woman driver gunning an engine to its fullest screaming capacity and realizing the American dream of the 1950s ads we remember subliminally – making one of these dream machines truly fly. When women buy cars in commercials in the 1990s, there is almost no effort to suggest erotic pleasure in handling a car, but all is tailored, as in the 1950s, to efficacy, economy, and prettiness.

90 *Indian Blood* belongs to *The Family Stories: A Continuing Serial Performance* that includes *San Juan Hill* (1983), *My Father and the Wars* (1985), *Indian Blood* (1987), and *Sally's Rape* (with Jeannie Hutchins, 1991). I first saw *Indian Blood* in 'An American Festival' at Cornell University Center for Theater Arts, September 1989. Jazz accompaniment was composed and performed by Ed Montgomery on sax and clarinet, Martin Aubert on guitar, April Greene on piano with vocals. I thank Robbie McCauley for providing me with a text, and Marilyn Rivchin for making a video available. Beginning in 1979 and through the 1980s, McCauley co-created performance pieces with Ed Montgomery and Sedition Ensemble, and in 1983 began work on her 'Family Stories' series. As she was generating and directing community collaboration projects, *The Buffalo Project* (1990), *The Mississippi Project* (1992), *The Boston Project* (1993), *The Other Weapon* (1994), she was co-creating 'Thought Music' performances with writer/ performers Laurie Carlos, Jessica Hagedorn, and visual artist John Woo. See Vicki [Vivian] Patraka, 'Robbie McCauley: Obsessing in Public. An Interview,' *The Drama Review* 37:2 (Summer 1993), pp. 25–55. See also Robbie McCauley, 'Thoughts on my Career, *The Other Weapon*, and Other Projects,' in Elin Diamond, ed., *Performance and Cultural Politics* (London: Routledge, 1996) pp. 265–282.

91 See n. 12.

92 See Timothy Murray's superb discussion of *métissage* (mixed blood), mourning, and colonization in McCauley's *Indian Blood* in *Discourse* (Spring 1994), pp. 29–45.

93 Benjamin, *Gesammelte Schriften*, vol. 5, p. 591. Cited in Buck-Morss, *Dialectics*,

p. 108.
94   McCauley, 'Thoughts on My Career,' p. 266.
95   Benjamin, *Gesammelte Schriften*, vol. 5, p. 592. Cited in Richard Wolin, *Walter Benjamin: An Aesthetic of Redemption* (Berkeley: University of California Press, 1994), p. xx.
96   McCauley, 'Thoughts on My Career,' p. 265.
97   Benjamin, 'Mimetic Faculty,' pp. 333–334.
98   McCauley, *Indian Blood*, p. 16.
99   See Sandra Richards, 'Caught in the Act of Social Definition: *On the Road* with Anna Deveare Smith,' in Lynda Hart and Peggy Phelan, eds, *Acting Out: Feminist Performances* (Ann Arbor: University of Michigan Press), pp. 35–53. Richards discusses audience anxiety provoked by a segment of Anna Deveare Smith's *On the Road* performances: because

> Smith has put on and discarded racial and gendered identities several times before arriving at this sequence [entitled 'Is Race a Trope?'] . . . racial identity of the character or fictional construct becomes blurred, lost somewhere on the radioactive American terrain between the likelihood of the original and the actuality of the visible.
>
> (46)

100 See Anthony Appiah, 'The Uncompleted Argument: Du Bois and the Illusion of Race,' *Critical Inquiry* 12 (Autumn 1885), pp. 21–37.
101 In *Sally's Rape*, a piece made, with Jeannie Hutchins, directly after *Indian Blood*, McCauley remembers her enslaved great-great-grandmother by stripping, climbing on an auction block and asking the audience to bid on her. After all performances, McCauley has a talkback session. At Rutgers University in 1993, the racially mixed student audience talked for over an hour about the connections the piece made available. For many, *Sally's Rape* was a history lesson.
102 Wolfarth, p. 82.
103 See Lerone Bennett, Jr, *The Shaping of Black America* (New York: Penguin, 1993), p. 88ff.
104 I saw this performance in New York in 1995. I thank Deb Margolin for her script of the show, a video, and numerous inspiring conversations about the work. Deb Margolin, co-founder of Split Britches (see n. 65) has been performing in solo pieces, starting with *Of All the Nerve* (1989), *970–DEBB* (1990), *Gestation* (1991), *The Breaks* (with Rae C. Wright, 1992), *Of Mice, Bugs and Women* (1994), *Carthieves! Joyrides!* (1995), and most recently *O Wholly Night and Other Jewish Solecisms* (1996). Apart from the vast bibliography on Split Britches, see Lynda Hart and Peggy Phelan, 'Queerer Than Thou: Being and Deb Margolin,' *Theatre Journal* 47:2 (May 1995), pp. 269–282.
105 Luce Irigaray, *This Sex Which Is Not One*, trans. Catherine Porter with Carolyn Burke (Ithaca, NY: Cornell University Press, 1977), p. 216. See Chapter 1, n. 6 on Deleuze and the simulacrum.
106 Cited in Asman, p. 49.
107 Ibid., p. 76.
108 Buck-Morss, *Dialectics*, p. 243.
109 Judith Butler, *Bodies That Matter: On the Discursive Limits of 'Sex'* (New York: Routledge, 1993), p. 47.
110 Irigaray, p. 301.
111 In *Ethique de la différence sexuelle* (Paris: Minuit, 1984), Irigaray writes that the maternal-feminine precedes 'all possibility of determining identity.' Cited in Margaret Whitford, *Luce Irigaray: Philosophy in the Feminine* (London: Routledge, 1991), p. 67. Perhaps I am perverse in forgiving Irigaray for using metaphors that

I would never use. But I think there's a strategy. Like Benjamin's pre-social moment of 'natural correspondence,' Irigaray's pre-social nature, as Elizabeth Grosz puts it, 'attempts to create alterity' (cited in Whitford, p. 202).

112 Naomi Schor, 'This Essentialism Which Is Not One: Coming to Grips With Irigaray,' *Differences* 1:2 (Summer 1989), p. 48.

113 Deb Margolin, 'N,' *Harper's Magazine* (April 1988), p. 47.

114 See n. 38.

115 Buck-Morss, *Dialectics*, p. 70.

116 Cited in Buck-Morss, *Dialectics*, pp. 256–257, along with her comment that Benjamin called *Le Paysan de Paris* the best book on Paris.

117 Benjamin, *Gesammelte Schriften*, vol. 5, p. 1023. Cited in Buck-Morss, *Dialectics*, p. 108.

118 Buck-Morss, *Dialectics*, p. 112. In Benjamin's and Adorno's notion of 'natural history,' nature and history were seen as dialectically intertwined – what seems natural is really historical (changing, and also mortal); what seems historical contains characteristics of nature (cyclical/repetition, and also material/sentient/suffering). Natural history was a conceptual lever against any sort of idealism, and was specifically mounted as a critique of Heidegger's notion that 'historicity is the "nature" of Being.' Buck-Morss, p. 59.

119 See Marling, pp. 148–149.

120 Cited in Alan Read, *Theatre and Everyday Life: An Ethics of Performance* (London: Routledge, 1993), p. 90. See Drucilla Cornell on ethical feminism and mimesis in Adorno, in *Beyond Accommodation: Ethical Feminism, Deconstruction, and the Law* (New York and London: Routledge, 1991), pp. 147–52.

121 Wohlfarth, pp. 79, 80.

122 Trinh T. Minh-ha, 'Not You/Like You: Post-Colonial Women and the Interlocking Questions of Identity and Difference,' in *Making Face, Making Soul* (San Francisco, Aunt Lute Books, 1990), p. 374.

Index

Lightning Source UK Ltd.
Milton Keynes UK
UKOW01f2020111017

310832UK00002B/168/P